ANNUAL EDITIONS

Archaeology
Ninth Edition

D0071328

EDITORS

Mari Pritchard Parker
Pasadena City College

Mari Pritchard Parker is a Registered Professional Archaeologist with more than 20 years of cultural resources management experience in coastal California, the Great Basin and the Desert Southwest. Ms Pritchard Parker earned a Bachelor's degree in Anthropology from California State University, Fullerton, in 1986 and a Master's degree in Archaeology from the University of California at Riverside in 1995.

Her interest is primarily in ground stone analysis and replication, textile conservation, and ceramic studies. She has served as guest editor for the *Pacific Coast Archaeological Society Quarterly* on two special issues on ground stone analysis. She is also the founder of the Milford Archaeological Research Institute, a non-profit organization dedicated to educating the public and future archaeologists in the study of archaeology and past lifeways of the Desert Southwest.

Elvio Angeloni
Pasadena City College

Elvio Angeloni received his BA from UCLA in 1963, his MA in anthropology from UCLA in 1965, and his MA in communication arts from Loyola Marymount University in 1976. He has produced several films, including *Little Warrior,* winner of the Cinemedia VI Best Bicentennial Theme, and *Broken Bottles,* shown on PBS. He served as an academic adviser on the instructional television series *Faces of Culture.* He received the Pasadena City College Outstanding Teacher Award in 2006. He is also the academic editor of *Annual Editions: Physical Anthropology, Classic Edition Sources: Anthropology* and co-editor of *Annual Editions: Archaeology* and *Roundtable Viewpoints: Physical Anthropology.* His primary area of interest has been indigenous peoples of the American Southwest.

Higher Education

Boston   Burr Ridge, IL   Dubuque, IA   New York   San Francisco   St. Louis
Bangkok   Bogotá   Caracas   Kuala Lumpur   Lisbon   London   Madrid   Mexico City
Milan   Montreal   New Delhi   Santiago   Seoul   Singapore   Sydney   Taipei   Toronto

ANNUAL EDITIONS: ARCHAEOLOGY, NINTH EDITION

1 2 3 4 5 6 7 8 9 0 QPD/QPD 0 9

ISBN 978–0–07–812774–8
MHID 0–07–812774–2
ISSN 1092–4760

Managing Editor: *Larry Loeppke*
Senior Managing Editor: *Faye Schilling*
Developmental Editor: *Debra Henricks*
Editorial Coordinator: *Mary Foust*
Editorial Assistant: *Nancy Meissner*
Production Service Assistant: *Rita Hingtgen*
Permissions Coordinator: *Lenny J. Behnke*
Senior Marketing Manager: *Julie Keck*
Marketing Communications Specialist: *Mary Klein*
Marketing Coordinator: *Alice Link*
Project Manager: *Sandy Wille*
Design Specialist: *Tara McDermott*
Senior Production Supervisor: *Laura Fuller*
Cover Graphics: *Kristine Jubeck*

Compositor: Laserwords Private Limited
Cover Image: © Glowimages (inset); © Philip Coblentz/Brand X Pictures/PictureQuest (background)

Library in Congress Cataloging-in-Publication Data
Main entry under title: Annual Editions: Archaeology. 9/e.
   1. Archaeology—Periodicals. I. Pritchard Parker, Mari; Angeloni, Elvio, *comp*. II. Title: Archaeology.
658'.05

www.mhhe.com

Editors/Advisory Board

Members of the Advisory Board are instrumental in the final selection of articles for each edition of ANNUAL EDITIONS. Their review of articles for content, level, currentness, and appropriateness provides critical direction to the editor and staff. We think that you will find their careful consideration well reflected in this volume.

Preface

In publishing ANNUAL EDITIONS we recognize the enormous role played by the magazines, newspapers, and journals of the public press in providing current, first-rate educational information in a broad spectrum of interest areas. Many of these articles are appropriate for students, researchers, and professionals seeking accurate, current material to help bridge the gap between principles and theories and the real world. These articles, however, become more useful for study when those of lasting value are carefully collected, organized, indexed, and reproduced in a low-cost format, which provides easy and permanent access when the material is needed. That is the role played by ANNUAL EDITIONS.

The ninth edition of *Annual Editions: Archaeology* has been compiled by its two editors with the intent of presenting a vivid overview of the field of archaeology as practiced today. It is our hope that these readings, in keeping with its previous editions will make the old bones, shards of pottery, and stone tools of the past pop into the present. The book's purpose is to present an approach in which archaeologists speak for themselves of their own special experiences. The student is shown that archaeology is a historical as well as a living, public science. The idea is to give the student the necessary basics in order to transform passive learning into active learning. This way, information is both perceived and conceptualized. Hopefully, the light bulb will go on when students read these articles.

This book is organized into five units, each of which contains several articles of various themes on "doing" archaeology. At the beginning of the book is the table of contents that provides a short synopsis of each article. This is followed by a topic guide that cross-references general areas of interest as they appear in the different articles. In addition, there are Internet references that can be used to further explore the articles in that unit.

Each unit is introduced by an overview that provides both a commentary on the unit topic and a few key points to provoke thought and discussion. It is highly recommended that the student reads these unit overviews, as they are presented with humor and also contain challenges and puzzles to solve.

The organization of this book is both suggestive and subjective. The articles may be assigned or read in any fashion that is deemed desirable. Each article stands on its own and may be assigned in conjunction with or in contrast to any other article. *Annual Editions: Archaeology* may serve as a supplement to a standard textbook for both introductory and graduate archaeology courses. It may also be used in general, undergraduate, or graduate courses in anthropology. The lay reader in anthropology may also find the collection of readings insightful.

It is the desire of those involved in the production of this book that each edition be a valuable and provocative teaching tool. We welcome your criticisms, advice, and suggestions in order to carefully hone new editions into finer artifacts of education.

We suggest that you use the postage-paid form at the end of this book for your comments and article ratings. We would be most grateful for the time you take to give your feedback. Each year these comments and ratings are carefully read by the editors in creating the next edition. Your responses would truly be appreciated and seriously considered.

Mari Pritchard Parker
Editor

Elvio Angeloni
Editor

Contents

UNIT 1
About Archaeologists and Archaeology

1. **The Awful Truth about Archaeology,** Dr. Lynne Sebastian,
Albuquerque Tribune, April 16, 2002

"You're an Archaeologist! That sounds soooo exciting!" Of course it sounds exciting because of the hyperbole and mystery perpetuated by T.V. shows, movies, and novels—professional archaeologists know better! Yes, the thrill of looking at the past is truly exciting. ***The process of discovery is slow, tedious, and frustrating*** especially when nothing is found. Digging square holes in the ground and carefully measuring artifacts, cataloging, taking notes, and hoping to publish something meaningful about the past—it is more of a work of love that has its inherent reward in knowledge. It is a work of love that has its inherent reward in knowledge.

2. **Archaeology: The Next 50 Years,** Brian Fagan, *Archaeology,*
September/October 2006

As Brian Fagan reflects upon how far the field of archaeology has come as well as where it is going, he finds that "a century of increasing involvement with **science** has produced a finer understanding of how archaeological sites were formed, how people exploited their surrounding landscapes, and even how they thought about the cosmos and the world around them. Many ***future discoveries*** will come from minute detective work far from the field, contributing to a much ***more detailed portrait of the past.***"

3. **All the King's Sons,** Douglas Preston, *The New Yorker,*
January 22, 1996

A well-told narrative of ***modern archaeology,*** Douglas Preston's article is based on ***scientific archaeology.*** It is not, however, a typical "scientific" or "monograph" report common to ***academic archaeology.*** This tale of archaeology, with all the immediacy and punch of being in the field, is wish fulfillment for students or laypersons of archaeology because it is about a spectacular find—the biggest archaeological site in ***Egypt*** since King Tut's tomb. No "blah-blah Egypt, blah-blah dummy," here.

4. **Maya Archaeologists Turn to the Living to Help Save the Dead,**
Michael Bawaya, *Science Magazine,* August 26, 2005

By enabling local residents, rather than outsiders, to serve as custodians of their own heritage, archaeologists have helped to instill in them ***a sense of identity*** and, instead of looting and destroying ***valuable sites,*** they are now ***dedicated to preserving them.***

5. **The Fantome Controversy,** Heather Pringle, *Archaeology,*
May/June 2006

As ***treasure hunting*** at marine archaeological sites becomes more common, the mercenary practices of ***a small number of professional underwater archaeologists*** are coming under fire. Not only are they helping ***private companies obtain government licenses*** and search for valuables; they are willing to accept the fact that such materials will be sold for a ***profit.*** For the professional archaeological community, this is simply immoral.

The concepts in bold italics are developed in the article. For further expansion, please refer to the Topic Guide.

UNIT 2
Problem Oriented Archaeology

The concepts in bold italics are developed in the article. For further expansion, please refer to the Topic Guide.

UNIT 3
Techniques in Archaeology

The concepts in bold italics are developed in the article. For further expansion, please refer to the Topic Guide.

UNIT 4
Historical Archaeology

The concepts in bold italics are developed in the article. For further expansion, please refer to the Topic Guide.

UNIT 5
Contemporary Archaeology

The concepts in bold italics are developed in the article. For further expansion, please refer to the Topic Guide.

The concepts in bold italics are developed in the article. For further expansion, please refer to the Topic Guide.

Correlation Guide

The *Annual Editions* series provides students with convenient, inexpensive access to current, carefully selected articles from the public press. **Annual Editions: Archaeology, 9/e** is an easy-to-use reader that presents articles on important topics such as *epistemology, ethnographic analogy, salvage and conservation,* and many more. For more information on *Annual Editions* and other *McGraw-Hill Contemporary Learning Series* titles, visit www.mhcls.com.

This convenient guide matches the units in **Annual Editions: Archaeology, 9/e** with the corresponding chapters in two of our best-selling McGraw-Hill Archaeology textbooks by Ashmore/Sharer and Price/Feinman.

Annual Editions: Archaeology, 9/e	**Discovering Our Past: A Brief Introduction to Archaeology, 5/e by Ashmore/Sharer**	**Images of the Past, 5/e by Price/Feinman**
Unit 1: About Archaeologists and Archaeology	**Chapter 1:** Introduction **Chapter 2:** Archaeology's Past **Chapter 3:** Contemporary Approaches to Archaeology	**Chapter 1:** Principles of Archaeology
Unit 2: Problem Oriented Archaeology	**Chapter 4:** How Archaeology Works	**Chapter 2:** The First Humans **Chapter 3:** Out of Africa: Homo Erectus **Chapter 4:** The Hunters **Chapter 7:** Native North Americans **Chapter 8:** Ancient Mesoamerica **Chapter 10:** States and Empires in Asia and Africa
Unit 3: Techniques in Archaeology	**Chapter 5:** Fieldwork **Chapter 7:** Dating the Past	**Chapter 1:** Principles of Archaeology **Chapter 5:** Postglacial Foragers
Unit 4: Historical Archaeology	**Chapter 5:** Fieldwork **Chapter 6:** Analyzing the Past **Chapter 8:** Reconstructing the Past **Chapter 9:** Understanding the Past	
Unit 5: Contemporary Archaeology	**Chapter 10:** Archaeology Today	**Chapter 1:** Principles of Archaeology **Chapter 4:** The Hunters **Chapter 12:** In Conclusion: The Past as Present and Future

Topic Guide

This topic guide suggests how the selections in this book relate to the subjects covered in your course. You may want to use the topics listed on these pages to search the Web more easily.

On the following pages a number of Web sites have been gathered specifically for this book. They are arranged to reflect the units of this Annual Editions reader. You can link to these sites by going to *http://www.mhcls.com*.

All the articles that relate to each topic are listed below the bold-faced term.

About archaeologists and archaeology

1. The Awful Truth about Archaeology
2. Archaeology: The Next 50 Years
3. All the King's Sons
4. Maya Archaeologists Turn to the Living to Help Save the Dead
5. The Fantome Controversy
6. Distinguished Lecture in Archaeology: Communication and the Future of American Archaeology
7. Prehistory *of* Warfare
9. Who Were the First Americans?
10. Poop Fossil Pushes Back Date for Earliest Americans
11. Archaeologists Rediscover Cannibals
12. A Coprological View of Ancestral Pueblo Cannibalism
19. Gritty Clues
30. Thracian Gold Fever
33. Earth Movers

Art and religion

3. All the King's Sons
11. Archaeologists Rediscover Cannibals
25. Where Was Jesus Born?

Burials, reburials and human remains

8. The Mystery of Unknown Man E
10. Poop Fossil Pushes Back Date for Earliest Americans
11. Archaeologists Rediscover Cannibals
14. New Women of the Ice Age
22. Profile of an Anthropologist: No Bone Unturned
24. Artful Surgery
27. Secrets of the Medici
29. Living through the Donner Party
30. Thracian Gold Fever
31. In Flanders Fields
32. The Past as Propaganda
37. Watery Tombs

Ceramic analysis

30. Thracian Gold Fever
33. Earth Movers

Classical and biblical archaeology

2. Archaeology: The Next 50 Years
3. All the King's Sons
8. The Mystery of Unknown Man E
18. The Maya Collapses
24. Artful Surgery
25. Where Was Jesus Born?
30. Thracian Gold Fever
37. Watery Tombs

Cognitive and ideological archaeology

6. Distinguished Lecture in Archaeology: Communication and the Future of American Archaeology

Cultural Resource Management (CRM)

4. Maya Archaeologists Turn to the Living to Help Save the Dead
31. In Flanders Fields

Epistemology (method and theory)

1. The Awful Truth about Archaeology
3. All the King's Sons
6. Distinguished Lecture in Archaeology: Communication and the Future of American Archaeology
14. New Women of the Ice Age
15. Woman the Toolmaker
27. Secrets of the Medici

Ethics and laws

3. All the King's Sons
4. Maya Archaeologists Turn to the Living to Help Save the Dead
5. The Fantome Controversy
30. Thracian Gold Fever

Ethnoarchaeology

11. Archaeologists Rediscover Cannibals
12. A Coprological View of Ancestral Pueblo Cannibalism
14. New Women of the Ice Age
17. Bushmen
29. Living through the Donner Party
30. Thracian Gold Fever
33. Earth Movers
37. Watery Tombs

Ethnographic analogy

11. Archaeologists Rediscover Cannibals
12. A Coprological View of Ancestral Pueblo Cannibalism
14. New Women of the Ice Age
17. Bushmen
29. Living through the Donner Party
37. Watery Tombs

Experimental archaeology

16. Yes, Wonderful Things
17. Bushmen

Forensic archaeology

8. The Mystery of Unknown Man E
24. Artful Surgery
28. Digging for Truth

Garbology

16. Yes, Wonderful Things

Gender and sex roles

3. All the King's Sons
14. New Women of the Ice Age
15. Woman the Toolmaker
29. Living through the Donner Party

History and historical archaeology

2. Archaeology: The Next 50 Years
5. The Fantome Controversy
8. The Mystery of Unknown Man E
11. Archaeologists Rediscover Cannibals
12. A Coprological View of Ancestral Pueblo Cannibalism

Internet References

The following Internet sites have been selected to support the articles found in this reader. These sites were available at the time of publication. However, because Web sites often change their structure and content, the information listed may no longer be available. We invite you to visit http://www.mhcls.com for easy access to these sites.

Annual Editions: Archaeology 9/e

General Sources

Anthropology Resources on the Internet
http://www.socsciresearch.com/r7.html

This site provides extensive Internet links that are primarily of anthropological relevance. The Education Index rated it "one of the best education-related sites on the Web."

Archaeological Institute of America
http://www.archaeological.org

This home page of the AIA describes the purpose of the nonprofit organization. Review this site for information about AIA and AIA/IAA–Canada and other archaeological-research institutions and organizations around the world.

How Humans Evolved
http://www.wwnorton.com/college/anthro/bioanth/

This site presents a good overview of human evolution, with links to Science and Nature magazines, access to e-mail chat groups, and other topics of archaeological interest.

Library of Congress
http://www.loc.gov

Examine this extensive Web site to learn about resource tools, library services/resources, exhibitions, and databases in many different subfields of archaeology.

Society for American Archaeology
http://www.saa.org

An international organization dedicated to the research, interpretation, and protection of the archaeological heritage of the Americas.

Society for Historical Archaeology
http://www.sha.org

The official website of the Society for Historical Archaeology. Historical Archaeology is the study of the material remains of past societies that also left behind historical documentary evidence. This subfield of archaeology studies the emergence, transformation, and nature of the Modern World.

The New York Times
http://www.nytimes.com/

Browsing through the extensive archives of the New York Times will provide you with a wide array of articles and information related to archaeology.

USD Anthropology
http://www.usd.edu/anth/

Many topics can be accessed from this site, such as South Dakota archaeology. Repatriation and reburial are just a few examples of the variety of information available.

UNIT 1: About Archaeologists and Archaeology

Anthropology, Archaeology, and American Indian Sites on the Internet
http://dizzy.library.arizona.edu/library/teams/sst/anthro/

This Web page points out a number of Internet sites of interest to archaeologists. Visit this page for links to electronic journals and more.

GMU Anthropology Department
http://www.gmu.edu/departments/anthro/

Look over this site for current listings of scientific papers dealing with anthropological and archaeological studies. The site provides a number of interesting links, such as a listing of archaeological fieldwork opportunities.

Smithsonian Institution Web Site
http://www.si.edu/

This site, which will provide access to many of the enormous resources of the Smithsonian, will give you a sense of the scope of anthropological and archaeological inquiry today.

Society for American Archaeology
www.saa.org

An international organization dedicated to the research, interpretation, and protection of the archaeological heritage of the Americas.

UNIT 2: Problem Oriented Archaeology

Archaeology Links (NC)
http://www.arch.dcr.state.nc.us/links.htm#stuff

North Carolina Archaeology provides this site, which has many links to sites of interest to archaeologists, such as the paleolithic painted cave at Vallon-Pont-d'Arc (Ardeche).

Archaeology Magazine
http://www.archaeology.org

This home page of Archaeology magazine, the official publication of the AIA, provides information about current archaeological events, staff picks of Web sites, and access to selected articles from current and past editions of the magazine.

UNIT 3: Techniques in Archaeology

American Anthropologist
http://www.aaanet.org

Check out this site—the home page of the American Anthropology Association—for general information about archaeology and anthropology as well as access to a wide variety of articles.

Internet References

NOVA Online/Pyramids—The Inside Story
http://www.pbs.org/wgbh/nova/pyramid/

Take a virtual tour of the pyramids at Giza through this interesting site. It provides information on the pharaohs for whom the tombs were built and follows a team of archaeologists as they excavate a bakery that fed the pyramid builders.

Radiocarbon Dating for Archaeology
http://www.rlaha.ox.ac.uk/orau/index.html

This Web site describes the advantages inherent in using radiocarbon dating to promote mass spectrometry over the older decay counting method.

UNIT 4: Historical Archaeology

GIS and Remote Sensing for Archaeology: Burgundy, France
http://www.informatics.org/france/france.html

This project has been an ongoing collaboration between Dr. Scott Madry from the Center for Remote Sensing and Spatial Analysis at Rutgers University and many other researchers. A period of over 2,000 years in the Arroux River Valley region of Burgundy is being analyzed to understand long-term interaction between the different cultures and the physical environment.

Society for Historical Archaeology
www.sha.org

The official website of the Society for Historical Archaeology. Historical Archaeology is the study of the material remains of past societies that also left behind historical documentary evidence. This subfield of archaeology studies the emergence, transformation, and nature of the Modern World.

Zeno's Forensic Page
http://forensic.to/forensic.html

A complete list of resources on forensics is here. It includes DNA/serology sources and databases, forensic-medicine anthropology sites, and related areas.

UNIT 5: Contemporary Archaeology

Archaeology and Anthropology: The Australian National University
http://online.anu.edu.au/AandA/

Browse through this home page of the Anthropology and Archaeology Departments of the Australian National University for information about topics in Australian and regional archaeology and to access links to other resource centers.

WWW: Classical Archaeology
http://www.archaeology.org/wwwarky/classical.html

This site provides information and links regarding ancient Greek and Roman archaeology.

Al Mashriq-Archaeology in Beirut
http://almashriq.hiof.no/base/archaeology.html

At this site the links to the fascinating excavations taking place in Beirut can be explored. Reports from the site, background material, discussion of the importance of the site, and information on other Lebanese sites are included.

American Indian Ritual Object Repatriation Foundation
http://www.repatriationfoundation.org/

Visit this home page of the American Indian Ritual Object Repatriation Foundation, which aims to assist in the return of sacred ceremonial material to the appropriate American Indian nation, clan, or family, and to educate the public.

ArchNet—WWW Virtual Library
http://archnet.asu.edu/archnet/

ArchNet serves as the World Wide Web Virtual Library for Archaeology. This site can provide you with access to a broad variety of archaeological resources available on the Internet, categorized by geographic region and subject.

Current Archaeology
http://www.archaeology.co.uk

This is the home page of Current Archaeology, Great Britain's leading archaeological magazine. Its various sections provide links about archaeology in Britain.

National Archaeological DataBase
http://www.cast.uark.edu/other/nps/nagpra/nagpra.html

Examine this site from the Archaeology and Ethnography Program of the NAD to read documents related to the Native American Graves Protection and Repatriation Act.

Society for Archaeological Sciences
http://www.socarchsci.org/

The Society for Archaeological Sciences provides this site to further communication among scholars applying methods from the physical sciences to archaeology.

UNIT 1

About Archaeologists and Archaeology

Unit Selections

1. **The Awful Truth about Archaeology,** Dr. Lynne Sebastian
2. **Archaeology: The Next 50 Years,** Brian Fagan
3. **All the King's Sons,** Douglas Preston
4. **Maya Archaeologists Turn to the Living to Help Save the Dead,** Michael Bawaya
5. **The Fantome Controversy,** Heather Pringle
6. **Distinguished Lecture in Archaeology: Communication and the Future of American Archaeology,** Jeremy A. Sabloff

Key Points to Consider

- How does modern archaeology differ from archaeology of the Nineteenth Century and why? Give some examples of what is meant by archaeological methods, fieldwork, theory, and ethics.

- How is culture viewed by anthropology?

- What is the general relationship between anthropology and archaeology? Please give specific examples.

- What is public archaeology? How could archaeologists better communicate with the public? What role should archaeology play in public education? Give some examples.

- What is the difference between academic and non-academic archaeologists? What is the potential for non-academic archaeologists?

- What is the biggest find in Egypt since King Tut-ankh-Amun's tomb? Why is digging in Egypt considered to be a cliché among archaeologists? Is this an example of academic archaeology? Give some examples.

- How is it possible to distinguish the fake objects from the genuine in today's museums?

Student Web Site
www.mhcls.com

Internet References

Anthropology, Archaeology, and American Indian Sites on the Internet
http://dizzy.library.arizona.edu/library/teams/sst/anthro/

GMU Anthropology Department
http://www.gmu.edu/departments/anthro/

Smithsonian Institution Web Site
http://www.si.edu/

Society for American Archaeology
www.saa.org

Ozymandias [1817]

I met a traveller from an antique land, who said: Two vast and trunkless legs of stone Stand in the desert. Near them, on the sand, Half sunk, a shattered visage lies, whose frown, And wrinkled lip, and sneer of cold command, Tell that its sculptor well those passions read. Which yet survive, stamped on these lifeless things, The hand that mocked them, and the heart that fed; And on the pedestal these words appear: "My name is Ozymandias, King of Kings: Look on my works, ye Mighty, and despair!"Nothing beside remains. Round the decay Of that colossal wreck, boundless and bare, The lone and level sands stretch far away.

—Percy Bysshe Shelley

So just who is an archaeologist? The job description presented by the mass media is very different from the reality of today's anthropological archaeologists. Archaeologists in the Americas, after all, are trained as anthropologists. Our goal is to reconstruct cultures of the past based on the material remains that managed to survive the "ravages of time." So today's archaeologists are concerned with the reconstruction of human behavior, not just with the collection of treasure objects.

If human behavior were a baseball game, the anthropologist would be in the broadcaster's booth. But long before the game was over, in a seeming paradox, the anthropologist would run into the stands to be a spectator, chow down on a good, fresh, steamy mustard-covered hot dog, and then rush onto the field to be a player and catch a high fly to left field. This is the eccentric nature of anthropology. This is why anthropology is so interesting.

If one compares anthropology, psychology, sociology, and history as four disciplines that study human nature, anthropology is the one that takes the giant step back and uses a 360-degree panoramic camera. The psychologist stands nose to nose with the individual person, the sociologist moves back for the group shot, and the historian goes back in time as well as space.

However, the anthropologist does all these things, standing well behind the others, watching and measuring, using the data of all these disciplines, but recombining them into the uniqueness of the anthropological perspective: much the way meiosis generates novel genetic combinations.

Anthropology is the science of human behavior that studies all humankind, starting with our biological and evolutionary origins as cultural beings and continues with the diversification of our cultural selves. Humankind is the single species that has evolved a culture as a unique way of adapt to the world. Academically, anthropology is divided into four major fields: cultural anthropology, physical anthropology, linguistics and archaeology. Anthropologists hold in common a shared concept of culture. The basic tenet that anthropologists share is to generate a behavioral science that can explain the differences and similarities between cultures. In order to achieve this, anthropologists view people within a cross-cultural perspective. This encompasses comparing the parts and parcels of all cultures, present and past, with each other. This is the holistic approach of anthropology: considering all things in all their manifestations. A grand task, indeed. One that requires, above all, learning to ask the "right" questions.

What is culture? Culture is the unique way in which the human species adapts to its total environment. Total environment includes everything that affects human beings—the physical environment that includes plants, animals, the weather; beliefs; values; a passing insult; or an opportunistic virus. Everything possible that human beings are capable of is by culture.

Culture is the human adaptive system. It is an ecology in which all people live in groups defined by time, space, and place. They pass on shared values and beliefs through common language(s), and manipulate things in their environment by making and using tools. Cultures change and evolve through time. And perhaps most enigmatically cultures, all cultures, be they high civilizations or small tribes, do eventually cease to exist.

Archaeology is the subfield of anthropology that studies these extinct cultures. Archaeologists dig up the physical remains, the tools, the houses, the garbage and the utensils of past cultures. And from this spare database, archaeologists attempt to reconstruct these past cultures in their material, social, and ideological aspects. Is this important to anthropology? Yes, this is anthropology. Because these once-living cultures represent approximately ninety-eight percent of all cultures that have ever existed. They tell us where we have been, when we are there again, and where we might go in the future.

How do archaeologists do this? Today the mass media is the major source of the epistemology in the modern world, and it underscores cultural values and also creates cultural myths by which all humans are made to live. The media is as much a response to our demands as we are to its manipulations. Its themes play a medley in our minds over and over again, until they fade into our unconscious only to be recycled again, pulled up, and laid before us like the ice cream man's musical chimes of our childhood. But the media mind is characterized by fuzzy thinking and skepticism. If minds are trained to be articulate, thought and action will follow suit. Scientific thinking involves a very strict set of rules and regulations that test the veracity of conclusions. A kind of operational language emerges, codified, similar to mathematics that allow apples to be compared only with apples.

Postmodernists may argue that knowledge is only knowable in a relative sense. But we know what we know in a very real pragmatic sense because we are, after all humans-the cultural animal. It is our way of knowing and surviving. Let us proceed now to see how archaeologists ply their magical trade.

The Awful Truth about Archaeology

Dr. Lynne Sebastian

"Ohhhh! You're an Archaeologist! That sounds soooo exciting!" Whenever I tell someone on a plane or at a dinner party what I do for a living, this is almost always the response that I get. Either that, or they want to talk to me about dinosaurs, and I have to explain gently that it is paleontologists who do dinosaurs; archaeologists study people who lived long ago.

The reason people think archaeology must be exciting is that they have spent WAY too much time watching The *Curse of the Mummy, Indiana Jones* and the *Temple of Doom,* and *Lara Croft, Tomb Raider* (do you suppose that she actually has that printed on her business cards?). Perhaps it is a flaw in my character or a lapse in my professional education, but I have never once recovered a golden idol or been chased through the jungle by thugs, and I appear to have been absent from graduate school on the day that they covered bullwhips, firearms, and the martial arts. I have not even, so far as I can tell, suffered from a curse, although I have had few nasty encounters with serpents, scorpions, and lightening.

I'm sure that members of every profession are exasperated by the way that they are portrayed in movies and on television, and archaeologists are no exception. Every time we see Sydney Fox (*Relict Hunter,* another great job title) fly off to an exotic country, follow the clues on the ancient map, and rip-off some fabulous object to bring home to the museum, we want to root for the bad guys who are trying to bring her career to an abrupt and permanent halt.

What would really happen if a mysterious man wearing an eye patch showed up at Sydney's university office and gave her the map, just before expiring as a result of slow-acting poison? Well, of course, first there would be a lot of unpleasantness with the campus police . . . but leaving that aside, she would spend months writing grant proposals to get funding for a research expedition and more months getting the needed permits and authorizations from the government of the exotic country. Then she would have to persuade the Dean and her department Chair to give her release time from teaching. And when she and her research team finally arrived in the exotic country, they would spend months meticulously mapping the site, painstakingly removing thin layers of soil from perfectly square holes, and recording every stone, every bit of stained earth, every piece of debris that they encountered, using photos, maps, sketches, and detailed written notes. Finally, at the end of the field season,

the team would return to the university with 70 boxes of broken pottery, bits of stone, and all manner of scientific samples to be washed and cataloged and analyzed. And in the end, all that material would be returned to a museum in the exotic country.

Now, of course, nobody would want to watch a TV show where even the beauteous Sydney did all that, but this kind of tedious, detailed work is one important aspect of "real" archaeology. Just about every archaeologist that I know has a copy of an old Calvin and Hobbs cartoon somewhere in his or her office. In it, Calvin, who has spent an exhausting day doing a make-believe archaeological excavation in his backyard, turns to Hobbs in disgust and says, "Archaeology has to be the most mind-numbing job in the world!!" And some days it is. Worse yet, it is detailed work that involves a lot of paperwork and delicate instruments but has to be done outdoors in every sort of adverse weather. When it is 20 degrees and you are hunched down in a square hole in the ground trying to write a description of layers of dirt with a pen that keeps freezing solid or when the wind is blowing sheets of sand straight sideways into your face while you are lying on your stomach using a dental pick to expose a broken shell bracelet so you can photograph it before you remove it—these are experiences that can cause a person to question her career choice.

But you know what? Archaeology really IS exciting, and not for any of the reasons that Indy or Lara would suggest. Archaeology is exciting because it connects with the past in a way that nothing else can, and sometimes that connection can be stunningly immediate and personal. I worked one year on the Hopi Reservation in Arizona, excavating a site that was going to be destroyed by road construction. We found that one of the three "pithouses" or semi-subterranean structures on the site appeared to have been cleaned out and closed up, presumably in the expectation that someone would return to live in it again. A flat slab had been placed over the ventilator opening, perhaps to keep out dirt and debris and critters, and the slab was sealed in place with wet mud. But no one came back, and eventually the small pithouse burned.

When we excavated the pithouse, we found the imprint of human hands, perfectly preserved in the mud, which had been hardened by the fire. That little house was built in AD 805, but I could reach out and place my hands in those handprints left there by someone a thousand years before. And more important, the Hopi school children who visited the site could place their small hands in those prints made by one of their ancestors, 50 generations removed. We lifted each one of the children into the pithouse, and let them do just that—like children everywhere, they were astonished that they were being encouraged to touch rather than being forbidden to do so.

Afterward we sat together on the site and talked about what life was like for that Hisatsinom (the Hopi term for the people we call Anasazi) person. We talked about food and looked at the burned corn kernels and the squash seeds that we had found. We talked about shelter and tools and looked at the three houses and the broken bits of stone and bone and pottery that we were recovering from the trash areas at the site. One of the houses had burned while it was occupied, and we looked at the fragments of the rolled up sleeping mats and baskets of corn and other possessions that the people had lost. We talked about the family that had lived there, how much the parents loved their children and how they must have worried about providing for them after such a terrible loss. And we talked about the migration stories that are a central part of Hopi oral history, and about what the Hopi elders had told us about the place of this particular site in those stories. I like to think that those children, who reached back across the centuries and touched the hand of their fifty-times-great grandmother, came away with a stronger sense of who they were and where they came from and a richer understanding of the oral traditions of their people.

But what if I had been not me, Dr. Science, purveyor of meticulous and mind-numbing archaeological techniques, but rather Lara Croft, Tomb Raider? If Lara had been rooting about in this site, searching for "treasures," she would have quickly dismissed that small pithouse, although she might have smashed that burned mud with the handprints in order to rip away the slab and check for hidden goodies behind it.

No, she would have focused on the other house, the one that burned while it was being used. She would have pulled out all those burned roof beams whose pattern of rings enabled us to learn that the houses were built in AD 805, probably using them for her campfire. She would have crushed the remnants of the burned sleeping mats and baskets of corn. She would never have noticed the stone griddle still in place on the hearth or the grease stains left by the last two corn cakes cooking on it when the fire started. She would have kicked aside the broken pieces of the pottery vessels that were crushed when the burning roof fell, the same pots that we put back together in the lab in order to estimate the size of the family and to recover traces of the items stored and cooked in them.

No, Lara would have missed all that we learned about that site and the people who made their homes there. Instead, she would have seized the single piece of pottery that didn't break in the fire and clutching it to her computer enhanced bosom, she would have stolen away into the night, narrowly escaping death and destruction at the hands of the rival gang of looters.

Is archaeology the most mind-numbing pursuit in the world, as Calvin claims? Or is it "sooo exciting" as my airline seatmates always exclaim? Both. And much more. What Lara and Indy and the others don't know is that archaeology is not about things, it is about people. It is about understanding life in the past, about understanding who we are and where we came from—not just where we came from as a particular cultural group, but what we share with all people in this time and in all the time that came before.

LYNNE SEBASTIAN is Director of Historic Preservation with the SRI Foundation, a private nonprofit dedicated to historic preservation, and an adjunct assistant professor of Anthropology at UNM. She is a former New Mexico State Archaeologist and State Historic Preservation Office, and she is currently the President of the Society for American Archaeology.

Archaeology: The Next 50 Years

BRIAN FAGAN

rdipithecus, the 4-million-year-old hominin; the 160,000-year-old Huerto skulls from Ethiopia, the earliest known modern humans; Stone age cave paintings from Chauvet cave; Egypt's Bahariya mummies, a spectacular cemetery of burials from the sixth century B.C. and the first and second centuries A.D.; and the Moche lords of Sipán in Peru: We are in the midst of a remarkable period of archaeological discovery. This is particularly true of Maya civilization, where a combination of decipherment and large-scale field research is yielding new perceptions of lord and commoner alike. The spectacular wall paintings from San Bartolo, Guatemala, hint that remarkable finds still lie ahead. They depict the Maya maize god and date to as early as 300 B.C., the earliest known Preclassic Maya art. The glyphs with the frieze are still undeciphered, but push back the beginnings of Maya writing more than three centuries. The same potential for stunning finds exists in the Andes, where the discovery of ceremonial centers at Caral and Buena Vista are revising long-held theories about the rise of complex societies along Peru's north coast. Even heavily researched areas such as the Southwest United States are yielding hitherto unknown pueblos.

This torrent of new discoveries raises a fascinating question. What major archaeological discoveries can we expect during the next half-century or so? Where will the truly sensational finds be made? What kinds of discoveries will radically transform our knowledge of the past? I believe we can make some intelligent forecasts.

After a century-and-a-half of archaeological discovery, we have a clear sense of more than 2.5 million years of history. We have a preliminary grasp of early human evolution, and a good sense of the world's early civilizations, life in classical Greece and Rome, the origins of agriculture and animal domestication, and early human behavior, even if many details remain unknown. What, then, will be the major research questions asked and answered in the next 50 years? And in what directions will new technologies take us? I suspect that today's major questions will remain, for we have barely scratched the surface of issues such as human origins, the appearance and spread of *Homo sapiens* during the late Ice Age, the first settlement of the Americas, and the origins of civilization.

Over the past 50 years, we moved from an era of pioneer discovery, of field seasons writ large, to a new archaeological world that relies heavily on technology, where discoveries often come on a much smaller scale. Twenty-first century archaeologists may rarely find cities and entire civilizations, but they'll be connoisseurs of exquisite and often arcane detail–studies of early human diet based on teeth, obscure details of Maya scripts, and changes in the distribution of ancient settlements. For all the big questions, we'll be increasingly concerned with crossing the T's and dotting the I's of the past. Obviously, an occasional spectacular site, the 400,000-year-old hunting camps found at Schöningen, Germany, for example will radically alter our perceptions of an entire era of the past. Thanks to Schöningen, we now know that the first Europeans were expert big-game hunters. More often, we'll find ourselves clarifying a pottery chronology in the American Southwest, deciphering the construction of a burial mound in central Europe, or puzzling over environmental change on the fringes of the Sahara Desert. Today's archaeologist lives in a world of mind-numbing detail, often important, frequently interesting. But it's often hard to discern the forest for the archaeological trees, partly because archaeology is now so specialized, and also because all of us suffer from information overload about the past dumped on us by the Web, newspapers, TV specials, and all the apparatus of modern global communications.

One certainty: More archaeological finds will be unearthed during the next half-century than during the entire 150 years or so that archaeologists have worked on the past.

One certainty: More archaeological finds will be unearthed during the next half-century than during the entire 150 years or so that archaeologists have worked on the past. This statement is a sure bet in an era when industrial activity and urban expansion uncover thousands of sites a year. Much of this development is on truly enormous scales, so the challenges of doing archaeology before the bulldozers arrive are truly overwhelming. Some of these projects have long lead times, especially when developers buy up land many years before they build on it. Just planning these developments takes years, and far-sighted some organizations are retaining archaeological companies to manage sites and other cultural resources as part of the planning process. Apart from everything else, it's cheaper. Proactive archaeology, rather than hasty salvage, has the potential to revolutionize much cultural resource management, but the widespread adoption of this strategy is, alas, a long way in the future.

It is in rapidly developing countries such as China, India, South Africa, and Thailand that the most important archaeological discoveries may be made.

A breakneck pace of development may continue in North America and Europe, but it is in rapidly developing countries such as China, India, South Africa, and Thailand that the most important archaeological discoveries may be made. China alone boasts of hundreds, if not thousands, of unexcavated and virtually unknown cities. Even once densely populated centers such as the Han city of Changan near X'ian remain little excavated. There are also, of course, important known sites that await scientific investigation, such as the burial mound of China's first emperor, Shihuangdi, who died in 221 B.C. His sepulcher is said to contain a map of China with the rivers outlined in mercury. Wisely, Chinese authorities have decided to wait until they have the resources and skills to excavate such a unique site. I doubt the mound will be opened in our lifetime—nor should it be: The finds are safe in the ground and a discovery of this importance and magnitude will require extraordinary conservation measures.

Sites such as Shihuangdi's burial mound are the tip of a huge archaeological iceberg. Excavations of Khmer cities and ceremonial centers such as Angkor Wat or Ta Proehm have hardly begun. We can expect spectacular discoveries from Khmer palaces and temples, and fascinating information on the changing settlement patterns in the hinterlands of the great centers. Myanmar is virtually unknown archaeological territory, with its Pyu cities and the spectacular city of Bagan of the eleventh to thirteenth century A.D. Indian archaeology offers open-ended prospects. Unexcavated Harappan towns and cities along the Saraswati River are but one tantalizing prospect. Central Asia's Neolithic and Bronze Age sites are still largely unknown, while the archaeology of the Silk Road remains a virtual mystery. Apart from these potentially spectacular discoveries, we still have much to learn about the archaeology of Siberia and the submerged landbridge of Beringia, which linked Asia with Alaska during the late Ice Age. And when was Australia first settled? We guess about 45,000 years ago, but we don't really know.

Many of the world's archaeological mysteries lie under the high post–Ice Age sea levels. The Danes are already actively engaged in underwater excavation of Neolithic sites in the shallow waters of the Baltic, digging shell middens, recovering canoes, and locating long-submerged houses. Someday, when our ability to carry out archaeological surveys underwater improves, we may be able to identify Paleoindian settlements on the steppe-tundra plains that once lined parts of southeast Alaska, and look for sites on Southeast Asia's continental shelf. A few tantalizing finds from British Columbia and elsewhere give us hope that we will, one day, have the technology to peer at Ice Age coasts and even, perhaps, to excavate submerged

shell middens and hunting camps now below Pacific waters. All this is, of course, quite apart from the advances in deep-sea detection that are already allowing archaeologists to examine ancient wrecks beyond diving range.

We can be sure that industrial development, and the cultural resource management that goes with it, will produce many important archaeological finds in coming years. As archaeology has increasingly become a profession, the chasm between managing cultural resources and purely academic research has tended to widen, especially since the scale much resource management work is now much larger of than in the past. The gap is certain to narrow in future years, as the training of professional archaeologists shifts to accommodate the common ground between academic and nonacademic. The focus of both academic and management research is shifting away from excavation to archaeological survey and the study of ancient landscapes. Landscape archaeology, or settlement archaeology as it is often called, has been in vogue since the 1960s, with notable studies of Peruvian river valleys, Roman landscapes, and an epochal 1970s survey of the Valley of Mexico, which chronicled the dramatic changes in population distributions with the rise of Aztec civilization in the fifteenth century A.D. But landscape archaeology extends far beyond just changing dots on a map to include sophisticated research involving geographic information systems that allow us to place the settlements of the past in the heart of a changing landscape that can be manipulated by a few computer keys. With such studies, we will learn a great deal about, for example, the smaller communities around the great Mississippian center at Cahokia. What was their relationship to ceremonial centers? How important were different agricultural soils and fishing grounds to individual communities? Or, in the Maya lowlands, we may be able to decipher the skein of Maya farming villages around Palenque, Tikal, and other centers. How did village layout change through the centuries? In what ways did such communities respond to exhausted agricultural soils or chronic droughts? And, for the first time, we may gain insights into the ways in which the people of the past perceived their landscapes—the landscapes of memory, if you will. Newer, more sophisticated computer-based maps of locations such as Stonehenge and Roman Wroxeter allow us to "walk" through ancient landscapes and study the visibility of stone circles in their original settings.

As landscape archaeology matures, and we acquire more comprehensive settlement data from new generations of surveys, we will be able to answer important questions about self-sustainability and the use of landscapes by communities. We will achieve a much better understanding of, say, the relationship between classical Athens and its hinterland, of the changes brought on the countryside by the Maya collapse, and of the ritual settings of ancient rock paintings and painted caves. Such research is not particularly spectacular by the standards of the Victorian archaeologist Austen Henry Layard, who excavated ancient Nineveh and Nimrud or Howard Carter of Tutankhamun fame, but crucial in a discipline whose task is not just to find, but to explain ancient human behavior.

The next half-century will see us digging more royal tombs, unraveling the domestication of cattle and other animals, studying women's roles and other social issues. But this time we will be far more sophisticated in our excavations and laboratory work, combining powerful medical science tools with genetics, or climatology with much better excavation and recording techniques. Scientific methods will become so refined that we will be able to look at the deceased as individuals, as peoples with intricate medical histories. Using both bones and DNA, we will literally stand alongside ancient hunters as they try to tame the formidable aurochs. The discoveries will often be cumulative rather than spectacular.

Using both bones and DNA, we will literally stand alongside ancient hunters as they try to tame the formidable aurochs.

Molecular biologists have already transformed the way in which we think about such major developments in the past as the spread of *Homo sapiens* from tropical Africa and the beginnings of agriculture in Europe, to say nothing of the origins of domesticated crops such as einkorn (the first domesticated wheat) in southeastern Turkey. Thanks to medical science, we know more about pharaoh Ramesses II's health than he did. A revolution in climatology using tree rings, ice cores, and other approaches is already having an impact on our understanding of important sites such as Chaco Canyon, New Mexico, where the abandonment of the canyon coincided with a major drought between A.D. 1130 and 1180. Bone strontium tells us that the Amesbury archer from southern England spent his childhood in Central Europe in about 2470 B.C. Now researchers are studying large numbers of Neolithic skeletons to understand how people moved across the landscape. A half-century's further research Will accumulate large numbers of individual strontium and DNA analyses—hundreds, if not thousands, of individual studies will come together in dazzling portraits of the past. Imagine reconstructing the first settlement of Britain by farmers through bone strontium! Envisage a study of the ancestral Pueblo abandonment of Chaco Canyon tied precisely to architectural stages of pueblos and drought cycles! Such revelations are not beyond the grounds of scientific possibility. Residue analysis and trace element studies already allow us to identify Tutankhamun's wines, reconstruct the funeral feast of King Midas of Gordion in about 700 B.C., and study ancient trade routes. Thanks to sophisticated plant and pollen analysis, we can recreate the vegetation under Bronze Age burial mounds near Avebury in southern England, down to the season.

During the next five decades our ability to be "time detectives," to unravel minute clues from the tiniest of finds, will advance exponentially. Ancient beetles offer open-ended chances to glimpse life in prehistoric settlements thousands of years ago. Their habitats are often so distinctive that by looking at their presence one can distinguish between human-occupied areas and natural habitats. Meticulous study of the timbers from the Bronze Age wooden circle at Seahenge in eastern England have established that 59 axes were used on the posts. The recent efforts at facial reconstruction of Tutankhamun or humbler folk such as wounded soldiers from England's War of the Roses represent a tremendous step forward in our understanding of our

forebears. Research in the laboratory today will be crude by the standards of tomorrow, for many of today's emerging methods such as strontium analysis will acquire much greater sophistication within a generation, allowing us to pinpoint individual life histories with remarkable precision. Science is cumulative. Tree-ring studies are an excellent example. Seventy-five years ago, the astronomer Andrew Douglass dated Southwestern pueblos in the world's first precise archaeological chronology. Today, we can reconstruct rainfall in medieval Europe, and date Stradivarius violins with refined versions of the same methodology.

Some of the greatest future revelations will revolve around self-sustainability. There is much talk about oil shortages and our dependence on fossil fuels, but all too few people talk about water. Archaeologist Vernon Scarborough has shown how Maya lords were expert hydrographers, who made sophisticated use of high water tables and aquifers to provide water to their cities. Many futurologists believe tomorrow's wars will revolve around water as much as they will territorial claims or weapons of mass destruction. Thanks to the new paleoclimatology, we can look for the first time at the intricate relationships between sudden, major climatic events such as El Niño or droughts and the continued viability of human societies of every kind. The short-term effects of a drought or hurricane may be catastrophic, but the subtler results such as major and minor social changes, shifting of capitals, or new agricultural methods, may surface years, or even generations, later, as a society adjusts to changed circumstances, the toppling of established leaders, or the undermining of royal credibility. Such was the case in Old Kingdom Egypt in about 2180 B.C., when a severe drought that almost dried up the Nile undermined the ancient doctrine of pharaonic infallibility and the state fell apart. Earthquakes and El Niño devastated the Moche state of coastal Peru during the mid-sixth century A.D. At the time, powerful warrior-priests with a rigid ideology ruled the state. Within a generation, I suspect that we'll have methods to decipher the ways in which Moche's rulers coped with the disaster. For instance, at Huaca de la Luna, the Moche's most sacred shrine, Steve Bourget has recently unearthed a plaza filled with sacrificial victims and evidence of an ideology adopted by the warrior-priests to reinforce their authority when El Niño struck. With luck, the lessons that come from such research will be listened to today.

Many futurologists believe tomorrow's wars will revolve around water as much as they will territorial claims or weapons of mass destruction.

A century of increasing involvement with science has produced a much finer-grained understanding of how archaeological sites were formed, how people exploited their surrounding landscapes, and even how they thought about the cosmos and the world around them. Many future discoveries will come from minute detective work far from the field, contributing to the even-more detailed portrait of the past. But the impact on the larger picture of our history will be immense, especially as the cumulative results of this work come into focus, perhaps a generation or more later. We will never, for example, acquire an instant portrait of the first Americans, much as some of us would like to paint one. Our understanding of this, and so many other "big picture" problems will come from hundreds of seemingly trivial, yet cumulatively extremely important, finds that will make up the archaeology of the future. And as part of this process, I believe that the most exciting discoveries will come not necessarily from the material remains of the past, but from the ancient intangibles, from the unwritten forces that have governed human behavior for nearly 200,000 years. In the next half-century, we'll come much closer to the ultimate goal of archaeology—understanding human diversity and ourselves in the context of more than 200 millennia. And that, in and of itself, is reason enough to study archaeology—to understand the world of the past and why human beings are so similar and yet so different.

BRIAN FAGAN is emeritus professor of anthropology at the University of California, Santa Barbara, and the author of many general books on archaeology.

From *Archaeology,* Sept/Oct 2006, pp. 19–23. Copyright © 2006 by Archaeological Institute of America. Reprinted by permission.

Annals of Archaeology

All the King's Sons

The biggest archaeological find in Egypt since King Tut's tomb is also the most unusual: it may explain the fate of most of Ramesses II's fifty-two sons, New Kingdom funerary practices, and pharaonic sex. What does it feel like to be the first person to enter such a place in three thousand years?

DOUGLAS PRESTON

On February 2, 1995, at ten in the morning, the archaeologist Kent R. Weeks found himself a hundred feet inside a mountain in Egypt's Valley of the Kings, on his belly in the dust of a tomb. He was crawling toward a long-buried doorway that no one had entered for at least thirty-one hundred years. There were two people with him, a graduate student and an Egyptian workman; among them they had one flashlight.

To get through the doorway, Weeks had to remove his hard hat and force his large frame under the lintel with his toes and fingers. He expected to enter a small, plain room marking the end of the tomb. Instead, he found himself in a vast corridor, half full of debris, with doorways lining either side and marching off into the darkness. "When I looked around with the flashlight," Weeks recalled later, "we realized that the corridor was tremendous. I didn't know *what* to think." The air was dead, with a temperature in excess of a hundred degrees and a humidity of one hundred per cent. Weeks, whose glasses had immediately steamed up, was finding it hard to breathe. With every movement, clouds of powder arose, and turned into mud on the skin.

The three people explored the corridor, stooping, and sometimes crawling over piles of rock that had fallen from the ceiling. Weeks counted twenty doorways lining the hundred-foot hallway, some opening into whole suites of rooms with vaulted ceilings carved out of the solid rock of the mountain. At the corridor's end, the feeble flashlight beam revealed a statue of Osiris, the god of resurrection: he was wearing a crown and holding crossed flails and sceptres; his body was bound like that of a mummy. In front of Osiris, the corridor came to a T, branching into two transverse passageways, each of them eighty feet long and ending in what looked like a descending staircase blocked with debris. Weeks counted thirty-two additional rooms off those two corridors.

The tomb was of an entirely new type, never seen by archaeologists before. "The architecture didn't fit any known pattern," Weeks told me. "And it was so *big*. I just couldn't make sense of it." The largest pharaonic tombs in the Valley contain ten or fifteen rooms at most. This one had at least sixty-seven—the total making it not only the biggest tomb in the Valley but possibly the biggest in all Egypt. Most tombs in the Valley of the Kings follow a standard architectural plan—a series of consecutive chambers and corridors like a string of boxcars shot at an angle into the bedrock, and ending with the burial vault. This tomb, with its T shape, had a warren of side chambers, suites, and descending passageways. Weeks knew from earlier excavations that the tomb was the resting place for at least four sons of Ramesses II, the pharaoh also known as Ramesses the Great—and, traditionally, as simply Pharaoh in the Book of Exodus. Because of the tomb's size and complexity, Weeks had to consider the possibility that it was a catacomb for as many as fifty of Ramesses' fifty-two sons—the first example of a royal family mausoleum in ancient Egypt.

Weeks had discovered the tomb's entrance eight years earlier, after the Egyptian government announced plans to widen the entrance to the Valley to create a bus turnaround at the end of an asphalt road. From reading old maps and reports, he had recalled that the entrance to a lost tomb lay in the area that was to be paved over. Napoleon's expedition to Egypt had noted a tomb there, and a rather feckless Englishman named James Burton had crawled partway inside it in 1825. A few years later, the archaeologist Sir John Gardner Wilkinson had given it the designation KV5, for Kings' Valley Tomb No. 5, when he numbered eighteen tombs there. Howard Carter—the archaeologist who discovered King Tutankhamun's tomb in 1922, two hundred feet farther on—dug two feet in, decided that KV5's entrance looked unimportant, and used it as a

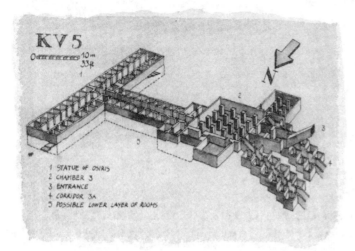

© Matteo Pericoli

A floor plan of KV5, which may be the largest tomb in Egypt and the only royal mausoleum. Ramesses II, the master builder of Thebes, now rests in the Cairo Museum.

Egyptian Museum of Antiquities, Cairo.

dumping ground for debris from his other excavations, thus burying it under ten feet of stone and dirt. The location of the tomb's entrance was quickly forgotten.

It took about ten days of channelling through Carter's heaps of debris for Weeks and his men to find the ancient doorway of KV5, and it proved to be directly across the path from the tomb of Ramesses the Great. The entrance lay at the edge of the asphalt road, about ten feet below grade and behind the rickety booths of T-shirt venders and fake-scarab-beetle sellers.

Plans for the bus turnaround were cancelled, and, over a period of seven years, Weeks and his workmen cleared half of the first two chambers and briefly explored a third one. The tomb was packed from floor to ceiling with dirt and rocks that had been washed in by flash floods. He uncovered finely carved reliefs on the walls, which showed Ramesses presenting various sons to the gods, with their names and titles recorded in hieroglyphics. When he reached floor level, he found thousands of objects: pieces of faience jewelry, fragments of furniture, a wooden fist from a coffin, human and animal bones, mummified body parts, chunks of sarcophagi, and fragments of the canopic jars used to hold the mummified organs of the deceased—all detritus left by ancient tomb robbers.

The third chamber was anything but modest. It was about sixty feet square, one of the largest rooms in the Valley, and was supported by sixteen massive stone pillars arranged in four rows. Debris filled the room to within about two feet of the ceiling, allowing just enough space for Weeks to wriggle around. At the back of the chamber, in the axis of the tomb, Weeks noticed an almost buried doorway. Still believing that the tomb was like others in the Valley, he assumed that the doorway merely led to a small, dead-end annex, so he didn't bother with it for several years—not until last February, when he decided to have a look.

Immediately after the discovery, Weeks went back to a four-dollar-a-night pension he shared with his wife, Susan, in the mud village of Gezira Bairat, showered off the tomb dust, and took a motorboat across the Nile to the small city of Luxor. He faxed a short message to Cairo, three hundred miles downriver. It was directed to his major financial supporter, Bruce Ludwig, who was attending a board meeting at the American University in Cairo, where Weeks is a professor. It read, simply, "Have made wonderful discovery in Valley of the Kings. Await your arrival." Ludwig instantly recognized the significance of the fax and the inside joke it represented: it was a close paraphrase of the telegram that Howard Carter had sent to the Earl of Carnarvon, his financial supporter, when he discovered Tutankhamun's tomb. Ludwig booked a flight to Luxor.

"That night, the enormousness of the discovery began to sink in," Weeks recalled. At about two o'clock in the morning, he turned to his wife and said, "Susan, I think our lives have changed forever."

The discovery was announced jointly by Egypt's Supreme Council of Antiquities, which oversees all archaeological work in the country, and the American University in Cairo, under whose aegis Weeks was working. It became the biggest archaeological story of the decade, making the front page of the *Times* and the cover of *Time*. Television reporters descended on the site. Weeks had to shut down the tomb to make the talk-show circuit. The London newspapers had a field day: the *Daily Mail* headlined its story "PHARAOH'S 50 SONS IN MUMMY OF ALL TOMBS," and one tabloid informed its readers that texts in the tomb gave a date for the Second Coming and the end of the world, and also revealed cures for AIDS and cancer.

The media also wondered whether the tomb would prove that Ramesses II was indeed the pharaoh referred to in Exodus. The speculation centered on Amun-her-khopshef, Ramesses' firstborn son, whose name is prominent on KV5's wall. According to the Bible, in order to force Egypt to free the Hebrews from bondage the Lord visited a number of disasters on the land, including the killing of all firstborn Egyptians from the pharaoh's son on down. Some scholars believe that if Amun-her-khopshef's remains are found it may be possible to show at what age and how he died.

Book publishers and Hollywood producers showed great interest in Weeks's story. He didn't respond at first, dismissing inquiries with a wave of the hand. "It's all *kalam fadi*," he said, using the Arabic phrase for empty talk. Eventually, however, so many offers poured in that he engaged an agent at William Morris to handle them; a book proposal will be submitted to publishers later this month.

In the fall, Weeks and his crew decided to impose a partial media blackout on the excavation site—the only way they could get any work done, they felt—but they agreed to let me accompany them near the end of the digging season. Just before I arrived, in mid-November, two mysterious descending corridors, with dozens of new chambers, unexpectedly came to light, and I had the good fortune to be the only journalist to see them.

The Valley of the Kings was the burial ground for the pharaohs of the New Kingdom, the last glorious period of Egyptian history. It began around 1550 B.C., when the Egyptians expelled the foreign Hyksos rulers from Lower Egypt and reëstablished a vast empire, stretching across the Middle East to Syria. It lasted half a millennium. Sixty years before Ramesses, the pharaoh Akhenaten overthrew much of the Egyptian religion and decreed that thenceforth Egyptians should worship only one god—Light, whose visible symbol was Aten, the disk of the sun. Akhenaten's revolution came to a halt at his death. Ramesses represented the culmination of the return to tradition. He was an exceedingly conservative man, who saw himself as the guardian of the ancient customs, and he was particularly zealous in erasing the heretic pharaoh's name from his temples and stelae, a task begun by his father, Seti I. Because Ramesses disliked innovation, his monuments were notable not for their architectural brilliance but for their monstrous size. The New Kingdom began a slow decline following his rule, and finally sputtered to an end with Ramesses XI, the last pharaoh buried in the Valley of the Kings.

The discovery of KV5 will eventually open for us a marvellous window on this period. We know almost nothing about the offspring of the New Kingdom pharaohs or what roles they played. After each eldest prince ascended the throne, the younger sons disappeared so abruptly from the record that it was once thought they were routinely executed. The burial chambers' hieroglyphics, if they still survive, may give us an invaluable account of each son's life and accomplishments. There is a remote possibility—it was suggested to me by the secretary-general of the Supreme Council of Antiquities, Professor Abdel-Halim Nur el-Din, who is an authority on women in ancient Egypt—that Ramesses' daughters might be buried in KV5 as well. (Weeks thinks the possibility highly unlikely.)

Before Weeks is done, he will probably find sarcophagi, pieces of funerary offerings, identifiable pieces of mummies, and many items with hieroglyphics on them. The tomb will add a new chapter to our understanding of Egyptian funerary traditions. And there is always a possibility of finding an intact chamber packed with treasure.

Ramesses the Great's reign lasted an unprecedented sixty-seven years, from 1279 to 1213 B.C. He covered the Nile Valley from Nubia to the delta with magnificent temples, statuary, and stelae, which are some of the grandest monuments the world has ever seen. Among his projects were the enormous forecourt at Luxor Temple; the Ramesseum; the cliffside temples of Abu Simbel; the great Hall of Columns at Karnak; and the city of Pi Ramesse. The two "vast and trunkless legs of stone" with a "shattered visage" in Shelley's poem "Ozymandias" were those of Ramesses—fragments of the largest statue in pharaonic history. Ramesses outlived twelve of his heirs, dying in his early nineties. The thirteenth crown prince, Merneptah, became pharaoh only in his sixties.

By the time Ramesses ascended the throne, at twenty-five, he had fathered perhaps ten sons and as many daughters. His father had started him out with a harem while he was still a teenager, and he had two principal wives, Nefertari and Istnofret. He later added several Hittite princesses to his harem, and probably his sister and two daughters. It is still debated whether the incestuous marriage of the pharaohs were merely ceremonial or actually consummated. If identifiable remains of Ramesses' sons are found in KV5, it is conceivable that DNA testing might resolve this vexing question.

In most pharaonic monuments we find little about wives and children, but Ramesses showed an unusual affection for his family, extolling the accomplishments of his sons and listing their names on numerous temple walls. All over Egypt, he commissioned statues of Nefertari (not to be confused with the more famous Nefertiti, who was Akhenaten's wife), "for whose sake the very sun does shine." When she died, in Year 24 of his reign, Ramesses interred her in the most beautiful tomb yet discovered in the Valley of the Queens, just south of the Valley of the Kings. The tomb survived intact, and its incised and painted walls are nearly as fresh as the day they were fashioned. The rendering of Nefertari's face and figure perhaps speaks most eloquently of Ramesses' love for her. She is shown making her afterlife journey dressed in a diaphanous linen gown, with her slender figure emerging beneath the gossamer fabric. Her face was painted using the technique of chiaroscuro—perhaps the first known example in the history of art of a human face being treated as a three-dimensional volume. The Getty Conservation Institute recently spent millions restoring the tomb. The Getty recommended that access to the tomb be restricted, in order to preserve it, but the Egyptian government has opened it to tourists, at thirty-five dollars a head.

The design of royal tombs was so fixed by tradition that they had no architect, at least as we use that term today. The tombs were laid out and chiseled from ceiling to floor, resulting in ceiling dimensions that are precise and floor dimensions that can vary considerably. All the rooms and corridors in a typical royal tomb had names, many of which we still do not fully understand: the First God's Passage, Hall of Hindering, Sanctuaries in Which the Gods Repose. The burial chamber was often called the House of Gold. Some tombs had a Hall of Truth, whose murals showed the pharaoh's heart being weighed in judgment by Osiris, with the loathsome god Ammut squatting nearby, waiting to devour it if it was found wanting. Many of the reliefs were so formulaic that they were probably taken from copybooks. Yet even within this rigid tradition breathtaking flights of creativity and artistic expression can be found.

Most of the tombs in the Valley were never finished: they took decades to cut, and the plans usually called for something more elaborate than the pharaoh could achieve during his rule. As a result, the burial of the pharaoh was often a panicky, ad-hoc affair, with various rooms in the tomb being adapted for other purposes, and decorations and texts painted in haste or omitted completely. (Some of the most beautiful inscriptions were those painted swiftly; they have a spontaneity and freshness of line rivalling Japanese calligraphy.)

From the time of Ramesses II on, the tombs were not hidden: their great doorways, which were made of wood, could be opened. It is likely that the front rooms of many tombs were regularly visited by priests to make offerings. This may have been particularly true of KV5, where the many side chambers perhaps served such a purpose. The burial chambers containing treasure, however, were always sealed.

Despite all the monuments and inscriptions that Ramesses left us, it is still difficult to bridge the gap of thirty-one hundred years and see Ramesses as a person. One thing we do know: the standard image of the pharaoh, embodied in Shelley's "frown, and wrinkled lip, and sneer of cold command," is a misconception. One of the finest works from Ramesses' reign is a statue of the young king now in the Museo Egizio, in Turin. The expression on his face is at once compassionate and other-worldly, not unlike that of a Giotto Madonna; his head is slightly bowed, as if to acknowledge his role as both leader and servant. This is not the face of a tyrant-pharaoh who press-ganged his people into building monuments to his greater glory. Rather, it is the portrait of a ruler who had his subjects' interests at heart, and this is precisely what the archaeological and historical records suggest about Ramesses. Most of the Egyptians who labored on the pharaoh's monuments did so proudly and were, by and large, well compensated. There is a lovely stela on which Ramesses boasts about how much he has given his workers, "so that they work for me with their full hearts." Dorothea Arnold, the head curator of the Egyptian Department at the Metropolitan Museum, told me, "The pharaoh was *believed* in. As to whether he was beloved, that is beside the point: he was *necessary.* He was life itself. He represented everything good. Without him there would be nothing."

Final proof of the essential humanity of the pharaonic system is that it survived for more than three thousand years. (When Ramesses ascended the throne, the pyramids at Giza were already thirteen hundred years old.) Egypt produced one of the most stable cultural and religious traditions the world has ever seen.

Very little lives in the Valley of the Kings now. It is a wilderness of stone and light—a silent, roofless sepulchre. Rainfall averages a quarter inch per year, and one of the hottest natural air temperatures on earth was recorded in the surrounding mountains. And yet the Valley is a surprisingly intimate place. Most of the tombs lie within a mere forty acres, and the screen of cliffs gives the area a feeling of privacy. Dusty paths and sun-bleached, misspelled signs add a pleasant, ramshackle air.

The Valley lies on the outskirts of the ancient city of Thebes, now in ruins. In a six-mile stretch of riverbank around the city, there are as many temples, palaces, and monuments as anywhere else on earth, and the hills are so pockmarked with the yawning pits and doorways of ancient tombs that they resemble a First World War battlefield. It is dangerous to walk or ride anywhere alone. Howard Carter discovered an important tomb when the horse he was riding broke through and fell into it. Recently, a Canadian woman fell into a tomb while hiking and fractured her leg; no one could hear her screams, and she spent the days leading up to her death writing postcards. One archaeologist had to clear a tomb that contained a dead cow and twenty-one dead dogs that had gone in to eat it.

Almost all the tombs lying open have been pillaged. A papyrus now in Italy records the trial of someone who robbed KV5 itself in 1150 B.C. The robber confessed under torture to plundering the tomb of Ramesses the Great and then going "across the path" to rob the tomb of his sons. Ancient plunderers often vandalized the tombs they robbed, possibly in an attempt to destroy the magic that supposedly protected them. They smashed everything, levered open sarcophagi, ripped apart mummies to get at the jewelry hidden in the wrappings, and sometimes threw objects against the walls with such force that they left dents and smudges of pure gold.

Nobody is sure why this particular valley, three hundred miles up the Nile from the pyramids, was chosen as the final resting place of the New Kingdom pharaohs. Egyptologists theorize that the sacred pyramidal shape of el-Qurn, the mountain at the head of the Valley of the Kings, may have been one factor. Another was clearly security: the Valley is essentially a small box canyon carved out of the barren heart of a desert mountain range; it has only one entrance, through a narrow gorge, and the surrounding cliffs echo and magnify any sounds of human activity, such as the tapping of a robber's pick on stone.

Contrary to popular belief, the tombs in the Valley are not marked with curses. King Tut's curse was invented by Arthur Weigall, an Egyptologist and journalist at the *Daily Mail,* who was furious that Carnarvon had given the London *Times* the exclusive on the discovery. Royal tombs did not need curses to protect them. Priests guarded the Valley night and day, and thieves knew exactly what awaited them if they were caught: no curse could compete with the fear of being impaled alive.

"There are a few curses on some private tombs and in some legal documents," James Allen, an Egyptologist with the Metropolitan Museum, told me. "The most extreme I know of is on a legal document of the Ramesside Period. It reads, 'As for the one who will violate it, he shall be seized for Amun-Ra. He shall be for the flame of Sekhmet. He is an enemy of Osiris, lord of Abydos, and so is his son, for ever and ever. May donkeys fuck him, may donkeys fuck his wife, may his wife fuck his son.' "

Some scholars today, looking back over the past two hundred years of archaeological activity, think a curse might have been a good idea: most of the archaeology done in the Valley has been indistinguishable from looting. Until the nineteen-sixties, those who had concessions to excavate there were allowed to keep a percentage of the spoils as "payment" for their work. In the fever of the treasure hunt, tombs were emptied without anyone bothering to photograph the objects found or to record their positions in situ, or even to note which tomb they came from. Items that had no market value were trashed. Wilkinson, the man who gave the tombs their numbers, burned three-thousand-year-old wooden coffins and artifacts to heat his house. Murals and reliefs were chopped out of walls. At dinner parties, the American lawyer Theodore M. Davis, who financed many digs in the Valley, used to tear up necklaces woven of ancient flowers and fabric to show how strong they were after three thousand years in a tomb. Pyramids were blasted open with explosives, and one tomb door was bashed in with a battering ram. Even Carter never published a proper scientific report on Tut's tomb. It is only in the last twenty-five years that real archaeology has come to Egypt, and KV5 will be one of the first tombs in the Valley of the Kings to be entirely excavated and documented according to proper archaeological techniques.

Fortunately, other great archaeological projects remain to be carried out with the new techniques. The Theban Necropolis is believed to contain between four thousand and five thousand tombs, of which only four hundred have been given numbers. More than half of the royal tombs in the Valley of the Kings have not been fully excavated, and of these only five have been properly documented. There are mysterious blocked passageways, hollow floors, chambers packed with debris, and caved-in rooms. King Tut's was by no means the last undiscovered pharaonic tomb in Egypt. In the New Kingdom alone, the tombs of Amosis, Amenhotep I, Tuthmosis II, and Ramesses VIII have never been identified. The site of the burial ground for the pharaohs of the entire Twenty-first Dynasty is unknown. And the richness and size of KV5 offer the tantalizing suggestion that other princely tombs of its kind are lying undiscovered beneath the Egyptian sands; Ramesses would surely not have been the only pharaoh to bury his sons in such style.

Work at KV5 in the fall season proceeds from six-thirty in the morning until one-thirty in the afternoon. Every day, to get to KV5 from my hotel in Luxor, I cross the Nile on the public ferry, riding with a great mass of fellaheen—men carrying goats slung around their necks, children lugging sacks of eggplants, old men squatting in their djellabas and smoking cigarettes or eating *leb* nuts—while the ancient diesel boat wheezes and blubs across the river. I am usually on the river in time to catch the sun rising over the shattered columns of Luxor Temple, along the riverbank. The Nile is still magical—crowded with feluccas, lined with date palms, and bearing on its current many clumps of blooming water hyacinths.

The ferry empties its crowds into a chaos of taxis, camels, donkeys, children begging for baksheesh, and hopeful guides greeting every tourist with a hearty "Welcome to Egypt!" In contrast to the grand hotels and boulevards of Luxor, the west bank consists of clusters of mud villages scattered among impossibly green fields of cane and clover, where the air is heavy with smoke and the droning prayers of the muezzin. Disembarkation is followed by a harrowing high-speed taxi ride to the Valley, the driver weaving past donkey carts and herds of goats, his sweaty fist pounding the horn.

On the first day of my visit, I find Kent Weeks sitting in a green canvas tent at the entrance to KV5 and trying to fit together pieces of a human skull. It is a cool Saturday morning in November. From the outside, KV5 looks like all the other tombs—a mere doorway in a hillside. Workmen in a bucket brigade are passing baskets filled with dirt out of the tomb's entrance and dumping them in a nearby pile, on which two men are squatting and sifting through the debris with small gardening tools. "Hmm," Weeks says, still fiddling with the skull. "I had this together a moment ago. You'll have to wait for our expert. He can put it together just like that." He snaps his fingers.

"Whose skull is it?"

"One of Ramesses' sons, I hope. The brown staining on it—here—shows that it might have come from a mummified body. We'll eventually do DNA comparisons with Ramesses and other members of his family."

Relaxing in the tent, Weeks does not cut the dapper, pugnacious figure of a Howard Carter, nor does he resemble the sickly, elegant Lord Carnarvon in waistcoat and watch chain. But because he is the first person to have made a major discovery in the Valley of the Kings since Carter, he is surely in their class. At fifty-four, he is handsome and fit, his ruddy face peering at the world through thick square glasses from underneath a Tilley hat. His once crisp shirt and khakis look like hell after an hour in the tomb's stifling atmosphere, and his Timberland shoes have reached a state of indescribable lividity from tomb dust.

Weeks has the smug air of a man who is doing the most interesting thing he could possibly do in life. He launches into his subject with such enthusiasm that one's first impulse is to flee. But as he settles back in his rickety chair with the skull in one hand and a glass of *yansoon* tea in the other, and yarns on about lost tombs, crazy Egyptologists, graverobbers, jackal-headed gods, mummies, secret passageways, and the mysteries of the Underworld, you begin to succumb. His conversation is laced with obscene sallies delivered with a schoolboy's relish, and you can tell he has not been to any gender-sensitivity training seminars. He can be disconcertingly blunt. He characterized one archaeologist as "ineffectual, ridiculously inept, and a wonderful source of comic relief," another as "a raving psychopath," and a third as "a dork, totally off the wall." When I asked if KV5 would prove that Ramesses was the Biblical Pharaoh, he responded with irritation: "I can almost guarantee you that we will *not* find anything in KV5 bearing on the Exodus question. All the speculation in the press assumed there *was* an exodus and that it was described accurately in the Bible. I don't believe it. There may have been Israelites in Egypt, but I sincerely doubt Exodus is an exact account of what occurred. At least I *hope* it wasn't—with the Lord striking down the firstborn of Egypt and turning the rivers to blood."

His is a rarefied profession: there are only about four hundred Egyptologists in the world, and only a fraction of them are archaeologists. (Most are art historians and philologists.) Egyptology is a difficult profession to break into; in a good year, there might be two job openings in the United States. It is the kind of field where the untimely death of a tenured figure sets the photocopying machines running all night.

"From the age of eight, I had no doubt: I wanted to be an Egyptologist," Weeks told me. His parents—one a policeman, the other a medical librarian—did not try to steer him into a sensible profession, and a string of teachers encouraged his interest. When Weeks was in high school, in Longview, Washington, he met the Egyptologist Ahmed Fakhry in Seattle, and Fakhry was so charmed by the young man that he invited him to lunch and mapped out his college career.

In 1963, Weeks's senior year at the University of Washington, one of the most important events in the history of Egyptology took place. Because of the construction of the High Dam at Aswan, the rising waters of the Nile began to flood Nubia; they would soon inundate countless archaeological sites, including the incomparable temples of Abu Simbel. UNESCO and the Egyptian and Sudanese governments issued an international plea for help. Weeks immediately wrote to William Kelly Simpson, a prominent Egyptologist at Yale who was helping to coördinate the salvage project, and offered his services. He received plane tickets by return mail.

"The farthest I'd been away from home was Disneyland, and here I was going to Nubia," Weeks said. "The work had to be done fast: the lake waters were already rising. I got there and suddenly found myself being told, 'Take these eighty workmen and go dig that ancient village.' The nearest settlement was Wadi Halfa, ninety miles away. The first words of Arabic I learned were 'Dig no deeper' and 'Carry the baskets faster.' "

Weeks thereafter made a number of trips to Nubia, and just before he set out on one of them he invited along as artist a young woman he had met near the mummy case at the University of Washington museum—Susan Howe, a solemn college senior with red hair and a deadpan sense of humor.

"We lived on the river on an old rat-infested dahabeah," Susan told me. "My first night on the Nile, we were anchored directly in front of Abu Simbel, parked right in front of Ramesses' knees. It was all lit up, because work was going on day and night." An emergency labor force was cutting the temple into enormous blocks and reassembling it on higher ground. "After five months, the beer ran out, the cigarettes ran out, the water was really hot, the temperature was a hundred and fifteen degrees in the shade, and there were terrible windstorms. My parents were just *desperate* to know when I was coming home. But I thought, Ah! This is the life! It was so romantic. The workmen sang songs and clapped every morning when we arrived. So we wrote home and gave our parents ten days' notice that we were going to get married."

They have now been married twenty-nine years. Susan is the artist and illustrator for many of Kent's projects, and has also worked for other archaeologists in Egypt. She spends much of her day in front of KV5, in the green tent, wearing a scarf and peach-colored Keds, while she makes precise scale drawings of pottery and artifacts. In her spare time, she wanders around Gezira Bairat, painting exquisite watercolors of doorways and donkeys.

Weeks eventually returned to Washington to get his M.A., and in 1971 he received a Ph.D. from Yale; his dissertation dealt with ancient Egyptian anatomical terminology. He landed a plum job as a curator in the Metropolitan Museum's Egyptian Department. Two years later, bored by museum work, he quit and went back to Egypt, and was shortly offered the directorship of Chicago House, the University of Chicago's research center in Luxor. The Weekses have two children, whom they reared partly in Egypt, sending them to a local Luxor school. After four years at Chicago House, Weeks took a professorship at Berkeley, but again the lure of Egypt was too strong. In 1987, he renounced tenure at Berkeley, took a large pay cut, and went back to Egypt as a professor of Egyptology at the American University in Cairo, where he has been ever since.

While in Nubia, Weeks excavated an ancient working-class cemetery, pulling some seven thousand naturally desiccated bodies out of the ground. In a study of diet and health, he and a professor of orthodontics named James Harris X-rayed many of these bodies. Then Weeks and Harris persuaded the Egyptian government to allow them to X-ray the mummies of the pharaohs, by way of comparison. A team of physicians, orthodontists, and pathologists studied the royal X-rays, hoping to determine such things as age at death, cause of death, diet, and medical problems. They learned that there was surprisingly little difference between the two classes in diet and health.

One finding caused an uproar among Egyptologists. The medical team had been able to determine ages at death for most of the pharaohs, and in some cases these starkly contradicted the standard chronologies of the Egyptologists. The mystery was eventually solved when the team consulted additional ancient papyri, which told how, in the late New Kingdom, the high priests realized that many of the tombs in the Valley of the Kings had been robbed. To prevent further desecration, they gathered up almost all the royal mummies (missing only King

Tut) and reburied them in two caches, both of which were discovered intact in the nineteenth century. "What we think happened is that the priests let the name dockets with some of the mummies fall off and put them back wrong," Weeks told me. It is also possible that the mixup occurred when the mummies were moved down the river to Cairo in the nineteenth century.

The team members analyzed the craniofacial characteristics of each mummy and figured out which ones looked most like which others. (Most of the pharaohs were related.) By combining these findings with age-at-death information, they were able to restore six of the mummies' proper names.

Weeks' second project led directly to the discovery of KV5. In 1979, he began mapping the entire Theban Necropolis. After an overview, he started with the Valley of the Kings. No such map had ever been done before. (That explains how KV5 came to be found and then lost several times in its history.) The Theban Mapping Project is to include the topography of the Valley and the three-dimensional placement of each tomb within the rock. The data are being computerized, and eventually Weeks will re-create the Valley on CD-s, which will allow a person to "fly" into any tomb and view in detail the murals and reliefs on its walls and ceilings.

Some Egyptologists I spoke with consider the mapping of the Theban Necropolis to be the most important archaeological project in Egypt, KV5 notwithstanding. A map of the Valley of the Kings is desperately needed. Some tombs are deteriorating rapidly, with murals cracking and falling to the floors, and ceilings, too, collapsing. Damage has been done by the opening of the tombs to outside air. (When Carter opened King Tut's tomb, he could actually hear "strange rustling, murmuring, whispering sounds" of objects as the new air began its insidious work of destruction. In other tombs, wooden objects turned into "cigar-ash.") Greek, Roman, and early European tourists explored the tombs with burning torches—and even lived in some tombs—leaving an oily soot on the paintings. Rapid changes in temperature and humidity generated by the daily influx of modern-day tourists have caused even greater damage, some of it catastrophic.

The gravest danger of all comes from flooding. Most of the tombs are now wide open. Modern alterations in the topography, such as the raising of the valley floor in order to build paths for the tourists, have created a highway directing floodwaters straight into the mouths of the tombs. A brief rain in November of 1994 generated a small flash flood that tore through the Valley at thirty miles an hour and damaged several tombs. It burst into the tomb of Bay, a vizier of the New Kingdom, with such force that it churned through the decorated chambers and completely ruined them. Layers of debris in KV5 indicate that a major flash flood occurs about once every three hundred years. If such a flood occurred tomorrow, the Valley of the Kings could be largely destroyed.

There is no master plan for preserving the Valley. The most basic element in such a plan is the completion of Weeks's map. Only then can preservationists monitor changes in the tombs

and begin channelling and redirecting floodwaters. For this reason, some archaeologists privately panicked when Weeks found KV5. "When I first heard about it," one told me, "I thought, Oh my God, that's it, Kent will never finish the mapping project."

Weeks promises that KV5 will not interfere with the Theban Mapping Project. "Having found the tomb, we've got an obligation to leave it in a good, stable, safe condition," he says. "And we have an obligation to publish. Public interest in KV5 has actually increased funding for the Theban Mapping Project."

At 9 A.M., the workmen laboring in KV5—there are forty-two of them—begin to file out and perch in groups on the hillside, to eat a breakfast of bread, tomatoes, green onions, and a foul cheese called *misht*. Weeks rises from his chair, nods to me, and asks, "Are you ready?"

We descend a new wooden staircase into the mountain and enter Chamber 1, where we exchange our sun hats for hard hats. The room is small and only half cleared. Visible tendrils of humid, dusty air waft in from the dim recesses of the tomb. The first impression I have of the tomb is one of shocking devastation. The ceilings are shot through with cracks, and in places they have caved in, dropping automobile-size pieces of rock. A forest of screw jacks and timbers holds up what is left, and many of the cracks are plastered with "tell-tales"—small seals that show if any more movement of the rock occurs.

The reliefs in Chamber 1 are barely visible, a mere palimpsest of what were once superbly carved and painted scenes of Ramesses and his sons adoring the gods, and panels of hieroglyphics. Most of the damage here was the result of a leaky sewer pipe that was laid over the tomb about forty years ago from an old rest house in the Valley. The leak caused salt crystals to grow and eat away the limestone walls. Here and there, however, one can still see traces of the original paint.

The decorations on the walls of the first two rooms show various sons being presented to the gods by Ramesses, in the classic Egyptian pose: head in profile, shoulders in frontal view, and torso in three-quarters view. There are also reliefs of tables laden with offerings of food for the gods, and hieroglyphic texts spelling out the names and titles of several sons and including the royal cartouche of Ramesses.

A doorway from Chamber 2 opens into Chamber 3—the Pillared Hall. It is filled with dirt and rock almost to the ceiling, giving one a simultaneous impression of grandeur and claustrophobia. Two narrow channels have been cut through the debris to allow for the passage of the workmen. Many of the pillars are split and shattered, and only fragments of decorations remain—a few hieroglyphic characters, an upraised arm, part of a leg. Crazed light from several randomly placed bulbs throws shadows around the room.

I follow Weeks down one of the channels. "This room is in such dangerous condition that we decided not to clear it," he says. "We call this channel the Mubarak trench. It was dug so that President Mubarak could visit the tomb without having to creep around on his hands and knees." He laughs.

When we are halfway across the room, he points out the words "James Burton 1825" smoked on the ceiling with the flame of a candle: it represents the Englishman's farthest point of penetration. Not far away is another graffito—this one in hieratic, the cursive form of hieroglyphic writing. It reads "Year 19"—the nineteenth year of Ramesses' reign. "This date gives us a *terminus ante quem* for the presence of Ramesses' workmen in this chamber," Weeks says.

He stops at one of the massive pillars. "And here's a mystery," he says, "Fifteen of the pillars in this room were cut from the native rock, but this one is a fake. The rock was carefully cut away—you can see chisel marks on the ceiling—and then the pillar was rebuilt out of stone and plastered to look like the others. Why?" He gives the pillar a sly pat. "Was something very large moved in here?"

I follow Weeks to the end of the trench—the site of the doorway that he crawled through in February. The door has been cleared, and we descend a short wooden staircase to the bottom of the great central corridor. It is illuminated by a string of naked light bulbs, which cast a yellow glow through a pall of dust. The many doors lining both sides of the corridor are still blocked with debris, and the stone floor is covered with an inch of dust.

At the far end of the corridor, a hundred feet away, stands the mummiform statue of Osiris. It is carved from the native rock, and only its face is missing. Lit from below, the statue casts a dramatic shadow on the ceiling. I try to take notes, but my glasses have fogged up, and sweat is dripping onto my notebook, making the ink run off the page. I can only stand and blink.

Nothing in twenty years of writing about archaeology has prepared me for this great wrecked corridor chiselled out of the living rock, with rows of shattered doorways opening into darkness, and ending in the faceless mummy of Osiris. I feel like a trespasser, a voyeur, grazing into the sacred precincts of the dead. As I stare at the walls, patterns and lines begin to emerge from the shattered stone: ghostly figures and faint hieroglyphics; animal-headed gods performing mysterious rites. Through doorways I catch glimpses of more rooms and more doorways beyond. There is a presence of death in this wrecked tomb that goes beyond those who were buried here; it is the death of a civilization.

With most of the texts on the walls destroyed or still buried under debris, it is not yet possible to determine what function was served by the dozens of side chambers. Weeks feels it likely, however, that they were *not* burial chambers, because the doorways are too narrow to admit a sarcophagus. Instead, he speculates they were chapels where the Theban priests could make offerings to the dead sons. Because the tomb departs so radically from the standard design, it is impossible even to speculate what the mysterious Pillared Hall or many of the other antechambers were for.

Weeks proudly displays some reliefs on the walls, tracing with his hand the figure of Isis and her husband, Osiris, and pointing out the ibis-headed god Thoth. "Ah!" he cries. "And here is a *wonderful* figure of Anubis and Hathor!" Anubis is the jackal-headed god of mummification, and Hathor a goddess associates with the Theban Necropolis. These were scenes to help guide Ramesses' sons through the rituals, spells, and incantations that would insure them a safe journey through the realm of death. The reliefs are exceedingly difficult to see; Susan Weeks told me later that she has sometimes had to stare at a wall for long periods—days, even—before she could pick out the shadow of a design. She is now in the process of copying these fragmentary reliefs on Mylar film, to help experts who will attempt to reconstruct the entire wall sequence and its accompanying test, and so reveal to us the purpose of the room or the corridor. KV5 will only yield up its secrets slowly, and with great effort.

"Here's Ramesses and one of his sons," Weeks says, indicating two figures standing hand in hand. "But, alas, the name is gone. Very disappointing!" He charges off down the corridor, raising a trail of dust, and comes to a halt at the statue of Osiris, poking his glasses back up his sweating nose. "Look at this. Spectacular! A three-dimensional statue of Osiris is very rare. Most tombs depict him painted only. We dug around the base here trying to find the face, but instead we found a lovely offering of nineteen clay figs."

He makes a ninety-degree turn down the left transverse corridor, snaking around a cave-in. The corridor runs level for some distance and then plunges down a double staircase with a ramp in the middle, cut from the bedrock, and ends in a wall of bedrock. Along the sides of this corridor we have passed sixteen more partly blocked doors.

"Now, here is something new," Weeks says. "You're the first outsider to see this. I hoped that this staircase would lead to the burial chambers. This kind of ramp was usually built to slide the sarcophagi down. But look! The corridor just ends in a blank wall. Why in the world would they build a staircase and ramp going nowhere? So I decided to clear the two lowest side chambers. We just finished last week."

He ushers me into one of the rooms. There is no light; the room is large and very hot.

"They were empty," Weeks says.

"Too bad."

"Take a look at this floor."

"Nice." Floors do not particularly excite me.

"It happens to be the finest plastered floor in the Valley of the Kings. They went to enormous trouble with this floor, laying down three coats of plaster at different times, in different colors. Why?" He pauses. "Now stamp on the floor."

I thump the floor. There is a hollow reverberation that shakes not only the floor but the entire room. "Oh, my God, there's something underneath there!" I exclaim.

"*Maybe,*" Weeks says, a large smile gathering on his face. "Who knows? It could be a natural cavity or crack, or it might be a passageway to a lower level."

"You mean there might be sealed burial chambers below?"

Weeks smiles again. "Let's not get ahead of ourselves. Next June, we'll drill some test holes and do it properly."

We scramble back to the Osiris statue.

"Now I'm going to take you to our latest discovery," Weeks says. "This is intriguing. *Very* fascinating."

We make our way through several turns back to the Pillared Hall. Weeks leads me down the other trench, which ends at the southwest corner of the hall. Here, earlier in the month, the workmen discovered a buried doorway that opened onto a steep descending passageway, again packed solid with debris. The workmen have now cleared the passageway down some sixty feet, exposing twelve more side chambers, and are still at work.

We pause at the top of the newly excavated passageway. A dozen screw jacks with timbers hold up its cracked ceiling. The men have finished breakfast and are back at work, one man picking away at the wall of debris at the bottom of the passageway while another scoops the debris into a basket made out of old tires. A line of workmen then pass the basket up the corridor and out of the tomb.

"I've called this passageway 3A," Weeks says. He drops his voice. "The incredible thing is that this corridor is heading toward the tomb of Ramesses himself. If it connects, that will be extraordinary. No two tombs were ever deliberately connected. This tomb just gets curiouser and curiouser."

Ramesses' tomb, lying a hundred feet across the Valley, was also wrecked by flooding and is now being excavated by a French team. "I would dearly love to surprise them," Weeks says. "To pop out one day and say *'Bonjour! C'est moi!'* I'd love to beat the French into their own tomb."

I follow him down the newly discovered corridor, slipping and sliding on the pitched floor. "Of course," he shouts over his shoulder, "the sons might also be buried *underneath* their father! We clearly haven't found the burial chambers yet, and it is my profound hope that one way or another this passageway will take us there."

We come to the end, where the workmen are picking away at the massive wall of dirt that blocks the passage. The forty-two men can remove about nine tons of dirt a day.

At the bottom, Weeks introduces me to a tall, handsome Egyptian with a black mustache and wearing a baseball cap on backward. "This is Muhammad Mahmud," Weeks says. "One of the senior workmen."

I shake his hand. "What do you hope to find down here?"

"Something very nice, *inshallah.*"

"What's in these side rooms?" I ask Weeks. All the doorways are blocked with dirt.

Weeks shrugs. "We haven't been in those rooms yet."

"Would it be possible . . . " I start to ask.

He grins. "You mean, would you like to be the first human being in three thousand years to enter a chamber in an ancient Egyptian tomb? Maybe Saturday."

As we are leaving the tomb, I am struck by the amount of work still unfinished. Weeks has managed to dig out only three rooms completely and clear eight others partway—leaving more than eighty rooms entirely untouched. What treasures lie under five or ten feet of debris in those rooms is anyone's guess. It will take from six to ten more years to clear and stabilize the tomb, and then many more years to publish the findings from it. As we emerge from the darkness, Weeks says, "I know what I'll be doing for the rest of my life."

One morning, I find a pudgy, bearded man sitting in the green tent and examining, Hamlet-like, the now assembled skull. He is the paleontologist Elwyn Simons, who has spent decades searching the sands of the Faiyum for primate ancestors of human beings. Susan Weeks once worked for him, and now he is a close friend of the couple, dropping in on occasion to look over bones from the tomb. Kent and Susan are both present, waiting to hear his opinions about the skull's sex. (Only DNA testing can confirm whether it's an actual son of Ramesses, of course.)

Simons rotates the skull, pursing his lips. "Probably a male, because it has fairly pronounced brow ridges," he says. "This"—he points to a hole punched in the top of the cranium—"was made post mortem. You can tell because the edges are sharp and there are no suppressed fractures."

Simons laughs, and sets the skull down. "You can grind this up and put it in your soup, Kent."

When the laughter has died down, I venture that I didn't get the joke.

"In the Middle ages, people filled bottles with powdered mummies and sold it as medicine," Simons explains.

"Or mummies were burned to power the railroad," Weeks adds. "I don't know how many miles you get per mummy, do you, Elwyn?"

While talk of mummies proceeds, a worker brings a tray of tea. Susan Weeks takes the skull away and puts another bone in front of Simons.

"That's the scapula of an artiodactyl. Probably a cow. The camel hadn't reached Egypt by the Nineteenth Dynasty."

The next item is a tooth.

"Artiodactyl again," he says, sipping his tea. "Goat or gazelle."

The identification process goes on.

The many animal bones found in KV5 were probably from offerings for the dead: valley tombs often contained sacrificed bulls, mummified baboons, birds, and cats, as well as steaks and veal chops.

Suddenly, Muhammad appears at the mouth of the tomb. "Please, Dr. Kent," he says, and starts telling Weeks in Arabic that the workers have uncovered something for him to see. Weeks motions for me to follow him into the dim interior. We put on our hard hats and duck through the first chambers into Corridor 3A. A beautiful set of carved limestone steps has appeared where I saw only rubble a few days before. Weeks kneels and brushes the dirt away, excited about the fine workmanship.

Muhammad and Weeks go to inspect another area of the tomb, where fragments of painted and carved plaster are being uncovered. I stay to watch the workmen digging in 3A. After a while, they forget I am there and begin singing, handing the baskets up the long corridor, their bare feet white with dust. A dark hole begins to appear between the top of the debris and the ceiling. It looks as if one could crawl inside and perhaps look farther down the corridor.

"May I take a look in there?" I ask.

One of the workmen hoists me up the wall of dirt, and I lie on my stomach and wriggle into the gap. I recall that archaeologists sometimes sent small boys into tombs through holes just like this.

Unfortunately, I am not a small boy, and in my eagerness I find myself thoroughly wedged. It is pitch-black, and I wonder why I thought this would be exciting.

"Pull me out!" I yell.

The Egyptians heave on my legs, and I come sliding down with a shower of dirt. After the laughter subsides, a skinny man named Nubie crawls into the hole. In a moment, he is back out, feet first. He cannot see anything; they need to dig more.

The workmen redouble their efforts, laughing, joking, and singing. Working in KV5 is a coveted job in the surrounding villages; Weeks pays his workmen four hundred Egyptian pounds a month (about a hundred and twenty-five dollars), four times what a junior inspector of antiquities makes and perhaps three times the average monthly income of an Egyptian family. Weeks is well liked by his Egyptian workers, and is constantly bombarded with dinner invitations from even his poorest laborers. While I was there, I attended three of these dinners. The flow of food was limitless, and the conversation competed with the bellowing of a water buffalo in an adjacent room or the braying of a donkey tethered at the door.

After the hole has been widened a bit, Nubie goes up again with a light and comes back down. There is great disappointment: it looks as though the passageway might come to an end. Another step is exposed in the staircase, along with a great deal of broken pottery. Weeks returns and examines the hole himself, without comment.

As the week goes by, more of Corridor 3A is cleared, foot by foot. The staircase in 3A levels out to a finely made floor, more evidence that the corridor merely ends in a small chamber. On Wednesday, however, Weeks emerges from the tomb smiling. "Come," he says.

The hole in 3A has now been enlarged to about two feet in diameter. I scramble up the dirt and peer inside with a light, choking on the dust. As before, the chiselled ceiling comes to an abrupt end, but below it lies what looks like a shattered door lintel.

"It's got to be a door," Weeks says, excited. "I'm afraid we're going to have to halt for the season at that doorway. We'll break through next June."

Later, outdoors, I find myself coughing up flecks of mud.

"Tomb cough," Weeks says cheerfully.

On Thursday morning, Weeks is away on business, and I go down into the tomb with Susan. At the bottom of 3A, we stop to watch Ahmed Mahmud Hassan, the chief supervisor of the crew, sorting through some loose dirt at floor level. Suddenly, he straightens up, holding a perfect alabaster statuette of a mummy.

"Madame," he says, holding it out.

Susan begins to laugh. "Ahmed, that's beautiful. Did you get that at one of the souvenir stalls?"

"No," he says. "I just found it." He points to the spot. "Here."

She turns to me. "They once put a rubber cobra in here. Everyone was terrified, and Muhammad began beating it with a rock."

"Madame," Ahmed says. "Look, please." By now, he is laughing, too.

"I see it," Susan says. "I hope it wasn't too expensive."

"Madame, please."

Susan takes it, and there is a sudden silence. "It's real," she says quietly.

"This is what I was telling Madame," Ahmed says, still laughing.

Susan slowly turns it over in her hands. "It's beautiful. Let's take it outside."

In the sunlight, the statuette glows. The head and shoulders still have clear traces of black paint, and the eyes look slightly crossed. It is an *ushabti*, a statuette that was buried only with the dead, meant to spare the deceased toil in the afterlife: whenever the deceased was called upon to do work, he would send the *ushabti* in his place.

That morning, the workmen also find in 3A a chunk of stone. Weeks hefts it. "This is very important," he says.

"How?"

"It's a piece of a sidewall of a sarcophagus that probably held one of Ramesses' sons. It's made out of serpentine, a valuable stone in ancient Egypt." He pulls out a tape measure and marks off the thickness of the rim. "It's eight-point-five centimetres, which, doubled, gives seventeen centimetres. Add to that the width of an average pair of human shoulders, and perhaps an inner coffin, and you could not have fitted this sarcophagus through any door to any of the sixty side chambers in that tomb." He pauses. "So, you see, this piece of stone is one more piece of evidence that we have yet to find the burial chambers."

Setting the stone down with a thud on a specimen mat, he dabs his forehead. He proceeds to lay out a theory about KV5. Ramesses had an accomplished son named Khaemwaset, who became the high priest of an important cult that worshipped a god represented by a sacred bull. In Year 16, Khaemwaset began construction of the Serapeum, a vast catacomb for the bulls, in Saqqara. The original design of the Serapeum is the only one that remotely resembles KV5's layout, and it might have been started around the same time. In the Serapeum, there are two levels: an upper level of offering chapels and a lower level for burials. "But," Weeks adds, throwing open his arms, "until we find the burial chambers it's *all* speculation."

On Friday, Bruce Ludwig arrives—a great bear of a man with white hair and a white beard. Dressed like an explorer, he is lugging a backpack full of French wine for the team.

Unlike Lord Carnarvon and other wealthy patrons who funded digs in the Valley of the Kings, Ludwig is a self-made man. His father owned a grocery store in South Dakota called Ludwig's Superette. Bruce Ludwig made his money in California real estate and is now a partner in a firm managing four billion dollars in pension funds. He has been supporting Weeks and the Theban Mapping Project for twelve years.

Over the past three, he has sunk a good deal of his own money into the project and has raised much more among his friends. Nevertheless, the cost of excavation continually threatens to outstrip the funds at hand. "The thing is, it doesn't take a Rockefeller or a Getty to be involved," he told me over a bottle of Château Lynch-Bages. "What I like to do is show other successful people that it won't cost a fortune and that it's just hugely rewarding. Buildings crumble and fall down, but when you put something in the books, it's there forever."

Ludwig's long-term support paid off last February, when he became one of the first people to crawl into the recesses of KV5. There may be better moments to come. "When I discover that door covered with unbroken Nineteenth Dynasty seals," Weeks told me, joking, "you bet I'll hold off until Bruce can get here."

Saturday, the workers' taxi picks the Weekses and me up before sunrise and then winds through a number of small villages, collecting workers as it goes along.

The season is drawing to a close, and Susan and Kent Weeks are both subdued. In the last few weeks, the probable number of rooms in the tomb has increased from sixty-seven to ninety-two, with no end in sight. Everyone is frustrated at having to lock up the tomb now, leaving the doorway at the bottom of 3A sealed, the plaster floor unplumbed, the burial chambers still not found, and so many rooms unexcavated.

Weeks plans to tour the United States lecturing and raising more funds. He estimates that he will need a quarter of a million dollars per year for the indefinite future in order to do the job right.

As we drive alongside sugarcane fields, the sun boils up over the Nile Valley through a screen of palms, burning into the mists lying on the fields. We pass a man driving a donkey cart loaded with tires, and whizz by the Colossi of Memnon, two enormous wrecked statues standing alone in a farmer's field. The taxi begins the climb to a village once famous for tomb robbing, some of whose younger residents now work for Weeks. The houses are completely surrounded by the black pits of tombs. The fragrant smell of dung fires drifts through the rocky streets.

Along the way, I talk with Ahmed, the chief supervisor. A young man with a handsome, aristocratic face, who comes from a prominent family in Gezira Bairat, he has worked for Weeks for about eight years. I ask him how he feels about working in the tomb.

Ahmed thinks for a moment, then says, "I forget myself in this tomb. It is so vast inside."

"How so?"

"I feel at home there. I know this thing. I can't express the feeling, but it's not so strange for me to be in this tomb. I feel something in there about myself. I am descended from these people who built this tomb. I can feel their blood is in me."

When we arrive in the Valley of the Kings, an inspector unlocks the metal gate in front of the tomb, and the workers file in, with Weeks leading the way. I wait outside to watch the sunrise. The tourists have not yet arrived, and if you screen out some signs you can imagine the Valley as it might have appeared when the pharaohs were buried here three thousand years ago. (The venders and rest house were moved last year.) As dawn strikes el-Qurn and invades the upper reaches of the canyon walls, a soft, peach-colored lights fills the air. The encircling cliffs lock out the sounds of the world; the black doorways of the tombs are like dead eyes staring out; and one of the guard huts of the ancient priests can still be seen perched at the cliff edge. The whole Valley becomes a slowly changing play of light and color, mountain and sky, unfolding in absolute stillness. I am given a brief, shivery insight into the sacredness of this landscape.

At seven, the tourists begin to arrive, and the spell is dispersed. The Valley rumbles to life with the grinding of diesel engines, the frantic expostulations of venders, and the shouting of guides leading groups of tourists. KV5 is the first tomb in the Valley, and the tourists begin gathering at the rope, pointing and taking pictures, while the guides impart the most preposterous misinformation about the tomb: that Ramesses had four hundred sons by only two wives, that there are eight hundred rooms in the tomb, that the greedy Americans are digging for gold but won't find any. Two thousand tourists a day stand outside the entrance to KV5.

I go inside and find Weeks in 3A, supervising the placement of more screw jacks and timbers. When he has finished, he turns to me. "You ready?" He points to the lowest room in 3A. "This looks like a good one for you to explore."

One of the workmen clears away a hole at the top of the blocked door for me to crawl through, and then Muhammad gives me a leg up. I shove a caged light bulb into the hold ahead of me and wriggle through. I can barely fit.

In a moment, I am inside. I sit up and look around, the light throwing my distorted shadow against the wall. There is three feet of space between the top of the debris and the ceiling, just enough for me to crawl around on my hands and knees. The room is about nine feet square, the walls finely chiselled from the bedrock. Coils of dust drift past the light. The air is just breathable.

I run my fingers along the ancient chisel marks, which are as fresh as if they were made yesterday, and I think of workmen who carved out this room, three millennia ago. Their only source of light would have been the dim illumination from wicks burning in a bowl of oil salted to reduce smoke. There was no way to tell the passage of time in the tomb: the wicks were cut to last eight hours, and when they guttered it meant that the day's work was done. The tombs were carved from the ceiling downward, the workers whacking off flakes of limestone with flint choppers, and then finishing the walls and ceilings with copper chisels and sandstone abrasive. Crouching in the hot stone chamber, I suddenly get a powerful sense of the enormous religious faith of the Egyptians. Nothing less could have motivated an entire society to pound these tombs out of rock.

Much of the Egyptian religion remains a mystery to us. It is full of contradictions, inexplicable rituals, and impenetrable texts. Amid the complexity, one simple fact stands out: it was a great human bargain with death. Almost everything that ancient Egypt has left us—the pyramids, the tombs, the temples—represents an attempt to overcome that awful mystery at the center of all our lives.

A shout brings me back to my senses.

"Find anything?" Weeks calls out.

"The room's empty," I say. "There's nothing in here but dust."

Maya Archaeologists Turn to the Living to Help Save the Dead

To preserve ancient sites, pioneering archaeologists are trying to improve the lives of the Maya people now living near the ruins.

MICHAEL BAWAYA

Archaeologist Jonathan Kaplan tries to spend as much time as possible exploring Chocolá, a huge Maya site in southern Guatemala dating from 1200 B.C.E. So far his team has mapped more than 60 mounds, identified dozens of monuments, and found signs of the emergence of Maya civilization, including large, sophisticated waterworks that likely required social organization to build.

But today, instead of digging, Kaplan is lunching with the mayor of a municipality that includes the impoverished town of Chocolá. Kaplan, a research associate with the Museum of New Mexico's Office of Archaeological Studies in Santa Fe, is trying to enlist the mayor's support for a land swap that would give farmers land of no archaeological value in exchange for land that holds Maya ruins. The local people he's trying to help, many of them descended from the ancient Maya, are "clinging by their fingers to survival," says Kaplan. So, working with a Guatemalan archaeologist, he has established a trash-removal service, hired an environmental scientist to help improve the drinking water, and developed plans for two museums to attract tourists.

Kaplan and others are in the vanguard of a movement called community archaeology. From Africa to Uzbekistan, researchers are trying to boost local people's quality of life in order to preserve the relics of their ancestors. In the Maya region, the situation is urgent; the vestiges of the ancient Maya may be destroyed in 5 to 10 years unless something is done to curb looting, logging, poaching, and oil exploration, says Richard Hansen, president of the Foundation for Anthropological Research & Environmental Studies and an archaeologist at Idaho State University in Pocatello. Hansen, Kaplan, and others are using archaeology as an engine for development, driving associated tourism and education projects. The resultant intertwining of research and development is such that "I cannot accomplish the one without the other," says Kaplan, "because poverty is preventing the people from attending to the ancient remains in a responsible fashion."

It wasn't always that way. Until fairly recently, Maya researchers were solely focused on the hunt for "stones and bones," says Hansen. Archaeologist Arthur Demarest of Vanderbilt University in Nashville, Tennessee, says researchers often excavated a site with the help of local workers, only to abandon them when the project ended. Those who lost their income often resorted to looting and slash-and-burn agriculture to survive. "In the wake of every archaeological project is an economic and social disaster," says Demarest.

He offers one of his own projects as an example of what not to do. After employing about 300 people in the early 1990s at several sites in the Petén, the vast tropical forest in northern Guatemala, Demarest left the government with a continuing development plan for the region, much of it federal land. But the federal government brought in outsiders to implement it. Desperate at having lost their jobs, the local people plundered the sites.

"From that, I learned a lot of lessons," Demarest says. "Archaeology transforms a region." In his view, archaeologists themselves must take responsibility for helping the locals succeed. "The days of Indiana Jones, when archaeologists could go to a place, excavate, and then leave without concern about the impact that their actions are having on the people in the area, are gone," he has said.

Today, Demarest embraces this responsibility as he excavates part of the great trade route that ran through much of the Maya region, including along the Pasión River and through Cancuen, an ancient city in central Guatemala. He says his project is successful because it operates "bottom up—we're working through the village." Using ethnographic studies of the Maya people and working with leaders from several villages, Demarest designed a research and community development plan that enables the local people, rather than outsiders, to serve as custodians of their own heritage. The communities choose projects—archaeology, restoration, ecotourism, etc.—and run them with the guidance of experts, earning more than they would by farming.

One successful enterprise is a boat service, run by the Maya, that ferries tourists down the Pasión River from the village of La Union to Cancuen, now a national park. In addition to generating revenue, the service attracted a variety of agencies that provided potable water, electricity, and school improvements to La Union. The World Bank cited the boat service as one of the 10 most innovative rural development projects in the world in 2003.

Demarest also helped establish a visitor center, an inn, a guide service, and a campground at the park's entrance. Three nearby villages collaboratively manage these operations, and the profits pay for water systems, school expansions, and medical supplies. "The only way these things are going to succeed is if it's theirs," says Demarest, who has raised nearly $5 million for community development at Cancuen. Last year, he became the first U.S. citizen to be awarded the National Order of Cultural Patrimony by the Guatemalan government.

Other archaeologists are trying to achieve similar results in their own field areas. Hansen is exploring the origins, the cultural and ecological dynamics, and the collapse of the Preclassic Maya (circa 2000 B.C.E. to 250 C.E.) in the Mirador Basin. His project has a budget of $1.2 million, with about $400,000 going to development and $800,000 to archaeology. He raised roughly half of the funds from the Global Heritage Fund, a nonprofit organization that helps preserve cultural heritage sites in developing countries. The project employs more than 200 people who earn above-average wages while getting training; Hansen's team has also installed a new water system and bought 40 computers to boost locals' computer skills.

Looting in the basin has been devastating in the past, so Hansen has hired 27 guards—most of them former looters. They make good guards, he says, "because they know the tricks of the trade." The project has instilled "a sense of identity" in some residents, although Hansen acknowledges that others continue to loot. "It is a long battle to win the hearts and minds of these people," he says.

Although both Demarest and Hansen have won generous grants for their work, they agree that finding funding for community archaeology is "horrific," as Hansen puts it. Kaplan makes do with about $130,000 each year for his "terribly underfunded" project, although his ideal would be about $800,000. Traditional funders, such as the U.S. National Science Foundation (NSF), pay for research but not community development, says Demarest. NSF, with its modest budget of $5 million to $6 million, is most interested in the "intellectual merit" of a project, agrees archaeology program director John Yellen, although he adds that the foundation does consider "broader impacts," including community development. Demarest, who is financed by some 20 organizations including the United States Agency for International Development and the Solar Foundation, says a big budget is a must for community projects: "You've got to have about $400,000 a season to do ethical archaeology."

But other researchers say it's possible to run such projects without big budgets. Archaeologist Anabel Ford of the University of California, Santa Barbara, who has been practicing small-scale community archaeology while studying land-use patterns at a large site called El Pilar on the Belize-Guatemala border since 1983, says that she can achieve her community development goals for as little as $12,000 a year. "I actually think it's not about tons of money," she says. "It's about consistency."

Ford operates on an annual budget of $30,000 to $75,000, with funding sources ranging from the Ford and MacArthur Foundations to her own pocket. Within El Pilar's lush tropical forest are numerous temples and other buildings that stand as high as 22 meters. Over the years, Ford has built a cultural center and a caretaker house, and El Pilar now attracts hundreds of ecotourists annually. Ford started an annual festival to celebrate cultural traditions and foster community involvement, and she's organizing a women's collective to sell local crafts. "We've built the first infrastructure at El Pilar since 1000 [C.E.]," she says.

Whether they operate with big money or on the cheap, community archaeologists face a delicate juggling act between development and research. Ford believes her academic career has suffered because of the time and effort she's invested in development projects. "I would have written much more substantive work on my research at El Pilar," she says, lamenting that she has yet to finish a book about her work. Kaplan and Demarest say that they spend about half their time on community development, leaving only half for archaeology.

As impressive and well-intentioned as these and other community archaeology projects seem, at least a few researchers are concerned about unintended consequences. "If you don't understand the local politics, you can really do damage," says Arlen Chase of the University of Central Florida in Orlando, who has investigated Caracol, a major Maya site in Belize, since 1984. It's difficult to determine just what archaeologists owe the community they work in, he adds. "This is a new endeavor, and we're learning how best to do it," agrees archaeologist Anne Pyburn, outgoing chair of the Ethics Committee of the American Anthropological Association.

Despite these concerns, Hansen and his colleagues seem convinced that they're making progress. Guatemalans who were "dedicated to looting and destroying these sites," Hansen says, are "now dedicated to preserving them."

MICHAEL BAWAYA is the editor of *American Archaeology*.

From *Science Magazine*, August 26, 2005, pp. 1317–1318. Copyright © 2007 by American Association for the Advancement of Science. Reproduced with permission from AAAS. www.sciencemag.org

The Fantome Controversy

HEATHER PRINGLE

On a foul night in late November 1814, a sleek man-of-war ran into serious trouble as it sailed to the British naval base at Halifax, Nova Scotia. Straying into shallow waters some 20 miles southwest of the port, HMS *Fantome* hit a rocky reef and sank in a matter of hours, as did two ships in the convoy she was escorting. Such maritime disasters along Nova Scotia's jagged, foggy coast were sadly common, but local residents took a particular interest in *Fantome*. The warship reputedly carried a unique cargo—plunder that British forces had taken before burning the White House on August 24, 1814.

Now, nearly 200 years later, *Fantome* lies at the center of an international controversy. To the dismay of many prominent nautical archaeologists, Nova Scotia has licensed a private treasure-hunting company to salvage what it believes to be *Fantome* and its convoy. Under this license, LeChameau Explorations Limited is free to sell for profit 90 percent of all the valuables it recovers, sparking fears that White House treasures may one day be auctioned on eBay to private collectors around the world. It's a prospect that disturbs U.S. government officials. "We'd like these artifacts returned," says State Department spokesperson Noel Clay.

More troubling still is the light this controversy sheds on the mercenary practices of a small group of professional archaeologists. Treasure hunting on marine archaeological sites is shockingly widespread in North America. Only Nova Scotia permits this practice in Canada, but all American states, except Texas and Maine, allow some degree of commercial exploitation. To obtain the necessary government licenses, some treasure hunters hire underwater archaeologists to help them in the search for valuables. In these cases, says Willis Stevens, a nautical archaeologist at Parks Canada, "you have an archaeologist who is working for a treasure hunter and who is quite willing to accept the fact that his material will be sold for profit. In the professional archaeological community, that is immoral." Certainly, it's a situation that infuriates Paul Johnston, curator of maritime history at the Smithsonian. Underwater sites, he explains, are "like the Wild West in the nineteenth century—an open frontier for those who want to exploit them."

Fantome is a worrisome case in point. The British raid on Washington took place during the War of 1812, a two-year-long battle between Britain and the United States over bitter trade differences. To humiliate the Americans, a British expedition sailed up Chesapeake Bay and marched to Washington, occupying the White House after American forces defending the capitol were routed. The First Lady, Dolley Madison, managed to flee to safety, reportedly taking the White House silver and a famous portrait of George Washington with her. "So what was left behind would have been household furniture, pretty much," says Bill Allman, the White House curator. As mementos, the British sailors and soldiers stole what were likely small, readily portable souvenirs from the White House, then set it and the Capitol ablaze. The next day, the troops marched back to Chesapeake Bay.

Surviving records paint a confusing picture of what eventually happened to these White House artifacts. Nova Scotian folklore, however, suggests that *Fantome* and its convoy were carrying these goods to Halifax when they sank, and during the 1960s, local divers reported finding American coins minted before 1814 in a region known as the Fantome Fangs. Drawn by these accounts, LeChameau Explorations Limited obtained an exclusive license under Nova Scotia's Treasure Trove Act to search for *Fantome*'s convoy and recover what might remain of the Ships. In a complex financial maneuver, the firm then sold the right to this license to a parent company owned by Sovereign Exploration Associates International.

Curtis Sprouse, chief operating officer of Sovereign Exploration, insists that his company is taking a scientific approach to the quest, and maintains that it will work closely with museums and make a documentary film about the wreck site. "I often tell people that we are in the preservation and presentation of history, that's our goal," he explains. In compliance with Nova Scotia's regulations, Sprouse and his colleagues have hired a conservator as well as an underwater archaeologist, James J. Sinclair, who previously took part in the commercial treasure-hunting operation on the famous Spanish galleon, *Nuestra Senora de Atocha*, which sank off the Florida coast in 1622 carrying at least 35 tons of silver and 161 pieces of gold. The recovery of *Atocha's* treasure came under harsh criticism from many nautical archaeologists for its crude recovery techniques. Sinclair declined, on the advice of lawyers, a request by ARCHAEOLOGY for an interview.

To date, Sinclair's team has surveyed the Nova Scotian wreck site, conducted an initial recovery of artifacts, and prepared a preliminary report on their work for the Nova Scotia Museum.

However, legal representatives of LeChameau Explorations Limited have insisted that ARCHAEOLOGY not make the contents of this scientific report public, citing "commercially sensitive information" in the document.

Fantome, however, is not the only historic ship that Sprouse and his colleagues are searching for. The company also holds exclusive rights to four other important wreck sites in Nova Scotia, including *Le Chameau,* a French merchant ship lost in 1725, and HMS *Tilbury,* a British naval vessel that sank in 1757, during the Seven Years' War. In addition, Sprouse states that the company has obtained—by arrangement with another private firm—licenses, permits, and rights to an additional 450 shipwreck sites, primarily in Nova Scotian waters. "No one," boasts Sprouse, "has ever done this on the type of scale that we are targeting."

Such business plans greatly worry heritage activists. One vocal critic, Halifax diver and documentary filmmaker John Wesley Chisholm, fears that the province's open-for-business attitude is destroying marine archaeological resources that should be preserved for all. The province's Treasure Trove legislation, he says, serves as little more than "a privateering act."

What is clearly needed, adds Chisholm, is stricter legislation to protect underwater sites from corporate bottom lines, as well as resources to hire provincial and state nautical archaeologists to enforce the regulations. Until then, concludes the filmmaker sadly, it's "come all ye pirates."

HEATHER PRINGLE is a freelance science journalist and author of *The Master Plan: Himmler's Scholars and the Holocaust.*

From *Archaeology,* May/June 2006, pp. 10–11. Copyright © 2006 by Heather Pringle. Courtesy of Archaeology Magazine and reprinted by permission of the author.

Distinguished Lecture in Archaeology
Communication and the Future of American Archaeology

What follows is the revised text of the Distinguished Lecture in Archaeology, presented at the 95th Annual Meeting of the American Anthropological Association, held in San Francisco, California, November, 1996.

JEREMY A. SABLOFF

I offer these remarks with somewhat ambivalent feelings. While it is an honor indeed to be asked to give the Archaeology Division's Distinguished Lecture, I nevertheless must admit that it is a daunting challenge. I have looked at many of the superb Distinguished Lectures that have been presented to you in recent years and subsequently published in the *American Anthropologist* and am very impressed with what our colleagues have had to say. Most of the recent talks have focused on aspects of the ongoing debates on modern archaeological theory and methods. I certainly could have continued this tradition, because, as many of you know, I have strong feelings about this topic. However, I decided to pursue a different, more general tack, which I hope you will agree is of equal importance.

In a few short years, we will be entering a new millennium. Will American archaeology survive in the twenty-first century? Of course it will. But will it continue to thrive in the new millennium? The answer to this question is a more guarded "yes." There are various causes for concern about the future health of archaeology. I would like to examine one of these concerns and offer some suggestions as to how this concern might be eased.

My theme will be archaeologists' communication with the public—or lack thereof—and, more specifically, the relevance of archaeology to non-professionals. In thinking about this theme, which has been a particular interest and concern of mine, it struck me how one of my favorite cartoons provided an important insight into the whole question of archaeological communication. I know that many of you have your office doors or bulletin boards festooned with a host of "Calvin and Hobbes," "Shoe," "Bloom County," "Doonesbury," or "Far Side" drawings that unerringly seem to pinpoint many of life's enduring paradoxes and problems. In particular, the "Far Side" cartoons by Gary Larson, who is now lamentably in early retirement like several of our master cartoonists, often resonate well with archaeologists' sensibilities. This cartoon, while not specifically targeting archaeologists or cultural anthropologists, as Larson often did pinpoint a central concern of my discussion.

While archaeologists may think they are talking clearly to the public, what the latter often hears, I believe, is "blah, blah, blah, *tomb*, blah, blah, blah *sacrifice*, blah, blah, blah, arrowhead."

I will argue that the field of American archaeology, despite some significant progress in the past decade, is still failing to effectively tell the public about how modern anthropological archaeology functions and about the huge gains archaeologists have made in understanding the development of ancient cultures through time and space.

More than 25 years ago, John Fritz and Fred Plog ended their article on "The Nature of Archaeological Explanation" (1970:412) with the famous assertion that "We suggest that unless archaeologists find ways to make their research increasingly relevant to the modern world, the modern world will find itself increasingly capable of getting along without archaeologists." Although Fritz and Plog had a very particular definition of relevance in mind relating to the development of laws of culture change, as did Fritz in his important article on "Relevance, Archaeology, and Subsistence Theory" (1973), if one adopts a broader view of the term *relevance,* then the thrust of their statement is just as important today—if not more so—than it was in 1970.

How can this be true? Archaeology appears to be thriving, if one counts number of jobs, money spent on archaeological field research, course enrollments, publications, and public fascination with the subject as measured in media coverage. But is the public interest, or, better yet, the public's interest, being served properly and satisfied in a productive and responsible fashion? With some important exceptions, I unfortunately would answer "no." Why do I think this to be the case?

In the nineteenth century, archaeology played an important public and intellectual role in the fledgling United States. Books concerned wholly or in part with archaeology were widely read and, as Richard Ford has indicated clearly in his article on "Archaeology Serving Humanity" (1973), archaeology played an important part in overthrowing the then-dominant Biblical view of human development in favor of Darwinian evolutionary theory. Empirical archaeological research, which excited public interest and was closely followed by the public, was able to provide data that indicated that human activities had considerable antiquity and that archaeological studies of the past could throw considerable light on the development of the modern world.

As is the case in most disciplines, as archaeology became increasingly professionalized throughout the nineteenth century and as academic archaeology emerged in the late-nineteenth and early-twentieth centuries, the communications gap between professionals and the public grew apace. This gap was accentuated because amateurs had always played an important part in the archaeological enterprise. As late as the 1930s, before academic archaeology really burgeoned, the gap between most amateurs and professionals was still readily bridgeable, I believe. The first article in *American Antiquity,* for example, was written by an amateur, and, as I have discussed in detail elsewhere, the founders of the journal hoped that it "would provide a forum for communication between these two groups" (Sabloff 1985:228). However, even a quick look today at *American Antiquity* will indicate that those earlier hopes have been dashed. It may be a terrific journal for professionals, but much of it would be nearly incomprehensible to non-professionals, except perhaps to the most devoted amateurs.

In 1924, Alfred Vincent Kidder published his landmark book *An Introduction to the Study of Southwestern Archaeology.* This highly readable volume both made key advances in scholarly understanding of the ancient Southwest and was completely accessible to the general public. As Gordon Willey (1967:299) has stated: "It is a rarity in that it introduces systematics to a field previously unsystematized, and, at the same time, it is vitally alive and unpedantic. . . . He wrote a book that was romantic but not ridiculous, scrupulously close to the facts but not a boring recital of them." How many regional archaeological syntheses could have that said of them today? Happily, the answer is not "none," and there is some evidence of a positive trend in the publication of more popularly oriented regional and site syntheses (see, for instance, Kolata 1993; Plog 1997; or Schele and Freidel 1990, among others). Marcus and Flannery's (1996) recent book on Zapotec civilization is a superb example of how such accessible writing can be combined with a clear, theoretically sophisticated approach, as well.

Kidder also was deeply concerned about the relevance of archaeology to the contemporary world and was not shy about expressing his belief that archaeology could and should play an important social role in the modern world (a view which is paralleled today by some post-processual [e.g., Hodder et al. 1995] and feminist [e.g., Spector 1993] concerns with humanizing archaeological narratives). Kidder's views were most clearly expressed by him at a 1940 symposium at the American Philosophical Society on "Characteristics of American Culture and Its Place in General Culture." As Richard Woodbury (1973:171) notes: "Kidder presented one of his most eloquent pleas for the importance of the anthropological understanding of the past through the techniques of archaeology." Kidder (1940:528), for example, states: "it is good for an archaeologist to be forced to take stock, to survey his field, to attempt to show what bearing his delvings into the past may have upon our judgement of present day life; and what service, if any, he renders the community beyond filling the cases of museums and supplying material for the rotogravure sections of the Sunday papers." Lamentably, his prescription for the practitioners of archaeology has not been well filled in the past half century.

The professionalization of archaeology over the course of this century obviously has had innumerable benefits. In the most positive sense, the discipline has little resemblance to the archaeology of 100 years ago. With all the advances in method, theory, and culture historical knowledge, archaeologists are now in a position to make important and useful statements about cultural adaptation and development that should have broad intellectual appeal. Ironically, though, one aspect of the professionalization of the discipline, what can be termed the academization of archaeology, is working against such broad dissemination of current advances in archaeological understanding of cultures of the past. The key factor, I am convinced, is that since World War II, and especially in the past few decades as archaeology rapidly expanded as an academic subject in universities and colleges throughout this country, the competition for university jobs and the institutional pressures to publish in quantity, in general, and in peer review journals, in particular, has led in part to the academic devaluation of popular writing and communication with the general public. Such activities just don't count or, even worse, count against you.

In addition, I believe that it is possible that some archaeologists, in their desire to prove the rigor and scientific standing of the discipline within the academy and among their non-anthropological colleagues and university administrators, have rejected or denigrated popular writing because it might somehow taint archaeology with a nonscientific "softness" from which they would like to distance the field.

If popular writing is frowned upon by some academics, then popularization in other media, such as television, can be treated even more derisively by these scholars, and consequently too few archaeologists venture into these waters. Why should the best known "archaeologist" to the public be an unrepentant looter like Indiana Jones? Is he the role model we want for our profession? When I turn on the television to watch a show with archaeological content, why should I be more than likely to see Leonard Nimoy and the repeated use of the term *mysterious?* It should be professional archaeologists routinely helping to write and perhaps even hosting many of the archaeology shows on television, not just—at best—popular science writers and Hollywood actors. In sum, I strongly feel that we need more accessible writing, television shows, videos, CD-ROMs, and the like with archaeologists heavily involved in all these enterprises.

Forty years ago, Geoffrey Bibby, in his best-selling book *The Testimony of the Spade,* wrote in his foreword (1956:vii):

It has long been customary to start any book that can be included under the comprehensive heading of "popular science" with an apology from the author to his fellow scientists for his desertion of the icy uplands of the research literature for the supposedly lower and supposedly lush fields of popular representation. This is not an apology, and it is not directed to archaeologists. In our day, when the research literature of one branch of knowledge has become all but incomprehensible to a researcher in another branch, and when the latest advances within any science can revolutionize—or end—our lives within a decade, the task of interpreting every science in language that can be understood by workers in other fields is no longer—if it ever was—a slightly disreputable sideline, but a first-priority duty.

Bibby was making a point that is similar to one made years ago by C. P. Snow (1959) that scholars in different disciplines do not read or are unable to read each others' works, but should! However, I believe that Bibby's argument can easily be expanded to include the lay public, which should be able to readily find out what archaeologists are doing. If they are interested in the subject, and they have no accessible professionally written sources to turn to—like *The Testimony of the Spade*—is it any surprise that they turn to highly speculative, non-professional sources? Unfortunately, Bibby's wise call has gone relatively unheeded. Where are all the *Testimony of the Spades* of this generation, or even the *Gods, Graves, and Scholars* (Ceram 1951)?

But even encouraging communication between archaeologists and the general public is not sufficient, I believe, to dispel the lack of popular understanding about the modern archaeological enterprise and the potential importance of archaeological knowledge. With all the problems that the world faces today, the conflicts and ethnic strife, the innumerable threats to the environment, and the inadequacy of food supplies in the face of rising populations, there never has been a more propitious time for archaeology's new insights into the nature of human development and diversity in time and space to be appreciated by people in all walks of life. In order for better communication to have a useful impact, I believe that the profession has to heed Fritz and Plog's call and strive to be relevant. Moreover, we should pursue relevance in both the general and specific senses of the term. In its broadest sense, *relevance* is "to the purpose; pertinent," according to *The American College Dictionary,* while in its more narrow definition, relevance according to *The Oxford English Dictionary,* means "pertinency to important current issues."

All things being equal, archaeology could be justified on the basis of its inherent interest. But all things are rarely equal, and therefore archaeological activities and their relevance to today's world do need justification. To what is archaeology pertinent? In the general sense, archaeology's main claim to relevance is its revelation of the richness of human experience through the study and understanding of the development of past cultures over the globe. Among the goals of such study is to foster awareness and respect of other cultures and their achievements. Archaeology can make itself relevant—pertinent—by helping its audiences appreciate past cultures and their accomplishments.

Why should we actively seek to fulfill such a goal? I firmly believe in the lessons of history. By appreciating the nature of cultures both past and present, their uniqueness and their similarities, their development, and their adaptive successes and failures, we have a priceless opportunity to better grapple with the future than is possible without such knowledge. For example, as many of you are aware, I have long argued that new understandings of the decline of Classic Maya civilization in the southern Maya lowlands in the eighth century A.D. can shed important light on the ability of the ancient Maya to sustain a complex civilization in a tropical rain-forest environment for over a millennium and the reasons why this highly successful adaptation ultimately failed (see Sabloff 1990). The potential implications for today's world are profound.

This form of striving for relevance is powerful and should have great appeal to the public, but it is not necessarily sufficient in terms of outreach goals for general audiences. Archaeology also needs to attempt to be relevant, where possible, in the narrower sense, too. As some of our colleagues in the Maya area, for instance, begin to take the new archaeological insights about sustainable agriculture and the potential for demographic growth and begin to directly apply them to modern situations, then archaeology clearly is becoming pertinent "to important current issues" (see, for example, Rice and Rice 1984).

In relation to this latter goal, I would argue that we need more "action archaeology," a term first coined by Maxine Klehidienst and Patty Jo Watson (1956) more than four decades ago (in the same year that *Testimony of the Spade* first appeared), but which I use in a more general way to convey the meaning of archaeology working *for* living communities, not just *in* them. One compelling example of such action archaeology is the field research of my colleague Clark Erickson, who has identified the remains of raised field agriculture in the Bolivian Amazon and has been studying the raised fields and other earthworks on the ground. He has been able to show that there was a complex culture in this area in Precolumbian times. Erickson also is working with local peasants in his field study area to show them how Precolumbian farmers successfully intensified their agricultural production and to indicate how the ancient raised field and irrigation techniques might be adapted to the modern situation so as to improve the current economic picture (see Erickson 1998). This is just one example of many that could be cited, including the close collaboration between archaeologists and Native American groups in, for example, the innovative research of my colleague Robert Preucel (1998) at Cochiti Pueblo, or in organizations like the Zuni Archaeological Project (see Anyon and Ferguson 1995), in the many pathbreaking modern garbage projects initiated by William L. Rathje and his colleagues (Rathje and Murphy 1992), in the thoughtful archaeological/environmental development project initiated by Anabel Ford and her collaborators at El Pilar in Belize and Guatemala (Ford 1998), or in cooperative projects between archaeologists and members of the local communities in locations such as Labrador or Belize that have been reported on by Stephen Loring and Marilyn Masson in recent Archaeology Division sections of the *AAA Newsletter* (October and November 1996). However, we need many more examples of such work. They should be the rule, not the exception.

This kind of work in archaeology parallels the continued growth of action anthropology among our cultural colleagues. The potential for collaboration among archaeologists and cultural anthropologists in this regard, as advocated, for example, by Anne Pybum and Richard Wilk (1995), is quite strong. Explorations of the possibilities of such cooperation should be particularly appropriate and of great importance to the Archaeology Division of the American Anthropological Association, which I know is interested in integrating archaeology within a general anthropological focus, and I urge the Division to pursue such an endeavor. Applied anthropology in its action form need not—and should not—be restricted to cultural anthropology.

It is depressing to note that the academic trend away from public communication appears to be increasing just as public interest in archaeology seems to be reaching new heights. Whatever the reasons for this growing interest, and clearly there are many potential reasons that could be and have been cited, including a turn to the past in times of current uncertainties, New Age ideological trends, or the growing accessibility of archaeological remains through travel, television, and video, there is no doubt that there is an audience out there that is thirsting for information about the past. But it does not appear that this interest is being well served, given the ratio of off-the-wall publications to responsible ones that one can find in any bookstore. I have written elsewhere (Sabloff 1982:7) that "Unfortunately, one of the prices we must pay for the privilege of sharing a free marketplace of ideas is the possibility that some writers will write unfounded speculation, some publishers will publish them, some bookstores will sell them, and some media will sensationalize them. In this way, unfounded speculations become widely spread among the general population of interested readers." I went on to suggest that "Perhaps the best solution to this problem is to help readers to become aware of the standards of scientific research so that scientific approaches can be better appreciated and pseudoscientific approaches can be read critically" (p. 7).

In order for this solution to work, however, archaeologists need to compete effectively in this free market. Why must we always run into the most outrageous pseudo-archaeology books (what Stephen Williams [1991] has termed "fantastic archaeology") in such visible places as airport news shops? I simply refuse to believe that among the large pool of professional archaeological writing talent that there aren't some of our colleagues who can write books that can replace *Chariots of the Gods?* (Von Däniken 1970). If we abandon much of the field of popular writing to the fringe, we should not be surprised at all that the public often fails to appreciate the significance of what we do. So what? Why does it matter if many archaeologists don't value public communication and much of the public lacks an understanding of archaeology and what archaeologists do and accomplish? There are two principal answers to this question, I believe. First, I strongly feel that we have a moral responsibility to educate the public about what we do. Good science and public education not only are compatible but should go hand in hand. The overwhelming majority of us, whether in the academic, government or business world, receive at least some public support in our work. I believe that we have a responsibility to give back to the public that provides us with grants, or contracts, or jobs. We need to share with them our excitement in our work and our insights into how peoples of the past lived and how our understandings of the past can inform us about the present and future; and we need to share all this in ways that everyone from young schoolchildren to committed amateur archaeologists can understand and appreciate.

Moreover, the better the public understands and appreciates what we do, what we know, and how we come to know it, the better it can assess the uses and—unfortunately—the abuses of archaeology, especially in political contexts. In this age of exploding ethnic conflicts, a public that has been educated to understand the nature of archaeological research and is thus able to cast a critical eye on how archaeological findings are used in modern political arenas clearly is preferable to people who lack such understanding. On a global scale, the use of archaeological myths in some of the former Soviet republics by various ethnic groups to justify repression of others is just one example—unfortunately!—of many kinds of abuses of archaeological data that could be cited (see Kohl and Fawcett 1995).

Second, there are eminently practical reasons for emphasizing and valuing public communication. Namely—and obviously—it is in our enlightened self-interest! As governmental, academic, and corporate budgets grow tighter and tighter, we are increasingly vying with innumerable groups and people, many with very compelling causes and needs, for extremely competitive dollars. If we don't make our case to the public about the significance of our work, then, in Fritz and Plog's (1970) words, we will surely find our public increasingly capable of getting along without us. How many of our representatives in Congress or in state legislatures really understand what archaeologists do and what they can contribute to the modern world? How many of them get letters from constituents extolling the virtues of the archaeological enterprise and urging them to support archaeological research both financially and through legislation? Unless we educate and work with our many publics, we are certain to find our sources of support, many of which have been taken for granted in recent years, rapidly drying up.

Let's turn our attention from the general problem to potential solutions. How can American archaeologists rectify the situation just described and particularly promote more popular writing by professional scholars? One answer is deceptively simple: we need to change our value system and our reward system within the academy. Just as Margaret Mead and other great anthropological popularizers have been sneered at by some cultural anthropologists, so colleagues like Brian Fagan, who has done so much to reach out to general readers (see, for example, Fagan 1977, 1984, 1987, 1991, and 1995, among many others), are often subject to similar snide comments. We need to celebrate those who successfully communicate with the public, not revile them. Ideally, we should have our leading scholars writing for the public, not only for their colleagues. Some might argue that popular writing would be a waste of their time. To the contrary, I would maintain that such writing is part of our collective academic responsibility. Who better to explain what is on the cutting edge of archaeological research than the field's leading practitioners? Moreover, we need to develop a significant number of our own Stephen Jay Goulds or Stephen Hawkings, not just a few.

Why do some scholars look down at archaeologists who are perceived as popularizers? There are probably a host of reasons, but one of them definitely is pure jealousy. Some archaeologists are jealous of their colleagues who successfully write popular books and articles because of the latter's writing skills. They also are jealous, I believe, of the visibility that popular communication brings those who enter this arena, and they are jealous of the monetary rewards that sometimes accompany popular success. But since such jealousy is not socially acceptable, it tends to be displaced into negative comments on the scholarly abilities of the popularizers.

Not only do we need to change our value system so that public communication is perceived in a positive light, more particularly, we need to change the academic evaluation and reward system for archaeologists (and others!), so that it gives suitable recognition to popular writing and public outreach. Clearly, these activities also can be counted as public service. But they further merit scholarly recognition. I also would include the curation of museum exhibits in this regard, especially ones that include catalogs or CD-ROMs that are accessible to broad audiences. Effective writing for general audiences requires excellent control of the appropriate theoretical, methodological, and substantive literature and the ability to comprehend and articulate clearly the core issues of the archaeology of an area, time period, or problem, and therefore should be subject to the same kind of qualitative academic assessment that ideally goes on today in any academic tenure, promotion, or hiring procedure. However, such a development would go against the current pernicious trend

that features such aspects as counting peer-review articles and use of citation indices. I strongly believe that the growing reliance on numbers of peer-review articles and the denigration of both popular and non-peer-review writing needs to be reversed. As in so many areas of life, quantity is being substituted for quality, while the measurement of quality becomes increasingly problematic. As the former editor of a major peer-review journal, as well as the editor of many multi-author volumes, I can assure you that the quality of chapters in edited books—often discounted as non-peer-reviewed writings—can be and frequently are of as high or higher quality than peer-reviewed articles. However, many faculty and administrators appear to be looking for formulae that short-change the qualitative evaluation of research and writing, no matter what form of publication. The whole academic system of evaluation for hiring, tenure, promotion, and salary raises needs to be rethought. In my opinion it is headed in the wrong direction, and the growing trend away from qualitative evaluation is especially worrisome.

As a call to action, in order to encourage popular writing among academics, particularly those with tenure, all of us need to lobby university administrators, department chairs, and colleagues about the value and importance of written communication with audiences beyond the academy. Academics should be evaluated on their popular as well as their purely academic writings. Clearly, what is needed is a balance between original research and popular communication. In sum, evaluations should be qualitative, not quantitative.

Concerning non-academic archaeologists, we need to raise the perceived value of general publications and public outreach in the cultural resource management arm of the profession and work toward having public reporting be routinely included in scopes of work of as many cultural resource management contracts as is feasible. In some areas, fortunately, such as in the National Parks Service or in some Colonial archaeological settings, such outreach already is valued. Positive examples like this need to be professionally publicized and supported.

I would be remiss if I didn't point out that there clearly is a huge irony here. The academic world obviously is becoming increasingly market-oriented with various institutions vying for perceived "stars" in their fields with escalating offers of high salaries, less teaching, better labs, more research funds, and so on, and most academics not only are caught up in this system but have bought into it. At the same time, those scholars who are most successful in the larger marketplace of popular ideas and the popular media and who make dollars by selling to popular audiences are frequently discounted and denigrated by the self-perceived "true scholars," who often have totally bought into the broad academic market economy and are busy playing this narrower market game!

To conclude, I hope that I have been able to stimulate some thought about what might appear to be a very simple problem but which in reality is quite complicated. In order to fulfill what I believe is one of archaeology's major missions, that of public education, we need to make some significant changes in our professional modes of operation. The Archaeology Division can form a common cause with many other units of the American Anthropological Association to realize this goal. This is a four-field problem with four-field solutions! The Society for American Archaeology has just endorsed public education and outreach as one of the eight principles of archaeological ethics. This Division can also play a key role in such endeavors by working within the American Anthropological Association and using its influence to help change the emphases of our professional lives and the reward systems within which we work. To reiterate, I strongly believe that we must change our professional value system so that public outreach in all forms, but especially popular writing, is viewed and supported in highly positive terms. We need to make this change. There are signs that the pendulum of general communication in the field of American archaeology is starting to swing in a positive direction. Let us all work to push it much further!

I am sure that we all have heard the clarion call to the American public—"will you help me to build a bridge the twenty-first century"—many, many times. It is my belief that, unfortunately, the bridge to the twenty-first century will be a shaky one indeed for archaeology and anthropology—perhaps even the proverbial bridge to nowhere!— unless we tackle the communication problem with the same energy and vigor with which we routinely debate the contentious issues of contemporary archaeological theory that past lecturers to this group have delineated for you. The fruits of our research and analyses have great potential relevance for the public at large. The huge, exciting strides in understanding the past that anthropological archaeology has made in recent years need to be brought to the public's attention both for our sakes and theirs.

References

Anyon, Roger, and T. J. Ferguson 1995 Cultural Resources Management at the Pueblo of Zuni, N.M., U.S.A. Antiquity 69 (266):913–930.

Bibby, Geoffrey 1956 The Testimony of the Spade. New York: Alfred A. Knopf.

Ceram, C. W. 1951 Gods, Graves, and Scholars: The Story of Archaeology. New York: Alfred A. Knopf.

Erickson, Clark L. 1998 Applied Archaeology and Rural Development: Archaeology's Potential Contribution to the Future. In Crossing Currents: Continuity and Change in Latin America. M. Whiteford and S. Whiteford, eds. pp. 34–45. Upper Saddle, NJ: Prentice-Hall.

Fagan, Brian M. 1977 Elusive Treasure: The Story of Early Archaeologists in the Americas. New York: Scribners. 1984 The Aztecs. New York: W. H. Freeman. 1987 The Great Journey: The Peopling of Ancient America. London: Thames and Hudson. 1991 Kingdoms of Gold, Kingdoms of Jade: The Americas before Columbus. London: Thames and Hudson. 1995 Time Detectives: How Archaeologists Use Technology to Recapture the Past. New York: Simon and Schuster.

Ford, Anabel, ed. 1998 The Future of El Pilar: The Integrated Research and Development Plan for the El Pilar Archaeological Reserve for Flora and Fauna, Belize-Guatemala. Department of State Publication 10507, Bureau of Oceans. and International Environmental and Scientific Affairs, Washington, DC.

Ford, Richard I. 1973 Archaeology Serving Humanity. In Research and Theory in Current Archaeology. Charles L. Redman, ed. Pp. 83–94. New York: John Wiley.

Fritz, John M. 1973 Relevance, Archaeology, and Subsistence Theory. In Research and Theory in Current Archaeology. Charles L. Redman, ed. Pp. 59–82. New York: John Wiley.

Fritz, John M., and Fred Plog 1970 The Nature of Archaeological Explanation. American Antiquity 35:405–12.

Hodder, Ian, Michael Shanks, Alexandra Alexandri, Victor Buchli, John Carman, Jonathan Last, and Gavin Lucas, eds. 1995 Interpreting Archaeology: Finding Meaning in the Past. New York: Routledge.

Kidder, Alfred V. 1924 An Introduction to the Study of Southwestern Archaeology, with a Preliminary Account of the Excavations at Pecos. Papers of the Southwestern Expedition, No. 1. Published for the Department of Archaeology, Phillips Academy, Andover. New Haven, CT: Yale University Press. 1940 Looking Backward. Proceedings of the American Philosophical Society 83:527–537.

Kleindienst, Maxine R., and Patty Jo Watson 1956 'Action Archaeology': The Archaeological Inventory of a Living Community. Anthropology Tomorrow 5:75–78.

Kohl, Philip L., and Clare Fawcett, eds. 1995 Nationalism, Politics, and the Practice of Archaeology. Cambridge: Cambridge University Press.

Kolata, Alan L. 1993 The Tiwanaku: Portrait of an Andean Civilization. Cambridge: Blackwell.

Marcus, Joyce, and Kent V. Flannery 1996 Zapotec Civilization: How Urban Society Evolved in Mexico's Oaxaca Valley. New York: Thames and Hudson.

Plog, Stephen 1997 Ancient Peoples of the American Southwest. London: Thames and Hudson.

Preucel, Robert W. 1998 The Kotyiti Research Project: Report of the 1996 Field Season. Report submitted to the Pueblo of Cochiti and the USDA Forest Service, Santa Fe National Forest, Santa Fe, NM.

Pyburn, Anne, and Richard Wilk 1995 Responsible Archaeology Is Applied Anthropology. In Ethics in American Archaeology: Challenges for the 1990s. Mark J. Lynott and Alison Wylie, eds. Pp. 71–76. Washington, DC: Society for American Archaeology.

Rathje, William L., and Cullen Murphy 1992 Rubbish!: The Archaeology of Garbage. New York: HarperCollins.

Rice, Don S., and Prudence M. Rice 1984 Lessons from the Maya. Latin American Research Review 19(3):7–34.

Sabloff, Jeremy A. 1982 Introduction. In Archaeology: Myth and Reality. Jeremy A. Sabloff, ed. Pp. 1–26. Readings from Scientific American. San Francisco: W. H. Freeman. 1985 American Antiquity's First Fifty Years: An Introductory Comment. American Antiquity 50:228–236. 1990: The New Archaeology and the Ancient Maya. A Scientific American Library Book. New York: W. H. Freeman.

Schele, Linda, and David A. Freidel 1990 A Forest of Kings: The Untold Story of the Ancient Maya. New York: Morrow.

Snow, C. P. 1959 The Two Cultures and the Scientific Revolution. Cambridge: Cambridge University Press.

Spector, Janet 1993 What This Awl Means: Feminist Archaeology at a Wahpeton Dakota Village. St. Paul: Minnesota Historical Society Press.

Von Däniken, Erich 1970 Chariots of the Gods? New York: G. P. Putnam's Sons.

Willey, Gordon R. 1967 Alfred Vincent Kidder, 1885–1963. In Biographical Memoirs, vol. 39. Published for the National Academy of Sciences. New York: Columbia University Press.

Williams, Stephen 1991 Fantastic Archaeology: The Wild Side of North American Prehistory. Philadelphia: University of Pennsylvania Press.

Woodbury, Richard B. 1973 Alfred V. Kidder. New York Columbia University Press.

JEREMY A. SABLOFF is from the University of Pennsylvania Museum of Archaeology and Anthropology Philadelphia, PA 19104

Acknowledgments—I am honored that I was asked to deliver the Archaeology Division's 1996 Distinguished Lecture and grateful to the Archaeology Division for its kind invitation to deliver this important talk. I wish to acknowledge the growing list of colleagues, only a few of which have been cited above, who have accepted the crucial challenge of writing for general public. May your numbers multiply! I also wish thank Paula L. W. Sabloff, Joyce Marcus, and the reviewer for this journal for their many insightful and helpful comments and suggestions, only some of which I have been able to take advantage of, that have certainly improved the quality of paper.

UNIT 2

Problem Oriented Archaeology

Unit Selections

Key Points to Consider

- Explain the causes of primitive warfare. Is warfare endemic to the human species?
- Who is the "Iceman?" What is the archaeological evidence that identifies him?
- Compare the major theories as to when modern humans migrated to the New World. Please cite the archaeological evidence.
- What new methods have been used by archaeologists to show that people began cultivating crops before they embraced full-scale farming? Cite examples.
- What was the advantage of the projectile point as compared to the tips of hand-thrown spears? What impact did this technological innovation have on human evolution?
- What is the archaeological evidence for human cannibalism? How widespread has it been?
- What role did women play in hunting and gathering in Ice-Age Europe? How does this view run contrary to what has been thought before?
- What does archaeology tell us about women as toolmakers in the Ice Age? Cite the archaeological evidence.
- Who is a "garbologist?" What kind of archaeology do they do? Cite examples.
- What does the excavation of hunter-gatherer peoples tell us about their past? Use the example of the Bushmen.
- What factors were involved in the collapse of the Mayan civilization? What lessons does this hold for the modern world?

Student Web Site

www.mhcls.com

Internet References

Archaeology Links (NC)
http://www.arch.dcr.state.nc.us/links.htm#stuff
Archaeology Magazine
http://www.archaeology.org

What are the goals of archaeology? What kinds of things motivate well-educated people to go out and dig square holes in the ground and sift through their diggings like flour for a cake? How do they know where to dig? What are they looking for? What do they do with the things they find? Let us drop in on an archaeology class at Metropolis University.

"Good afternoon, class. I'm Dr. Penny Pittmeyer. Welcome to Introductory Archaeology. Excuse me, young lady. Yes, you in the back, wearing the pith helmet. I don't think you'll need to bring that shovel to class this semester. We aren't going to be doing any digging."

A moan like that of an audience who had just heard a bad pun sounded throughout the classroom. Eyes bugged out, foreheads receded, sweat formed on brow ridges, and mouths formed into alphabet-soup at this pronouncement.

"That's right, no digging. You are here to learn about archaeology." "But archaeology is digging. So what are we going to do all semester? Sheesh!" protested a thin young man with stern, steel granny glasses and a straight, scraggly beard, wearing a stained old blue work shirt and low slung 501's with an old, solid, and finely tooled leather belt and scuffed cowboy boots. A scratched trowel jutted from his right back pocket where the seam was half torn away.

Dr. Pittmeyer calmly surveyed the class and quietly repeated, "You are here to learn about archaeology." In a husky, compelling voice, she went on. "Archaeology is not digging, nor is it just about Egyptian ruins or lost civilizations. It's a science. First you have to learn the basics of that science. Digging is just a technique. Digging comes later. Digging comes after you know why you are going to dig."

"No Egyptian ruins . . . ," a plaintive echo resonated through the still classroom.

"You can have your ruins later. Take a class in Egyptian archaeology—fine, fine! But this class is the prerequisite to all those other classes. I hate to be the one to tell you this, people, but there ain't no Indiana Jones! I would have found him by now if there were." Dr. Pittmeyer said this with a slightly lopsided smile. But a veiled look in her light eyes sent an "uh-oh" that the students felt somewhere deep in their guts. They knew that the woman had something to teach them. And teach them she would!

Dr. Pittmeyer half sat on the old desk at the front of the classroom. Leaning one elbow on the podium to her right, she picked up a tall, red, opaque glass, and took a long and satisfying drink from it. Behind her large-framed black glasses, her eyes brightened noticeably. She wiped away an invisible mustache from her upper lip and settled onto the desk, holding the red glass in her left hand and letting it sway slightly as she unhurriedly looked over the students. Her left eyebrow rose unconsciously.

The quiet lengthened so that the students filling out the Day-Glo-orange drop cards stopped writing, conscious of the now-loud silence in the room.

"OK! LET'S GO!" Dr. Pittmeyer said with a snap like a whip swinging over their heads. The startled students went straight-backed in unison.

"Archaeology is a science, ladies and gentlemen. It's part of the larger science of anthropology. The goals of both are to understand and predict human behavior. Let's start by looking at an area or subfield of archaeology that we may designate as problem-oriented archaeology. Humans evolved in Africa, Asia, and Europe, or what we refer to as the Old World."

Dr. Pittmeyer simultaneously turned out the lights and clicked on an overhead projector and wrote rapidly with a harshly bright, purple pen in a hieroglyphic-like scrawl. Dangling from her neck was a microphone that was plugged into a speaker that was then plugged back into the overhead projector which in turn was plugged into an old, cracked socket, the single electric outlet offered by the ancient high-ceilinged, asbestos-filled room.

Doubtful students suddenly felt compelled to take notes in the dim light provided by the irregularities of old-fashioned thick blinds that did not quite close completely.

"In the New World, in the Americas, from Alaska down to the tip of Tierra del Fuego, we only have well documented evidence that the first people lived here about 15,000–11,000 years ago. In contrast people have been living in the Old World for 200,000 years or more—people in the sense of Homo sapiens. "So what took them so long to get here?" a perplexed female voice asked.

"Please let me point out that your question contains a very telling assumption. You said what took them so long to get here. The question is moot because these early peoples were not trying to get here. We're talking about the Paleolithic era—people were migratory. They hunted and collected their food every day. They followed their food resources usually in seasonal patterns but within fairly local areas. So it is a non-question. Let me explain, please.

"In archaeology, you have to ask the right questions before you can get any useful answers. That is why archaeologists dig—not to make discoveries, but to answer questions. Now, here's what I want you to do. Go home and try to think of yourself back into the Paleolithic. Its 35,000 years ago, and mostly you hang out with your family and other close relatives. You get your food and shelter on a daily basis, and you have some free time, too. Everyone cooperates to survive. The point is that wherever you are, you are there. There is no place to try to get to. There is no notion of private property or ownership of land. Nobody needs to conquer anybody. There are no cities, no freeways, no clocks, and no rush. Think about it. It's a concept of life without measurements or urgencies."

"But they must have been pretty stupid back that long ago!" the young man with the beard, now nibbling his trowel, protested. "Please think about that assumption! No, these were people just like you and me. If they were here today, they probably could program their VCRs. These were people with many skills and accomplishments. They met their needs as we meet ours. But they had something we might envy. They were already there no matter where they were! There's a lot to be learned from our prehistoric ancestors."

"But, frankly, tomorrow's another day." Alone in the classroom, Dr. Penny Pittmeyer finished her soda and allowed her eyes to glaze over as the forgotten Day-Glo-orange drop cards fluttered to the floor. She stared far back in time where she saw intelligent people living a simple life in peace—or so she hoped.

Prehistory *of* Warfare

Humans have been at each others' throats since the dawn of the species.

STEVEN A. LEBLANC

In the early 1970s, working in the El Morro Valley of west-central New Mexico, I encountered the remains of seven large prehistoric pueblos that had once housed upwards of a thousand people each. Surrounded by two-story-high walls, the villages were perched on steep-sided mesas, suggesting that their inhabitants built them with defense in mind. At the time, the possibility that warfare occurred among the Anasazi was of little interest to me and my colleagues. Rather, we were trying to figure out what the people in these 700-year-old communities farmed and hunted, the impact of climate change, and the nature of their social systems—not the possibility of violent conflict.

One of these pueblos, it turned out, had been burned to the ground; its people had clearly fled for their lives. Pottery and valuables had been left on the floors, and bushels of burned corn still lay in the storerooms. We eventually determined that this site had been abandoned, and that immediately afterward a fortress had been built nearby. Something catastrophic had occurred at this ancient Anasazi settlement, and the survivors had almost immediately, and at great speed, set about to prevent it from happening again.

Thirty years ago, archaeologists were certainly aware that violent, organized conflicts occurred in the prehistoric cultures they studied, but they considered these incidents almost irrelevant to our understanding of past events and people. Today, some of my colleagues are realizing that the evidence I helped uncover in the El Morro Valley is indicative warfare endemic throughout the entire Southwest, with its attendant massacres, population decline, and area abandonments that forever changed the Anasazi way of life.

When excavating eight-millennia-old farm villages in southeastern Turkey in 1970, I initially marveled how similar modern villages were to ancient ones, which were occupied at a time when an abundance of plants and animals made warfare quite unnecessary. Or so I thought. I knew we had discovered some plaster sling missiles (one of our workmen showed me how shepherds used slings to hurl stones at predators threatening their sheep). Such missiles were found at many of these sites, often in great quantities, and were clearly not intended for protecting flocks of sheep; they were exactly the same size and shape as later Greek and Roman sling stones used for warfare.

The so-called "donut stones" we had uncovered at these sites were assumed to be weights for digging sticks, presumably threaded on a pole to make it heavier for digging holes to plant crops. I failed to note how much they resembled the round stone heads attached to wooden clubs—maces—used in many places of the world exclusively for fighting and still used ceremonially to signify power. Thirty years ago, I was holding mace heads and sling missiles in my hands, unaware of their use as weapons of war.

We now know that defensive walls once ringed many villages of this era, as they did the Anasazi settlements. Rooms were massed together behind solid outside walls and were entered from the roof. Other sites had mud brick defensive walls, some with elaborately defended gates. Furthermore, many of these villages had been burned to the ground, their inhabitants massacred, as indicated by nearby mass graves.

Certainly for those civilizations that kept written records or had descriptive narrative art traditions, warfare is so clearly present that no one can deny it. Think of Homer's *Iliad* or the Vedas of South India, or scenes of prisoner sacrifice on Moche pottery. There is no reason to think that warfare played any less of a role in prehistoric societies for which we have no such records, whether they be hunter-gatherers or farmers. But most scholars studying these cultures still are not seeing it. They should assume warfare occurred among the people they study, just as they assume religion and art were a normal part of human culture. Then they could ask more interesting questions, such as: What form did warfare take? Can warfare explain some of the material found in the archaeological record? What were people fighting over and why did the conflicts end?

Today, some scholars know me as Dr. Warfare. To them, I have the annoying habit of asking un-politic questions about their research. I am the one who asks why the houses at a particular site were jammed so close together and many catastrophically burned. When I suggest that the houses were crowded behind defensive walls that were not found because no one was looking for them, I am not terribly appreciated. And I don't win any popularity contests when I suggest that twenty-mile-wide zones with no sites in them imply no-man's lands—clear evidence for warfare—to archaeologists who have explained a region's history without mention of conflict.

> **Scholars should assume warfare occurred among the people they study, just as they assume religion was a normal part of human culture. Then they would ask more interesting questions, such as: What form did warfare take? Why did people start and stop fighting?**

Virtually all the basic textbooks on archaeology ignore the prevalence or significance of past warfare, which is usually not discussed until the formation of state-level civilizations such as ancient Sumer. Most texts either assume or actually state that for most of human history there was an abundance of available resources. There was no resource stress, and people had the means to control population, though how they accomplished this is never explained. The one archaeologist who has most explicitly railed against this hidden but pervasive attitude is Lawrence Keeley of the University of Illinois, who studies the earliest farmers in Western Europe. He has fund ample evidence of warfare as farmers spread west, yet most of his colleagues still believe the expansion was peaceful and his evidence a minor aberration, as seen in the various papers in Barry Cunliffe's *The Oxford Illustrated Prehistory of Europe* (1994) or Douglas Price's *Europe's First Farmers* (2000). Keeley contends that "prehistorians have increasingly pacified the past," presuming peace or thinking up every possible alternative explanation for the evidence they cannot ignore. In his *War Before Civilization* (1996) he accused archaeologists of being in denial on the subject.

Witness archaeologist Lisa Valkenier suggesting in 1997 that hilltop constructions along the Peruvian coast are significant because peaks are sacred in Andean cosmology. Their enclosing walls and narrow guarded entries may have more to do with restricting access to the *huacas,* or sacred shrines, on top of the hills than protecting defenders and barring entry to any potential attackers. How else but by empathy can one formulate such an interpretation in

an area with a long defensive wall and hundreds of defensively located fortresses, some still containing piles of sling missiles ready to be used; where a common artistic motif is the parading and execution of defeated enemies; where hundreds were sacrificed; and where there is ample evidence of conquest, no-man's lands, specialized weapons, and so on?

A talk I gave at the Mesa Verde National Park last summer, in which I pointed out that the over 700-year-old cliff dwellings were built in response to warfare, raised the hackles of National Park Service personnel unwilling to accept anything but the peaceful Anasazi message peddled by their superiors. In fact, in the classic book *Indians of Mesa Verde,* published in 1961 by the park service, author Don Watson first describes the Mesa Verde people as "peaceful farming Indians," and admits that the cliff dwellings had a defensive aspect, but since he had already decided that the inhabitants were peaceful, the threat must have been from a new enemy—marauding nomadic Indians. This, in spite of the fact that there is ample evidence of Southwestern warfare for more than a thousand years before the cliff dwellings were built, and there is no evidence for the intrusion of nomadic peoples at this time.

Of the hundreds of research projects in the Southwest, only one—led by Jonathan Haas and Winifred Creamer of the Field Museum and Northern Illinois University, respectively—deliberately set out to research prehistoric warfare. They demonstrated quite convincingly that the Arizona cliff dwellings of the Tsegi Canyon area (known best for Betatakin and Kiet Siel ruins) were defensive, and their locations were not selected for ideology or because they were breezier and cooler in summer and warmer in the winter, as was previously argued by almost all Southwestern archaeologists.

For most prehistoric cultures, one has to piece together the evidence for warfare from artifactual bits and pieces. Most human history involved foragers, and so they are particularly relevant. They too were not peaceful. We know from ethnography that the Inuit (Eskimo) and Australian Aborigines engaged in warfare. We've also discovered remains of prehistoric bone armor in the Arctic, and skeletal evidence of deadly blows to the head are well documented among the prehistoric Aborigines. Surprising to some is the skeletal evidence for warfare in prehistoric California, once thought of as a land of peaceful acorn gatherers. The prehistoric people who lived in southern Californian had the highest incident of warfare deaths known anywhere in the world. Thirty percent of a large sample of males dating to the first centuries A.D. had wounds or died violent deaths. About half that number of women had similar histories. When we remember that not all warfare deaths leave skeletal evidence, this is a staggering number.

There was nothing unique about the farmers of the Southwest. From the Neolithic farmers of the Middle East and Europe to the New Guinea highlanders in the twentieth century, tribally organized farmers probably had the most intense warfare of any type of society. Early villages in China, the Yucatán, present-day Pakistan, and Micronesia were well fortified. Ancient farmers in coastal Peru had plenty of forts. All Polynesian societies had warfare, from the smallest islands like Tikopia, to Tahiti, New Zealand (more than four thousand prehistoric forts), and Hawaii. No-man's lands separated farming settlements in Okinawa, Oaxaca, and the southeastern United States. Such societies took trophy heads and cannibalized their enemies. Their skeletal remains show ample evidence of violent deaths. All well-studied prehistoric farming societies had warfare. They may have had intervals of peace, but over the span of hundreds of years there is plenty of evidence for real, deadly warfare.

When farmers initially took over the world, they did so as warriors, grabbing land as they spread out from the Levant through the Middle East into Europe, or from South China down through Southeast Asia. Later complex societies like the Maya, the Inca, the Sumerians, and the Hawaiians were no less belligerent. Here, conflict took on a new dimension. Fortresses, defensive walls hundreds of miles long, and weapons and armor expertly crafted by specialists all gave the warfare of these societies a heightened visibility.

Demonstrating the prevalence of warfare is not an end in itself. It is only the first step in understanding why there was so much of it, why it was "rational" for everyone to engage in it all the time. I believe the question of warfare links to the availability of resources.

There is a danger in making too much of the increased visibility of warfare we see in these complex societies. This is especially true for societies with writing. When there are no texts, it is easy to see no warfare. But the opposite is true. As soon as societies can write, they write about warfare. It is not a case of literate societies having warfare for the first time, but their being able to write about what had been going on for a long time. Also, many of these literate societies link to European civilization in one way or another, and so this raises the specter of Europeans being warlike and spreading war to inherently peaceful people elsewhere, a patently false but prevalent notion. Viewing warfare from their perspective of literate societies tells us nothing about the thousands of years of human societies that were not civilizations—that is, almost all of human history. So we must not rely too much on the small time slice represented by literate societies if we want to understand warfare in the past.

The Maya were once considered a peaceful society led by scholarly priests. That all changed when the texts written by their leaders could be read, revealing a long history of warfare and conquest. Most Mayanists now accept that there was warfare, but many still resist dealing with its scale or implications. Was there population growth that resulted in resource depletion, as throughout the rest of the world? We would expect the Maya to have been fighting each other over valuable farmlands as a consequence, but Mayanist Linda Schele concluded in 1984 that "I do not think it [warfare] was territorial for the most part," this even though texts discuss conquest, and fortifications are present at sites like El Mirador, Calakmul, Tikal, Yaxuná, Uxmal, and many others from all time periods. Why fortify them, if no one wanted to capture them?

Today, more Maya archaeologists are looking at warfare in a systematic way, by mapping defensive features, finding images of destruction, and dating these events. A new breed of younger scholars is finding evidence of warfare throughout the Maya past. Where are the no-man's lands that almost always open up between competing states because they are too dangerous to live in? Warfare must have been intimately involved in the development of Maya civilization, and resource stress must have been widespread.

Demonstrating the prevalence of warfare is not an end in itself. It is only the first step in understanding why there was so much, why it was "rational" for everyone to engage in it all the time. I believe the question of warfare links to the availability of resources.

During the 1960s, I lived in Western Samoa as a Peace Corps volunteer on what seemed to be an idyllic South Pacific Island—exactly like those painted by Paul Gauguin. Breadfruit and coconut groves grew all around my village, and I resided in a thatched-roof house with no walls beneath a giant mango tree. If ever there was a Garden of Eden, this was it. I lived with a family headed by an extremely intelligent elderly chief named Sila. One day, Sila happened to mention that the island's trees did not bear fruit as they had when he was a child. He attributed the decline to the possibility that the presence of radio transmissions had affected production, since Western Samoa (now known as Samoa) had its own radio station by then. I suggested that what had changed was not that there was less fruit but that there were more mouths to feed. Upon reflection, Sila decided I was probably right. Being an astute manager, he was already taking the precaution of expanding his farm plots into some of the last remaining farmable land on the island, at considerable cost and effort, to ensure adequate food for his growing family. Sila was aware of his escalating provisioning problems but was not quite able to grasp the overall demographic situation. Why was this?

The simple answer is that the rate of population change in our small Samoan village was so gradual that during an adult life span growth was not dramatic enough to be fully comprehended. The same thing happens to us all the time. Communities grow and change composition, and often only after the process is well advanced do we recognize just how significant the changes have been—and we have the benefit of historic documents, old photographs, long life spans, and government census surveys. All human societies can grow substantially over time, and all did whenever resources permitted. The change may seem small in one person's lifetime, but over a couple of hundred years, populations can and do double, triple, or quadruple in size.

The consequences of these changes become evident only when there is a crisis. The same can be said for environmental changes. The forests of Central America were being denuded and encroached upon for many years, but it took Hurricane Mitch, which ravaged most of the region in late October 1998, to produce the dramatic flooding and devastation that fully demonstrated the magnitude of the problem: too many people cutting down the forest and farming steep hillsides to survive. The natural environment is resilient and at the same time delicate, as modern society keeps finding out. And it was just so in the past.

From foragers to farmers to more complex societies, when people no longer have resource stress they stop fighting. When climate greatly improves, warfare declines. The great towns of Chaco Canyon were built during an extended warm–and peaceful–period.

These observations about Mother Nature are incompatible with popular myths about peaceful people living in ecological balance with nature in the past. A peaceful past is possible only if you live in ecological balance. If you live in a Garden of Eden surrounded by plenty, why fight? By this logic, warfare is a sure thing when natural resources run dry. If someone as smart as Sila couldn't perceive population growth, and if humans all over Earth continue to degrade their environments, could people living in the past have been any different?

A study by Canadian social scientists Christina Mesquida and Neil Wiener has shown that the greater the proportion of a society is composed of unmarried young men, the greater the likelihood of war. Why such a correlation? It is not because the young men are not married; it is because they cannot get married. They are too poor to support wives and families. The idea that poverty breeds war is far from original. The reason poverty exists has remained the same since the beginning of time: humans have invariably over-exploited their resources because they have always outgrown them.

There is another lesson from past warfare. It stops. From foragers to farmers, to more complex societies, when people no longer have resource stress they stop fighting. When the climate greatly improves, warfare declines. For example, in a variety of places the medieval warm interval of ca. 900–1100 improved farming conditions. The great towns of Chaco Canyon were built at this time, and it was the time of archaeologist Stephen Lekson's *Pax Chaco*—the longest period of peace in the Southwest. It is no accident that the era of Gothic cathedrals was a response to similar climate improvement. Another surprising fact is that the amount of warfare has declined over time. If we count the proportion of a society that died from warfare, and not the size of the armies, as the true measure of warfare, then we find that foragers and farmers have much higher death rates—often approaching 25 percent of the men—than more recent complex societies. No complex society, including modern states, ever approached this level of warfare.

If warfare has ultimately been a constant battle over scarce resources, then solving the resource problem will enable us to become better at ridding ourselves of conflict.

There have been several great "revolutions" in human history: control of fire, the acquisition of speech, the agricultural revolution, the development of complex societies. One of the most recent, the Industrial Revolution, has lowered the birth rate and increased available resources. History shows that peoples with strong animosities stop fighting after adequate resources are established and the benefits of cooperation recognized. The Hopi today are some of the most peaceful people on earth, yet their history is filled with warfare. The Gebusi of lowland New Guinea, the African !Kung Bushmen, the Mbuti Pygmies of central Africa, the Sanpoi and their neighbors of the southern Columbia River, and the Sirionno of Amazonia are all peoples who are noted for being peaceful, yet archaeology and historical accounts provide ample evidence of past warfare. Sometimes things changed in a generation; at other times it took longer. Adequate food and opportunity does not instantly translate into peace, but it will, given time.

The fact that it can take several generations or longer to establish peace between warring factions is little comfort for those engaged in the world's present conflicts. Add to this a recent change in the decision-making process that leads to war. In most traditional societies, be they forager bands, tribal farmers, or even complex chiefdoms, no individual held enough power to start a war on his own. A consensus was needed; pros and cons were carefully weighed and hotheads were not tolerated. The risks to all were too great. Moreover, failure of leadership was quickly recognized, and poor leaders were replaced. No Hitler or Saddam Hussein would have been tolerated. Past wars were necessary for survival, and therefore were rational; too often today this is not the case. We cannot go back to forager-band-type consensus, but the world must work harder at keeping single individuals from gaining the power to start wars. We know from archaeology that the amount of warfare has declined markedly over the course of human history and that peace can prevail under the right circumstances. In spite of the conflict we see around us, we are doing better, and there is less warfare in the world today than there ever has been. Ending it may be a slow process, but we are making headway.

© 2003 by STEVEN A. LEBLANC. Portions of this article were taken from his book *Constant Battles,* published in April 2003 by St. Martin's Press. LeBlanc is director of collections at Harvard University's Peabody Museum of Archaeology and Ethnology. For further reading visit www.archaeology.org.

The Mystery of Unknown Man E

Was a mummy found in less-than-royal wrappings a disgraced prince who plotted to murder his father, Ramesses III?

BOB BRIER

On a day at the end of June 1886, Gaston Maspero, head of the Egyptian Antiquities Service, was unwrapping the mummies of kings and queens found in a cache at Deirel Bahri, near the Valley of the Kings. Inside a plain, undecorated coffin that offered no clues to the deceased's identity, Maspero found something that shocked him. There, wrapped in a sheepskin—a ritually unclean object for ancient Egyptians—was a young man, hands and feet bound, who seemed to be screaming. There was no incision on the left abdomen, through which the embalmers normally removed the internal organs; the man had not been afforded the traditional mummification. Maspero was convinced there had been foul play, as he wrote in *Les Momies Royales de Deir-el-Bahari* (1889):

> All those who saw him first hand thought that [he] looked as though he had been poisoned. The contraction of the abdomen and stomach, the desperate movement with which the head is thrown back, the expression of excruciating pain spread over the face hardly allow for any other explanation.

Daniel Fouquet, the physician who examined the mummy at the time, agreed that he had been poisoned and said, "the last convulsions of horrid agony can, after thousands of years, still be seen." A chemist named Mathey who did some analyses on the mummy, felt that "the wretched man must have been deliberately asphyxiated—most likely by being buried alive."

All three investigators had let their imaginations run wild. A quarter century later, the mummy was examined by the anatomist Grafton Elliott Smith, who was far more experienced than Maspero, Fouquet, and Mathey. Smith quickly dismissed their theories about the cause of death, pointing out in *The Royal Mummies* (1912) that "a corpse that was dead of any complaint might fall into just such an attitude as this body has assumed." The real questions remain to this day, Who is this mummy, and how did his unembalmed body, wrapped in a sheepskin and buried in an unmarked coffin, come to rest with the greatest kings and queens of Egypt?

Many have speculated about the identity of Unknown Man E (designated such by Maspero, who assigned letters to each of the half dozen anonymous mummies in the cache). We know from the royal archives of the Hittite Empire, found a century ago at Bogazkoy in central Turkey, that a prince was sent to Egypt to marry the widow of Tutankhamun, but he was murdered on the border of Egypt. Some have suggested that Unknown Man E is that prince, and that is why he, a foreigner, was buried in a sheepskin. As evidence, they point to the Egyptian papyrus Known as "The Tale of Sinuhe." In it, the pharaoh tries to convince Sinuhe, a former friend and confidant who has been living abroad, to return to Egypt. The king says, "You shall not die in a foreign land. . . you shall not be placed in a sheepskin as they make your grave."

Another explanation that has been offered is that Unknown Man E was an important personage who died abroad, perhaps on a military campaign in a region with limited knowledge of, or access to, mummification technology. The local priests did what they could to preserve the body, added the sheepskin because it was appropriate in their beliefs, and shipped it home.

Maspero suggested that the mummy was that of Prince Pentewere, the son of Ramesses III (1185–1153 B.C.) who was involved in a conspiracy against his father ("The Harem Conspiracy,"). The conspirators, including Queen Tiy and her son Pentewere, were caught and either executed or, in the case of the highest-ranking ones, such as Pentewere, allowed to take their own lives. But would a convicted criminal be buried with the royal family?

Much of the speculation about Unknown Man E stemmed from the fact that no one had seen the mummy in nearly a hundred years. All we have had to go on are the early reports and a few photos taken more than a century ago. In late 2004, with the permission and assistance of Egypt's Supreme Council of Antiquities, I had the opportunity to examine him. My hope was that we might find clues to the date, cause of death, and identification of the mummy and explain how such a burial could happen. While I cannot prove with the current evidence that this is the mummy of Pentewere, that identification seems to fit the curious facts of Unknown Man E.

For more than 75 years, tourists had walked by Unknown Man E as he lay in his plain wooden coffin on the second floor of the Egyptian Museum in Cairo. For our preliminary examination, the coffin was brought down to a room on the museum's ground floor and for the first time in nearly a century the lid was removed. Would the mummy still be intact? Our first glimpse of Unknown Man E was reassuring. He looked very much as he did in the old photos, a sign that the mummy was in good condition. By his side was the famous sheepskin.

Museum staff members carefully removed Unknown Man E and placed him on an examination table. Much of what we found confirmed some of the observations of Smith and the earlier investigators. He was approximately 5 feet 9 inches tall and quite muscular. Because his mouth was gaping open, we could examine his teeth, which were free of cavities and showed little sign of wear. His lower third molars (wisdom teeth) were in, but his uppers had not yet descended, placing his age at the time of death as early twenties. His fingernails were well cared for, as were his toenails, which were hennaed—indications that he was upper class. We found no external evidence of a cause of death, such as a wound or trauma.

As our examination proceeded, a picture of his unusual preparation for the next world emerged. Although neither the internal organs nor the brain had been removed, the early investigators noticed some attempt to preserve the body. Natron—a natural combination of salt and baking soda used by ancient embalmers to dehydrate the deceased—had been sprinkled on the body. We noticed a black material on the teeth, and closer inspection showed some of it had pooled in the back of his throat. This is probably resin, a standard ingredient in mummification. Normally it was poured via the nasal passages into the cranium after the brain was removed to cauterize the area.

Remains of the leather bands used to tie the hands and feet together were in the coffin. We could see that they had dug into the flesh when it was still soft—before the body was mummified—certainly an unusual finding.

Smith had described a strange white coating that encrusted the body and matted the hair as "cheese-like." Analysis by Mathey showed that it was partly organic and partly inorganic. The organic part was human fat and results from a process that occurs naturally in some cadavers. The fats in the body migrate to the surface and turn to soap, called "grave wax" by early observers of the phenomenon. The inorganic substance that was mixed with the fat proved to be natron. Because his internal organs were not removed, there was still considerable moisture in his body when he was wrapped. (Moisture is necessary for the "grave wax" to form.) His body was sprinkled with natron in an attempt to preserve him and this mixed with the fat beneath the bandages. It is evidence of a hurried burial.

Clearly the traditional 70-day mummification process was not followed. The internal organs and brain were not removed

The Harem Conspiracy

Ramesses III had successfully defended Egypt against several invasions in his earlier years, earning his reputation as the last great pharaoh. But later in his reign there were signs of discontent. The workers at Deir el-Medineh, who were responsible for the royal tombs, went on strike for back pay. The old pharaoh no longer commanded the respect that he once did. Perhaps sensing Ramesses was not long to rule, factions must have begun jockeying for power. The legitimate heir was Prince Ramesses, son of Iset, one of the pharaoh's two principal wives. But Tiy, a secondary queen, plotted to overthrow Ramesses III and place her son Pentewere on the throne. Involved in the plot were women in the harem, palace functionaries, officials in charge of the harem, scribes and guards, and a commander of Nubian bowmen and a general. An assassination attempt miscarried, and the coup failed. Ramessses ordered the trial of the conspirators, but died soon after it began. Egyptians never revealed details about a king's death, so we can't be certain, but it appears he might have survived an attack only to succumb to the wounds or infection some days later.

Records of the trials have been preserved on papyrus scrolls, giving us details of the plot and the fate of those who took part in it. The plot was complex: the assassination of Ramesses III would be accompanied by a military uprising. Magic would be employed to ensure its success; several of the conspirators were adept in this area, as the records reveal that one of them made "magical scrolls for hindering and terrifying, and to make some gods of wax, and some people for enfeebling the limbs of people." But the uprising collapsed, and more than a dozen conspirators were caught and convicted and either took their own lives or were executed. We do not know what happened to Queen Tiy. We do know, however, what happened to Pentewere, the prince who would be king. He, along with some high court officials, was permitted to commit suicide: "They took their own lives, and no punishment was executed upon them." Being permitted to commit suicide, probably by poison, was a kindness. Execution was usually by impalement on a wooden stake.

—B.B.

and the body was not dehydrated in natron for 35 days. Yet there was some attempt at mummification. Undoubtedly he was someone of high status who for some reason could not be given the full treatment.

There is nothing about the mummification, such as it was, that allows us to date Unknown Man E. All earlier reports agreed that the wrappings seemed to be of a style prevalent prior to the 21st Dynasty (1064–940 B.C.). Smith suggested the earlier 18th Dynasty, possibly because of the style of bandage wrapping. But the wrappings were never photographed and are now gone, so that evidence is lost.

Once we emptied the coffin, we could see clearly that it was not originally made for Unknown Man E. Inside it, areas at the foot and by the shoulders had been crudely hacked away to make room for the tall, broad man, and its floor was still littered with shavings.

Was there anything to be learned from the objects buried with Unknown Man E? Maspero had described the mummy as being sewn into a sheepskin, but close examination of the skin seems to contradict this. It is clearly too small to have wrapped around and enveloped a full-size man. Furthermore, the edges had no holes from sewing, nor were we able to find remains of thread. At most, the mummy was covered with the skin, not sewn into it.

When he was first discovered, Unknown Man E's ears still contained simple gold earrings, and there were two walking sticks in the coffin with him. The earrings had been removed by Smith's day, and the walking sticks were not in the coffin when we opened it. Because they are just simple hoops, the earrings don't help us date the mummy. They indicate the mummy was of a high-status individual but not necessarily royal, as wealthy commoners also wore gold. The fact that they were not taken by the embalmers suggests someone who cared about him oversaw his burial. The walking sticks, another indication of status, might be more helpful. Numerous examples of royal walking sticks were found in Tutankhamun's tomb, and if those found with Unknown Man E could be located, they might aid in determining the time of burial more precisely.

Once we emptied the coffin, we could see clearly that it was not originally made for Unknown Man E. Inside it, areas at the foot and by the shoulders had been crudely hacked away to make room for the tall, broad man, and its floor was still littered with shavings. Again, a sign of a hasty burial; they hadn't even swept up the shavings. The coffin is of pre-21st Dynasty date, possibly as early as the 18th Dynasty, but that doesn't help us date the mummy. It may have been an available coffin that was hastily adapted for Unknown Man E's burial. Although it was unmarked and not richly decorated, the coffin was of imported cedar wood and well crafted, not an inexpensive receptacle for the body. It suggests that whoever oversaw the burial was a person of wealth and status.

Interpreting the evidence of the mummy, its coffin, and the objects found with it requires an understanding of the royal mummy cache in which it was found. In the 21st Dynasty, an official inspection revealed that the tombs in the Valley of the Kings had been robbed, their coffins smashed and treasures looted. To preserve the mummies—some of which had been torn apart by looters seeking jewels and gold among the linen bandages—the priests in charge of the royal burials rewrapped them, placed them in new coffins, and moved them to a secret tomb off a secluded path near the temple of Queen Hatshepsut at Deir el-Bahri.

The tomb was considered safe enough that the 21st Dynasty ruler Pinedjem I used it for his own burial around 1026 B.C., as did Pinedjem II half a century later. During this period, the priests placed the unmarked coffin with Unknown Man E in the tomb along with the damaged royal mummies. There it remained—one of 40 mummies, including some of Egypt's greatest pharaohs—undisturbed for three millennia.

In the 1870s, spectacular objects began appearing on the Egyptian antiquities market, including a Book of the Dead that had been buried with Henettowey, the wife of Pinedjem I. The artifacts were traced to the three Rassoul brothers from the village of Gourna, near the Valley of the Kings. One of the brothers eventually confessed and took Maspero's assistant, Emile Brugsch, to the tomb in June 1881. Brugsch worked quickly, removing all the coffins and funerary equipment in just six days. Virtually no record was made of the coffins, mummies, and objects before they were taken out of the tomb.

So, how do we interpret the evidence we have? I believe we can take it at face value. The 21st Dynasty priests repackaged many of the mummies in the cache, so the wrappings, objects, and coffins associated with a particular mummy may, or may not, be its original ones. But the priests were chiefly concerned with the mummies that had been damaged by ancient tomb robbers, and there is no evidence of damage to Unknown Man E. Furthermore, everyone who saw the wrappings agreed that they seemed to be of a style prior to the 21st Dynasty. This suggests that Unknown Man E was in his original burial trappings when discovered. Was the mummy disturbed by the Rassoul bothers? They probably never touched the coffin in the years they plundered the tomb. It was not rich enough—there were much more posh ones around. And if they had opened the coffin and rifled the mummy, they would have discovered and taken the gold earrings.

If we take the mummy, coffin, wrappings, and artifacts as all belonging together, we can then make the following observations based on earlier examinations and the one I conducted last year. Unknown Man E was:

1. a robust young man with no external indication of cause of death
2. a high-status individual (coffin quality, earrings, walking sticks, and presence in royal cache)
3. buried quickly but with some care (limited mummification, coffin crudely adapted, coffin quality, earrings not pilfered)
4. left unnamed deliberately (no identification on coffin or wrappings, as normally found)
5. buried with a sheepskin covering his mummy
6. originally buried between the later 18th Dynasty and before the 21st (coffin and wrapping style).

With these observations in mind, we can return to the proposed identifications of Unknown Man E: murdered Hittite prince, nobleman, or royal who died while away from Egypt, or Pentewere of the conspiracy against Ramesses III.

I believe the first two can be ruled out. If you commit a murder, you dispose of the body—you don't keep it. So it is highly unlikely that we have a murdered Hittite prince buried with Egyptian kings and queens. If for some diplomatic reason the Egyptians had buried the prince, we might expect an official record of it in the Hittite archives or something identifying his mummy. And the unnamed mummy and coffin speak against this being a high-ranking individual who died while abroad. So, for the evidence that we have available to us today, the story of Pentewere fits best.

How could Pentewere, guilty of trying to overthrow his father, come to be buried in the royal cache at Deir el-Bahri? We might imagine that after the prince committed suicide, someone who cared for him—he had plenty of brothers and sisters, and likely had followers who were not implicated in the conspiracy—paid an embalmer to do what he could quickly and covertly. Natron was placed on the body, resin was poured into the mouth, and the body was wrapped. Then an available coffin was bought and crudely enlarged to accommodate Pentewere's large frame. Two of his walking sticks, perhaps favored possessions, were placed in the coffin with him. Now, where could he be buried?

We know that Ramesses III died soon after the attempted coup and before the trial of the conspirators had ended. Thus when Pentewere committed suicide, Ramesses' tomb must have been open, with frantic preparations being made to receive the king's mummy and funerary equipment. It is possible that someone was bribed and the coffin containing Pentewere was placed in a corner of a side chamber where it was hidden behind the furniture and other things the pharaoh was taking to the next world. From there, the priests of the 21st Dynasty gathered the unmarked coffin of Unknown Man E, moving it to Deir el-Bahri more than a century later.

This scenario is highly speculative, and the identification of Unknown Man E as Pentewere is far from certain. But it does take into account the known facts about the mummy and does not involve any far-fetched assumptions. Clearly a more thorough study of Unknown Man E will provide additional evidence and might lead to a more certain identification.

There are many analytical techniques available that did not exist a hundred years ago and could answer questions that my visual examination of the mummy could not. For example, carbon dating could place him in a particular dynasty. The soapy "grave wax" material must be from the time of his burial and it, as well as the leather bands from the hands and feet, can be sampled and dated this way without harming the mummy. Carbon dating could also verify that the sheepskin is from the same time as the mummy.

If permitted, analysis of tissue from the mummy could reveal many things. We could determine whether or not Unknown Man E grew up in Egypt. Was poison the cause of death? Mathey found no evidence, but he was looking for modern types such as strychnine. Unknown Man E's DNA could be compared with that of Ramesses III—if DNA analysis of mummies were far enough advanced. For now, blood typing is a better bet, and we could compare results from Unknown Man E with Ramesses III.

In fact, the Supreme Council of Antiquities is currently planning a detailed examination and CT scanning of all the royal mummies in the Egyptian Museum. And Zahi Hawass, Secretary General of the Supreme Council, has promised that Unknown Man E will be the first.

BOB BRIER is Senior Research Fellow at the C.W. Post Campus of Long Island University and is also a contributing editor to ARCHAEOLOGY.

From *Archaeology,* March/April 2006, pp. 36–42. Copyright © 2006 by Archaeological Institute of America. Reprinted by permission.

Who Were the First Americans?

MICHAEL D. LEMONICK AND ANDREA DORFMAN

It was clear from the moment Jim Chatters first saw the partial skeleton that no crime had been committed—none recent enough to be prosecutable, anyway. Chatters, a forensic anthropologist, had been called in by the coroner of Benton County, Wash., to consult on some bones found by two college students on the banks of the Columbia River, near the town of Kennewick. The bones were obviously old, and when the coroner asked for an opinion, Chatters' off-the-cuff guess, based on the skull's superficially Caucasoid features, was that they probably belonged to a settler from the late 1800s. Then a CT scan revealed a stone spear point embedded in the skeleton's pelvis, so Chatters sent a bit of finger bone off to the University of California at Riverside for radiocarbon dating. When the results came back, it was clear that his estimate was dramatically off the mark. The bones weren't 100 or even 1,000 years old. They belonged to a man who had walked the banks of the Columbia more than 9,000 years ago.

In short, the remains that came to be known as Kennewick Man were almost twice as old as the celebrated Iceman discovered in 1991 in an Alpine glacier, and among the oldest and most complete skeletons ever found in the Americas. Plenty of archaeological sites date back that far, or nearly so, but scientists have found only about 50 skeletons of such antiquity, most of them fragmentary. Any new find can thus add crucial insight into the ongoing mystery of who first colonized the New World—the last corner of the globe to be populated by humans. Kennewick Man could cast some much needed light on the murky questions of when that epochal migration took place, where the first Americans originally came from and how they got here.

U.S. government researchers examined the bones, but it would take almost a decade for independent scientists to get a good look at the skeleton. Although it was found in the summer of 1996, the local Umatilla Indians and four other Columbia Basin tribes almost immediately claimed it as ancestral remains under the Native American Graves Protection and Repatriation Act *(see box)*, demanding that the skeleton be reburied without the desecration of scientific study. A group of researchers sued, starting a legal tug-of-war and negotiations that ended only last summer, with the scientists getting their first extensive access to the bones. And now, for the first time, we know the results of that examination.

What the Bones Revealed

It was clearly worth the wait. The scientific team that examined the skeleton was led by forensic anthropologist Douglas Owsley of the Smithsonian Institution's National Museum of Natural History. He has worked with thousands of historic and prehistoric skeletons, including those of Jamestown colonists, Plains Indians and Civil War soldiers. He helped identify remains from the Branch Davidian compound in Texas, the 9/11 attack on the Pentagon and mass graves in Croatia.

In this case, Owsley and his team were able to nail down or make strong guesses about Kennewick Man's physical attributes. He stood about 5 ft. 9 in. tall and was fairly muscular. He was clearly right-handed: the bones of the right arm are markedly larger than those of the left. In fact, says Owsley, "the bones are so robust that they're bent," the result, he speculates, of muscles built up during a lifetime of hunting and spear fishing.

An examination of the joints showed that Kennewick Man had arthritis in the right elbow, both knees and several vertebrae but that it wasn't severe enough to be crippling. He had suffered plenty of trauma as well. "One rib was fractured and healed," says Owsley, "and there is a depression fracture on his forehead and a similar indentation on the left side of the head." None of those fractures were fatal, though, and neither was the spear jab. "The injury looks healed," says Owsley. "It wasn't a weeping abscess." Previous estimates had Kennewick Man's age as 45 to 55 when he died, but Owsley thinks he may have been as young as 38. Nothing in the bones reveals what caused his demise.

But that's just the beginning of an impressive catalog of information that the scientists have added to what was already known—all the more impressive given the limitations placed on the team by the U.S. Army Corps of Engineers, which is responsible for the skeleton because the Corps has jurisdiction over the federal land on which it was found. The researchers had to do nearly all their work at the University of Washington's Burke Museum, where Kennewick Man has been housed in a locked room since 1998, under the watchful eyes of representatives of both the Corps and the museum, and according to a strict schedule that had to be submitted in advance. "We only had 10 days to do everything we wanted to do," says Owsley. "It was like a choreographed dance."

Perhaps the most remarkable discovery: Kennewick Man had been buried deliberately. By looking at concentrations of

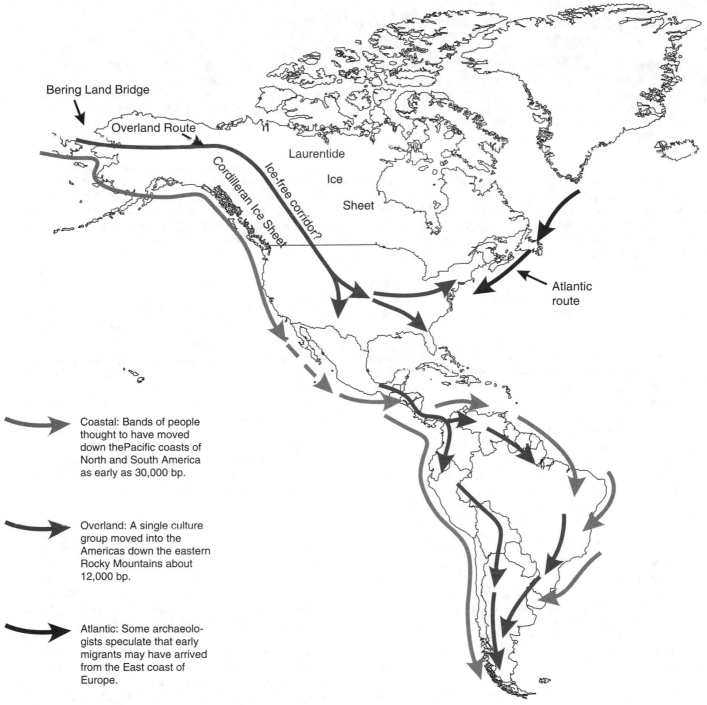

Bering Land Bridge

Overland Route

Cordilleran Ice Sheet

Ice-free corridor?

Laurentide

Ice

Sheet

Atlantic route

Coastal: Bands of people thought to have moved down thePacific coasts of North and South America as early as 30,000 bp.

Overland: A single culture group moved into the Americas down the eastern Rocky Mountains about 12,000 bp.

Atlantic: Some archaeologists speculate that early migrants may have arrived from the East coast of Europe.

Hypothesized routes for the first settlement of the Americas.

calcium carbonate left behind as underground water collected on the underside of the bones and then evaporated, scientists can tell that he was lying on his back with his feet rolled slightly outward and his arms at his side, the palms facing down—a position that could hardly have come about by accident. And there was no evidence that animal scavengers had been at the body.

The researchers could also tell that Kennewick Man had been buried parallel to the Columbia, with his left side toward the water: the bones were abraded on that side by water that eroded the bank and eventually dumped him out. It probably happened no more than six months before he was discovered, says team member Thomas Stafford, a research geochemist based in Lafayette, Colo. "It wouldn't have been as much as a year," he says. "The bones would have been more widely dispersed."

The deliberate burial makes it especially frustrating for scientists that the Corps in 1998 dumped hundreds of tons of boulders, dirt and sand on the discovery site—officially as part of a project to combat erosion along the Columbia River, although some scientists suspect it was also to avoid further conflict with

The Legal Battle: Who Should Own the Bones?

The Pawnee Indians tell a mordant story about the kinds of things scientists discover when they study sacred remains. After decades of watching researchers plunder its burial grounds for bodies and artifacts, the tribe finally forced Nebraska researchers and museums to return the items in 1989. Once the treasures were back in hand, the Pawnees asked the scientists what they had learned.

"You ate corn," they answered.

Kennewick Man, the most talked-about Native American remains uncovered in recent memory, may be revealing a lot more than that. But if it's a mother lode for scientists, it's also been a massive headache for the Federal Government, local tribes and the lawyers who represent them. At issue is the Native American Graves Protection and Repatriation Act (NAGPRA), a 1990 law intended to make up in some way for the generations of scientific strip-mining Indian lands have endured, by either selectively protecting artifacts still in Native American hands or returning those that have been carried off.

NAGPRA probably seemed straightforward enough to the legislators' eyes. It requires Indians who want to protect an artifact to show by a preponderance of archaeological, geological, historical or other evidence that they have some cultural affiliation to it. But what appears clear to lawyers can be devilishly hard to apply.

For one thing, the older an artifact is, the harder it becomes to show the neat nexus of affiliations that the law requires. "The evidence collapses as you go back in time," Says Pat Barker, an archaeologist for the Bureau of Land Management (BLM) in Nevada, who is working on a similar case. "The first 500 years is pretty solid, by 1,000 it's getting dicey, and by 10,000 most of that stuff you just can't get at."

That would put Kennewick Man—more than 9,000 years old—firmly in the hands of the scientists. But lawyers and archaeologists aren't theologians, and for a lot of Native Americans, spirituality is what protecting artifacts is all about.

"Archaeologists always tell us where we came from," says Rochanne Downs, a coordinator for the dozens of Indian tribes that have banded together in the Great Basin Inter-Tribal NAGPRA Coalition. "Well, we know where we came from. Our people were made from mud, and then the tribes were sent out. Sometimes people think that's funny, but when I look at the immaculate Conception, that seems kind of odd to me." Not all Indians believe in the ancient-clay idea, but if those who do are going to be shown the same respect as the adherents of any other faith, then the age of the find becomes immaterial. "We don't have a prehistory," says Downs. "We have one continuous history."

Human remains that are returned to tribes are treated reverently. Several weeks ago, the Umatilla tribe in Washington reinterred 240 remains in a massive burial accompanied by traditional ceremonies and moving words from tribal elders. "It was hard to describe," says Audie Huber, a Native American—though not an Umatilla—who has monitored the Kennewick case for several tribes. "The sense of relief was palpable."

What makes these disputes more difficult is that modern archaeological methods often guarantee that an artifact will—in the eyes of the Indians at least—be defiled. Not only is the find seized from sacred land, but radiocarbon dating (which was used to estimate the age of Kennewick Man) requires that a portion of the find be destroyed. "We're always presented as antiscience Luddites," says Huber. "But we don't like seeing remains pulverized and irradiated."

Finally, ticklish as any NAGPRA case can be, the extreme age and importance of Kennewick Man practically guaranteed that it would be beset by legal maneuvering. Soon after the find was announced in 1996, the Umatilla tribes of Oregon and Washington claimed it. Eight anthropologists immediately sued for the right to study it, and archaeologists for the National Park Service were called in to study the skeleton and help settle the dispute. They found in favor of the Umatillas, but a federal district court disagreed, as did a circuit court, citing a lack of cultural and genetic evidence to link the bones to the claimants.

That stunned the tribes, since NAGPRA does not include a DNA requirement. Last year Senator John McCain proposed an amendment that might have smoothed things over by broadening NAGPRA to include Indians who were ever indigenous to a particular region. The measure appeared headed for approval until the Interior Department objected to it—a move that helped scuttle the change and only inflamed the situation further. Even if the McCain measure had passed, the Indians see it as merely a first step, citing another recent case in which the BLM ignored a NAGPRA committee recommendation without even a court ruling. "With NAGPRA," says Downs, "you get a judgment but no enforcement." With as many as 118,000 sets of Native American remains still awaiting repatriation, that problem is not going away.

The pity is that even in its current, imperfect state, NAGPRA can work (to date, about 30,000 remains and half a million funerary objects have been returned to tribes), provided that everyone turns down the heat and tries to reach consensus. However much knowledge scientists pry from the Kennewick bones, the goodwill lost and the contentious precedents set may make the next generation of NAGPRA cases a lot less friendly than the last.

—Jeffrey Kluger.
Reported by Dan Cray/Los Angeles.

the local tribes. Kennewick Man's actual burial pit had already been washed away by the time Stafford visited the site in December 1997, but a careful survey might have turned up artifacts that could have been buried with him. And if his was part of a larger burial plot, there's now no way for archaeologists to locate any contemporaries who might have been interred close by.

Still, the bones have more secrets to reveal. They were never fossilized, and a careful analysis of their carbon and nitrogen composition, yet to be performed, should reveal plenty about Kennewick Man's diet. Says Stafford: "We can tell if he ate nothing but plants, predominantly meat or a mixture of the two." The researchers may be able to determine whether he preferred meat or fish. It's even possible that DNA could be extracted and analyzed someday.

While the Corps insisted that most of the bones remain in the museum, it allowed the researchers to send the skull fragments and the right hip, along with its embedded spear point, to a lab in Lincolnshire, Ill., for ultrahigh resolution CT scanning. The process produced virtual slices just 0.39 mm (about 0.02 in.) thick—"much more detailed than the ones made of King Tut's mummy," says Owsley. The slices were then digitally recombined into 3-D computer images that were used to make exact copies out of plastic. The replica of the skull has already enabled scientists to clear up a popular misconception that dates back to the initial reports of the discovery.

Was Kennewick Man Caucasian?

Thanks to Chatters' mention of Caucasoid features back in 1996, the myth that Kennewick Man might have been European never quite died out. The reconstructed skull confirms that he was not—and Chatters never seriously thought otherwise. "I tried my damnedest to curtail that business about Caucasians in America early," he says. "I'm not talking about today's Caucasians. I'm saying they had 'Caucasoid-like' characteristics. There's a big difference." Says Owsley: "[Kennewick Man] is not North American looking, and he's not tied in to Siberian or Northeast Asian populations. He looks more Polynesian or more like the Ainu [an ethnic group that is now found only in northern Japan but in prehistoric times lived throughout coastal areas of eastern Asia] or southern Asians."

That assessment will be tested more rigorously when researchers compare Kennewick Man's skull with databases of several thousand other skulls, both modern and ancient. But provisionally, at least, the evidence fits in with a revolutionary new picture that over the past decade has utterly transformed anthropologists' long-held theories about the colonization of the Americas.

Who Really Discovered America?

The conventional answer to that question dates to the early 1930s, when stone projectile points that were nearly identical began to turn up at sites across the American Southwest. They suggested a single cultural tradition that was christened Clovis, after an 11,000-year-old-plus site near Clovis, N.M. And because no older sites were known to exist in the Americas, scientists assumed that the Clovis people were the first to arrive. They came, according to the theory, no more than 12,000 years B.P. (before the present), walking across the dry land that connected modern Russia and Alaska at the end of the last ice age, when sea level was hundreds of feet lower than it is today. From there, the earliest immigrants would have made their way south through an ice-free corridor that geologists know cut through what are now the Yukon and Mackenzie river valleys, then along

the eastern flank of the Canadian Rockies to the continental U.S. and on to Latin America.

That's the story textbooks told for decades—and it's almost certainly wrong. The first cracks in the theory began appearing in the 1980s, when archaeologists discovered sites in both North and South America that seemed to predate the Clovis culture. Then came genetic and linguistic analyses suggesting that Asian and Native American populations diverged not 12,000 years ago but closer to 30,000 years ago. Studies of ancient skulls hinted that the earliest Americans in South America had different ancestors from those in the North. Finally, it began to be clear that artifacts from Northeast Asia dating from just before the Clovis period and South American artifacts of comparable age didn't have much in common with Clovis artifacts.

Those discoveries led to all sorts of competing theories, but few archaeologists or anthropologists took them seriously until 1997. In that year, a blue-ribbon panel of researchers took a hard look at evidence presented by Tom Dillehay, then at the University of Kentucky, from a site he had been excavating in Monte Verde, Chile. After years of skepticism, the panel finally affirmed his claim that the site proved humans had lived there 12,500 years ago. "Monte Verde was the turning point," says David Meltzer, a professor of prehistory at Southern Methodist University in Dallas who was on the panel. "It broke the Clovis barrier."

Why? Because if people were living in southern Chile 12,500 years ago, they must have crossed over from Asia considerably earlier, and that means they couldn't have used the ice-free inland corridor; it didn't yet exist. "You could walk to Fairbanks," says Meltzer. "It was getting south from Fairbanks that was a problem." Instead, many scientists now believe, the earliest Americans traveled down the Pacific coast—possibly even using boats. The idea has been around for a long time, but few took it seriously before Monte Verde.

One who did was Jon Erlandson, an archaeologist at the University of Oregon, whose work in Daisy Cave on San Miguel Island in California's Channel Island chain uncovered stone cutting tools that date to about 10,500 years B.P., proving that people were traveling across the water at least that early. More recently, researchers at the Santa Barbara Museum of Natural History redated the skeletal remains of an individual dubbed Arlington Springs Woman, found on another of the Channel Islands, pushing her age back to about 11,000 years B.P. Farther south, on Cedros Island off the coast of Baja California, U.C. at Riverside researchers found shell middens—heaps of kitchen waste, essentially—and other materials that date back to the same period as Daisy Cave. Down in the Andes, researchers have found coastal sites with shell middens dating to about 10,500 years B.P.

And in a discovery that offers a sharp contrast to the political hoopla over Kennewick Man, scientists and local Tlingit and Haida tribes cooperated so that researchers could study skeletal remains found in On Your Knees Cave on Prince of Wales Island in southern Alaska. "There's no controversy," says Erlandson, who has investigated cave sites in the same region. "It hardly ever hits the papers." Of about the same vintage as Kennewick Man and found at around the same time, the Alaskan bones, along with other artifacts in the area, lend strong support to the coastal-migration theory. "Isotopic analysis of the human remains," says James Dixon, the University of Colorado at Boulder anthropologist who found them, "demonstrates that the individual—a young male in his early 20s—was raised primarily on a diet of seafood."

Cruising Down the Kelp Highway

Erlandson has found one more line of evidence that supports the migration theory. While working with a group of marine ecologists, he was startled to learn that there were nearly continuous kelp forests growing just offshore all the way from Japan in the western Pacific to Alaska and down the West Coast to Baja California, then (with a gap in the tropics) off the coast of South America. In a paper presented three weeks ago, he outlined the potential importance to the earliest Americans of what he calls the "kelp highway."

"Most of the early sites on the west coast are found adjacent to kelp forests, even in Peru and Chile," he says. "The thing about kelp forests is they're extremely productive." They not only provide abundant food, from fish, shellfish, seals and otters that thrive there, but they also reduce wave energy, making it easier to navigate offshore waters. By contrast, the inland route along the ice-free corridor would have presented travelers with enormous ecological variability, forcing them to adapt to new conditions and food sources as they traveled.

Unfortunately, the strongest evidence for the coastal theory lies offshore, where ancient settlements would have been submerged by rising seas over the past 10,000 years or so. "Artifacts have been found on the continental shelves," says Dixon, "so I'm quite confident there's material out there." But you need submersible craft to search, and, he says, that type of research is a very hard sell to the people who own and operate that kind of equipment. "The maritime community is interested in shipwrecks and treasures. A little bit of charcoal and some rocks on the ocean floor is not very exciting to them."

Multiple Migrations

Even if the earliest Americans traveled down the coast, that doesn't mean they couldn't have come through the interior as well. Could there have been multiple waves of migration along a variety of different routes? One way scientists have tried to get a handle on that question is through genetics. Their studies have focused on two different types of evidence extracted from the cells of modern Native Americans: mitochondrial DNA, which resides outside the nuclei of cells and is passed down only through the mother; and the Y chromosome, which is passed down only from father to son. Since DNA changes subtly over the generations, it serves as a sort of molecular clock, and by measuring differences between populations, you can gauge when they were part of the same group.

Or at least you can try. Those molecular clocks are still rather crude. "The mitochondrial DNA signals a migration up to 30,000 years ago," says research geneticist Michael Hammer of

the University of Arizona. "But the Y suggests that it occurred within the last 20,000 years." That's quite a discrepancy. Nevertheless, Hammer believes that the evidence is consistent with a single pulse of migration.

Theodore Schurr, director of the University of Pennsylvania's Laboratory of Molecular Anthropology, thinks there could have been many migrations. "It looks like there may have been one primary migration, but certain genetic markers are more prevalent in North America than in South America," Schurr explains, suggesting secondary waves. At this point, there's no definitive proof of either idea, but the evidence and logic lean toward multiple migrations. "If one migration made it over," Dillehay, now at Vanderbilt University, asks rhetorically, "why not more?"

Out of Siberia?

Genetics also points to an original homeland for the first Americans—or at least it does to some researchers. "Skeletal remains are very rare, but the genetic evidence suggests they came from the Lake Baikal region" of Russia, says anthropologist Ted Goebel of the University of Nevada at Reno, who has worked extensively in that part of southern Siberia. "There is a rich archaeological record there," he says, "beginning about 40,000 years ago." Based on what he and Russian colleagues have found, Goebel speculates that there were two northward migratory pulses, the first between 28,000 and 20,000 years ago and a second sometime after 17,000 years ago. "Either one could have led to the peopling of the Americas," he says.

Like just about everything else about the first Americans, however, this idea is open to vigorous debate. The Clovis-first theory is pretty much dead, and the case for coastal migration appears to be getting stronger all the time. But in a field so recently liberated from a dogma that has kept it in an intellectual straitjacket since Franklin Roosevelt was President, all sorts of ideas are suddenly on the table. Could prehistoric Asians, for example, have sailed directly across the Pacific to South America? That may seem far-fetched, but scientists know that people sailing from Southeast Asia reached Australia some 60,000 years ago. And in 1947 the explorer Thor Heyerdahl showed it was possible to travel across the Pacific by raft in the other direction.

At least a couple of archaeologists, including Dennis Stanford of the Smithsonian, even go so far as to suggest that the earliest Americans came from Europe, not Asia, pointing to similarities between Clovis spear points and blades from France and Spain dating to between 20,500 and 17,000 years B.P. (Meltzer, Goebel and another colleague recently published a paper calling this an "outrageous hypothesis," but Dillehay thinks it's possible.)

All this speculation is spurring a new burst of scholarship about locations all over the Americas. The Topper site in South Carolina, Cactus Hill in Virginia, Pennsylvania's Meadowcroft, the Taima-Taima waterhole in Venezuela and several rock shelters in Brazil all seem to be pre-Clovis. Dillehay has found several sites in Peru that date to between 10,000 and 11,000 years

B.P. but have no apparent links to the Clovis culture. "They show a great deal of diversity," he says, "suggesting different early sources of cultural development in the highlands and along the coast."

It's only by studying those sites in detail and continuing to search for more evidence on land and offshore that these questions can be fully answered. And as always, the most valuable evidence will be the earthly remains of the ancient people themselves. In one 10-day session, Kennewick Man has added immeasurably to anthropologists' store of knowledge, and the next round of study is already under way. If scientists treat those bones with respect and Native American groups acknowledge the importance of unlocking their secrets, the mystery of how and when the New World was populated may finally be laid to rest.

From *Time*, March 13, 2006, pp. 45–52. Copyright © 2006 by Time Inc. Reprinted by permission via Rightslink.

Poop Fossil Pushes Back Date for Earliest Americans

RANDOLPH E. SCHMID

New evidence shows humans lived in North America more than 14,000 years ago, 1,000 years earlier than had previously been known.

Discovered in a cave in Oregon, fossil feces yielded DNA indicating these early residents were related to people living in Siberia and East Asia, according to a report in an online edition of the journal *Science*.

"This is the first time we have been able to get dates that are undeniably human, and they are 1,000 years before Clovis," said Dennis L. Jenkins, a University of Oregon archaeologist, referring to the Clovis culture, well known for its unique spear-points that have been studied previously.

Humans are widely believed to have arrived in North America from Asia over a land-bridge between Alaska and Siberia during a warmer period. A variety of dates has been proposed and some are in dispute.

Few artifacts were found in the cave, leading Jenkins to speculate that these people stayed there only a few days at a time before moving on, perhaps following game animals or looking for other food.

The petrified poop—coprolites to scientists—is yielding a look at the diet of these ancient Americans, Jenkins said.

While the analysis is not yet complete, he said there are bones of squirrels, bison hair, fish scales, protein from birds and dogs and the remains of plants such as grass and sunflowers.

The oldest of several coprolites studied is 14,340 calendar years old, said co-author Eske Willerslev, director of the Center for Ancient Genetics at Denmark's University of Copenhagen.

"The Paisley Cave material represents, to the best of my knowledge, the oldest human DNA obtained from the Americas," he said. "Other pre-Clovis sites have been claimed, but no human DNA has been obtained."

The date for the new coprolites is similar to that of Monte Verde in southern Chile, where human artifacts have been discovered, added Willerslev.

Jenkins said it isn't clear exactly who these people living in the Oregon caves were, since there were few artifacts found. He said there was one stone tool, a hand tool used perhaps to polish or grind or mash bones or fat.

"We are not saying that these people were of a particular ethnic group. At this point, we know they most likely came from Siberia or Eastern Asia, and we know something about what they were eating, which is something we can learn from coprolites. We're talking about human signature," he said.

"If you are looking for the first people in North America, you are going to have to step back more than 1,000 years beyond Clovis to find them," Jenkins said.

The Clovis culture has been dated to between 13,200 and 12,900 calendar years ago and is best known by the tools left behind.

Michael Waters, director of the Center for the Study of the First Americans at Texas A&M University, said the find, along with indications of human presence at other locations, adds to the evidence for a pre-Clovis human presence in North America.

"The genetic evidence from the coprolites from Paisley Caves is also consistent with the current genetic data for the peopling of the Americas—that the earliest inhabitants of the Americas came from Northeast Asia," added Waters, who was not part of the research team.

Anthropologist Ripan Malhi of the University of Illinois, Urbana-Champaign, said this data along with material from Alaska provide increasing "evidence that ancestors of Native Americans used a coastal route during the colonization of the Americas." Malhi was not part of the research team.

Jenkins said that discoveries like those in the Oregon caves "help us to reconstruct the American past."

"Our heritage is really important and it is important to the majority of the American public. If you don't know where you come from, it's hard to have a feeling of community, of participation."

To make sure the Oregon cave material hadn't been contaminated with modern DNA, the researchers tested more than 50 people who worked at the site. The DNA testing indicated that the feces belonged to Native Americans in two groups that can be traced to Siberia and East Asia.

In their paper the researchers dated the coprolites at 12,300 "carbon years" before the present. Prior to 3,000 years ago, carbon years differed from calendar years, resulting in the date of approximately 14,300 calendar years for the coprolites.

The research was funded by the Museum of Natural and Cultural History, University of Oregon; Association of Oregon Archaeologists and the Marie Curie Actions program.

Archaeologists Rediscover Cannibals

At digs around the world, researchers have unearthed strong new evidence that people ate their own kind from the early days of human evolution through recent prehistory.

ANN GIBBONS

When Arizona State University bioarchaeologist Christy G. Turner II first looked at the jumbled heap of bones from 30 humans in Arizona in 1967, he was convinced that he was looking at the remains of a feast. The bones of these ancient American Indians had cut marks and burns, just like animal bones that had been roasted and stripped of their flesh. "It just struck me that here was a pile of food refuse," says Turner, who proposed in *American Antiquity* in 1970 that these people from Polacca Wash, Arizona, had been the victims of cannibalism.

But his paper was met with "total disbelief," says Turner. "In the 1960s, the new paradigm about Indians was that they were all peaceful and happy. So, to find something like this was the antithesis of the new way we were supposed to be thinking about Indians"—particularly the Anasazi, thought to be the ancestors of living Pueblo Indians. Not only did Turner's proposal fly in the face of conventional wisdom about the Anasazi culture, but it was also at odds with an emerging consensus that earlier claims of cannibalism in the fossil record rested on shaky evidence. Where earlier generations of archaeologists had seen the remains of cannibalistic feasts, current researchers saw bones scarred by ancient burial practices, war, weathering, or scavenging animals.

To Turner, however, the bones from Polacca Wash told a more disturbing tale, and so he set about studying every prehistoric skeleton he could find in the Southwest and Mexico to see if it was an isolated event. Now, 30 years and 15,000 skeletons later, Turner is putting the final touches on a 1500-page book to be published next year by the University of Utah press in which he says, "Cannibalism was practiced intensively for almost four centuries" in the Four Corners region. The evidence is so strong that Turner says "I would bet a year of my salary on it."

He isn't the only one now betting on cannibalism in prehistory. In the past decade, Turner and other bioarchaeologists have put together a set of clear-cut criteria for distinguishing the marks of cannibalism from other kinds of scars. "The analytical rigor has increased across the board," says paleoanthropologist Tim D. White of the University of California, Berkeley. Armed with the new criteria, archaeologists are finding what they say are strong signs of cannibalism throughout the fossil record. This summer, archaeologists are excavating several sites in Europe where the practice may have occurred among our ancestors, perhaps as early as 800,000 years ago. More recently, our brawny cousins, the Neandertals, may have eaten each other. And this behavior wasn't limited to the distant past—strong new evidence suggests that in addition to the Anasazi, the Aztecs of Mexico and the people of Fiji also ate their own kind in the past 2500 years.

These claims imply a disturbing new view of human history, say Turner and others. Although cannibalism is still relatively rare in the fossil record, it is frequent enough to imply that extreme hunger was not the only driving force. Instead of being an aberration, practiced only by a few prehistoric Donner Parties, killing people for food may have been standard human behavior—a means of social control, Turner suspects, or a mob response to stress, or a form of infanticide to thin the ranks of neighboring populations.

Not surprisingly, some find these claims hard to stomach: "These people haven't explored all the alternatives," says archaeologist Paul Bahn, author of the *Cambridge Encyclopedia* entry on cannibalism. "There's no question, for example, that all kinds of weird stuff is done to human remains in mortuary practice"—and in warfare. But even the most prominent skeptic of earlier claims of cannibalism, cultural anthropologist William Arens of the State University of New York, Stony Brook, now admits the case is stronger: "I think the procedures are sounder, and there is more evidence for cannibalism than before."

White learned how weak most earlier scholarship on cannibalism was in 1981, when he first came across what he thought might be a relic of the practice—a massive skull of an early human ancestor from a site called Bodo in Ethiopia. When he got his first look at this 600,000-year-old skull on a museum

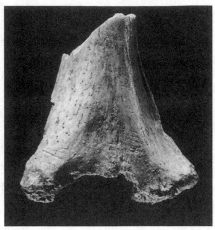

T. D. White/Berkeley
Unkind cuts. A Neandertal bone from Vindija Cave, Croatia.

Photos By: C. Turner/Arizona State University

Cannibals house? The Peasco Blanco great house at Chaco Canyon, New Mexico, where some bones bear cut marks (upper left); others were smashed, perhaps to extract marrow.

table, White noticed that it had a series of fine, deep cut marks on its cheekbone and inside its eye socket, as if it had been defleshed. To confirm his suspicions, White wanted to compare the marks with a "type collection" for cannibalism—a carefully studied assemblage of bones showing how the signature of cannibalism differs from damage by animal gnawing, trampling, or excavation.

"We were naïve at the time," says White, who was working with archaeologist Nicholas Toth of Indiana University in Bloomington. They learned that although the anthropological literature was full of fantastic tales of cannibalistic feasts among early humans at Zhoukoudian in China, Krapina cave in Croatia, and elsewhere, the evidence was weak—or lost.

Indeed, the weakness of the evidence had already opened the way to a backlash, which was led by Arens. He had deconstructed the fossil and historical record for cannibalism in a book called *The Man-Eating Myth: Anthropology and Anthropophagy* (Oxford, 1979). Except for extremely rare cases of starvation or insanity, Arens said, none of the accounts of cannibalism stood up to scrutiny—not even claims that it took place among living tribes in Papua New Guinea (including the Fore, where cannibalism is thought to explain the spread of the degenerative brain disease kuru). There were no reliable eye witnesses for claims of cannibalism, and the archaeological evidence was circumstantial. "I didn't deny the existence of cannibalism," he now says, "but I found that there was no good evidence for it. It was bad science."

Physical anthropologists contributed to the backlash when they raised doubts about what little archaeological evidence there was (*Science,* 20 June 1986, p. 1479). Mary Russell, then at Case Western Reserve University in Cleveland, argued, for example, that cut marks on the bones of 20 Neandertals at

Krapina Cave could have been left by Neandertal morticians who were cleaning the bones for secondary burial, and the bones would have been smashed when the roof caved in, for example. In his 1992 review in the *Cambridge Encyclopedia,* Bahn concluded that cannibalism's "very existence in prehistory is hard to swallow."

Rising from the Ashes

But even as some anthropologists gave the ax to Krapina and other notorious cases, a new, more rigorous case for cannibalism in prehistory was emerging, starting in the American Southwest. Turner and his late wife, Jacqueline Turner, had been systematically studying tray after tray of prehistoric bones in museums and private collections in the United States and Mexico. They had identified a pattern of bone processing in several hundred specimens that showed little respect for the dead. "There's no known mortuary practice in the Southwest where the body is dismembered, the head is roasted and dumped into a pit unceremoniously, and other pieces get left all over the floor," says Turner, describing part of the pattern.

White, meanwhile, was identifying other telltale signs. To fill the gap he discovered when he looked for specimens to compare with the Bodo skull, he decided to study in depth one of the bone assemblages the Turners and others had cited. He chose Mancos, a small Anasazi pueblo on the Colorado Plateau from A.D. 1150, where archaeologists had recovered the scattered and broken remains of at least 29 individuals. The project evolved into a landmark book, *Prehistoric Cannibalism at Mancos* (Princeton, 1992). While White still doesn't know why the Bodo skull was defleshed—"it's a black box," he says—he extended the blueprint for identifying cannibalism.

In his book, White describes how he painstakingly sifted through 2106 bone fragments, often using an electron microscope to identify cut marks, burn traces, percussion and anvil damage, disarticulations, and breakages. He reviewed how to distinguish marks left by butchering from those left by animal gnawing, trampling, or other wear and tear. He also proposed a new category of bone damage, which he called "pot polish"—shiny abrasions on bone tips that come from being stirred in pots (an idea he tested by stirring deer bones in a replica of an Anasazi pot). And he outlined how to compare the remains of suspected victims with those of ordinary game animals at other sites to see if they were processed the same way.

When he applied these criteria to the Mancos remains, he concluded that they were the leavings of a feast in which 17 adults and 12 children had their heads cut off, roasted, and broken open on rock anvils. Their long bones were broken—he believes for marrow—and their vertebral bodies were missing, perhaps crushed and boiled for oil. Finally, their bones were dumped, like animal bones.

In their forthcoming book, the Turners describe a remarkably similar pattern of bone processing in 300 individuals from 40 different bone assemblages in the Four Corners area of the Southwest, dating from A.D. 900 to A.D. 1700. The strongest case, he says, comes from bones unearthed at the Peñasco Blanco great house at Chaco Canyon in New Mexico, which was the highest center of the Anasazi culture and, he argues, the home of cannibals who terrorized victims within 100 miles of Chaco Canyon, where most of the traumatized bones have been excavated. "Whatever drove the Anasazi to eat people, it happened at Chaco," says Turner.

The case for cannibalism among the Anasazi that Turner and White have put together hasn't swayed all the critics. "These folks have a nice package, but I don't think it proves cannibalism," says Museum of New Mexico archaeologist Peter Bullock. "It's still just a theory."

But even critics like Bullock acknowledge that Turner and White's studies, along with work by the University of Colorado, Boulder's, Paolo Villa and colleagues at another recent site, Font-brégoua Cave in southeastern France (*Science*, 25 July 1986, p. 431), have raised the standards for how to investigate a case of cannibalism. In fact, White's book has become the unofficial guidebook for the field, says physical anthropologist Carmen Pijoan at the Museum of Anthropology in Mexico City, who has done a systematic review of sites in Mexico where human bones were defleshed. In a forthcoming book chapter, she singles out three sites where she applied diagnostic criteria outlined by Turner, White, and Villa to bones from Aztec and other early cultures and concludes that all "three sites, spread over 2000 years of Mexican prehistory, show a pattern of violence, cannibalism, and sacrifice through time."

White's book "is my bible," agrees paleontologist Yolanda Fernandez-Jalvo of the Museum of Natural History in Madrid, who is analyzing bones that may be the oldest example of cannibalism in the fossil record—the remains of at least six individuals who died 800,000 years ago in an ancient cave at Atapuerca in northern Spain.

Age-Old Practices

The Spanish fossils have caused considerable excitement because they may represent a new species of human ancestor (*Science*, 30 May, pp. 1331 and 1392). But they also show a pattern familiar from the more recent sites: The bones are highly fragmented and are scored with cut marks, which Fernandez-Jalvo thinks were made when the bodies were decapitated and the bones defleshed. A large femur was also smashed open, perhaps for marrow, says Fernandez-Jalvo, and the whole assemblage had been dumped, like garbage. The treatment was no different from that accorded animal bones at the site. The pattern, says Peter Andrews, a paleo-anthropologist at The Natural History Museum, London, is "pretty strong evidence for cannibalism, as opposed to ritual defleshing." He and others note, however, that the small number of individuals at the site and the absence of other sites of similar antiquity to which the bones could be compared leave room for doubt.

A stronger case is emerging at Neandertal sites in Europe, 45,000 to more than 130,000 years old. The new criteria for recognizing cannibalism have not completely vindicated the earlier claims about Krapina Cave, partly because few animal bones are left from the excavation of the site in 1899 to compare with the Neandertal remains. But nearby Vindija Cave, excavated in the 1970s, did yield both animal and human remains. When White and Toth examined the bones recently, they found that both sets showed cut marks, breakage, and disarticulation, and had been dumped on the cave floor. It's the same pattern seen at Krapina, and remarkably similar to that at Mancos, says White, who will publish his conclusions in a forthcoming book with Toth. Marseilles prehistorian Alban DeFleur is finding that Neandertals may also have feasted on their kind in the Moula-Guercy Cave in the Ardeche region of France, where animal and Neandertal bones show similar processing. Taken together, says White, "the evidence from Krapina, Vindija, and Moula is strong."

Not everyone is convinced, however. "White does terrific analysis, but he hasn't proved this is cannibalism," says Bahn. "Frankly, I don't see how he can unless you find a piece of human gut [with human bone or tissue in it]." No matter how close the resemblance to butchered animals, he says, the cut marks and other bone processing could still be the result of mortuary practices. Bullock adds that warfare, not cannibalism, could explain the damage to the bones.

White, however, says such criticism resembles President Clinton's famous claim about marijuana: "Some [although not all] of the Anasazi and Neandertals processed their colleagues. They skinned them, roasted them, cut their muscles off, severed their joints, broke their long bones on anvils with hammerstones, crushed their spongy bones, and put the pieces into pots." Borrowing a line from a review of his book, White says: "To say they didn't eat them is the archaeological equivalent of saying Clinton lit up and didn't inhale."

White's graduate student David DeGusta adds that he has compared human bones at burial sites in Fiji and at a nearby trash midden from the last 2000 years. The intentionally buried bones were less fragmentary and had no bite marks, burns, percussion pits, or other signs of food processing. The human bones in the trash midden, however, were processed like those of pigs. "This site really challenges the claim that these assemblages of bones are the result of mortuary ritual," says DeGusta.

After 30 years of research, Turner says it is a modern bias to insist that cannibalism isn't part of human nature. Many other species eat their own, and our ancestors may have had their own "good" reasons—whether to terrorize subject peoples, limit their neighbors' offspring, or for religious or medicinal purposes. "Today, the only people who eat other people outside of starving are the crazies," says Turner. "We're dealing with a world view that says this is bad and always has been bad. . . . But in the past, that view wasn't necessarily the group view. Cannibalism could have been an adaptive strategy. It has to be entertained."

A Coprological View of Ancestral Pueblo Cannibalism

Debate over a single fecal fossil offers a cautionary tale of the interplay between science and culture.

KARL J. REINHARD

As the object of my scientific study, I've chosen coprolites. It's not a common choice, but to a paleonutritionist and archaeoparasitologist, a coprolite—a sample of ancient feces preserved by mineralization or simple drying—is a scientific bonanza. Analysis of coprolites can shed light on both the nutrition of and parasites found in prehistoric cultures. Dietary reconstructions from the analysis of coprolites can inform us about, for example, the origins of modern Native American diabetes. With regard to parasitology; coprolites hold information about the ancient emergence and spread of human infectious disease. Most sensational, however, is the recent role of coprolite analysis in debates about cannibalism.

Most Americans know the people who lived on the Colorado Plateau from 1200 B.C. onward as the Anasazi, a Navajo (or Dine) word. The modern Pueblo people in Arizona and New Mexico, who are their direct descendants, prefer the description Ancestral Pueblo or Old Ones. Because the image of this modern culture could be tainted by the characterization of their ancestors, it's especially important that archaeologists and physical anthropologists come to the correct conclusion about cannibalism. This is the story of my involvement in that effort.

When a coprolite arrived in my laboratory for analysis in 1997, I didn't imagine that it would become one of the most contentious finds in archaeological history. Banks Leonard, the Soil Systems archaeologist who directed excavation of the site at Cowboy Wash, Utah, explained to me that there was evidence of unusual dietary activity by the prehistoric individual who deposited the coprolite. He or she was possibly a cannibal.

I had been aware of the cannibalism controversy for a number of years, and I was interested in evaluating evidence of such activity. But from my scientific perspective, it was simply another sample that would provide a few more data points in my reconstruction of ancient diet from a part of the Ancestral Pueblo region that was unknown to me.

The appearance of the coprolite was unremarkable—in fact, it was actually a little disappointing. It looked like a plain cylinder of tan dirt with no obvious macrofossils or visible dietary inclusions. I have analyzed hundreds of Ancestral and pre-Ancestral Pueblo coprolites that were more interesting. Indeed, I have surveyed tens of thousands more that, to my experienced eye, held greater scientific promise. Yet this one coprolite, when news of it hit the media, undid 20 years of my research on the Ancestral Pueblo diet. On a broader scale, it caused the archaeological community to rethink our perception of the nature of this prehistoric culture and to question what is reasonable scientific proof.

Cannibalism, Without Question

In the arid environment of the U.S. Southwest, feces dried in ancient times provide a 9,000-year record of gastronomic traditions. This record allows me and a few other thick-skinned researchers to trace dietary history in the deserts. (I say "thick-skinned," because analysts generally don't last long in this specialty. Many have done one coprolite study, only to move on to a more socially acceptable archaeological specialty.)

From the mid-1980s to the mid-'90s, I had characterized the Ancestral Pueblo lifestyle as a combination of hunting and gathering mixed with agriculture based on the analysis of about 500 coprolites from half a dozen sites. Before me, Gary Fry, then at Youngstown State University, had come to the same conclusion in work he published during the '70s and '80s, based on the analysis of a large number of Ancestral Pueblo coprolites from many sites. These people were finely attuned to the diverse and complicated habitats of the Colorado Plateau for plant gathering, as well as for plant cultivation. The Ancestral Pueblo certainly ate meat—many kinds of meat—but never had there been any indication of cannibalism in any coprolite analysis from any site.

The evidence for cannibalism at Cowboy Wash has been widely published. A small number of people were undoubtedly killed, disarticulated and their flesh exposed to heat and boiling. This took place in a pit house typical of the Ancestral Pueblo circa 1200 A.D. At the time of the killings, the appearance of the pit house must have been appallingly gruesome. Human blood residue was found on stone tools, and I imagine that the disarticulation of the corpses must have left a horrifying splatter of blood around the room. But the most conclusive evidence of cannibalism did not come from the room where the corpses were dismembered. It came from a nearby room where someone had defecated on the hearth around the time that the killings took place. The feces was preserved as a coprolite and would turn out to be the conclusive evidence of cannibalism.

My analysis of the coprolite was not momentous. I could determine from its general morphology that it was indeed from a human being. However, the tiny fragment that I rehydrated and examined by several microscopic techniques contained none of the typical plant foods eaten by the Ancestral Pueblo. Background pollen of the sort that would have been inhaled or drunk was the only plant residue that I found. Thus, I concluded that the coprolite did not represent normal Ancestral Pueblo diet. It seemed to represent a purely meat meal, something that is unheard of from Ancestral Pueblo coprolite analyses.

After analyzing the Cowboy Wash coprolite, I took a half-year sabbatical as a Fulbright scholar in Brazil. When I returned, I learned that my analysis had been superseded by a new technology. Richard Marlar from the University of Colorado School of Medicine and colleagues had taken over direct analysis of the coprolite using an enzyme-linked immunosorbent assay to detect human myoglobin, and their work had confirmed and expanded my analysis. The coprolite was from a human who had eaten another human. The technical paper appeared in *Nature* and was followed by articles in the *New Yorker, Discover, Southwestern Lore* and the *Smithsonian,* among many others. The articles became the focus of a veritable explosion of media pieces in the press, on radio and television, and on the Internet, amounting to an absolute attack on Ancestral Pueblo culture.

Initially, I sat and watched the media feeding frenzy and Internet chat debates with a sense of awe and post-sabbatical detachment. My original report suggesting the coprolite was not of Ancestral Pueblo origin went largely unnoticed. The few journalists who did call me for an opinion proved uninterested in publishing it. In some cases it was too far to fly to Nebraska to film; in others my opinion didn't fit into the context of the debate. Well, I have looked at more Ancestral Pueblo feces than any other human being, and I do have an opinion: The Ancestral Pueblo were not cannibalistic. Cannibalism just doesn't make sense as a pattern of diet for people so exquisitely adapted to droughts by centuries of hunting-gathering traditions and agricultural innovation.

Then a media quote knocked me out of my stupor. Arizona State University anthropologist (emeritus) Christy G. Turner II, commenting in an interview about a book he co-authored on Ancestral Pueblo cannibalism, said, "I'm the guy who brought down the Anasazi." Perhaps to temper Turner's broad generalization, Brian Billman (a coauthor of the Marlar *Nature* paper) of the University of North Carolina at Chapel Hill, suggested that a period of drought brought on emergency conditions that resulted in cannibalism. Beyond the scientific quibbling about who ate whom and why, I am amazed at the vortex of debate

around the Coyote Wash coprolite. The furor over that one coprolite represents a new way of thinking about the Ancestral Pueblo and archaeological evidence.

What Did the Ancestral Pueblo Eat?

To me, a specialist in Ancestral Pueblo diet, neither Turner's nor Billman's explanation made sense. So, in the years since the *Nature* paper appeared in 2000, I have renewed my analyses of Ancestral Pueblo coprolites to understand just what they did eat in times of drought. And let me say emphatically that Ancestral Pueblo coprolites are not composed of the flesh of their human victims. Some of their dietary practices were, perhaps, peculiar. I still recall in wonderment the inch-diameter deer vertebral centrum that I found in one sample. It was swallowed whole. The consumption of insects, snakes and lizards brought the Ancestral Pueblo notice in the children's book *It Was Disgusting and I Ate It.* But looking beyond such peculiarities, their diet was delightfully diverse and testifies to the human ability to survive in the most extreme environments. To me, diet is one of the most fundamental bases of civilization, and the Ancestral Pueblo possessed a complicated cuisine. They were gastronomically civilized.

Widespread analysis of coprolites by "paleoscatologists" began in the 1960s and culminated in the '70s and '80s when graduate students worked staunchly on their coprological theses and dissertations. From Washington State University to Northern Arizona University to Texas A & M and many more, Ancestral Pueblo coprolites were rehydrated, screened, centrifuged and analyzed. Richard Hevly, Glenna Williams-Dean, John Jones, Mark Stiger, Linda Scott-Cummings, Kate Aasen, Gary Fry, Karen Clary, Molly Toll and Vaughn Bryant, Jr., to name a few, joined me in puzzling over Ancestral Pueblo culinary habits. In their conscientious and rigorous research, the same general theme emerged. The Ancestral Pueblo were very well adapted to the environment, both in times of feast and in times of famine.

In general, the Ancestral Pueblo diet was the culmination of a long period of victual tradition that began around 9,000 years ago, when people on the Colorado Plateau gave up hunting big animals and started collecting plants and hunting smaller animals. Prickly pear cactus, yucca, grain from dropseed grass, seeds from goosefoot and foods from 15 other wild plants dominated pre-Ancestral Pueblo life. One of the truly interesting dietary patterns that emerged in the early time and continued through the Ancestral Pueblo culture was the consumption of pollen-rich foods. Cactus and yucca buds and other flowers were the sources of this pollen. Rabbit viscera probably provided a source of fungal spores of the genus *Endogane,* although I doubt that these people knew they were eating the spores when they ate the rabbits. The pre-Ancestral Pueblo people adapted to starvation from seasonal food shortages by eating yucca leaf bases and prickly pear pads and the few other plants that were available in such lean times.

Prey for the pre-Ancestral Pueblo people included small animals such as rabbits, lizards, mice and insects. In tact, most pre-Ancestral Pueblo coprolites contain the remains of small animals. My analysis of these remains shows that small animals, especially rabbits and mice, were a major source of protein in summer and winter, good times and bad.

The Ancestral Pueblo *per se* descended from this hunter-gatherer tradition. Coprolite analysis shows that they were largely vegetarian, and plant foods of some sort are present in every Ancestral Pueblo coprolite I have analyzed. But these later people also expanded on their predecessors' cuisine. They cultivated maize, squash and eventually beans. Yet they continued to collect a wide diversity of wild plants. They actually ate more species of wild plants—more than 50—than their ancestors who were totally dependent on wild species.

Adapting to the Environment

In 1992, I presented a series of hypotheses addressing why the Ancient Pueblo ate so many species of wild plants. Later, Mark Stiger of Western State College and I went to work on the problem using a statistical method that he devised. We determined that the Ancestral Pueblo encouraged the growth of edible weedy species in the disturbances caused by cultivation and village life. In doing so, they increased the spectrum of wild edible plants available to them, often using them to spice cultivated plants. Rocky Mountain beeweed, purslane and groundcherry were especially important in conjunction with maize. Corn smut was another important condiment. In fact, maize, purslane, beeweed and corn smut appear as the earliest components of a distinct cuisine in the earliest Ancestral Pueblo coprolites I have analyzed, from Turkey Pen Cave, Utah. These coprolites are about 1,500 years old. The maize-beeweed-corn smut-purslane association remained a central feature of Ancestral Pueblo cuisine at most sites to the latest periods of the culture. Importantly, they also ate wild plants to offset seasonal shortages, especially in winter when their stores of cultivated food were exhausted. Thus, retaining a diverse array of wild plants in the mix helped them adapt to food shortages.

Paul Minnis of the University of Oklahoma applied a different statistical test to address a different problem. He analyzed coprolite findings from Arizona, New Mexico, Utah and Colorado to see if people in different regions had distinct dietary traditions. Paul showed that the Ancient Pueblo adapted to the environmental variability of the Colorado Plateau by adjusting their agricultural, hunting and gathering habits to the natural resources available. Ancient Pueblo from Glen Canyon, Utah, had a slightly different dietary tradition from those of Inscription House, Arizona; those of Mesa Verde, Colorado; and those of Chaco Canyon, New Mexico. Later, in separate work, he identified how these people adapted to bad times. He found that the Ancestral Pueblo had "starvation foods," such as yucca and prickly pear, to get through poor times. These were a legacy from their hunter-gatherer ancestors.

Sometimes Ancestral Pueblo groups developed dietary traditions that required trade or foraging in areas remote from their home. Sara LeRoy-Toren, with the Lincoln High School Science Focus Program, and I are analyzing coprolites from Salmon Ruin, which was built along the San Juan River between the modern towns of Farmington and Bloomfield, New Mexico. It was abandoned by its original occupants and reoccupied by people from the San Juan River Valley. Our analysis is from the San Juan occupation, which was generally a time of abundance for both agriculture and gathered foods.

These coprolites reflect the Ancestral Pueblo tradition and contain juniper berries and cactus buds from areas local to the site, but they also contain piñon nuts that must have been harvested some miles away. We also calculated the number of pollen grains per gram of Salmon Ruin coprolites and found both maize and beeweed pollen in quantities as large as millions of grains per gram. Importantly, the maize pollen is shredded in a manner consistent with pollen eaten in corn meal, so maize was eaten both fresh off the cob and in the form of stored flour, although most of the macroscopic remains from Salmon Ruin are in the ground form.

One of my former graduate students, Dennis Danielson, now at the Central Identification Laboratory at the Joint POW/MIA Accounting Command, found phytoliths—microscopic crystals produced in plant cells—in the Salmon Ruin coprolites. More than half of the Salmon Ruin coprolites contain phytoliths from yucca-type plants and cactus, a legacy of pre-Ancestral Pueblo gathering adaptation to the desert. Denny eventually found phytoliths from these wild plants in coprolites from other Ancestral Pueblo sites. These gathered plants predominated in his analyses and reaffirmed that the Ancestral Pueblo could adapt to drought by turning to edible desert plants that were adapted to extremely dry conditions.

But were these plants actually what the Ancestral Pueblo ate in times of drought, rather that just a routine part of their diet? Denny and I analyzed coprolites from the last occupation of Antelope House in Canyon de Chelly, Arizona. All archaeological, climatological and biological analyses indicate that the last occupation was a time of ecological collapse. The level of anemia in skeletons from this time and region is the highest known among the Ancestral Pueblo. Archaeological surveys show that the mesas around the canyon were abandoned as people moved into the canyon to have access to water. The levels of parasitism, especially with crowd diseases, elevated; parasites were present in one-quarter of the 180 Antelope House coprolites I studied.

The coprolites at Antelope House record the adaptation to this environmental collapse and drought. Phytoliths from prickly pear and yucca leaf bases were present in 92 percent of the coprolites. The Ancestral Pueblo at Antelope House had clearly resorted to reliance on desert starvation foods. Yet their diet still lacked desperate monotony, as they ate wild plants from moist areas. Pollen occurs at concentrations in the hundreds of thousands to tens of millions of pollen grains per gram in the Antelope House coprolites. The main sources of pollen and spores were cattail, horsetail, beeweed and maize, but the diet at Antelope House included the greatest diversity of wild plants—27 species—ever recorded in Ancestral Pueblo coprolite studies. By contrast, only 16 wild species were identified in Salmon Ruin coprolites.

As for meat, my colleagues Mark Sutton, with California State University, Bakersfield, and Richard Marlar have found chemical signals in Ancestral Pueblo coprolites of bighorn sheep, rabbits, dogs and rodents. But as for cannibalism, Richard looked for human muscle indicators in the Salmon Ruin coprolites and found none. At Antelope House, Mark found protein residue of rabbit, rodents, dog, big horn sheep and pronghorn. There were also human protein residues present, but they were from intestinal cells shed by the body. The Ancestral Pueblo at Antelope House suffered parasitism from hookworms and hookworm-like organisms that would have resulted in excess shedding of intestinal cells. In fact, one Antelope House coprolite I analyzed was a mass of excreted parasitic worms mixed with seeds. Stable carbon and stable-nitrogen isotope analyses of the bones of these people from many sites indicate that, although they did eat meat, they were 70 percent herbivorous.

Every coprolite researcher who has worked with Ancestral Pueblo material has found animal bone. Kristin Sobolik of the University of Maine has shown that these people ate a particularly large number of lizard- and mouse-sized animals. This reliance on small animals was a remarkable adaptation to the Southwestern deserts, where small animals are most numerous and therefore a reliable source of protein—something the Ancestral Pueblo relied on feast or famine, just as their predecessors had.

Life on the Edge

Compared with other agricultural traditions I have studied in other parts of the world, the Ancestral Pueblo were rarely far from agricultural failure. My students and I have examined coprolites from the most primitive and advanced cultures in the Andes, from the earliest Chinchorros to the latest Incas. In the Andes, too, there is a long history of hunting and gathering that preceded agriculture. Once agriculture was established, however, 90 percent of the food species of Andean peoples were cultivated. This stands in meaningful contrast to the Ancestral Pueblo, whose food species remained predominantly wild. I think this is because they were on the very northern fringe of the region conducive to agriculture and couldn't rely on consistent productivity of their cultivated plots from year to year. Therefore, they maintained the hunter-gatherer dietary traditions to supplement, or replace if necessary, cultivated plants. Complete caloric dependence on cultivated plants, as took place in the Andes, was simply impossible for the Ancestral Pueblo.

Furthermore, these people often survived times of drought without cultural perturbations such as cannibalism. In my experience, the most poignant example of drought adaptation was seen in the analysis of a partially mummified child from Glen Canyon, Arizona. The child was buried during a long drought period, from 1210 to 1260 A.D. Archaeologist Steve Dominguez of the Midwest Archaeological Center directed the analysis of many specialists including myself and my students, Danielson and Kari Sandness. Burial offerings included a wide variety of ceramic, gourd and basketry artifacts. Compared with burial goods of other Ancestral Pueblo, these were consistent with those of average-status individuals. The drought did not disrupt the standard burial traditions for this three-to-four-year-old, yet x rays showed that this child survived seven episodes of starvation. The cause of death is unknown for this otherwise healthy child.

Analysis of the intestinal contents of the child provided insights into adaptation to drought. About 20 coprolites were excavated, and all of them were composed of a wild grass known as "rice grass." In the absence of cultivated foods, the child was provided with an alternative, and equally nutritious, wild food. Dominguez summarized the findings from the research succinctly:

> Investigations in nearby areas indicate that this was a period of environmental degradation and that Anasazi populations may have experienced nutritional stress or other consequent forms of physiological stress. Studies of both prehistoric populations and living populations suggest that a number of methods were employed to support individuals through periods of stress, and to promote the well-being of the group.

Was the Cannibal Ancestral Pueblo?

Work by numerous investigators thus shows that the Ancestral Pueblo possessed remarkable ecological adaptability; if they resorted to cannibalism because of environmental stress, it was a highly atypical response. Further, burial excavations demonstrate that they maintained their traditions even in times of drought. Besides, beyond a single sample, hundreds of coprolite analyses find not even a hint of cannibalism. Overwhelmingly, the Ancestral Pueblo were primarily herbivorous. Why, then, does one coprolite from the northern reaches of the Ancestral Pueblo domain come to characterize an entire culture? A number of researchers were incredulous at the hysteria created by the Cowboy Wash cannibal coprolite. Vaughn Bryant, Jr., at Texas A & M, e-mailed his disbelief to our small specialist community. From his experience in the study of Western diets, cannibalism was simply not plausible. Karen Clary, with the University of Texas at Austin, also e-mailed her concerns with the findings as well as with the unbridled sensationalism.

Both coprolite and skeletal evidence examined by Utah State University bio-archaeologist Patricia Lambert do show that Ancestral Pueblo of Cowboy Wash were victims of violence and cannibalism—there's little question about it. But that doesn't mean that the cannibal(s) were Ancestral Pueblo. Mark Sutton and I found that these people invariably ate plant foods when they ate meat; it was a feature of their cuisine. The complete lack of plant matter in the Cowboy Wash coprolite tells me that it was not from an individual who observed the Ancestral Pueblo dietary tradition. To date, none of the principal investigators involved in the Cowboy Wash analysis have implicated residents or even Ancestral Pueblo from another location as the perpetrators of the violence. In short, I don't know who killed and ate the residents of Cowboy Wash, but I am sure the cannibal wasn't an Ancestral Pueblo.

The Peaceful People Concept

Christy Turner's quote in the popular media puzzled me. Why would anyone want to bring down an ancient culture, especially Turner, whose work is characterized by attention to detail, meticulous analytical procedures and, most of all, accumulation of mountains of data to support his conclusions? One of my most striking memories of any scientist was an afternoon chat I had with Turner regarding his work with dental traits to trace migrations to the New World. His office was packed with neat columns of computer printouts from data collected from thousands of skulls. That same afternoon, the conversation turned to his study of cannibalism. I asked him specifics about his methods and found that he approached this area of research with the same exhaustive thoroughness he applied to his dental work. At no time did he indicate that he intended to "bring down the Anasazi."

Then I read the book that Turner cowrote, *Man Corn,* and I realized that it was not the Ancestral Pueblo culture that he brought down. He was after our archaeological biases in how we reconstruct the nature of Ancestral Pueblo culture. To understand how that one coprolite came to be considered ironclad evidence of cannibalism among the Ancestral Pueblo, it's necessary to understand how these people have been characterized by anthropologists and archaeologists at various times over the past 50 or so years.

The view of the Ancestral Pueblo as peaceful people took root in the 1960s and '70s. Earlier work had shown that violence, and perhaps even cannibalism, had taken place among the Ancestral Pueblo. But in the '60s and '70s—a time of social volatility, seemingly suffused in the violence of combat and revolt—modern American culture was searching for examples of nonviolent social systems. Academia sought out paradigms of peacefulness from other regions, other times and even other species. The Ancestral Pueblo became one of those "paragons of peace," as did the San Bushmen and wild chimpanzees. Elizabeth Marshall Thomas published her book about the bushmen, *The Harmless People,* in 1959, and anthropologists took to highlighting the nonviolence of hunter-gatherers. This was when the "New Archaeology" emerged as a replacement for previous approaches. Students were discouraged from reading archaeological research that dated from before 1960; thus the earlier work that described evidence of violence was ignored.

Excavations during the 1970s were very counter-cultural in appearance and philosophy. Scholarly excavation camps often had the flavor of hippie communes. In that atmosphere, evidence of violence was largely dismissed both in the field and during the analysis phase. I recall participating in three excavations in which houses had burned and people perished within them. This seemed like pretty good evidence that all was not tranquil with the peaceful people, but such fires were explained as accidental. Once, when we discovered arrow points in a skeleton in a burned house, the evidence of violence was not deemed conclusive because the arrow points had not penetrated bone. At the time, I wondered whether we were being a little too quick to dismiss the possibility of violence; the alternative was that these people were remarkably negligent with their hearths and weapons. I began to think of the Ancestral Pueblo as peaceful but fatally accident prone.

Those claiming evidence of cannibalism among ancient American cultures were excluded from presenting their findings at the Pecos Conference, the regional meeting for Southwestern archaeologists. This caused quite a furor. A symposium on the subject of violence and cannibalism had been scheduled for the meeting, and the participants arrived, but the symposium was canceled at the last minute. In 20 years of participating in scientific meetings, this is the only instance I can recall of a scheduled event being canceled for purely political reasons.

In the '80s and '90s, the paragons of peaceful society began to fall—and fall in a big way. First, violence was acknowledged among the Maya, held as the Mesoamerican counterweight to the undoubtedly violent and cannibalistic Aztec prior to ascendance of the peaceful people. Violence and cannibalism were then documented among wild chimpanzees, the behavioral analogues to ancestral human beings. The evidence of conflict among the Ancestral Pueblo became so overwhelming that it was the focus of a 1995 Society of American Archaeology symposium, the proceedings of which were published in the book, *Deciphering Anasazi Violence.* The Ancestral Pueblo cannibalism argument was formalized in University of California, Berkeley anthropologist Tim White's 1992 book *Prehistoric Cannibalism at Mancos 5Mtumr2346.* In each case, physical anthropology alone, or in combination with scientific archaeology, brought down the peaceful paradigm with the weight of scientific evidence. Turner produced much of that evidence.

Cannibalism at Other Sites?

In *Man Corn,* Turner carefully stated that he thought the Ancestral Pueblo were victims of terrorism imposed on them by a more violent and cannibalistic culture. The book reviews skeletal evidence of violence at more than 76 sites in the Ancestral Pueblo region. He believes that violence and cannibalism were introduced by migrants from central Mexico, where there is a long tradition of violence, human sacrifice and cannibalism.

Of the sites Turner discusses, I have first-hand experience with one, Salmon Ruin, where I spent three seasons excavating and later reconstructing the parasite ecology and diet of this large pueblo's occupants as part of my thesis and dissertation research. He focuses on a high structure called a kiva at the center of the three-story pueblo. Initially it was thought that the bodies of two adults and 35 children were burned in the tower kiva. His analysis indicates that these bodies were disarticulated and cannibalized. However, there are other interpretations.

In 1977, I discussed the tower kiva finds with the excavation director, the late Cynthia Irwin-Williams, who was then with Eastern New Mexico State University. She believed that the children were sent to the highest place in the pueblo with two adults when the structure caught fire. As the fire went out of control, they were trapped there.

Another explanation was offered to me by Larry Baker, director of the Salmon Ruin Museum. He told me that a new analysis of the bones showed that the people in the tower kiva were long dead when their bodies burned. Furthermore, there is evidence in the burned bones that the bodies had at least partly decomposed. It may be that the bodies were placed in the tower as part of a mortuary custom after the pueblo was abandoned. When the pueblo burned, so did the bodies.

More recently, Nancy Akins, with the Museum of New Mexico, reanalyzed the human remains and stratigraphy of the tower kiva. She found that only 20 children and 4 adults were represented. Some of the bodies were deliberately cremated and others partially burned. Some remains showed that the bodies were dry before they were burned. This analysis suggests a complex series of mortuary events preceding the burning of the tower kiva and surrounding rooms. Analysis of the stratigraphy shows that they were not burned simultaneously but were deposited in different episodes. In this view, the evidence suggests a previously unknown mortuary practice rather than trauma and cannibalism.

I conclude that when analyzing the remains of the Ancestral Pueblo, it is important to consider that recent work shows that their mortuary practices were more complicated than we previously thought—and that complex mortuary practices should come as no surprise and constitute ambiguous evidence. Prehistoric people in Chile, the Chinchorros, not only disarticulated the dead, but also rearticulated the cleaned bones in vegetation and clay "statues." In Nebraska, disarticulation and burning of bones was done as a part of mortuary ritual. Closer to the Ancestral Pueblo, the Sinagua culture of central Arizona cremated their dead. Thus disarticulated skeletal remains and burning fall short of proving cannibalism.

What We Can Learn

Because the members of extinct cultures cannot speak for themselves, the nature of cultural reconstruction easily becomes colored by the projections of the archaeological community and the inclination of the media to oversimplify or even sensationalize. The Ancestral Pueblo, once thought to be peaceful, have now become, especially in the lay mind, violent cannibals. Neither depiction is fair. They had a level of violence typical of most human populations—present but not excessive. Is that really so surprising?

Perhaps more astonishing is how unquestioning our culture can be in tearing down its icons. Much as we scientists may prefer to stick to the field or the laboratory, shunning the bright lights, we bear a responsibility to present our data in a way that reduces the opportunity for exaggeration. Our findings must be qualified in the context of alternative explanations. As such, the Cowboy Wash coprolite offers us a cautionary tale.

Bibliography

Billman, B. R., P. M. Lambert and L. B. Leonard. 2000. Cannibalism, warfare, and drought in the Mesa Verde Region during the Twelfth Century A.D. *American Antiquity* 65:145–178.

Bryant, V. M., Jr., and G. Williams-Dean. 1975. The coprolites of man. *Scientific American* 232:100–109.

Dongoske, K. K., D. L. Martin and T. J. Ferguson. 2000. Critique of the claim of cannibalism at Cowboy Wash. *American Antiquity* 65:179–190.

Fry, G. F. 1980. Prehistoric diet and parasites in the desert west of North America. In; *Early Native Americans,* ed. F. L. Browman. The Hague: Mouton Press, pp. 325–339.

Fry, G. F., and H. J. Hall. 1986. Human coprolites. In: *Archaeological Investigations at Antelope House,* ed. D. P. Morris. Washington, D. C.: U.S. Government Printing Office, pp. 165–188.

Lambert, P. M., L. B. Leonard, B. R. Billman, R. A. Marlar, M. E. Newman and K. J. Reinhard. 2000. Response to the critique of the claim of cannibalism at Cowboy Wash. *American Antiquity* 65:397–406.

Marlar, R., B. Billman, B. Leonard, P. Lambert and K. Reinhard. 2000. Fecal evidence of cannibalism. *Southwestern Lore* 4:14–22.

Reinhard, K. J. 1992. Patterns of diet, parasitism, anemia in prehistoric west North American. In: *Diet, Demography, and Disease: Changing Perspectives on Anemia,* ed. P. Stuart-Macadann and S. Kent. New York: Aldine de Gruyter, pp. 219–258.

Reinhard, K. J., and V. M. Bryant, Jr. 1992a. Coprolite analysis: A biological perspective on archaeology. In: *Advances in Archaeological Method and Theory 4,* ed. M. D. Schiffer. Tucson: University of Arizona Press, pp. 245–288.

Reinhard, K. J., and D. R. Danielson. 2005. Pervasiveness of phytoliths in prehistoric southwestern diet and implications for regional and temporal trends for dental mircowear. *Journal of Archaeological Science* 32:981–988.

Scott, L. 1979. Dietary inferences from Hoy House coprolites: A palynological interpretation. *The Kiva* 44:257–281.

Sobolik, K. 1993. Direct evidence for the importance of small animals to prehistoric diets: A review of coprolite studies. *North American Archaeologist* 14:227–243.

Sutton, M. Q., and K. J. Reinhard, 1995. Cluster analysis of coprolites from Antelope House:. Implications for Anasazi diet and culture. *Journal of Archaeological Science* 22:741–750.

KARL J. REINHARD is a professor in the School of Natural Resources at the University of Nebraska and a Fulbright Commission Senior Specialist in Archaeology for 2004–2009. The main focus of his career since earning his Ph.D. from Texas A&M has been to find explanations for modern patterns of disease in the archaeological and historic record. He also developed a new specialization called archaeoparasitology, which attempts to understand the evolution of parasitic disease.

Modern Humans Made Their Point

ANN GIBBONS

Long before guns gave European explorers a decisive advantage over indigenous peoples, our ancestors had their own technological innovation that allowed them to dominate the Stone Age competition: the projectile point, launched from bows or spear throwers. Paleolithic hunters shooting spears or arrows tipped with these small stone points could stay at a safe distance while hunting a wide assortment of prey—or other humans, says archaeologist John Shea of Stony Brook University in New York. Projectile launchers might even be the key to modern humans' triumph when they entered the Neandertal territory of Europe about 40,000 years ago, Shea proposed in his talk. Neandertals lacked projectiles until it was too late, and they could heft their heavier spears only as far as they could throw them. "Projectile points were such an important invention, like gunpowder, that it would have given the bearers a huge advantage," says archaeologist Alison Brooks of George Washington University in Washington, D.C.

In two separate studies, Shea and Brooks showed that modern humans were using light-weight points associated with projectile launchers by 40,000 years ago. Shea and Brooks both think these new weapons were invented first in Africa, although they disagree about the timing. They agree that modern humans had a technological advantage when they left Africa and spread around the globe. "These lightweight points show up more than 50,000 years ago in Africa," says Stan Ambrose of the University of Illinois, Urbana-Champaign, who heard Shea's talk. "They may have helped modern humans get out of Africa."

The challenge in pinpointing when projectiles were invented is that few of the launchers themselves survive, because they were made of materials that disintegrate over time. The oldest known bow is only 11,000 years old, and the oldest known spear thrower is about 18,000 years old, but archaeologists suspect that the technology is much older. So they try to distinguish projectile points from those used on the tips of hand-thrown spears. One criterion is size: Projectile points must be small and light to soar fast enough to kill. "You wouldn't go up to a Cape buffalo with those tiny points on a thrusting spear," says Brooks.

Shea and Brooks each surveyed points from around the world, setting an upper limit on the size and weight of points considered projectiles. Shea set an upper limit on cross sections at the tip, whereas Brooks set a limit on weight. Shea found that projectile points were wide-spread by 40,000 years ago; earlier points didn't meet his criteria. He proposed that the points were developed for warfare and may have hastened the extinction of Neandertals.

Brooks found that points from 50,000 to 90,000 years ago in three regions of Africa met her criteria. She noted that there was a "grammar and an order" to assembling these tools—one that required extensive social networks in order to exchange technology and specialized materials. She thinks that projectiles made modern humans more efficient hunters who could shoot small game and live in varied terrain. "They didn't have to kill [Neandertals]," says Brooks. "They just had to outcompete them."

New Women of the Ice Age

Forget about hapless mates being dragged around by macho mammoth killers. The women of Ice Age Europe, it appears, were not mere cavewives but priestly leaders, clever inventors, and mighty hunters.

HEATHER PRINGLE

The Black Venus of Dolní Vestonice, a small, splintered figurine sensuously fashioned from clay, is an envoy from a forgotten world. It is all soft curves, with breasts like giant pillows beneath a masked face. At nearly 26,000 years old, it ranks among the oldest known portrayals of women, and to generations of researchers, it has served as a powerful—if enigmatic—clue to the sexual politics of the Ice Age.

Excavators unearthed the Black Venus near the Czech village of Dolní Vestonice in 1924, on a hillside among charred, fractured mammoth bones and stone tools. (Despite its nickname, the Black Venus is actually reddish—it owes its name to the ash that covered it when it was found.) Since the mid-nineteenth century, researchers had discovered more than a dozen similar statuettes in caves and open-air sites from France to Russia. All were cradled in layers of earth littered with stone and bone weaponry, ivory jewelry, and the remains of extinct Ice Age animals. All were depicted naked or nearly so. Collectively, they came to be known as Venus figurines, after another ancient bare-breasted statue, the Venus de Milo. Guided at least in part by prevailing sexual stereotypes, experts interpreted the meaning of the figurines freely. The Ice Age camps that spawned this art, they concluded, were once the domain of hardworking male hunters and secluded, pampered women who spent their days in idleness like the harem slaves so popular in nineteenth-century art.

Over the next six decades, Czech archeologists expanded the excavations at Dolní Vestonice, painstakingly combing the site square meter by square meter. By the 1990s they had unearthed thousands of bone, stone, and clay artifacts and had wrested 19 radiocarbon dates from wood charcoal that sprinkled camp floors. And they had shaded and refined their portrait of Ice Age life. Between 29,000 and 25,000 years ago, they concluded, wandering bands had passed the cold months of the year repeatedly at Dolní Vestonice. Armed with short-range spears, the men appeared to have been specialists in hunting tusk-wielding mammoths and other big game, hauling home great mountains of meat to feed their dependent mates and children. At night men feasted on mammoth steaks, fed their fires with mammoth bone, and fueled their sexual fantasies with tiny figurines of women carved from mammoth ivory and fired from clay. It was the ultimate man's world.

Or was it? Over the past few months, a small team of American archeologists has raised some serious doubts. Amassing critical and previously overlooked evidence from Dolní Vestonice and the neighboring site of Pavlov, Olga Soffer, James Adovasio, and David Hyland now propose that human survival there had little to do with manly men hurling spears at big-game animals. Instead, observes Soffer, one of the world's leading authorities on Ice Age hunters and gatherers and an archeologist at the University of Illinois in Champaign-Urbana, it depended largely on women, plants, and a technique of hunting previously invisible in the archeological evidence—net hunting. "This is not the image we've always had of Upper Paleolithic macho guys out killing animals up close and personal," Soffer explains. "Net hunting is communal, and it involves the labor of children and women. And this has lots of implications."

Many of these implications make her conservative colleagues cringe because they raise serious questions about the focus of previous studies. European archeologists have long concentrated on analyzing broken stone tools and butchered big-game bones, the most plentiful and best preserved relics of the Upper Paleolithic era (which stretched from 40,000 to 12,000 years ago). From these analyses, researchers have developed theories about how these societies once hunted and gathered food. Most researchers ruled out the possibility of women hunters for biological reasons. Adult females, they reasoned, had to devote themselves to breast-feeding and tending infants. "Human babies have always been immature and dependent," says Soffer. "If women are the people who are always involved with biological reproduction and the rearing of the young, then that is going to constrain their behavior. They have to provision that child. For fathers, provisioning is optional."

To test theories about Upper Paleolithic life, researchers looked to ethnography, the scientific description of modern and historical cultural groups. While the lives of modern hunters do not exactly duplicate those of ancient hunters, they supply valuable clues to universal human behavior. "Modern ethnography cannot be used to clone the past," says Soffer. "But people have always had to solve problems. Nature and social relationships present problems to people. We use ethnography to look for theoretical insights into human behavior, test them with ethnography, and if they work, assume that they represent a universal feature of human behavior."

But when researchers began turning to ethnographic descriptions of hunting societies, they unknowingly relied on a very incomplete literature. Assuming that women in surviving hunting societies were homebodies who simply tended hearths and suckled children, most early male anthropologists spent their time with male informants. Their published ethnographies brim with descriptions of males making spears and harpoons and heaving these weapons at reindeer, walruses, and whales. Seldom do they mention the activities of women. Ethnography, it seemed, supported theories of ancient male big-game hunters. "When they talked about primitive man, it was always 'he,'" says Soffer. "The 'she' was missing."

Recent anthropological research has revealed just how much Soffer's colleagues overlooked. By observing women in the few remaining hunter-gatherer societies and by combing historical accounts of tribal groups more thoroughly, anthropologists have come to realize how critical the female half of the population has always been to survival. Women and children have set snares, laid spring traps, sighted game and participated in animal drives and surrounds—forms of hunting that endangered neither young mothers nor their offspring. They dug starchy roots and collected other plant carbohydrates essential to survival. They even hunted, on occasion, with the projectile points traditionally deemed men's weapons. "I found references to Inuit women carrying bows and arrows, especially the blunt arrows that were used for hunting birds," says Linda Owen, an archeologist at the University of Tübingen in Germany.

The revelations triggered a volley of new research. In North America, Soffer and her team have found tantalizing evidence of the hunting gear often favored by women in historical societies. In Europe, archeobotanists are analyzing Upper Paleolithic hearths for evidence of plant remains probably gathered by women and children, while lithics specialists are poring over stone tools to detect new clues to their uses. And the results are gradually reshaping our understanding of Ice Age society. The famous Venus figurines, say archeologists of the new school, were never intended as male pornography: instead they may have played a key part in Upper Paleolithic rituals that centered on women. And such findings, pointing toward a more important role for Paleolithic women than had previously been assumed, are giving many researchers pause.

Like many of her colleagues, Soffer clearly relishes the emerging picture of Upper Paleolithic life. "I think life back then was a hell of a lot more egalitarian than it was with your later peasant societies," she says. "Of course the Paleolithic women were pulling their own weight." After sifting through Ice Age research for nearly two decades, Soffer brings a new critical approach to the notion—flattering to so many of her male colleagues—of mighty male mammoth hunters. "Very few archeologists are

hunters," she notes, so it never occurred to most of them to look into the mechanics of hunting dangerous tusked animals. They just accepted the ideas they'd inherited from past work.

But the details of hunting bothered Soffer. Before the fifth century B.C., no tribal hunters in Asia or Africa had ever dared make their living from slaying elephants; the great beasts were simply too menacing. With the advent of the Iron Age in Africa, the situation changed. New weapons allowed Africans to hunt elephants and trade their ivory with Greeks and Romans. A decade ago, keen to understand how prehistoric bands had slaughtered similar mammoths, Soffer began studying Upper Paleolithic sites on the Russian and Eastern European plains. To her surprise, the famous mammoth bone beds were strewn with cumbersome body parts, such as 220-pound skulls, that sensible hunters would generally abandon. Moreover, the bones exhibited widely differing degrees of weathering, as if they had sat on the ground for varying lengths of time. To Soffer, it looked suspiciously as if Upper Paleolithic hunters had simply camped next to places where the pachyderms had perished naturally—such as water holes or salt licks—and mined the bones for raw materials.

If one of these Upper Paleolithic guys killed a mammoth, and occasionally they did, they probably didn't stop talking about it for ten years.

Soffer began analyzing data researchers had gathered describing the sex and age ratios of mammoths excavated from four Upper Paleolithic sites. She found many juveniles, a smaller number of adult females, and hardly any males. The distribution mirrored the death pattern other researchers had observed at African water holes, where the weakest animals perished closest to the water and the strongest farther off. "Imagine the worst time of year in Africa, which is the drought season," explains Soffer. "There is no water, and elephants need an enormous amount. The ones in the worst shape—your weakest, your infirm, your young—are going to be tethered to that water before they die. They are in such horrendous shape, they don't have any extra energy to go anywhere. The ones in better shape would wander off slight distances and then keel over farther away. You've got basket cases and you've got ones that can walk 20 feet."

To Soffer, the implications of this study were clear. Upper Paleolithic bands had pitched their camps next to critical resources such as ancient salt licks or water holes. There the men spent more time scavenging bones and ivory from mammoth carcasses then they did risking life and limb by attacking 6,600-pound pachyderms with short-range spears. "If one of these Upper Paleolithic guys killed a mammoth, and occasionally they did," concedes Soffer dryly, "they probably didn't stop talking about it for ten years."

But if Upper Paleolithic families weren't often tucking into mammoth steaks, what were they hunting and how? Soffer found the first unlikely clue in 1991, while sifting through hundreds of tiny clay fragments recovered from the Upper Paleolithic site of Pavlov, which lies just a short walk from Dolní Vestonice. Under a magnifying lens, Soffer noticed something strange on a few of the fragments: a series of parallel lines impressed on their surfaces. What could have left such a regular pattern? Puzzled, Soffer photographed the pieces, all of which had been unearthed from a zone sprinkled with wood charcoal that was radiocarbon-dated at between 27,000 and 25,000 years ago.

When she returned home, Soffer had the film developed. And one night on an impulse, she put on a slide show for a visiting colleague, Jim Adovasio. "We'd run out of cable films," she jokes. Staring at the images projected on Soffer's refrigerator, Adovasio, an archeologist at Mercyhurst College in Pennsylvania and an expert on ancient fiber technology, immediately recognized the impressions of plant fibers. On a few, he could actually discern a pattern of interlacing fibers—weaving.

Without a doubt, he said, he and Soffer were gazing at textiles or basketry. They were the oldest—by nearly 7,000 years—ever found. Just how these pieces of weaving got impressed in clay, he couldn't say. "It may be that a lot of these [materials] were lying around on clay floors," he notes. "When the houses burned, the walked-in images were subsequently left in the clay floors."

Soffer and Adovasio quickly made arrangements to fly back to the Czech Republic. At the Dolní Vestonice branch of the Institute of Archaeology, Soffer sorted through nearly 8,400 fired clay pieces, weeding out the rejects. Adovasio made positive clay casts of 90. Back in Pennsylvania, he and his Mercyhurst colleague David Hyland peered at the casts under a zoom stereomicroscope, measuring warps and wefts. Forty-three revealed impressions of basketry and textiles. Some of the latter were as finely woven as a modern linen tablecloth. But as Hyland stared at four of the samples, he noted something potentially more fascinating: impressions of cordage bearing weaver's knots, a technique that joins two lengths of cord and that is commonly used for making nets of secure mesh. It looked like a tiny shred of a net bag, or perhaps a hunting net. Fascinated, Soffer expanded the study. She spent six weeks at the Moravian Museum in Brno, sifting through the remainder of the collections from Dolní Vestonice. Last fall, Adovasio spied the telltale impression of Ice Age mesh on one of the new casts.

The mesh, measuring two inches across, is far too delicate for hunting deer or other large prey. But hunters at Dolní Vestonice could have set nets of this size to capture hefty Ice Age hares, each carrying some six pounds of meat, and other furbearers such as arctic fox and red fox. As it turns out, the bones of hares and foxes litter camp floors at Dolní Vestonice and Pavlov. Indeed, this small game accounts for 46 percent of the individual animals recovered at Pavlov. Soffer, moreover, doesn't rule out the possibility of turning up bits of even larger nets. Accomplished weavers in North America once knotted mesh with which they captured 1,000-pound elk and 300-pound bighorn sheep. "In fact, when game officials have to move sheep out west, it's by nets," she adds. "You throw nets on them and they just lie down. It's a very safe way of hunting."

Illustration by Ron Miller

Nets made Ice Age hunting safe enough for entire communities to participate, and they captured everything from hares and foxes to deer and sheep.

In many historical societies, she observes, women played a key part in net hunting since the technique did not call for brute strength nor did it place young mothers in physical peril. Among Australian aborigines, for example, women as well as men knotted the mesh, laboring for as much as two or three years on a fine net. Among native North American groups, they helped lay out their handiwork on poles across a valley floor. Then the entire camp joined forces as beaters. Fanning out across the valley, men, women, and children alike shouted and screamed, flushing out game and driving it in the direction of the net. "Everybody and their mother could participate," says Soffer. "Some people were beating, others were screaming or holding the net. And once you got the net on these animals, they were immobilized. You didn't need brute force. You could club them, hit them any old way."

People seldom returned home empty-handed. Researchers living among the net-hunting Mbuti in the forests of Congo report that they capture game every time they lay out their woven traps, scooping up 50 percent of the animals encountered. "Nets are a far more valued item in their panoply of food-producing things than bows and arrows are," says Adovasio. So lethal are these traps that the Mbuti generally rack up more meat than they can consume, trading the surplus with neighbors. Other net hunters traditionally smoked or dried their catch and stored it for leaner times. Or they polished it off immediately in large ceremonial feasts. The hunters of Dolní Vestonice and Pavlov, says Soffer, probably feasted during ancient rituals. Archeologists unearthed no evidence of food storage pits at either site. But there is much evidence of ceremony. At Dolní Vestonice, for example, many clay figurines appear to have been ritually destroyed in secluded parts of the site.

Soffer doubts that the inhabitants of Dolní Vestonice and Pavlov were the only net makers in Ice Age Europe. Camps stretching from Germany to Russia are littered with a notable abundance of small-game bones, from hares to birds like ptarmigan. And at least some of their inhabitants whittled bone tools that look much like the awls and net spacers favored by historical

Illustration by Ron Miller

Once animals were caught in the nets, hunters could beat them to death with whatever was handy.

net makers. Such findings, agree Soffer and Adovasio, reveal just how shaky the most widely accepted reconstructions of Upper Paleolithic life are. "These terribly stilted interpretations," says Adovasio, "with men hunting big animals all the time and the poor females waiting at home for these guys to bring home the bacon—what crap."

In her home outside Munich, Linda Owen finds other faults with this traditional image. Owen, an American born and raised, specializes in the microscopic analysis of stone tools. In her years of work, she often noticed that many of the tools made by hunters who roamed Europe near the end of the Upper Paleolithic era, some 18,000 to 12,000 years ago, resembled pounding stones and other gear for harvesting and processing plants. Were women and children gathering and storing wild plant foods?

Most of her colleagues saw little value in pursuing the question. Indeed, some German archeologists contended that 90 percent of the human diet during the Upper Paleolithic era came from meat. But as Owen began reading nutritional studies, she saw that heavy meat consumption would spell death. To stoke the body's cellular engines, human beings require energy from protein, fat, or carbohydrates. Of these, protein is the least efficient. To burn it, the body must boost its metabolic rate by 10 percent, straining the liver's ability to absorb oxygen. Unlike carnivorous animals, whose digestive and metabolic systems are well adapted to a meat-only diet, humans who consume more than half their calories as lean meat will die from protein

poisoning. In Upper Paleolithic times, hunters undoubtedly tried to round out their diets with fat from wild game. But in winter, spring, and early summer, the meat would have been very lean. So how did humans survive?

Owen began sifting for clues through anthropological and historical accounts from subarctic and arctic North America. These environments, she reasoned, are similar to that of Ice Age Europe and pose similar challenges to their inhabitants. Even in the far north, Inuit societies harvested berries for winter storage and gathered other plants for medicines and for fibers. To see if any of the flora that thrived in Upper Paleolithic Europe could be put to similar uses, Owen drew up a list of plants economically important to people living in cold-climate regions of North America and Europe and compared it with a list of species that botanists had identified from pollen trapped in Ice Age sediment cores from southern Germany. Nearly 70 plants were found on both lists. "I came up with just a fantastic list of plants that were available at that time. Among others, there were a number or reeds that are used by the Eskimo and subarctic people in North America for making baskets. There are a lot of plants with edible leaves and stems, and things that were used as drugs and dyes. So the plants were there."

The chief plant collectors in historical societies were undoubtedly women. "It was typically women's work," says Owen. "I did find several comments that the men on hunting expeditions would gather berries or plants for their own meals, but they did not participate in the plant-gathering expeditions. They might go along, but they would be hunting or fishing."

Were Upper Paleolithic women gathering plants? The archeological literature was mostly silent on the subject. Few archeobotanists, Owen found, had ever looked for plant seeds and shreds in Upper Paleolithic camps. Most were convinced such efforts would be futile in sites so ancient. At University College London, however, Owen reached a determined young archeobontanist, Sarah Mason, who had analyzed a small sample of charcoal-like remains from a 26,390-year-old hearth at Dolní Vestonice.

The sample held more than charcoal. Examining it with a scanning electron microscope, Mason and her colleagues found fragments of fleshy plant taproots with distinctive secretory cavities—trademarks of the daisy and aster family, which boasts several species with edible roots. In all likelihood, women at Dolní Vestonice had dug the roots and cooked them into starchy meals. And they had very likely simmered other plant foods too. Mason and her colleagues detected a strange pulverized substance in the charred sample. It looked as if the women had either ground plants into flour and then boiled the results to make gruel or pounded vegetable material into a mush for their babies. Either way, says Soffer, the results are telling. "They're stuffing carbohydrates."

Owen is pursuing the research further. "If you do look," she says, "you can find things." At her urging, colleagues at the University of Tübingen are now analyzing Paleolithic hearths for botanical remains as they unearth them. Already they have turned up more plants, including berries, all clearly preserved after thousands of years. In light of these findings, Owen suggests that it was women, not men, who brought home most of

Illustration by Ron Miller

The clay figurines at Dolní Vestonice may have been used in divination rituals.

the calories to Upper Paleolithic families. Indeed, she estimates that if Ice Age females collected plants, bird eggs, shellfish, and edible insects, and if they hunted or trapped small game and participated in the hunting of large game—as northern women did in historical times—they most likely contributed 70 percent of the consumed calories.

Moreover, some women may have enjoyed even greater power, judging from the most contentious relics of Ice Age life: the famous Venus figurines. Excavators have recovered more than 100 of the small statuettes, which were crafted between 29,000 and 23,000 years ago from such enduring materials as bone, stone, antler, ivory, and fired clay. The figurines share a strange blend of abstraction and realism. They bare prominent breasts, for example, but lack nipples. Their bodies are often minutely detailed down to the swaying lines of their backbones and the tiny rolls of flesh—fat folds—beneath their shoulder blades, but they often lack eyes, mouths, and any facial expression. For years researchers viewed them as a male art form. Early anthropologists, after all, had observed only male hunters carving stone, ivory, and other hard materials. Females were thought to lack the necessary strength. Moreover, reasoned experts, only men would take such loving interest in a woman's body. Struck by the voluptuousness of the small stone, ivory, and clay bodies, some researchers suggested they were Ice Age erotica, intended to be touched and fondled by their male makers. The idea still lingers. In the 1980s, for example, the well-known American paleontologist Dale Guthrie wrote a scholarly article comparing the postures of the figurines with the provocative poses of *Playboy* centerfolds.

But most experts now dismiss such contentions. Owen's careful scouring of ethnographic sources, for example, revealed that women in arctic and subarctic societies did indeed work stone and ivory on occasion. And there is little reason to suggest the figurines figured as male erotica. The Black Venus, for example, seems to have belonged to a secret world of ceremony and ritual far removed from everyday sexual life.

The evidence, says Soffer, lies in the raw material from which the Black Venus is made. Clay objects sometimes break or explode when fired, a process called thermal-shock fracturing. Studies conducted by Pamela Vandiver of the Smithsonian Institution have demonstrated that the Black Venus and other human and animal figurines recovered from Dolní Vestonice—as well as nearly 2,000 fired ceramic pellets that litter the site—were made from a local clay that is resistant to thermal-shock fracturing. But many of the figurines, including the celebrated Black Venus, bear the distinctive jagged branching splinters created by thermal shock. Intriguingly, the fired clay pellets do not.

Curious, Vandiver decided to replicate the ancient firing process. Her analysis of the small Dolní Vestonice kilns revealed that they had been fired to temperatures around 1450 degrees Fahrenheit—similar to those of an ordinary hearth. So Vandiver set about making figurines of local soil and firing them in a similar earthen kiln, which a local archeological crew had built nearby. To produce thermal shock, she had to place objects larger than half an inch on the hottest part of the fire; moreover, the pieces had to be so wet they barely held their shape.

To Vandiver and Soffer, the experiment—which was repeated several times back at the Smithsonian Institution—suggests that thermal shock was no accident. "Stuff can explode naturally in the kiln," says Soffer, "or you can make it explode. Which was going on at Dolní Vestonice? We toyed with both ideas. Either we're dealing with the most inept potters, people with two left hands, or they are doing it on purpose. And we reject the idea that they were totally inept, because other materials didn't explode. So what are the odds that this would happen only with a very particular category of objects?"

These exploding figurines could well have played a role in rituals, an idea supported by the location of the kilns. They are situated far away from the dwellings, as ritual buildings often are. Although the nature of the ceremonies is not clear, Soffer speculates that they might have served as divination rites for discerning what the future held. "Some stuff is going to explode. Some stuff is not going to explode. It's evocative, like picking petals off a daisy. She loves me, she loves me not."

Moreover, ritualists at Dolní Vestonice could have read significance into the fracturing patterns of the figurines. Many historical cultures, for example, attempted to read the future by a related method called scapulimancy. In North America, Cree ceremonialists often placed the shoulder blade, or scapula, of a desired animal in the center of a lodge. During the ceremonies, cracks began splintering the bone: a few of these fractures leaked droplets of fat. To Cree hunters, this was a sign that they would find game if they journeyed in the direction indicated by the cracks.

Venus figurines from other sites also seem to have been cloaked in ceremony. "They were not just something made to look pretty," says Margherita Mussi, an archeologist at the University of Rome-La Sapienza who studies Upper Paleolithic figurines. Mussi notes that several small statuettes from the Grimaldi Cave carvings of southern Italy, one of the largest troves of Ice Age figurines ever found in Western Europe, were carved from rare materials, which the artists obtained with great difficulty, sometimes through trade or distant travel. The statuettes were laboriously whittled and polished, then rubbed with ocher, a pigment that appears to have had ceremonial significance, suggesting that they could have been reserved for special events like rituals.

The nature of these rites is still unclear. But Mussi is convinced that women took part, and some archeologists believe they stood at the center. One of the clearest clues, says Mussi, lies in a recently rediscovered Grimaldi figurine known as Beauty and the Beast. This greenish yellow serpentine sculpture portrays two arched bodies facing away from each other and joined at the head, shoulders, and lower extremities. One body is that of a Venus figurine. The other is a strange creature that combines the triangular head of a reptile, the pinched waist of a wasp, tiny arms, and horns. "It is clearly not a creature of this world," says Mussi.

The pairing of woman and supernatural beast, adds Mussi, is highly significant. "I believe that these women were related to the capacity of communicating with a different world," she says. "I think they were believed to be the gateway to a different dimension." Possessing powers that far surpassed others in their communities, such women may have formed part of a spiritual elite, rather like the shamans of ancient Siberia. As intermediaries between the real and spirit worlds, Siberian shamans were said to be able to cure illnesses and intercede on behalf of others for hunting success. It is possible that Upper Paleolithic women performed similar services for their followers.

Although the full range of their activities is unlikely ever to be known for certain, there is good reason to believe that Ice Age women played a host of powerful roles—from plant collectors and weavers to hunters and spiritual leaders. And the research that suggests those roles is rapidly changing our mental images of the past. For Soffer and others, these are exciting times. "The data do speak for themselves," she says finally. "They answer the questions we have. But if we don't envision the questions, we're not going to see the data."

HEATHER PRINGLE lives in Vancouver, British Columbia. "I love how this article overturns the popular image of the role of women in the past," says Pringle, who specializes in writing about archaeology. "It was fun to write and a delight to research." Pringle is the author of *In Search of Ancient North America*.

Woman the Toolmaker

A day in the life of an Ethiopian woman who scrapes hides the old-fashioned way.

STEVEN A. BRANDT AND KATHRYN WEEDMAN

On the edge of the western escarpment of the Ethiopian Rift Valley, we sit in awe, not of the surrounding environment—some of the world's most spectacular scenery—but of an elderly woman deftly manufacturing stone scrapers as she prepares food, answers an inquisitive child, and chats with a neighbor. She smiles at us, amused and honored by our barrage of questions and our filming of her activities.

In our world of electronic and digital gadgetry, it is surprising to meet someone who uses stone tools in their everyday life. Yet, over the past three decades, researchers have identified a handful of ethnic groups in Ethiopia's southern highlands whose artisans live by making stone scrapers and processing animal hides.

In 1995, with colleagues from Ethiopia's Authority for Research and Conservation of Cultural Heritage and the University of Florida, we surveyed the highlands and, much to our surprise, identified hundreds of stone tool makers in ten different ethnic groups.

The Konso, one group we surveyed, grow millet and other crops on terraces and raise livestock that provide the skins for the hide workers. While hide working in virtually all of the other groups is conducted by men who learn from their fathers, among the Konso the hide workers are women, taught by their mothers or other female relatives.

In archaeological writings, scholarly and popular, stone toolmaking has generally been presented as a male activity; *Man the Toolmaker* is the title of one classic work. This is despite the fact that Australian Aboriginal, North American Inuit (Eskimo), and Siberian women, among others, have been reported in recent times to have made flaked-stone artifacts. The Konso hide workers are probably the only women in the world still making stone tools on a regular basis. They provide a unique opportunity for ethnoarchaeology, the study of the material remains of contemporary peoples. In the past two summers, our team returned to study the women hide workers, following them with our notebooks and cameras, and observing them as they went through their daily lives.

One Konso woman we studied is Sokate, a respected and energetic grandmother now in her 70s. Our many questions amuse Sokate, but she is polite and patient with us. When we ask why only 31 of the 119 Konso hide workers are men, she can only laugh and say that hide working has always been women's work.

After an early morning rain, Sokate strides through her village's terraced millet fields to the same riverbed in which her mother and grandmother searched for chert, a flakeable stone similar to flint. She uses a digging stick to pry stones loose. After almost an hour, Sokate picks up a small nodule of chert. She places it on a large, flat basalt rock. Lifting another large piece of basalt, she brings it down onto the nodule several times, striking off many pieces. Sokate selects ten of the flakes and places them into the top ruffle of her skirt, folding it into her waistband. She also tucks in three pieces of usable quartz, found with the aid of accompanying children.

Returning home, Sokate is greeted by children, goats, and chickens. She picks up the iron tip of a hoe, and, sitting on a goat hide in front of her house, strikes flakes off a chert nodule she collected earlier. She then picks up a wooden bowl filled with scraper components—wooden handles, used stone scrapers, small, unused flakes—and puts the new chert and quartz flakes in it. Moving to the hearth area in front of her house, she takes a flake from the bowl. Resting the flake directly along the edge of a large basalt block that serves as a hearthstone and an anvil, she strikes the flake's edges with the hoe tip, shaping it into a scraper that will fit into the socket of the wooden handle. Although she has access to iron, Sokate tells us that she prefers using stone because it is sharper, more controllable, and easier to resharpen than iron, or even glass. But not all Konso hide workers share her opinion, and in fact, there are now only 21 of them who still use stone regularly.

She places the handle, passed down to her from her mother, into the ashes of the hearth, warming the acacia tree gum (mastic) that holds the scraper in its socket. When the mastic becomes pliable, Sokate pulls the old, used-up scraper out of the socket, then places the end of the handle back into the ashes. After a few minutes, she takes it out and removes some of the old mastic with a stick. On an earthenware sherd, she mixes fresh resin she collected earlier in the day with ashes and heats it. Winding it onto a stick, she drips it into the socket. Sokate then puts a new scraper into the socket, patting the resin down around it with her index finger, making certain that it is set at the proper 90-degree angle to the haft.

Local farmers and other artisans bring Sokate hides to scrape, paying her with grain or money. The morning she is going to scrape a cow hide, Sokate brushes it with a mixture of water and juice from the enset plant, or false banana. If the hide is too dry, removing the fat from its inner side is difficult. After the hide is saturated, she latches one end of it to a tree or post so the hide is slightly above the ground. Squatting or kneeling, she holds the hide taut with her feet to facilitate scraping it. Then with both hands holding the wooden handle, she scrapes the cow hide in long strokes, using a "pull" motion. Goat hides are laid flat on the ground with Sokate sitting with one leg on top of the hide and the other underneath to keep it taut. She scrapes a got hide with short strokes and a "push" motion away from her body, giving better control of the scraper with the thin goat skin.

Sokate removes the fatty inner layer, shaving off long strips in a rhythmic motion. When the edge of her tool becomes dull, usually after about 60 strokes, she resharpens it. Most of the small chips she removes from the scraper to resharpen it fall into a wooden bowl or gourd. Her barefoot grandchildren periodically dump the sharp chips onto the communal trash pile just outside the village. Sokate uses the scraper until it becomes too dull for scraping and too small to resharpen further. She'll wear out two or three scraping a single cattle hide, one or two for a goat hide.

Many hide-working activities take place in Konso compounds, which are often surrounded by stone walls. A broken pot on the roof indicates the father of a household is a first-born son, a person of higher status.

After Sokate scrapes the hide, she spreads a reddish, oily paste of ground castor beans and pieces of red ocher over it. She then folds the hide over and works the mixture into it. After a few days, the skin is soft. Cow hides are then made into bedding, sandals, straps, belts, and musical instruments, while goat hides are made into bags and (now much more rarely) clothing. During harvest time, the demand for goat hides increases because more bags are needed to carry agricultural goods. Sokate then sends her granddaughter to tell the hide's owner that it is ready.

Sokate and the other Ethiopian hide workers say they are proud of their profession, as they play important economic and social roles within their villages. In addition to hide working, they may also be responsible for announcing births, deaths, and meetings, and for performing puberty initiation ceremonies and other ritual activities. Despite the usefulness of their craft and other duties in the community, Konso hide workers and other artisans, such as ironsmiths and potters, have low social status. Farmers hold them in low esteem and consider them polluted, probably because their crafts involve contact with items that are thought to be impure, like the skins of dead animals. They cannot marry outside of their artisan group, usually cannot own land, and are often excluded from political and judicial life.

Clearly, the Konso hide workers are a rich source of information from which we can address a range of questions: Can excavations of abandoned hide worker compounds provide insights into the identification of social inequality and ranking? How and in what social contexts is stone toolmaking learned? Can we differentiate women's activities from men's on the basis of stone tools?

There is a sense of urgency in our work. Many of the hide workers are elderly and have not taught their children their craft; the influx of plastic bags and Western furnishings have greatly reduced demand for their products. And many of the hide workers have abandoned the use of stone in favor of bottle glass: why hike two hours for chert when you can just walk down the road and pick up pieces of glass? We want to complete our study of the Konso hide workers as soon as possible and begin studying other groups in southern Ethiopia whose hide workers are still using flaked stone, for after 2.5 million years of stone tool use and probably more than 100,000 years of scraping hides with stone, humanity's first and longest-lasting cultural tradition is rapidly being lost.

STEVEN A. BRANDT and KATHRYN WEEDMAN are in the department of anthropology at the University of Florida, Gainseville. Their work is supported by funds from the National Science Foundation.

Yes, Wonderful Things

William Rathje and Cullen Murphy

On a crisp October morning not long ago the sun ascended above the Atlantic Ocean and turned its gaze on a team of young researchers as they swarmed over what may be the largest archaeological site in the world. The mound they occupied covers three thousand acres and in places rises more than 155 feet above a low-lying island. Its mass, estimated at 100 million tons, and its volume, estimated at 2.9 billion cubic feet, make it one of the largest man-made structures in North America. And it is known to be a treasure trove—a Pompeii, a Tikal, a Valley of the Kings—of artifacts from the most advanced civilization the planet has ever seen. Overhead sea gulls cackled and cawed, alighting now and then to peck at an artifact or skeptically observe an archaeologist at work. The surrounding landscape still supported quail and duck, but far more noticeable were the dusty, rumbling wagons and tractors of the New York City Department of Sanitation.

The site was the Fresh Kills landfill, on Staten Island, in New York City, a repository of garbage that, when shut down, in the year 2005, will have reached a height of 505 feet above sea level, making it the highest geographic feature along a fifteen-hundred-mile stretch of the Atlantic seaboard running north from Florida all the way to Maine. One sometimes hears that Fresh Kills will have to be closed when it reaches 505 feet so as not to interfere with the approach of aircraft to Newark Airport, in New Jersey, which lies just across the waterway called Arthur Kill. In reality, though, the 505-foot elevation is the result of a series of calculations designed to maximize the landfill's size while avoiding the creation of grades so steep that roads built upon the landfill can't safely be used.

Fresh Kills was originally a vast marshland, a tidal swamp. Robert Moses's plan for the area, in 1948, was to dump enough garbage there to fill the marshland up—a process that would take, according to one estimate, until 1968—and then to develop the site, building houses, attracting light industry, and setting aside open space for recreational use. ("The Fresh Kills landfill project," a 1951 report to Mayor Vincent R. Impelliteri observed, "cannot fail to affect constructively a wide area around it. It is at once practical and idealistic.") Something along these lines may yet happen when Fresh Kills is closed. Until then, however, it is the largest active landfill in the world. It is twenty-five times the size of the Great Pyramid of Khufu at Giza, forty times the size of the Temple of the Sun at Teotihuacan. The volume of Fresh Kills is approaching that of the Great Wall of China, and by one estimate will surpass it at some point in the next few years. It is the sheer physical stature of Fresh Kills in the hulking world of landfills that explains why archaeologists were drawn to the place.

To the archaeologists of the University of Arizona's Garbage Project, which is now entering its twentieth year, landfills represent valuable lodes of information that may, when mined and interpreted, produce valuable insights—insights not into the nature of some past society, of course, but into the nature of our own. Garbage is among humanity's most prodigious physical legacies to those who have yet to be born; if we can come to understand our discards, Garbage Project archaeologists argue, then we will better understand the world in which we live. It is this conviction that prompts Garbage Project researchers to look upon the steaming detritus of daily existence with the same quiet excitement displayed by Howard Carter and Lord George Edward Carnarvon at the unpillaged, unopened tomb of Tutankhamun.

"Can you see anything?" Carnarvon asked as Carter thrust a lighted candle through a hole into the gloom of the first antechamber. "Yes," Carter replied. "Wonderful things."

Garbage archaeology can be conducted in several ways. At Fresh Kills the method of excavation involved a mobile derrick and a thirteen-hundred-pound bucket auger, the latter of which would be sunk into various parts of the landfill to retrieve samples of garbage from selected strata. At 6:15 A.M. Buddy Kellett of the company Kellett's Well Boring, Inc., which had assisted with several previous Garbage Project landfill digs, drove one of the company's trucks, with derrick and auger collapsed for travel, straight up the steep slope of one of the landfill mounds. Two-thirds of the way up, the Garbage Project crew directed Kellett to a small patch of level ground. Four hydraulic posts were deployed from the stationary vehicle, extending outward to keep it safely moored. Now the derrick was raised. It supported a long metal rod that in turn housed two other metal rods; the apparatus, when pulled to its full length, like a telescope, was capable of penetrating the landfill to a depth of ninety-seven feet—enough at this particular spot to go clear through its bottom and into the original marsh that Fresh Kills had been (or into what was left of it). At the end of the rods was the auger, a large bucket made of high-tension steel: four feet high, three feet in diameter, and open at the bottom like a cookie cutter, with six graphite-and-steel teeth around the bottom's circumference. The bucket would spin at about thirty revolutions per minute and with such force that virtually nothing could impede its descent. At a Garbage Project excavation in Sunnyvale, California, in 1988, one of the first things the bucket hit in the cover dirt a few feet below the surface of the Sunnyvale Landfill was the skeleton of a car. The bucket's teeth snapped the axle, and drilled on.

The digging at Fresh Kills began. Down the whirring bucket plunged. Moments later it returned with a gasp, laden with garbage that, when released, spewed a thin vapor into the chill autumnal air. The smell was pungent, somewhere between sweet and disagreeable. Kellett's rig operator, David Spillers, did his job with the relaxation that comes of familiarity, seemingly oblivious to the harsh grindings and sharp clanks. The rest of the archaeological crew, wearing cloth aprons and heavy rubber gloves, went about their duties with practiced efficiency and considerable speed. They were veteran members of the Garbage Project's A-Team—its landfill-excavating arm—and had been through it all before.

Again a bucketful of garbage rose out of the ground. As soon as it was dumped Masakazu Tani, at the time a Japanese graduate student in anthropology at the University of Arizona (his Ph.D. thesis, recently completed, involves identifying activity areas in ancient sites on the basis of distributions of litter), plunged a thermometer into the warm mass. "Forty-three degrees centigrade," Tani called out. The temperature (equivalent to 109.4 degrees Fahrenheit) was duly logged. The garbage was then given a brusque preliminary examination to determine its generic source and, if possible, its date of origin. In this case the presence of telltale domestic items, and of legible newspapers, made both tasks easy. Gavin Archer, another anthropologist and a research associate of the Garbage Project, made a notation in the running log that he would keep all day long: "Household, circa 1977." Before the next sample was pulled up Douglas Wilson, an anthropologist who specializes in household hazardous waste, stepped up to the auger hole and played out a weighted tape measure, eventually calling out, "Thirty-five feet." As a safety precaution, Wilson, like any other crew member working close to the sunken shaft on depth-measure duty, wore a leather harness tethered to a nearby vehicle. The esophagus created by the bucket auger was just large enough to accept a human being, and anyone slipping untethered a story or two into this narrow, oxygen-starved cavity would die of asphyxiation before any rescue could be attempted.

Most of the bucketfuls of garbage received no more attention than did the load labeled "Household, circa 1977." Some basic data were recorded for tracking purposes, and the garbage was left on a quickly accumulating backdirt pile. But as each of what would finally be fourteen wells grew deeper and deeper, at regular intervals (either every five or every ten feet) samples were taken and preserved for full-dress analysis. On those occasions Wilson Hughes, the methodical and serenely ursine co-director and field supervisor of the Garbage Project, and the man responsible for day-to-day logistics at the Fresh Kills dig, would call out to the bucket operator over the noise of the engine: "We'll take the next bucket." Then Hughes and

Wilson would race toward the rig in a running crouch, like medics toward a helicopter, a plywood sampling board between them. Running in behind came a team of microbiologists and civil engineers assembled from the University of Oklahoma, the University of Wisconsin, and Procter & Gamble's environmental laboratory. They brought with them a variety of containers and sealing devices to preserve samples in an oxygen-free environment—an environment that would allow colonies of the anaerobic bacteria that cause most of the biodegradation in landfills (to the extent that biodegradation occurs) to survive for later analysis. Behind the biologists and engineers came other Garbage Project personnel with an assortment of wire mesh screens and saw horses.

Within seconds of the bucket's removal from the ground, the operator maneuvered it directly over the sampling board, and released the contents. The pile was attacked first by Phillip Zack, a civil engineering student from the University of Wisconsin, who, as the temperature was being recorded, directed portions of the material into a variety of airtight conveyances. Then other members of the team moved in—the people who would shovel the steaming refuse atop the wire mesh; the people who would sort and bag whatever didn't go through the mesh; the people who would pour into bags or cannisters or jars whatever did go through the mesh; the people who would label everything for the trip either back to Tucson and the Garbage Project's holding bins or to the laboratories of the various microbiologists. (The shortest trip was to the trailer-laboratory that Procter & Gamble scientists had driven from Cincinnati and parked at the edge of the landfill.) The whole sample-collection process, from dumping to sorting to storing, took no more than twelve minutes. During the Fresh Kills dig it was repeated forty-four times at various places and various depths.

As morning edged toward afternoon the bucket auger began to near the limits of its reach in one of the wells. Down through the first thirty-five feet, a depth that in this well would date back to around 1984, the landfill had been relatively dry. Food waste and yard waste—hot dogs, bread, and grass clippings, for example—were fairly well preserved. Newspapers remained intact and easy to read, their lurid headlines ("Woman Butchered-Ex-Hubby Held") calling to mind a handful of yesterday's tragedies. Beyond thirty-five feet, however, the landfill became increasingly wet, the garbage increasingly unidentifiable. At sixty feet, a stratum in this well containing garbage from the 1940s and 1950s, the bucket grabbed a sample and pulled it toward the surface. The Garbage Project team ran forward with their equipment, positioning themselves underneath. The bucket rose majestically as the operator sat at the controls, shouting something over the noise. As near as anyone can reconstruct it now, he was saying, "You boys might want to back off some, 'cause if this wind hits that bucket. . . ." The operator broke off because the wind did hit that bucket, and the material inside—a gray slime, redolent of putrefaction—thoroughly showered the crew. It would be an exaggeration to suggest that the victims were elated by this development, but their curiosity was certainly piqued, because on only one previous excavation had slime like this turned up in a landfill. What was the stuff made of? How had it come to be? What did its existence mean? The crew members doggedly collected all the usual samples, plus a few extra bottles of slime for special study. Then they cleaned themselves off.

It would be a blessing if it were possible to study garbage in the abstract, to study garbage without having to handle it physically.[1] But that is not possible. Garbage is not mathematics. To understand garbage you have to touch it, to feel it, to sort it, to smell it. You have to pick through hundreds of tons of it, counting and weighing all the daily newspapers, the telephone books; the soiled diapers, the foam clamshells that once briefly held hamburgers, the lipstick cylinders coated with grease, the medicine vials still encasing brightly colored pills, the empty bottles of scotch, the half-full cans of paint and muddy turpentine, the forsaken toys, the cigarette butts. You have to sort and weigh and measure the volume of all the organic matter, the discards from thousands of plates: the noodles and the Cheerios and the tortillas; the pieces of pet food that have made their own gravy; the hardened jelly doughnuts, bleeding from their side wounds; the half-eaten bananas, mostly still within their peels, black and incomparably sweet in the embrace of final decay. You have to confront sticky green mountains of yard waste, and slippery brown hills of potato peels, and brittle ossuaries of chicken bones and T-bones. And then, finally, there are the "fines," the vast connecting mixture of tiny bits of paper, metal, glass, plastic, dirt, grit, and former nutrients that suffuses every landfill like a kind of grainy lymph. To understand garbage you need thick gloves and a mask and some booster shots. But the yield in knowledge—about people and their behavior as well as about garbage itself—offsets the grim working conditions.

To an archaeologist, ancient garbage pits or garbage mounds, which can usually be located within a short distance from any ruin, are always among the happiest of finds, for they contain in concentrated form the artifacts and comestibles and remnants of behavior of the people who used them. While every archaeologist dreams of discovering spectacular objects, the bread-and-butter work of archaeology involves the most common and routine kinds of discards. It is not entirely fanciful to define archaeology as the discipline that tries to understand old garbage, and to learn from that garbage something about ancient societies and ancient behaviors. The eminent archaeologist Emil Haury once wrote of the aboriginal garbage heaps of the American Southwest: "Whichever way one views the mounds—as garbage piles to avoid, or as symbols of a way of life—they nevertheless are features more productive of information than any others." When the British archaeologist Sir Leonard Woolley, in 1916, first climbed to the top of the ancient city of Carchemish, on the Euphrates River near the modern-day Turkish-Syrian border, he moistened his index finger and held it in the air. Satisfied, he scanned the region due south of the city—that is, downwind—pausing to draw on his map the location of any mounds he saw. A trench dug through the largest of these mounds revealed it to be the

garbage dump Woolley was certain it was, and the exposed strata helped establish the chronological sequence for the Carchemish site as a whole. Archaeologists have been picking through ancient garbage ever since archaeology became a profession, more than a century ago, and they will no doubt go on doing so as long as garbage is produced.

Several basic points about garbage need to be emphasized at the outset. First, the creation of garbage is an unequivocal sign of a human presence. From Styrofoam cups along a roadway and urine bags on the moon there is an uninterrupted chain of garbage that reaches back more than two million years to the first "waste flake" knocked off in the knapping of the first stone tool. That the distant past often seems misty and dim is precisely because our earliest ancestors left so little garbage behind. An appreciation of the accomplishments of the first hominids became possible only after they began making stone tools, the debris from the production of which, along with the discarded tools themselves, are now probed for their secrets with electron microscopes and displayed in museums not as garbage but as "artifacts." These artifacts serve as markers—increasingly frequent and informative markers—of how our forebears coped with the evolving physical and social world. Human beings are mere placeholders in time, like zeros in a long number; their garbage seems to have more staying power, and a power to inform across the millennia that complements (and often substitutes for) that of the written word. The profligate habits of our own country and our own time—the sheer volume of the garbage that we create and must dispose of—will make our society an open book. The question is: Would we ourselves recognize our story when it is told, or will our garbage tell tales about us that we as yet do not suspect?

That brings up a second matter: If our garbage, in the eyes of the future, is destined to hold a key to the past, then surely it already holds a key to the present. This may be an obvious point, but it is one whose implications were not pursued by scholars until relatively recently. Each of us throws away dozens of items every day. All of these items are relics of specific human activities—relics no different in their inherent nature from many of those that traditional archaeologists work with (though they are, to be sure, a bit fresher). Taken as a whole the garbage of the United States, from its 93 million households and 1.5 million retail outlets and from all of its schools, hospitals, government offices, and other public facilities, is a mirror of American society. Of course, the problem with the mirror garbage offers is that, when encountered in a garbage can, dump, or landfill, it is a broken one: our civilization is reflected in billions of fragments that may reveal little in and of themselves. Fitting some of the pieces back together requires painstaking effort—effort that a small number of archaeologists and natural scientists have only just begun to apply.

A third point about garbage is that it is not an assertion but a physical fact—and thus may sometimes serve as a useful corrective. Human beings have over the centuries left many accounts describing their lives and civilizations. Many of these are little more than self-aggrandizing advertisements. The remains of the tombs, temples, and palaces of the elite are filled with personal histories as recorded by admiring relatives and fawning retainers. More such information is carved into obelisks and stelae, gouged into clay tablets, painted or printed on papyrus and paper. Historians are understandably drawn to written evidence of this kind, but garbage has often served as a kind of tattle-tale, setting the record straight.

It had long been known, for example, that French as well as Spanish forts had been erected along the coast of South Carolina during the sixteenth century, and various mounds and depressions have survived into our own time to testify to their whereabouts. Ever since the mid-nineteenth century a site on the tip of Parris Island, South Carolina, has been familiarly known as the site of a French outpost, built in 1562, that is spelled variously in old documents as Charlesfort, Charlesforte, and Charles Forte. In 1925, the Huguenot Society of South Carolina successfully lobbied Congress to erect a monument commemorating the building of Charlesfort. Subsequently, people in nearby Beaufort took up the Charlesfort theme, giving French names to streets, restaurants, and housing developments. Gift shops sold kitschy touristiana with a distinctly Gallic flavor. Those restaurants and gift shops found themselves in an awkward position when, in 1957, as a result of an analysis of discarded matter discovered at Charlesfort, a National Park Service historian, Albert Manucy, suggested that the site was of Spanish origin. Excavations begun in 1979 by the archaeologist Stanley South, which turned up such items as discarded Spanish olive jars and broken majolica pottery from Seville, confirmed Manucy's view: "Charlesfort," South established, was actually Fort San Marcos, a Spanish installation built in 1577 to protect a Spanish town named Santa Elena. (Both the fort and the town had been abandoned after only a few years.)

Garbage, then, represents physical fact, not mythology. It underscores a point that can not be too greatly emphasized: Our private worlds consist essentially of two realities—mental reality, which encompasses beliefs, attitudes, and ideas, and material reality, which is the picture embodied in the physical record. The study of garbage reminds us that it is a rare person in whom mental and material realities completely coincide. Indeed, for the most part, the pair exist in a state of tension, if not open conflict.

Americans have always wondered, sometimes with buoyant playfulness, what their countrymen in the far future will make of Americans "now." In 1952, in a monograph he first circulated privately among colleagues and eventually published in *The Journal of Irreproducible Results,* the eminent anthropologist and linguist Joseph H. Greenberg—the man who would one day sort the roughly one thousand known Native American languages into three broad language families—imagined the unearthing of the so-called "violence texts" during an excavation of the Brooklyn Dodgers' Ebbets Field in the year A.D. 2026; what interpretation, he wondered, would be given to such newspaper reports as "Yanks Slaughter Indians" and "Reese made a sacrifice in the infield"? In 1979 the artist and writer David Macaulay published *Motel of the*

Mysteries, an archaeological site-report setting forth the conclusions reached by a team of excavators in the year A.D. 4022 who have unearthed a motel dating back to 1985 (the year, Macaulay wrote, in which "an accidental reduction in postal rates on a substance called third- and fourth-class mail literally buried the North Americans under tons of brochures, fliers, and small containers called FREE"). Included in the report are illustrations of an archaeologist modeling a toilet seat, toothbrushes, and a drain stopper (or, as Macaulay describes them, "the Sacred Collar . . . the magnificent 'plasticus' ear ornaments, and the exquisite silver chain and pendant"), all assumed to be items of ritual or personal regalia. In 1982 an exhibit was mounted in New York City called "Splendors of the Sohites"—a vast display of artifacts, including "funerary vessels" (faded, dusky soda bottles) and "hermaphrodite amulets" (discarded pop-top rings), found in the SoHo section of Manhattan and dating from the Archaic Period (A.D. 1950–1961), the Classical Period (1962–1975), and the Decadent Period (1976–c.1980).

Greenberg, Macaulay, and the organizers of the Sohites exhibition all meant to have some fun, but there is an uneasy undercurrent to their work, and it is embodied in the question: What are we to make of ourselves? The Garbage Project, conceived in 1971, and officially established at the University of Arizona in 1973, was an attempt to come up with a new way of providing serious answers. It aimed to apply *real* archaeology to this very question; to see if it would be possible to investigate human behavior "from the back end," as it were. This scholarly endeavor has come to be known as garbology, and practitioners of garbology are known as garbologists. The printed citation (dated 1975) in the *Oxford English Dictionary* for the meaning of "garbology" as used here associates the term with the Garbage Project.

In the years since its founding the Garbage Project's staff members have processed more than 250,000 pounds of garbage, some of it from landfills but most of it fresh out of garbage cans in selected neighborhoods. All of this garbage has been sorted, coded, and catalogued—every piece, from bottles of furniture polish and egg-shaped pantyhose packaging to worn and shredded clothing, crumpled bubble-gum wrappers, and the full range of kitchen waste. A unique database has been built up from these cast-offs, covering virtually every aspect of American life: drinking habits, attitudes toward red meat, trends in the use of convenience foods, the strange ways in which consumers respond to shortages, the use of contraceptives, and hundreds of other matters.[2]

The antecedents of the Garbage Project in the world of scholarship and elsewhere are few but various. Some are undeniably dubious. The examination of fresh refuse is, of course, as old as the human species—just watch anyone who happens upon an old campsite, or a neighbor scavenging at a dump for spare parts or furniture. The first systematic study of the components of America's garbage dates to the early 1900s and the work of the civil engineers Rudolph Hering (in New York) and Samuel A. Greeley (in Chicago), who by 1921 had gathered enough information from enough cities to compile *Collection and Disposal of Municipal Refuse,* the first textbook on urban trash management. In academe, not much happened after that for quite some time. Out in the field, however, civil engineers and solid-waste managers did now and again sort and weigh fresh garbage as it stood in transit between its source and destination, but their categories were usually simple: paper, glass, metal. No one sorted garbage into detailed categories relating to particular consumer discard patterns. No one, for example, kept track of phenomena as specific as the number of beer cans thrown away versus the number of beer bottles, or the number of orange-juice cans thrown away versus the number of pounds of freshly squeezed oranges, or the amount of candy thrown away in the week after Halloween versus the amount thrown away in the week after Valentine's Day. And no one ever dug into the final resting places of most of America's garbage: dumps (where garbage is left in the open) and sanitary landfills (where fresh garbage is covered every night with six to eight inches of soil).

Even as America's city managers over the years oversaw—and sometimes desperately attempted to cope with—the disposal of ever-increasing amounts of garbage, the study of garbage itself took several odd detours—one into the world of the military, another into the world of celebrity-watching, and a third into the world of law enforcement.

The military's foray into garbology occurred in 1941, when two enlisted men, Horace Schwerin and Phalen Golden, were forced to discontinue a survey they were conducting among new recruits about which aspects of Army life the recruits most disliked. (Conducting polls of military personnel was, they had learned, against regulations.) Schwerin and Golden had already discovered, however, that the low quality of the food was the most frequently heard complaint, and they resolved to look into this one matter with an investigation that could not be considered a poll. What Schwerin and Golden did was to station observers in mess halls to record the types of food that were most commonly wasted and the volume of waste by type of food. The result, after 2.4 million man-meals had been observed, was a textbook example of how garbage studies can produce not only behavioral insights but also practical benefits. Schwerin and Golden discovered that 20 percent of the food prepared for Army mess halls was eventually thrown away, and that one reason for this was simply excess preparation. Here are some more of their findings, as summarized in a wartime article that appeared in the *The Saturday Evening Post:*

> Soldiers ate more if they were allowed to smoke in the mess hall. They ate more if they went promptly to table instead of waiting on line outside—perhaps because the food became cold. They ate more if they fell to on their own initiative instead of by command. They cared little for soups, and 65 percent of the kale and nearly as much of the spinach went into the garbage can. Favorite desserts were cakes and cookies, canned fruit, fruit salad, and gelatin. They ate ice cream in almost any amount that was served to them.

"That, sergeant, is an excellent piece of work," General George C. Marshall, the Army chief of staff, told Horace Schwerin after hearing a report by Schwerin on the research findings. The Army adopted many of Schwerin and Golden's recommendations, and began saving some 2.5 million pounds of food a day. It is perhaps not surprising to learn that until joining the Army Horace Schwerin had been in market research, and, among other things, had helped CBS to perfect a device for measuring audience reaction to radio shows.

The origins of an ephemeral branch of garbage studies focused on celebrities—"peeping-Tom" garbology, one might call it—seem to lie in the work of A. J. Weberman. Weberman was a gonzo journalist and yippie whose interest in the songs of Bob Dylan, and obsession with their interpretation, in 1970 prompted him to begin stealing the garbage from the cans left out in front of Dylan's Greenwich Village brownstone on MacDougal Street. Weberman didn't find much—some soiled Pampers, some old newspapers, some fast-food packaging from a nearby Blimpie Base, a shopping list with the word vanilla spelled "vanilla." He did, however, stumble into a brief but highly publicized career. This self-proclaimed "garbage guerrilla" quickly moved on to Neil Simon's garbage (it included a half-eaten bagel, scraps of lox, the Sunday Times), Muhammad Ali's (an empty can of Luck's collard greens, and empty roach bomb), and Abbie Hoffman's (a summons for hitchhiking, an unused can of deodorant, an estimate of the cost for the printing of *Steal This Book,* and the telephone numbers of Jack Anderson and Kate Millet). Weberman revealed many of his findings in an article in *Esquire* in 1971. It was antics such as his that inspired a prior meaning of the term "garbology," one very different from the definition established today.

Weberman's work inspired other garbage guerrillas. In January of 1975, the *Detroit Free Press* Sunday magazine reported on the findings from its raids on the garbage of several city notables, including the mayor, the head of the city council, the leader of a right-wing group, a food columnist, a disk jockey, and a prominent psychiatrist. Nothing much was discovered that might be deemed out of the ordinary, save for some of the contents of the garbage taken from a local Hare Krishna temple: a price tag from an Oleg Cassini garment, for example, and four ticket stubs from the Bel-Aire Drive-In Theater, which at the time was showing *Horrible House on the Hill* and *The Night God Screamed.* Six months after the *Free Press* exposé, a reporter for the *National Enquirer,* Jay Gourley, drove up to 3018 Dumbarton Avenue, N.W., in Washington, D.C., and threw the five garbage bags in front of Secretary of State Henry A. Kissinger's house into the trunk of his car. Secret Service agents swiftly blocked Gourley's departure, but after a day of questioning allowed him to proceed, the garbage still in the trunk. Among Gourley's finds: a crumpled piece of paper with a dog's teeth marks on it, upon which was written the work schedules of the Secret Service agents assigned to guard the Secretary; empty bottles of Seconal and Maalox; and a shopping list, calling for a case of Jack Daniel's, a case of Ezra Brooks bourbon, and a case of Cabin Still bourbon. Gourley later returned most of the garbage to the Kissingers—minus, he told reporters, "several dozen interesting things."

After the Kissinger episode curiosity about the garbage of celebrities seems to have abated. In 1977 the *National Enquirer* sent a reporter to poke through the garbage of President Jimmy

Carter's press secretary, Jody Powell. The reporter found so little of interest that the tabloid decided not to publish a story. In 1980 Secret Service agents apprehended A. J. Weberman as he attempted to abduct former President Richard Nixon's garbage from behind an apartment building in Manhattan. Weberman was released, without the garbage.

The third detour taken by garbage studies involves police work. Over the years, law enforcement agents looking for evidence in criminal cases have also been more-than-occasional students of garbage; the Federal Bureau of Investigation in particular has spent considerable time poring over the household trash of people in whom it maintains a professional interest. ("We take it on a case-by-case basis," an FBI spokesman says.) One of the biggest criminal cases involving garbage began in 1975 and involved Joseph "Joe Bananas" Bonanno, Sr., a resident of Tucson at the time and a man with alleged ties to organized crime that were believed to date back to the days of Al Capone. For a period of three years officers of the Arizona Drug Control District collected Bonanno's trash just before the regular pickup, replacing it with "fake" Bonanno garbage. (Local garbagemen were not employed in the operation because some of them had received anonymous threats after assisting law enforcement agencies in an earlier venture.) The haul in evidence was beyond anyone's expectations: Bonanno had apparently kept detailed records of his various transactions, mostly in Sicilian. Although Bonanno had torn up each sheet of paper into tiny pieces, forensic specialists with the Drug Control District, like archaeologists reconstructing ceramic bowls from potsherds, managed to reassemble many of the documents and with the help of the FBI got them translated. In 1980 Bonanno was found guilty of having interfered with a federal grand jury investigation into the business operations of his two sons and a nephew. He was eventually sent to jail.

Unlike law-enforcement officers or garbage guerrillas, the archaeologists of the Garbage Project are not interested in the contents of any particular individual's garbage can. Indeed, it is almost always the case that a given person's garbage is at once largely anonymous and unimaginably humdrum. Garbage most usefully comes alive when it can be viewed in the context of broad patterns, for it is mainly in patterns that the links between artifacts and behaviors can be discerned.

The seed from which the Garbage Project grew was an anthropology class conducted at the University of Arizona in 1971 that was designed to teach principles of archaeological methodology. The University of Arizona has long occupied a venerable place in the annals of American archaeology and, not surprisingly, the pursuit of archaeology there to this day is carried on in serious and innovative ways. The class in question was one in which students undertook independent projects aimed precisely at showing links between various kinds of artifacts and various kinds of behavior. For example, one student, Sharon Thomas, decided to look into the relationship between a familiar motor function ("the diffusion pattern of ketchup over hamburgers") and a person's appearance, as manifested in clothing. Thomas

took up a position at "seven different hamburger dispensaries" and, as people came in to eat, labeled them "neat" or "sloppy" according to a set of criteria relating to the way they dressed. Then she recorded how each of the fifty-seven patrons she studied—the ones who ordered hamburgers—poured ketchup over their food. She discovered that sloppy people were far more likely than neat people to put ketchup on in blobs, sometimes even stirring it with their fingers. Neat people, in contrast, tended to apply the ketchup in patterns: circles, spirals, and crisscrosses. One person (a young male neatly dressed in a body shirt, flared pants, and patent-leather Oxfords) wrote with ketchup what appeared to be initials.

Two of the student investigations, conducted independently by Frank Ariza and Kelly Allen, led directly to the Garbage Project. Ariza and Allen, wanting to explore the divergence between (or correlation of) mental stereotypes and physical realities, collected garbage from two households in an affluent part of Tucson and compared it to garbage from two households in a poor and, as it happens, Mexican-American part of town. The rich and poor families, each student found, ate about the same amount of steak and hamburger, and drank about the same amount of milk. But the poor families, they learned, bought more expensive child-education items. They also bought more household cleansers. What did such findings mean? Obviously the sample—involving only four households in all—was too small for the results even to be acknowledged as representative, let alone to provide hints as to what lay behind them. However, the general nature of the research effort itself—comparing garbage samples in order to gauge behavior (and, what is more, gauging behavior unobtrusively, thereby avoiding one of the great biases inherent in much social science)—seemed to hold great promise.

A year later, in 1972, university students, under professorial direction, began borrowing samples of household garbage from different areas of Tucson, and sorting it in a lot behind a dormitory. The Garbage Project was under way. In 1973, the Garbage Project entered into an arrangement with the City of Tucson, whereby the Sanitation Division, four days a week, delivered five to eight randomly selected household pickups from designated census tracts to an analysis site that the Division set aside for the Project's sorters at a maintenance yard. (Wilson Hughes, who as mentioned earlier is the Garbage Project's co-director, was one of the first undergraduate garbage sorters.) In 1984 operations were moved to an enclosure where many of the university's dumpsters are parked, across the street from Arizona Stadium.

The excavation of landfills would come much later in the Garbage Project's history, when to its focus on issues of garbage and human behavior it added a focus on issues of garbage management. The advantage in the initial years of sorting fresh garbage over excavating landfills was a basic but important one: In landfills it is often quite difficult and in many cases impossible to get some idea, demographically speaking, of the kind of neighborhood from which any particular piece of garbage has come. The value of landfill studies is therefore limited to advancing our understanding of garbage in the aggregate. With fresh garbage, on the other hand, one can have demographic precision down to the level of a few city blocks, by directing pickups to specific census districts and cross-tabulating the findings with census data.

Needless to say, deciding just which characteristics of the collected garbage to pay attention to posed a conceptual challenge, one that was met by Wilson Hughes, who devised the "protocol" that is used by the Garbage Project to this day. Items found in garbage are sorted into one of 150 specific coded categories that can in turn be clustered into larger categories representing food (fresh food versus prepared, health food versus junk food), drugs, personal and household sanitation products, amusement-related or educational materials, communications-related materials, pet-related materials, yard-related materials, and hazardous materials. For each item the following information is recorded on a standardized form: the date on which it was collected; the census tract from which it came; the item code (for example, 001, which would be the code for "Beef"); the item's type (for example, "chuck"); its original weight or volume (in this case, derived from the packaging); its cost (also from the packaging); material composition of container; brand (if applicable); and the weight of any discarded food (if applicable). The information garnered over the years from many thousands of such forms, filled out in pursuit of a wide variety of research objectives, constitutes the Garbage Project's database. It has all been computerized and amounts to some two million lines of data drawn from some fifteen thousand household-refuse samples. The aim here has been not only to approach garbage with specific questions to answer or hypotheses to prove but also to amass sufficient quantities of information, in a systematic and open-minded way, so that with the data on hand Garbage Project researchers would be able to answer any future questions or evaluate any future hypotheses that might arise. In 1972 garbage was, after all, still terra incognita, and the first job to be done was akin to that undertaken by the explorers Lewis and Clark.

From the outset the Garbage Project has had to confront the legal and ethical issues its research involves: Was collecting and sorting someone's household garbage an unjustifiable invasion of privacy? This very question has over the years been argued repeatedly in the courts. The Fourth Amendment unequivocally guarantees Americans protection from unreasonable search and seizure. Joseph Bonanno, Sr., tried to invoke the Fourth Amendment to prevent his garbage from being used as evidence. But garbage placed in a garbage can in a public thoroughfare, where it awaits removal by impersonal refuse collectors, and where it may be picked over by scavengers looking for aluminum cans, by curious children or neighbors, and by the refuse collectors themselves (some of whom do a thriving trade in old appliances, large and small), is usually considered by the courts to have been abandoned. Therefore, the examination of the garbage by outside parties cannot be a violation of a constitutional right. In the Bonanno case, U.S. District Court Judge William Ingram ruled that investigating garbage for evidence of a crime may carry a "stench," but was not illegal. In 1988, in *California v. Greenwood,* the U.S. Supreme Court ruled by a margin of six to two that the police were entitled to conduct a warrantless search of a suspected drug dealer's garbage—a search that led to drug

paraphernalia, which led in turn to warrants, arrests, and convictions. As Justice Byron White has written, "The police cannot reasonably be expected to avert their eyes from evidence of criminal activity that could have been observed by any member of the public."

Legal issues aside, the Garbage Project has taken pains to ensure that those whose garbage comes under scrutiny remain anonymous. Before obtaining garbage for study, the Project provides guarantees to communities and their garbage collectors that nothing of a personal nature will be examined and that no names or addresses or other personal information will be recorded. The Project also stipulates that all of the garbage collected (except aluminum cans, which are recycled) will be returned to the community for normal disposal.

As noted, the Garbage Project has now been sorting and evaluating garbage, with scientific rigor, for two decades. The Project has proved durable because its findings have supplied a fresh perspective on what we know—and what we think we know—about certain aspects of our lives. Medical researchers, for example, have long made it their business to question people about their eating habits in order to uncover relationships between patterns of diet and patterns of disease. These researchers have also long suspected that people—honest, well-meaning people—may often be providing information about quantities and types and even brands of food and drink consumed that is not entirely accurate. People can't readily say whether they trimmed 3.3 ounces or 5.4 ounces of fat off the last steak they ate, and they probably don't remember whether they had four, five, or seven beers in the previous week, or two eggs or three. The average person just isn't paying attention. Are there certain patterns in the way in which people wrongly "self-report" their dietary habits? Yes, there are, and Garbage Project studies have identified many of them.

Garbage archaeologists also know how much edible food is thrown away; what percentage of newspapers, cans, bottles, and other items aren't recycled; how loyal we are to brandname products and which have earned the greatest loyalty; and how much household hazardous waste is carted off to landfills and incinerators. From several truckloads of garbage and a few pieces of ancillary data—most importantly, the length of time over which the garbage was collected—the Garbage Project staff can reconstruct the community from which it came with a degree of accuracy that the Census Bureau might in some neighborhoods be unable to match.

Garbage also exposes the routine perversity of human ways. Garbage archaeologists have learned, for example, that the volume of garbage that Americans produce expands to fill the number of receptacles that are available to put it in. They have learned that we waste more of what is in short supply than of what is plentiful; that attempts by individuals to restrict consumption of certain foodstuffs are often counterbalanced by extra and inadvertent consumption of those same foodstuffs in hidden form; and that while a person's memory of what he has eaten and drunk in a given week is inevitably wide of the mark, his guess as to what a family member or even neighbor has eaten and drunk usually turns out to be more perceptive.

Some of the Garbage Project's research has prompted unusual forays into arcane aspects of popular culture. Consider the matter of those "amulets" worn by the Sohites—that is, the once-familiar detachable pop-top pull tab. Pull tabs first became important to the Garbage Project during a study of household recycling practices, conducted on behalf of the federal Environmental Protection Agency during the mid-1970s. The question arose: If a bag of household garbage contained no aluminum cans, did that mean that the household didn't dispose of any cans or that it had recycled its cans? Finding a way to answer that question was essential if a neighborhood's recycling rate was to be accurately determined. Pull tabs turned out to hold the key. A quick study revealed that most people did not drop pull tabs into the cans from which they had been wrenched; rather, the vast majority of people threw the tabs into the trash. If empty cans were stored separately for recycling, the pull tabs still went out to the curb with the rest of the garbage. A garbage sample that contained several pull tabs but no aluminum cans was a good bet to have come from a household that recycled.

All this counting of pull tabs prompted a surprising discovery one day by a student: Pull tabs were not all alike. Their configuration and even color depended on what kind of beverage they were associated with and where the beverage had been canned. Armed with this knowledge, Garbage Project researchers constructed an elaborate typology of pull tabs, enabling investigators to tease out data about beverage consumption—say, beer versus soda, Michelob versus Schlitz—even from samples of garbage that contained not a single can. Detachable pull tabs are no longer widely used in beverage cans, but the pull-tab typology remains useful even now. Among other things, in the absence of such evidence of chronology as a newspaper's dateline, pull tabs can reliably help to fix the dates of strata in a landfill. In archaeological parlance objects like these that have been widely diffused over a short period of time, and then abruptly disappear, are known as horizon markers.

The unique "punch-top" on Coors beer cans, for example, was used only between March of 1974 and June of 1977. (It was abandoned because some customers complained that they cut their thumbs pushing the holes open.) In landfills around the country, wherever Coors beer cans were discarded, punch-top cans not only identify strata associated with a narrow band of dates but also separate two epochs one from another. One might think of punch-tops playfully as the garbage equivalent of the famous iridium layer found in sediment toward the end of the Cretaceous Era, marking the moment (proponents of the theory believe) when a giant meteor crashed into the planet Earth, exterminating the dinosaurs.

All told, the Garbage Project has conducted nine full-scale excavations of municipal landfills in the United States and two smaller excavations associated with special projects. In the fall of 1991 it also excavated four sites in Canada, the data from which remains largely unanalyzed (and is not reflected in this book). The logistics of the landfill excavations are complex, and they have been overseen in all cases by Wilson Hughes. What is involved? Permission must be obtained from a raft of local officials and union leaders; indemnification notices must be provided to assure local authorities that the Garbage Project carries sufficient insurance against injury; local universities must be scoured for a supply of students to supplement the Garbage Project team; in many cases construction permits, of all things, must be obtained in advance of digging. There is also the whole matter of transportation, not only of personnel but also of large amounts of equipment. And there is the matter of personal accommodation and equipment storage. The time available for excavation is always limited, sometimes extremely so; the research program must be compressed to fit it, and the staff must be "tasked" accordingly. When the excavation has been completed the samples need to be packed and shipped—frequently on ice—back to headquarters or to specialized laboratories. All archaeologists will tell you that field work is mostly laborious, not glamorous; a landfill excavation is archaeology of the laborious kind.

For all the difficulties they present, the Garbage Project's landfill digs have acquired an increasing timeliness and relevance as concerns about solid-waste disposal have grown. Even as the Garbage Project has trained considerable attention on garbage as an analytical tool it has also taken up the problem of garbage itself—garbage as a problem, garbage as symbolized by *Mobro 4000,* the so-called "garbage barge," which sailed from Islip, Long Island, on March 22, 1987, and spent the next fifty-five days plying the seas in search of a place to deposit its 3,168 tons of cargo. Strange though it may seem, although more than 70 percent of America's household and commercial garbage ends up in landfills, very little reliable data existed until recently as to a landfill's contents and biological dynamics. Much of the conventional wisdom about garbage disposal consists of assertions that turn out, upon investigation, to be simplistic or misleading: among them, the assertion that, as trash, plastic, foam, and fast-food packaging are causes for great concern, that biodegradable items are always more desirable than nonbiodegradable ones, that on a per capita basis the nation's households are generating a lot more garbage than they used to, and that we're physically running out of places to put landfills.

This is not to say that garbage isn't a problem in need of serious attention. It is. But if they are to succeed, plans of action must be based on garbage realities. The most critical part of the garbage problem in America is that our notions about the creation and disposal of garbage are often riddled with myth. There are few other subjects of public significance on which popular and official opinion is so consistently misinformed. . . .

Gaps—large gaps—remain in our knowledge of garbage, and of how human behavior relates to it, and of how best to deal with it. But a lighted candle has at least been seized and thrust inside the antechamber.

Notes

1. A note on terminology. Several words for the things we throw away—"garbage," "trash," "refuse," "rubbish"—are used synonymously in casual speech but in fact have different meanings. *Trash* refers specifically to discards that are at least theoretically "dry"—newspapers, boxes, cans, and so on.

Garbage refers technically to "wet" discards—food remains, yard waste, and offal. *Refuse* is an inclusive term for both the wet discards and the dry. *Rubbish* is even more inclusive: It refers to all refuse plus construction and demolition debris. The distinction between wet and dry garbage was important in the days when cities slopped garbage to pigs, and needed to have the wet material separated from the dry; it eventually became irrelevant, but may see a revival if the idea of composting food and yard waste catches on. We will frequently use "garbage" in this book to refer to the totality of human discards because it is the word used most naturally in ordinary speech. The word is etymologically obscure, though it probably derives from Anglo-French, and its earliest associations have to do with working in the kitchen.

2. A question that always comes up is: What about garbage disposers? Garbage disposers are obviously capable of skewing the data in certain garbage categories, and Garbage Project researchers can employ a variety of techniques to compensate for the bias that garbage disposers introduce. Studies were conducted at the very outset of the Garbage Project to determine the discard differential between households with and without disposers, and one eventual result was a set of correction factors for various kinds of garbage (primarily food), broken down by subtype. As a general rule of thumb, households with disposers end up discarding in their trash about half the amount of food waste and food debris as households without disposers. It should be noted, however, that the fact that disposers have ground up some portion of a household's garbage often has little relevance to the larger issues the Garbage Project is trying to address. It means, for example, not that the Garbage Project's findings about the extent of food waste are invalid, but merely that its estimates are conservative.

Bushmen

John Yellen

I followed Dau, kept his slim brown back directly in front of me, as we broke suddenly free from the dense Kalahari bush and crossed through the low wire fence that separated Botswana from Namibia to the West. For that moment while Dau held the smooth wires apart for me, we were out in the open, in the full hot light of the sun and then we entered the shadows, the tangled thickets of arrow grass and thorn bush and mongongo trees once again. As soon as the bush began to close in around us again, I quickly became disoriented, Dau's back my only reference point.

Even then, in that first month of 1968, while my desert boots retained their luster, I knew enough to walk behind, not next to Dau. I had expected the Kalahari Desert to be bare open sand. I had imagined myself looking out over vast stretches that swept across to the horizon. But to my surprise, I found that the dunes were covered with trees and that during the rains the grasses grew high over my head. The bare sand, where I could see it, was littered with leaves, and over these the living trees and brush threw a dappled pattern of sunlight and shade. To look in the far distance and maintain a sense of direction, to narrow my focus and pick a way between the acacia bushes and their thorns, and then to look down, just in front of my feet to search out menacing shapes, was too much for me. Already, in that first month, the Bushmen had shown me a puff adder coiled motionless by the base of an acacia tree, but not until Cumsa the Hunter came up close to it, ready to strike it with his spear, could I finally see what all those hands were pointing at.

As Dau walked, I tried to follow his lead. To my discomfort I knew that many of these bushes had thorns—the Kalahari cloaks itself in thorns—some hidden close to the ground just high enough to rake across my ankles and draw blood when I pushed through, others long and straight and white so they reflected the sun. That morning, just before the border fence, my concentration had lagged and I found myself entangled in wait-a-bit thorns that curved backwards up the branch. So I stopped and this short, brown-skinned Bushman pushed me gently backwards to release the tension, then worked the branch, thorn by thorn from my shirt and my skin.

In the mid-1960s, the South African government had decided to accurately survey the Botswana border, mark it with five-strand fence, and cut a thin firebreak on either side. At intervals they constructed survey towers, strange skeletal affairs, like oil drilling rigs, their tops poking well above the highest mongongo trees. It was to one of these that Dau led me across the border, through the midday sun. Although he would not climb it himself, since it was a white man's tower, he assumed I would. I followed his finger, his chain of logic as I started rather hesitantly up the rusted rungs. I cleared the arrow grass, the acacia bushes, finally the broad leafy crowns of the mongongo nut trees. Just short of the top I stopped and sat, hooked my feet beneath the rung below, and wrapped my arms around the metal edges of the sides.

For a month now I had copied the maps—the lines and the circles the !Kung tribesmen had drawn with their fingers in the sand. I had listened and tried to transcribe names of those places, so unintelligible with their clicks, their rising and falling tones. I had walked with Dau and the others to some of those places, to small camps near ephemeral water holes, but on the ground it was too confusing, the changes in altitude and vegetation too subtle, the sun too nearly overhead to provide any sense of where I was or from where I had come.

For the first time from the tower, I could see an order to the landscape. From up there on the tower, I could see that long thin border scar, could trace it off to the horizon to both the north and south. But beyond that, no evidence, not the slightest sign of a human hand. The Bushmen camps were too few in number, too small and well-hidden in the grass and bush to be visible from here. Likewise, the camp where we anthropologists lived, off to the east at the Dobe waterhole, that also was too small to see.

As Dau had intended, from my perch on that tower I learned a lot. At least now I could use the dunes, the shallow valleys, to know whether I was walking east and west or north and south.

In those first years with the Dobe Bushmen, I did gain at least a partial understanding of that land. And I learned to recognize many of those places, the ones that rate no name at all but are marked only by events—brief, ephemeral happenings that leave no mark on the land. I learned to walk with the Bushmen back from a hunt or a trip for honey or spear-shaft wood and listen. They talked, chattered almost constantly, decorating the bus, these no-name places as they went, putting ornaments of experience on them: "See that tree there, John? That's where we stopped, my brother and I, long before he was married, when he killed a kudu, a big female. We stopped under that tree, hung the meat up there and rested in the shade. But the flies were so bad, the biting flies, that we couldn't stay for long."

It took me a long time to realize that this chatter was not chatter at all, to understand that those remarks were gifts, a private map shared only among a few, an overlay crammed with fine, spidery writing on top of the base map with its named waterholes and large valleys, a map for friends to read. Dau would see a porcupine burrow, tiny, hidden in the vastness of the bush. And at night he could sit by the fire and move the others from point to point across the landscape to that small opening in the ground.

But as an archeologist, I had a task to do—to name those places and to discover what life had been like there in the past. "This place has a name now," I told Dau when I went back in 1976. Not

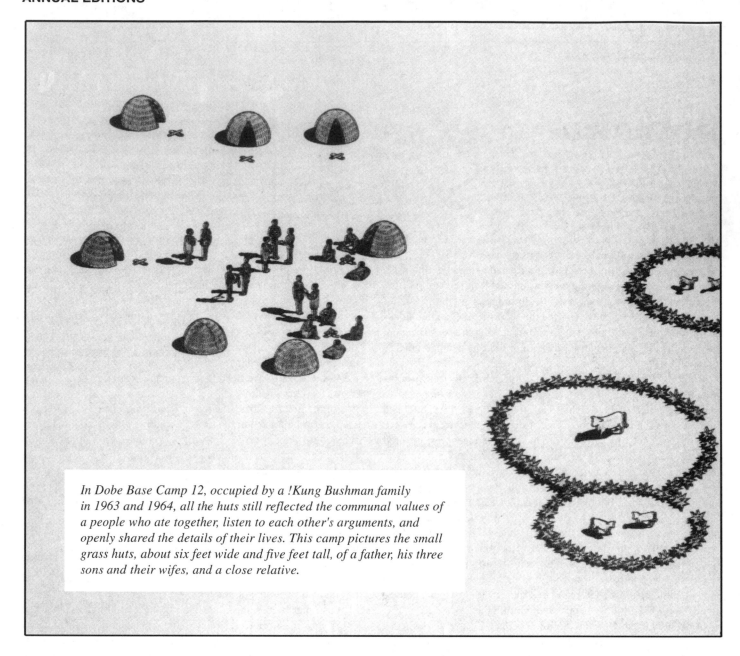

*In Dobe Base Camp 12, occupied by a !Kung Bushman family
in 1963 and 1964, all the huts still reflected the communal values of
a people who ate together, listen to each other's arguments, and
openly shared the details of their lives. This camp pictures the small
grass huts, about six feet wide and five feet tall, of a father, his three
sons and their wifes, and a close relative.*

the chicken camp, because when I was there I kept 15 chickens, or the cobra camp, for the cobra we killed one morning among the nesting hens, but Dobe Base Camp 18. Eighteen because it's the eighteenth of these old abandoned camps I've followed you to in the last three days. See? That's what goes into this ledger, this fat bound book in waterproof ballpoint ink. We could get a reflector in here—a big piece of tin like some metal off a roof and get some satellite or a plane to photograph it. We could tell just where it is then, could mark it on one of those large aerial maps down to the nearest meter if we wanted.

We came back to these camps, these abandoned places on the ground, not once but month after month for the better part of a year. Not just Dau and myself but a whole crew of us, eight Bushmen and I, to dig, to look down into the ground. We started before the sun was too high up in the sky, and later Dau and I sat in the shade sipping thick, rich tea. I asked questions and he talked.

"One day when I was living here, I shot a kudu: an adult female. Hit it with one arrow in the flank. But it went too far and we never found it. Then another day my brother hit a wildebeest, another

adult female and that one we got. We carried it back to camp here and ate it."

"What other meat did you eat here, Dau?"

"One, no two, steenbok, it was."

1948: 28 years ago by my counting was when Dau, his brothers, his family were here. How could he remember the detail? This man sat in the shade and recalled trivial events that have repeated themselves in more or less the same way at so many places over the last three decades.

We dug day after day in the old camps—and found what Dau said we should. Bones, decomposing, but still identifiable: bones of wildebeest and steenbok among the charcoal and mongongo nut shells.

We dug our squares, sifting through the sand for bones. And when I dumped the bones, the odd ostrich eggshell bead, the other bits and pieces out onto the bridge table to sort, so much of what my eyes and ears told me was confirmed in this most tangible form. If excavation in one square revealed the bones of a wildebeest or kudi or other large antelope, then the others would contain them as

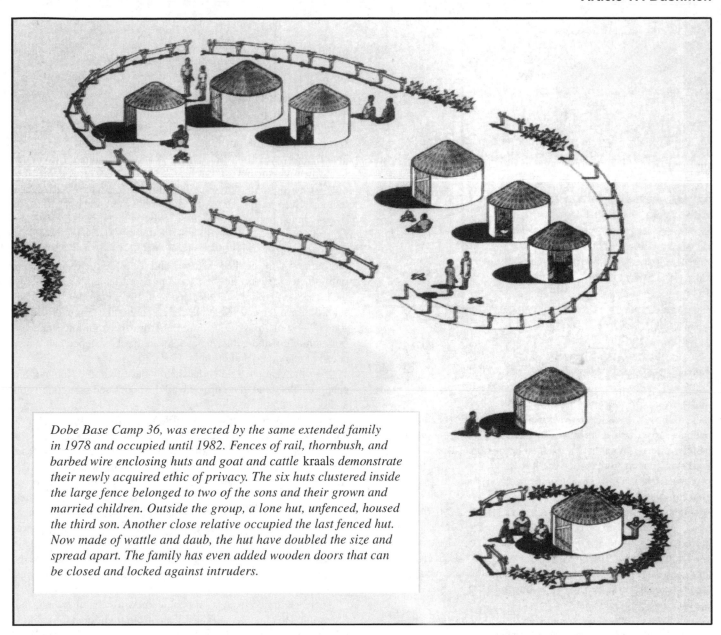

Dobe Base Camp 36, was erected by the same extended family in 1978 and occupied until 1982. Fences of rail, thornbush, and barbed wire enclosing huts and goat and cattle kraals demonstrate their newly acquired ethic of privacy. The six huts clustered inside the large fence belonged to two of the sons and their grown and married children. Outside the group, a lone hut, unfenced, housed the third son. Another close relative occupied the last fenced hut. Now made of wattle and daub, the hut have doubled the size and spread apart. The family has even added wooden doors that can be closed and locked against intruders.

well. In an environment as unpredictable as the Kalahari, where the game was hard to find and the probability of failure high, survival depended on sharing, on spreading the risk. And the bones, distributed almost evenly around the individual family hearths confirmed that. What also impressed me was how little else other than the bones there was. Most archeological sites contain a broad range of debris. But in those years the Bushmen owned so little. Two spears or wooden digging sticks or strings of ostrich eggshell beads were of no more use than one. Better to share, to give away meat or extra belongings and through such gifts create a web of debts, of obligations that some day would be repaid. In 1948, even in 1965, to accumulate material goods made no sense.

When it was hot, which was most of the year, I arranged the bridge table and two chairs in a patch of nearby shade. We sat there with the bound black and red ledger and dumped the bones in a heap in the center of the table, then sorted them out. I did the easy stuff, separated out the turtle shells, the bird bones, set each in a small pile around the table's edge. Dau did the harder part, separated the steenbok from the duiker, the wildebeest from kudu, held

small splintered bone fragments and turned them over and over in his hands. We went through the piles then, one by one, moved each in its turn to the center of the table, sorted them into finer categories, body part by body part, bone by bone. Cryptic notes, bits of data that accumulated page by page. The bones with their sand and grit were transformed into numbers in rows and columns, classes and subclasses which would, I hoped, emerge from some computer to reveal a grander order, a design, an underlying truth.

Taphonomy: That's the proper term for it. The study of burial and preservation. Archeologists dig lots of bones out of the ground, not just from recent places such as these but from sites that span the millions of years of mankind's existence. On the basis of the bones, we try to learn about those ancient people. We try to reconstruct their diet, figure out how the animals were hunted, how they were killed, butchered, and shared.

What appealed to me about the Dobe situation, why I followed Dau, walked out his youth and his early manhood back and forth around the waterhole was the neat, almost laboratory situation Dobe offered. A natural experiment. I could go to a modern camp,

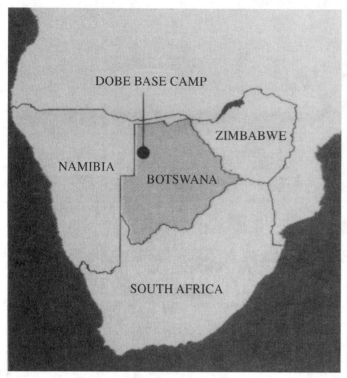

© J. Wisenbaugh

collect those discarded food bones even before the jackals and hyenas had gotten to them, examine and count them, watch the pattern emerge. What happened then to the bones after they'd been trampled, picked over, rained on, lain in the ground for five years? Five years ago? Dobe Base Camp 21, 1971. I could go there, dig up a sample and find out.

What went on farther and farther back in time? Is there a pattern? Try eight years ago. 1968, DBC 18. We could go there to the cobra camp and see. Thirty-four years ago? The camp where Tsaa with the beautiful wife was born. One can watch, can see how things fall apart, can make graphs, curves, shoot them back, watch them arc backwards beyond Dau, beyond Dau's father, back into the true archeological past.

We dug our way through the DBCs, back into the early 1940s, listening day after day to the South African soap operas on the short-wave radio, and our consumption of plastic bags went down and down. Slim pickings in the bone department. And the bones we did find tended to be rotten: They fragmented, fell apart in the sieve.

So we left the 1940s, collapsed the bridge table and the folding chairs and went to that site that played such a crucial role for anthropologists: DBC 12, the 1963 camp where those old myths about hunters and gatherers came up against the hard rock of truth.

They built this camp just after Richard Lee, the pioneer, arrived. They lived there through the winter and hunted warthog with spears and a pack of dogs so good they remember each by name to this day. Richard lived there with them. He watched them—what they did, what they ate, weighed food on his small scale slung with a rope from an acacia tree. He weighed people, sat in camp day after day with his notebook and his wristwatch and scale. He recorded times: when each person left camp in the morning, when each returned for the day.

In this small remnant group, one of the last in the world still living by hunting and gathering, it should be possible, he believed, to

see a reflection, a faint glimmer of the distant universal past of all humanity, a common condition that had continued for millions and millions of years. He went there because of that and for that reason, later on, the rest of us followed him.

What he found in that desert camp, that dry, hard land, set the anthropological world back on its collective ear. What his scale and his wristwatch and his systematic scribbles showed was that we were fooled, that we had it all wrong. To be a hunter and gatherer wasn't that bad after all. They didn't work that hard, even in this land of thorns: For an adult, it came to less time than a nine-to-five office worker puts in on the job. They lived a long time, too, didn't wear out and die young but old-looking, as we had always thought. Even in this camp, the camp with the good hunting dogs, it was plants, not meat, which provided the staff of life. Women walked through the nut groves and collected nuts with their toes, dug in the molapos and sang to each other through the bush. Unlike the game, which spooked so easily and followed the unpredictable rains, the nuts, roots, and berries were dependable, there in plenty, there for the picking. Another distinguished anthropologist, Marshall Sahlins, termed those DBC 12 people "the original affluent society"—something quite different from the traditional conception of hunting and gathering as a mean, hard existence half a step ahead of starvation and doom.

Over the years that name has held—but life in the Kalahari has changed. That kind of camp, with all the bones and mongongo nuts and dogs, is no more.

By the mid-1970s, things were different at Dobe. Diane Gelburd, another of the anthropologists out there then, only needed to look around her to see how the Bushman lifestyle had changed from the way Richard recorded it, from how Sahlins described it. But what had changed the people at DBC 12 who believed that property should be commonly held and shared? What had altered their system of values? That same winter Diane decided to find out.

She devised a simple measure of acculturation that used pictures cut from magazines: an airplane, a sewing machine, a gold mine in South Africa. (Almost no one got the gold mine right.) That was the most enjoyable part of the study. They all liked to look at pictures, to guess.

Then she turned from what people knew to what they believed. She wanted to rank them along a scale, from traditional to acculturated. So again she asked questions:

"Will your children be tattooed?"

To women: "If you were having a difficult childbirth and a white doctor were there, would you ask for assistance?"

To men: "If someone asked you for permission to marry your daughter would you demand (the traditional) bride service?"

Another question so stereotyped that in our own society one would be too embarrassed to ask it: "Would you let your child marry someone from another tribe—a Tswana or a Herero—a white person?"

First knowledge, then belief, and finally material culture. She did the less sensitive questions first. "Do you have a field? What do you grow? What kind of animals do you have? How many of what?" Then came the hard part: She needed to see what people actually owned. I tagged along with her one day and remember the whispers inside one dark mud hut. Trunks were unlocked and hurriedly unpacked away from the entrance to shield them from sight. A blanket spread out on a trunk revealed the secret wealth that belied their statements: "Me? I have nothing." In the semidarkness she made her inventory. Then the trunks were hastily repacked and relocked with relief.

She went through the data, looked at those lists of belongings, itemized them in computer printouts. Here's a man who still hunts. The printout shows it. He has a bow and quiver and arrows on which the poison is kept fresh. He has a spear and snares for birds. He has a small steenbok skin bag, a traditional carryall that rests neatly under his arm.

He also has 19 goats and two donkeys, bought from the Herero or Tswana, who now get Dobe Bushmen to help plant their fields and herd their cows. They pay in livestock, hand-me-down clothing, blankets, and sometimes cash. He has three large metal trunks crammed full: One is packed to the top with shoes, shirts, and pants, most well-worn. He has two large linen mosquito nets, 10 tin cups, and a metal file. He has ropes of beads: strand upon strand—over 200 in all, pounds of small colored glass beads made in Czechoslovakia that I had bought in Johannesburg years earlier. He has four large iron pots and a five-gallon plastic jerry can. He has a plow, a gift from the anthropologists. He has a bridle and bit, light blankets, a large tin basin. He has six pieces of silverware, a mirror and hairbrush, two billycans. His wife and his children together couldn't carry all that. The trunks are too heavy and too large for one person to carry so you would have to have two people for each. What about the plow, those heavy iron pots? Quite a job to carry those through bush, through the thick thorns.

But here is the surprising part. Talk to that man. Read the printout. See what he knows, what he believes. It isn't surprising that he speaks the Herero language and Setswana fluently or that he has worked for the Herero, the anthropologists. Nothing startling there. A budding Dobe capitalist. But then comes the shock: He espouses the traditional values.

"Bushmen share things, John. We share things and depend on each other, help each other out. That's what makes us different from the black people."

But the same person, his back to the door, opens his trunks, unlocks them one by one, lays out the blankets, the beads, then quickly closes each before he opens the next.

Multiply that. Make a whole village of people like that, and you can see the cumulative effect: You can actually measure it. As time goes on, as people come to own more possessions; the huts move farther and farther apart.

In the old days a camp was cosy, intimate and close. You could sit there by one fire and look into the other grass huts, see what the other people were doing, what they were making or eating. You heard the conversations, the arguments and banter.

We ask them why the new pattern?

Says Dau: "It's because of the livestock that we put our huts this way. They can eat the grass from the roofs and the sides of our houses. So we have to build fences to keep them away and to do that, you must have room between the huts."

I look up from the fire, glance around the camp, say nothing. No fences there. Not a single one around any of the huts, although I concede that one day they probably will build them. But why construct a lot of separate small fences, one around each hut? Why not clump the huts together the way they did in the old days and make a single large fence around the lot? Certainly a more efficient approach. Why worry about fences now in any case? The only exposed grass is on the roofs, protected by straight mud walls and nothing short of an elephant or giraffe could eat it.

Xashe's answer is different. Another brief reply. An attempt to dispose of the subject politely but quickly. "It's fire, John. That's what we're worried about. If we put our houses too close together, if one catches fire, the others will burn as well. We don't want one fire to burn all our houses down. That's why we build them so far apart."

But why worry about fire now? What about in the old days when the huts were so close, cheek by jowl? Why is it that when the huts were really vulnerable, when they were built entirely of dried grass, you didn't worry about fires then?

You read Diane's interviews and look at those lists of how much people own. You see those shielded mud huts with doors spaced, so far apart. You also listen to the people you like and trust. People who always have been honest with you. You hear their explanations and realize the evasions are not for you but for themselves. You see things they can't. But nothing can be done. It would be ludicrous to tell these brothers: "Don't you see, my friends, the lack of concordance between your values and the changing reality of your world?"

Now, years after the DBC study, I sit with data spread out before me and it is so clear. Richard's camp in 1963: just grass huts, a hearth in front of each. Huts and hearths in a circle, nothing more. 1968: more of the same. The following year though the first *kraal* appears, just a small thorn enclosure, some acacia bushes cut and dragged haphazardly together for their first few goats. It's set apart way out behind the circle of huts. On one goes, from plot to plot, following the pattern from year to year. The huts change from grass to mud. They become larger, more solidly built. Goats, a few at first, then more of them. So you build a fence around your house to keep them away from the grass roofs. The *kraals* grow larger, move in closer to be incorporated finally into the circle of huts itself. The huts become spaced farther and farther apart, seemingly repelled over time, one from the next. People, families move farther apart.

The bones tell the same story. 1947: All the bones from wild animals, game caught in snares or shot with poisoned arrows—game taken from the bush. By 1964 a few goat bones, a cow bone or two, but not many. Less than 20 percent of the total. Look then at the early 1970s and watch the line on the graph climb slowly upwards—by 1976 over 80 percent from domesticated stock.

But what explains the shattering of this society? Why is this hunting and gathering way of life, so resilient in the face of uncertainty, falling apart? It hasn't been a direct force—a war, the ravages of disease. It is the internal conflicts, the tensions, the inconsistencies, the impossibility of reconciling such different views of the world.

At Dobe it is happening to them all together. All of the huts have moved farther apart in lockstep, which makes it harder for them to see how incompatible the old system is with the new. But Rakudu, a Bushman who lived at the Mahopa waterhole eight miles down the valley from Dobe, was a step ahead of the rest. He experienced, before the rest of them, their collective fate.

When I was at the Cobra Camp in 1969, Rakudu lived down near Mahopa, off on his own, a mile or so away from the pastoral Herero villages. He had two hats and a very deep bass voice, both so strange, so out of place in a Bushman. He was a comical sort of man with the hats and that voice and a large Adam's apple that bobbed up and down.

The one hat must have been a leftover from the German-Herero wars because no one in Botswana wore a hat like that—a real pith helmet with a solid top and rounded brim. It had been cared for over the years because, although soiled and faded, it still retained the original strap that tucks beneath the chin. The second hat was also unique—a World War I aviator's hat, one of those leather sacks that fits tightly over the head and buckles under the chin. Only the goggles were missing.

I should have seen then how out of place the ownership of two hats was in that hunter-gatherer world. Give two hats like that to any of the others and one would have been given away on the spot. A month or two later, the other would become a gift as well. Moving goods as gifts and favors along that chain of human ties. That was the way to maintain those links, to keep them strong.

When I went to Rakudu's village and realized what he was up to, I could see that he was one of a kind. The mud-walled huts in his village made it look like a Herero village—not a grass hut in sight. And when I came, Rakudu pulled out a hand-carved wood and leather chair and set it in the shade. This village was different from any of the Bushman camps I had seen. Mud huts set out in a circle, real clay storage bins to hold the corn—not platforms in a tree—and *kraals* for lots of goats and donkeys. He had a large field, too, several years before the first one appeared at Dobe.

Why shouldn't Bushmen do it—build their own villages, model their subsistence after the Herero? To plant a field, to tend goats, to build mud-walled houses like that was not hard to do. Work for the Herero a while and get an axe, accumulate the nucleus of a herd, buy or borrow the seeds. That year the rains were long and heavy. The sand held the water and the crickets and the birds didn't come. So the harvest was good, and I could sit there in the carved chair and look at Rakudu's herd of goats and their young ones and admire him for his industry, for what he had done.

Only a year later I saw him and his eldest son just outside the Cobra Camp. I went over and sat in the sand and listened to the negotiations for the marriage Rakudu was trying to arrange. His son's most recent wife had run away, and Rakudu was discussing a union between his son and Dau the Elder's oldest daughter who was just approaching marriageable age. They talked about names and Dau the Elder explained why the marriage couldn't take place. It was clear that the objection was trivial, that he was making an excuse. Even I could see that his explanation was a face-saving gesture to make the refusal easier for all of them.

Later I asked Dau the Elder why he did it. It seemed like a good deal to me. "Rakudu has all that wealth, those goats and field. I'd think that you would be anxious to be linked with a family like that. Look at all you have to gain. Is the son difficult? Did he beat his last wife?"

"She left because she was embarrassed. The wife before her ran away for the same reason and so did the younger brother's wife," he said. "Both brothers treated their wives well. The problem wasn't that. It was when the wives' relatives came. That's when it became so hard for the women because Rakudu and his sons are such stingy men. They wouldn't give anything away, wouldn't share anything with them. Rakudu has a big herd just like the Herero, and he wouldn't kill goats for them to eat."

Not the way Bushmen should act toward relatives, not by the traditional value system at least. Sharing, the most deeply held Bushman belief, and that man with the two hats wouldn't go along. Herero are different. You can't expect them to act properly, to show what is only common decency; you must take them as they are. But someone like Rakudu, a Bushman, should know better than that. So the wives walked out and left for good.

But Rakudu understood what was happening, how he was trapped—and he tried to respond. If you can't kill too many goats from the herd that has become essential to you, perhaps you can find something else of value to give away. Rakudu thought he had an answer.

He raised tobacco in one section of his field. Tobacco, a plant not really adapted to a place like the northern Kalahari, has to be weeded, watered by hand, and paid special care. Rakudu did that and for one year at least harvested a tobacco crop.

Bushmen crave tobacco and Rakudu hoped he had found a solution—that they would accept tobacco in place of goats, in place of mealie meal. A good try. Perhaps the only one open to him. But, as it turned out, not good enough. Rakudu's son could not find a wife.

Ironic that a culture can die yet not a single person perish. A sense of identity, of a shared set of rules, of participation in a single destiny binds individuals together into a tribe or cultural group. Let that survive long enough, let the participants pass this sense through enough generations, one to the next, create enough debris, and they will find their way into the archeological record, into the study of cultures remembered only by their traces left on the land.

Rakudu bought out. He, his wife, and his two sons sold their goats for cash, took the money and walked west, across the border scar that the South Africans had cut, through the smooth fence wire and down the hard calcrete road beyond. They became wards of the Afrikaaners, were lost to their own culture, let their fate pass into hands other than their own. At Chum kwe, the mission station across the border 34 miles to the west, they were given numbers and the right to stand in line with the others and have mealie meal and other of life's physical essentials handed out to them. As wards of the state, that became their right. When the problems, the contradictions of your life are insoluble, a paternalistic hand provides one easy out.

Dau stayed at Dobe. Drive there today and you can find his mud-walled hut just by the waterhole. But he understands: He has married off his daughter, his first-born girl to a wealthy Chum kwe man who drives a tractor—an old man, more than twice her age, and by traditional Bushmen standards not an appropriate match. Given the chance, one by one, the others will do the same.

JOHN YELLEN, director of the anthropology program at the National Science Foundation, has returned to the Kalahari four times since 1968.

From *Science*, May 1985. Copyright © 1985 by John Yellen. Reprinted by permission of the author.

The Maya Collapses

**Mysteries of lost cities ■ The Maya environment ■ Maya agriculture ■
Maya history ■ Copán ■ Complexities of collapses ■ Wars and droughts ■
Collapse in the southern lowlands ■ The Maya message ■**

JARED DIAMOND

By now, millions of modern tourists have visited ruins of the ancient Maya civilization that collapsed over a thousand years ago in Mexico's Yucatán Peninsula and adjacent parts of Central America. All of us love a romantic mystery, and the Maya offer us one at our doorstep, almost as close for Americans as the Anasazi ruins. To visit a former Maya city, we need only board a direct flight from the U.S. to the modern Mexican state capital city of Mérida, jump into a rental car or minibus, and drive an hour on a paved highway [map, p. 161, omitted].

Today, many Maya ruins, with their great temples and monuments, still lie surrounded by jungle, far from current human settlement [Plate 12, omitted]. Yet they were once the sites of the New World's most advanced Native American civilization before European arrival, and the only one with extensive deciphered written texts. How could ancient peoples have supported urban societies in areas where few farmers eke out a living today? The Maya cities impress us not only with that mystery and with their beauty, but also because they are "pure" archaeological sites. That is, their locations became depopulated, so they were not covered up by later buildings as were so many other ancient cities, like the Aztec capital of Tenochtitlan (now buried under modern Mexico City) and Rome.

Maya cities remained deserted, hidden by trees, and virtually unknown to the outside world until rediscovered in 1839 by a rich American lawyer named John Stephens, together with the English draftsman Frederick Catherwood. Having heard rumors of ruins in the jungle, Stephens got President Martin Van Buren to appoint him ambassador to the Confederation of Central American Republics, an amorphous political entity then extending from modern Guatemala to Nicaragua, as a front for his archaeological explorations. Stephens and Catherwood ended up exploring 44 sites and cities. From the extraordinary quality of the buildings and the art, they realized that these were not the work of savages (in their words) but of a vanished high civilization. They recognized that some of the carvings on the stone monuments constituted writing, and they correctly guessed that it related historical events and the names of people. On his return,

Stephens wrote two travel books, illustrated by Catherwood and describing the ruins, that became best sellers.

A few quotes from Stephens's writings will give a sense of the romantic appeal of the Maya: "The city was desolate. No remnant of this race hangs round the ruins, with traditions handed down from father to son and from generation to generation. It lay before us like a shattered bark in the midst of the ocean, her mast gone, her name effaced, her crew perished, and none to tell whence she came, to whom she belonged, how long on her journey, or what caused her destruction.... Architecture, sculpture, and painting, all the arts which embellish life, had flourished in this overgrown forest; orators, warriors, and statesmen, beauty, ambition, and glory had lived and passed away, and none knew that such things had been, or could tell of their past existence.... Here were the remains of a cultivated, polished, and peculiar people, who had passed through all the stages incident to the rise and fall of nations; reached their golden age, and perished.... We went up to their desolate temples and fallen altars; and wherever we moved we saw the evidence of their taste, their skill in arts.... We called back into life the strange people who gazed in sadness from the wall; pictured them, in fanciful costumes and adorned with plumes of feather, ascending the terraces of the palace and the steps leading to the temples.... In the romance of the world's history nothing ever impressed me more forcibly than the spectacle of this once great and lovely city, overturned, desolate, and lost, ... overgrown with trees for miles around, and without even a name to distinguish it." Those sensations are what tourists drawn to Maya ruins still feel today, and why we find the Maya collapse so fascinating.

The Maya story has several advantages for all of us interested in prehistoric collapses. First, the Maya written records that have survived, although frustratingly incomplete, are still useful for reconstructing Maya history in much greater detail than we can reconstruct Easter Island, or even Anasazi history with its tree rings and packrat middens. The great art and architecture of Maya cities have resulted in far more archaeologists studying the Maya than would have been the case if they had just been illiterate hunter-gatherers living in archaeologically invisible hovels. Climatologists and paleoecologists have recently been able to recognize several signals of ancient climate and environmental changes that contributed to the Maya collapse.

Finally, today there are still Maya people living in their ancient homeland and speaking Maya languages. Because much ancient Maya culture survived the collapse, early European visitors to the homeland recorded information about contemporary Maya society that played a vital role in our understanding ancient Maya society. The first Maya contact with Europeans came already in 1502, just 10 years after Christopher Columbus's "discovery" of the New World, when Columbus on the last of his four voyages captured a trading canoe that may have been Maya. In 1527 the Spanish began in earnest to conquer the Maya, but it was not until 1697 that they subdued the last principality. Thus, the Spanish had opportunities to observe independent Maya societies for a period of nearly two centuries. Especially important, both for bad and for good, was the bishop Diego de Landa, who resided in the Yucatán Peninsula for most of the years from 1549 to 1578. On the one hand, in one of history's worst acts of cultural vandalism, he burned all Maya manuscripts that he could locate in his effort to eliminate "paganism," so that only four survive today. On the other hand, he wrote a detailed account of Maya society, and he obtained from an informant a garbled explanation of Maya writing that eventually, nearly four centuries later, turned out to offer clues to its decipherment.

A further reason for our devoting a chapter to the Maya is to provide an antidote to our other chapters on past societies, which consist disproportionately of small societies in somewhat fragile and geographically isolated environments, and behind the cutting edge of contemporary technology and culture. The Maya were none of those things. Instead, they were culturally the most advanced society (or among the most advanced ones) in the pre-Columbian New World, the only one with extensive preserved writing, and located within one of the two heartlands of New World civilization (Mesoamerica). While their environment did present some problems associated with its karst terrain and unpredictably fluctuating rainfall, it does not rank as notably fragile by world standards, and it was certainly less fragile than the environments of ancient Easter Island, the Anasazi area, Greenland, or modern Australia. Lest one be misled into thinking that crashes are a risk only for small peripheral societies in fragile areas, the Maya warn us that crashes can also befall the most advanced and creative societies.

From the perspective of our five-point framework for understanding societal collapses, the Maya illustrate four of our points. They did damage their environment, especially by deforestation and erosion. Climate changes (droughts) did contribute to the Maya collapse, probably repeatedly. Hostilities among the Maya themselves did play a large role. Finally, political/cultural factors, especially the competition among kings and nobles that led to a chronic emphasis on war and erecting monuments rather than on solving underlying problems, also contributed. The remaining item on our five-point list, trade or cessation of trade with external friendly societies, does not appear to have been essential in sustaining the Maya or in causing their downfall. While obsidian (their preferred raw material for making into stone tools), jade, gold, and shells were imported into the Maya area, the latter three items were non-essential luxuries. Obsidian tools remained widely distributed in the Maya area long after the political collapse, so obsidian was evidently never in short supply.

To understand the Maya, let's begin by considering their environment, which we think of as "jungle" or "tropical rainforest." That's not true, and the reason why not proves to be important. Properly speaking, tropical rainforests grow in high-rainfall equatorial areas that remain wet or humid all year round. But the Maya homeland lies more than a thousand miles from the equator, at latitudes 17° to 22°N, in a habitat termed a "seasonal tropical forest." That is, while there does tend to be a rainy season from May to October, there is also a dry season from January through April. If one focuses on the wet months, one calls the Maya homeland a "seasonal tropical forest"; if one focuses on the dry months, one could instead describe it as a "seasonal desert."

From north to south in the Yucatán Peninsula, rainfall increases from 18 to 100 inches per year, and the soils become thicker, so that the southern peninsula was agriculturally more productive and supported denser populations. But rainfall in the Maya homeland is unpredictably variable between years; some recent years have had three or four times more rain than other years. Also, the timing of rainfall within the year is somewhat unpredictable, so it can easily happen that farmers plant their crops in anticipation of rain and then the rains do not come when expected. As a result, modern farmers attempting to grow corn in the ancient Maya homelands have faced frequent crop failures, especially in the north. The ancient Maya were presumably more experienced and did better, but nevertheless they too must have faced risks of crop failures from droughts and hurricanes.

Although southern Maya areas received more rainfall than northern areas, problems of water were paradoxically more severe in the wet south. While that made things hard for ancient Maya living in the south, it has also made things hard for modern archaeologists who have difficulty understanding why ancient droughts would have caused bigger problems in the wet south than in the dry north. The likely explanation is that a lens of freshwater underlies the Yucatán Peninsula, but surface elevation increases from north to south, so that as one moves south the land surface lies increasingly higher above the water table. In the northern peninsula the elevation is sufficiently low that the ancient Maya were able to reach the water table at deep sinkholes called cenotes, or at deep caves; all tourists who have visited the Maya city of Chichén Itzá will remember the great cenotes there. In low-elevation north coastal areas without sinkholes, the Maya may have been able to get down to the water table by digging wells up to 75 feet deep. Water is readily available in many parts of Belize that have rivers, along the Usumacinta River in the west, and around a few lakes in the Petén area of the south. But much of the south lies too high above the water table for cenotes or wells to reach down to it. Making matters worse, most of the Yucatán Peninsula consists of karst, a porous sponge-like limestone terrain where rain runs straight into the ground and where little or no surface water remains available.

How did those dense southern Maya populations deal with their resulting water problem? It initially surprises us that many of their cities were not built next to the few rivers but instead on promontories in rolling uplands. The explanation is that the Maya excavated depressions, modified natural depressions, and then plugged up leaks in the karst by plastering the bottoms of the depressions in order to create cisterns and reservoirs, which collected rain from large plastered catchment basins and stored it for use in the dry season. For example, reservoirs at the Maya city of Tikal held enough water to meet the drinking water needs of about 10,000 people for a period of 18 months. At the city of Coba the Maya built dikes around a lake in order to raise its level and make their water supply more reliable. But the inhabitants of Tikal and other cities dependent on reservoirs for drinking water would still have been in deep trouble if 18 months passed without rain in a prolonged drought. A shorter drought in which they exhausted their stored food supplies might already have gotten them in deep trouble through starvation, because growing crops required rain rather than reservoirs.

Of particular importance for our purposes are the details of Maya agriculture, which was based on crops domesticated in Mexico—especially corn with beans being second in importance. For the elite as well as commoners, corn constituted at least 70% of the Maya diet, as deduced from isotope analyses of ancient Maya skeletons. Their sole domestic animals were the dog, turkey, Muscovy duck, and a stingless bee yielding honey, while their most important wild meat source was deer that they hunted, plus fish at some sites. However, the few animal bones at Maya archaeological sites suggest that the quantity of meat available to the Maya was low. Venison was mainly a luxury food for the elite.

It was formerly believed that Maya farming was based on slash-and-burn agriculture (so-called swidden agriculture) in which forest is cleared and burned, crops are grown in the resulting field for a year or a few years until the soil is exhausted, and then the field is abandoned for a long fallow period of 15 or 20 years until regrowth of wild vegetation restores fertility to the soil. Because most of the landscape under a swidden agricultural system is fallow at any given time, it can support only modest population densities. Thus, it was a surprise for archaeologists to discover that ancient Maya population densities, estimated from numbers of stone foundations of farmhouses, were often far higher than what swidden agriculture could support. The actual values are the subject of much dispute and evidently varied among areas, but frequently cited estimates reach 250 to 750, possibly even 1,500, people per square mile. (For comparison, even today the two most densely populated countries in Africa, Rwanda and Burundi, have population densities of only about 750 and 540 people per square mile, respectively.) Hence the ancient Maya must have had some means of increasing agricultural production beyond what was possible through swidden alone.

Many Maya areas do show remains of agricultural structures designed to increase production, such as terracing of hill slopes to retain soil and moisture, irrigation systems, and arrays of canals and drained or raised fields. The latter systems, which are well attested elsewhere in the world and which require a lot of labor to construct, but which reward the labor with increased food production, involve digging canals to drain a waterlogged area, fertilizing and raising the level of the fields between the canals by dumping muck and water hyacinths dredged out of canals onto the fields, and thereby keeping the fields themselves from being inundated. Besides harvesting crops grown over the fields, farmers with raised fields also "grow" wild fish and turtles in the canals (actually, let them grow themselves) as an additional food source. However, other Maya areas, such as the well-studied cities of Copán and Tikal, show little archaeological evidence of terracing, irrigation, or raised- or drained-field systems. Instead, their inhabitants must have used archaeologically invisible means to increase food production, by mulching, floodwater farming, shortening the time that a field is left fallow, and tilling the soil to restore soil fertility, or in the extreme omitting the fallow period entirely and growing crops every year, or in especially moist areas growing two crops per year.

Socially stratified societies, including modern American and European society, consist of farmers who produce food, plus non-farmers such as bureaucrats and soldiers who do not produce food but merely consume the food grown by the farmers and are in effect parasites on farmers. Hence in any stratified society the farmers must grow enough surplus food to meet not only their own needs but also those of the other consumers. The number of non-producing consumers that can be supported depends on the society's agricultural productivity. In the United States today, with its highly efficient agriculture, farmers make up only 2% of our population, and each farmer can feed on the average 125 other people (American non-farmers plus people in export markets overseas). Ancient Egyptian agriculture, although much less efficient than modern mechanized agriculture, was still efficient enough for an Egyptian peasant to produce five times the food required for himself and his family. But a Maya peasant could produce only twice the needs of himself and his family. At least 70% of Maya society consisted of peasants. That's because Maya agriculture suffered from several limitations.

First, it yielded little protein. Corn, by far the dominant crop, has a lower protein content than the Old World staples of wheat and barley. The few edible domestic animals already mentioned included no large ones and yielded much less meat than did Old World cows, sheep, pigs, and goats. The Maya depended on a narrower range of crops than did Andean farmers (who in addition to corn also had potatoes, high-protein quinoa, and many other plants, plus llamas for meat), and much narrower again than the variety of crops in China and in western Eurasia.

Another limitation was that Maya corn agriculture was less intensive and productive than the Aztecs' *chinampas* (a very productive type of raised-field agriculture), the raised fields of the Tiwanaku civilization of the Andes, Moche irrigation on the coast of Peru, or fields tilled by animal-drawn plows over much of Eurasia.

Still a further limitation arose from the humid climate of the Maya area, which made it difficult to store corn beyond a year, whereas the Anasazi living in the dry climate of the U.S. Southwest could store it for three years.

Finally, unlike Andean Indians with their llamas, and unlike Old World peoples with their horses, oxen, donkeys, and camels, the Maya had no animal-powered transport or plows. All overland transport for the Maya went on the backs of human porters. But if you send out a porter carrying a load of corn to accompany an army into the field, some of that load of corn is required to feed the porter himself on the trip out, and some more to feed him on the trip back, leaving only a fraction of the load available to feed the army. The longer the trip, the less of the load is left over from the porter's own requirements. Beyond a march of a few days to a week, it becomes uneconomical to send porters carrying corn to provision armies or markets. Thus, the modest productivity of Maya agriculture, and their lack of draft animals, severely limited the duration and distance possible for their military campaigns.

We are accustomed to thinking of military success as determined by quality of weaponry, rather than by food supply. But a clear example of how improvements in food supply may decisively increase military success comes from the history of Maori New Zealand. The Maori are the Polynesian people who were the first to settle New Zealand. Traditionally, they fought frequent fierce wars against each other, but only against closely neighboring tribes. Those wars were limited by the modest productivity of their agriculture, whose staple crop was sweet potatoes. It was not possible to grow enough sweet potatoes to feed an army in the field for a long time or on distant marches. When Europeans arrived in New Zealand, they brought potatoes, which beginning around 1815 considerably increased Maori crop yields. Maori could now grow enough food to supply armies in the field for many weeks. The result was a 15-year period in Maori history, from 1818 until 1833, when Maori tribes that had acquired potatoes and guns from the English sent armies out on raids to attack tribes hundreds of miles away that had not yet acquired potatoes and guns. Thus, the potato's productivity relieved previous limitations on Maori warfare, similar to the limitations that low-productivity corn agriculture imposed on Maya warfare.

Those food supply considerations may contribute to explaining why Maya society remained politically divided among small kingdoms that were perpetually at war with each other, and that never became unified into large empires like the Aztec Empire of the Valley of Mexico (fed with the help of their *chinampa* agriculture and other forms of intensification) or the Inca Empire of the Andes (fed by more diverse crops carried by llamas over well-built roads). Maya armies and bureaucracies remained small and unable to mount lengthy campaigns over long distances. (Even much later, in 1848, when the Maya revolted against their Mexican overlords and a Maya army seemed to be on the verge of victory, the army had to break off fighting and go home to harvest another crop of corn.) Many Maya kingdoms held populations of only up to 25,000 to 50,000 people, none over half a million, within a radius of two or three days' walk from the king's palace. (The actual numbers are again highly controversial among archaeologists.) From the tops of the temples of some Maya kingdoms, it was possible to see the temples of the nearest kingdom. Maya cities remained small (mostly less than one square mile in area), without the large populations and big markets of Teotihuacán and Tenochtitlán in the Valley of Mexico, or of Chan-Chan and Cuzco in Peru, and without archaeological evidence of the royally managed food storage and trade that characterized ancient Greece and Mesopotamia.

Now for a quick crash-course in Maya history. The Maya area is part of the larger ancient Native American cultural region known as Mesoamerica, which extended approximately from Central Mexico to Honduras and constituted (along with the Andes of South America) one of the two New World centers of innovation before European arrival. The Maya shared much in common with other Mesoamerican societies not only in what they possessed, but also in what they lacked. For example, surprisingly to modern Westerners with expectations based on Old World civilizations, Mesoamerican societies lacked metal tools, pulleys and other machines, wheels (except locally as toys), boats with sails, and domestic animals large enough to carry loads or pull a plow. All of those great Maya temples were constructed by stone and wooden tools and by human muscle power alone.

Of the ingredients of Maya civilization, many were acquired by the Maya from elsewhere in Mesoamerica. For instance, Mesoamerican agriculture, cities, and writing first arose outside the Maya area itself, in valleys and coastal lowlands to the west and southwest, where corn and beans and squash were domesticated and became important dietary components by 3000 B.C., pottery arose around 2500 B.C., villages by 1500 B.C., cities among the Olmecs by 1200 B.C., writing appeared among the Zapotecs in Oaxaca around or after 600 B.C., and the first states arose around 300 B.C. Two complementary calendars, a solar calendar of 365 days and a ritual calendar of 260 days, also arose outside the Maya area. Other elements of Maya civilization were either invented, perfected, or modified by the Maya themselves.

Within the Maya area, villages and pottery appeared around or after 1000 B.C., substantial buildings around 500 B.C., and writing around 400 B.C. All preserved ancient Maya writing, constituting a total of about 15,000 inscriptions, is on stone and pottery and deals only with kings, nobles, and their conquests [Plate 13, omitted]. There is not a single mention of commoners. When Spaniards arrived, the Maya were still using bark paper coated with plaster to write books, of which the sole four that escaped Bishop Landa's fires turned out to be treatises on astronomy and the calendar. The ancient Maya also had had such bark-paper books, often depicted on their pottery, but only decayed remains of them have survived in tombs.

The famous Maya Long Count calendar begins on August 11, 3114 B.C.—just as our own calendar begins on January 1 of the first year of the Christian era. We know the significance to us of that day-zero of our calendar: it's the supposed beginning of the year in which Christ was born. Presumably the Maya also attached some significance to their own day zero, but we don't know what it was. The first preserved Long Count date is only A.D. 197 for a monument in the Maya area and 36 B.C. outside the Maya area, indicating that the Long Count calendar's day-zero was backdated to August 11, 3114 B.C. long after the facts; there was no writing anywhere in the New World then, nor would there be for 2,500 years after that date.

Our calendar is divided into units of days, weeks, months, years, decades, centuries, and millennia: for example, the date of February 19, 2003, on which I wrote the first draft of this paragraph, means the 19th day of the second month in the third year of the first decade of the first century of the third millennium beginning with the birth of Christ. Similarly, the Maya Long Count calendar named dates in units of days (*kin*), 20 days (*uinal*), 360 days (*tun*), 7,200 days or approximately 20 years (*katunn*), and 144,000 days or approximately 400 years (*baktun*). All of Maya history falls into baktuns 8, 9, and 10.

The so-called Classic period of Maya civilization begins in baktun 8, around A.D. 250, when evidence for the first kings and dynasties appears. Among the glyphs (written signs) on Maya monuments, students of Maya writing recognized a few dozen, each of which was concentrated in its own geographic area, and which are now considered to have had the approximate meaning of dynasties or kingdoms. In addition to Maya kings having their own name glyphs and palaces, many nobles also had their own inscriptions and palaces. In Maya society the king also functioned as high priest carrying the responsibility to attend to astronomical and calendrical rituals, and thereby to bring rain and prosperity, which the king claimed to have the supernatural power to deliver because of his asserted family relationship to the gods. That is, there was a tacitly understood quid pro quo: the reason why the peasants supported the luxurious lifestyle of the king and his court, fed him corn and venison, and built his palaces was because he had made implicit big promises to the peasants. As we shall see, kings got into trouble with their peasants if a drought came, because that was tantamount to the breaking of a royal promise.

From A.D. 250 onwards, the Maya population (as judged from the number of archaeologically attested house sites), the number of monuments and buildings, and the number of Long Count dates on monuments and pottery increased almost exponentially, to reach peak numbers in the 8th century A.D. The largest monuments were erected towards the end of that Classic period. Numbers of all three of those indicators of a complex society declined throughout the 9th century, until the last known Long Count date on any monument fell in baktun 10, in the year A.D. 909. That decline of Maya population, architecture, and the Long Count calendar constitutes what is known as the Classic Maya collapse.

As an example of the collapse, let's consider in more detail a small but densely built city whose ruins now lie in western Honduras at a site known as Copán, and described in two recent books by archaeologist David Webster. For agricultural purposes the best land in the Copán area consists of five pockets of flat land with fertile alluvial soil along a river valley, with a tiny total area of only 10 square miles; the largest of those five pockets, known as the Copán pocket, has an area of only 5 square miles. Much of the land around Copán consists of steep hills, and nearly half of the hill area has a slope above 16% (approximately double the slope of the steepest grade that you are likely to encounter on an American highway). Soil in the hills is less fertile, more acidic, and poorer in phosphate than valley soil. Today, corn yields from valley-bottom fields are two or three times those of fields on hill slopes, which suffer rapid erosion and lose three-quarters of their productivity within a decade of farming.

As judged by numbers of house sites, population growth in the Copán Valley rose steeply from the 5th century up to a peak estimated at around 27,000 people at A.D. 750–900. Maya written history at Copán begins in the year with a Long Count date corresponding to A.D. 426, when later monuments record retrospectively that some person related to nobles at Tikal and Teotihuacán arrived. Construction of royal monuments glorifying kings was especially massive between A.D. 650 and 750. After A.D. 700, nobles other than kings also got into the act and began erecting their own palaces, of which there were about twenty by the year A.D. 800, when one of those palaces is known to have consisted of 50 buildings with room for about 250 people. All of those nobles and their courts would have increased the burden that the king and his own court imposed on the peasants. The last big buildings at Copán were put up around A.D. 800, and the last Long Count date on an incomplete altar possibly bearing a king's name has the date of A.D. 822.

Archaeological surveys of different types of habitats in the Copán Valley show that they were occupied in a regular sequence. The first area farmed was the large Copán pocket of valley bottomland, followed by occupation of the other four bottomland pockets. During that time the human population was growing, but there was not yet occupation of the hills. Hence that increased population must have been accommodated by intensifying production in the bottomland pockets by some combination of shorter fallow periods, double-cropping, and possibly some irrigation.

By the year A.D. 650, people started to occupy the hill slopes, but those hill sites were cultivated only for about a century. The percentage of Copán's total population that was in the hills, rather than in the valleys, reached a maximum of 41%, then declined until the population again became concentrated in the valley pockets. What caused that pullback of population from the hills? Excavation of the foundations of buildings in the valley floor showed that they became covered with sediment during the 8th century, meaning that the hill slopes were getting eroded and probably also leached of nutrients. Those acidic infertile hill soils were being carried down into the valley and blanketing the more fertile valley soils, where they would have reduced agricultural yields. This ancient quick abandonment of hillsides coincides with modern Maya experience that fields in the hills have low fertility and that their soils become rapidly exhausted.

The reason for that erosion of the hillsides is clear: the forests that formerly covered them and protected their soils were being cut down. Dated pollen samples show that the pine forests originally covering the upper elevations of the hill slopes were eventually all cleared. Calculation suggests that most of those felled pine trees were being burned for fuel, while the rest were used for construction or for making plaster. At other Maya sites from the pre-Classic era, where the Maya went overboard in lavish use of thick plaster on buildings, plaster production may have been a major cause of deforestation. Besides causing sediment accumulation in the valleys and depriving valley inhabitants of wood supplies, that deforestation may have begun to cause a "man-made drought" in the valley bottom because forests play a major role in water cycling, such that massive deforestation tends to result in lowered rainfall.

Hundreds of skeletons recovered from Copán archaeological sites have been studied for signs of disease and malnutrition, such as porous bones and stress lines in the teeth. These skeletal signs show that the health of Copán's inhabitants deteriorated from A.D. 650 to 850, both among the elite and among the commoners, although the health of commoners was worse.

Recall that Copán's population was increasing steeply while the hills were being occupied. The subsequent abandonment of all of those fields in the hills meant that the burden of feeding the extra population formerly dependent on the hills now fell increasingly on the valley floor, and that more and more people were competing for the food grown on those 10 square miles of valley bottomland. That would have led to fighting among the farmers themselves for the best land, or for any land, just as in modern Rwanda (Chapter 10). Because Copán's king was failing to deliver on his promises of rain and prosperity in return for the power and luxuries that he claimed, he would have been the scapegoat for this agricultural failure. That may explain why the last that we hear from any Copán king is A.D. 822 (that last Long Count date at Copán), and why the royal palace was burned around A.D. 850. However, the continued production of some luxury goods suggest that some nobles managed to carry on with their lifestyle after the king's downfall, until around A.D. 975.

To judge from datable pieces of obsidian, Copán's total population decreased more gradually than did its signs of kings and nobles. The estimated population in the year A.D. 950 was still around 15,000, or 54% of the peak population of 27,000. That population continued to dwindle, until there are no more signs of anyone in the Copán Valley by around A.D. 1250. The reappearance of pollen from forest trees thereafter provides independent evidence that the valley became virtually empty of people, and that the forests could at last begin to recover.

The general outline of Maya history that I have just related, and the example of Copán's history in particular, illustrates why we talk about "the Maya collapse." But the story grows more complicated, for at least five reasons.

First, there was not only that enormous Classic collapse, but at least two previous smaller collapses at some sites, one around the year A.D. 150 when El Mirador and some other Maya cities collapsed (the so-called pre-Classic collapse), the other (the so-called Maya hiatus) in the late 6th century and early 7th century, a period when no monuments were erected at the well-studied site of Tikal. There were also some post-Classic collapses

in areas whose populations survived the Classic collapse or increased after it—such as the fall of Chichén Itzá around 1250 and of Mayapán around 1450.

Second, the Classic collapse was obviously not complete, because there were hundreds of thousands of Maya who met and fought the Spaniards—far fewer Maya than during the Classic peak, but still far more people than in the other ancient societies discussed in detail in this book. Those survivors were concentrated in areas with stable water supplies, especially in the north with its cenotes, the coastal lowlands with their wells, near a southern lake, and along rivers and lagoons at lower elevations. However, population otherwise disappeared almost completely in what previously had been the Maya heartland in the south.

Third, the collapse of population (as gauged by numbers of house sites and of obsidian tools) was in some cases much slower than the decline in numbers of Long Count dates, as I already mentioned for Copán. What collapsed quickly during the Classic collapse was the institution of kingship and the Long Count calendar.

Fourth, many apparent collapses of cities were really nothing more than "power cycling": i.e., particular cities becoming more powerful, then declining or getting conquered, and then rising again and conquering their neighbors, without changes in the whole population. For example, in the year 562 Tikal was defeated by its rivals Caracol and Calakmul, and its king was captured and killed. However, Tikal then gradually gained strength again and finally conquered its rivals in 695, long before Tikal joined many other Maya cities in the Classic collapse (last dated Tikal monuments A.D. 869). Similarly, Copán grew in power until the year 738, when its king Waxaklahuun Ub'aah K'awil (a name better known to Maya enthusiasts today by its unforgettable translation of "18 Rabbit") was captured and put to death by the rival city of Quirigua, but then Copán thrived during the following half-century under more fortunate kings.

Finally, cities in different parts of the Maya area rose and fell on different trajectories. For example, the Puuc region in the northwest Yucatán Peninsula, after being almost empty of people in the year 700, exploded in population after 750 while the southern cities were collapsing, peaked in population between 900 and 925, and then collapsed in turn between 950 and 1000. El Mirador, a huge site in the center of the Maya area with one of the world's largest pyramids, was settled in 200 B.C. and abandoned around A.D. 150, long before the rise of Copán. Chichén Itzá in the northern peninsula grew after A.D. 850 and was the main northern center around 1000, only to be destroyed in a civil war around 1250.

Some archaeologists focus on these five types of complications and don't want to recognize a Classic Maya collapse at all. But this overlooks the obvious facts that cry out for explanation: the disappearance of between 90 and 99% of the Maya population after A.D. 800, especially in the formerly most densely populated area of the southern lowlands, and the disappearance of kings, Long Count calendars, and other complex political and cultural institutions. That's why we talk about a Classic Maya collapse, a collapse both of population and of culture that needs explaining.

Two other phenomena that I have mentioned briefly as contributing to Maya collapses require more discussion: the roles of warfare and of drought.

Archaeologists for a long time believed the ancient Maya to be gentle and peaceful people. We now know that Maya warfare was intense, chronic, and unresolvable, because limitations of food supply and transportation made it impossible for any Maya principality to unite the whole region in an empire, in the way that the Aztecs and Incas united Central Mexico and the Andes, respectively. The archaeological record shows that wars became more intense and frequent towards the time of the Classic collapse. That evidence comes from discoveries of several types over the last 55 years: archaeological excavations of massive fortifications surrounding many Maya sites; vivid depictions of warfare and captives on stone monuments, vases [Plate 14, omitted], and on the famous painted murals discovered in 1946 at Bonampak; and the decipherment of Maya writing, much of which proved to consist of royal inscriptions boasting of conquests. Maya kings fought to take one another captive, one of the unfortunate losers being Copán's King 18 Rabbit. Captives were tortured in unpleasant ways depicted clearly on the monuments and murals (such as yanking fingers out of sockets, pulling out teeth, cutting off the lower jaw, trimming off the lips and fingertips, pulling out the fingernails, and driving a pin through the lips), culminating (sometimes several years later) in the sacrifice of the captive in other equally unpleasant ways (such as tying the captive up into a ball by binding the arms and legs together, then rolling the balled-up captive down the steep stone staircase of a temple).

Maya warfare involved several well-documented types of violence: wars between separate kingdoms; attempts of cities within a kingdom to secede by revolting against the capital; and civil wars resulting from frequent violent attempts by would-be kings to usurp the throne. All of these types were described or depicted on monuments, because they involved kings and nobles. Not considered worthy of description, but probably even more frequent, were fights between commoners over land, as overpopulation became excessive and as land became scarce.

The other phenomenon important to understanding Maya collapses is the repeated occurrence of droughts, studied especially by Mark Brenner, David Hodell, the late Edward Deevey, and their colleagues at the University of Florida, and discussed in a recent book by Richardson Gill. Cores bored into layers of sediments at the bottoms of Maya lakes yield many measurements that let us infer droughts and environmental changes. For example, gypsum (a.k.a. calcium sulfate) precipitates out of solution in a lake into sediments when lake water becomes concentrated by evaporation during a drought. Water containing the heavy form of oxygen known as the isotope oxygen-18 also becomes concentrated during droughts, while water containing the lighter isotope oxygen-16 evaporates away. Molluscs and crustacea living in the lake take up oxygen to lay down in their shells, which remain preserved in the lake sediments, waiting for climatologists to analyze for those oxygen isotopes long after the little animals have died. Radiocarbon dating of a sediment layer identifies the approximate year when the drought or rainfall conditions inferred from those gypsum and oxygen isotope measurements were prevailing. The same lake sediment cores provide palynologists with information about deforestation (which shows up as a decrease in pollen from forest trees at the expense of an increase in grass pollen), and also soil erosion (which shows up as a thick clay deposit and minerals from the washed-down soil).

Based on these studies of radiocarbon-dated layers from lake sediment cores, climatologists and paleoecologists conclude that the Maya area was relatively wet from about 5500 B.C. until 500 B.C. The following period from 475 to 250 B.C., just before the rise of pre-Classic Maya civilization, was dry. The pre-Classic rise may have been facilitated by the return of wetter conditions after 250 B.C., but then a drought from A.D. 125 until A.D. 250 was associated with the pre-Classic collapse at El Mirador and other sites. That collapse was followed by the resumption of wetter conditions and of the buildup of Classic Maya cities, temporarily interrupted by a drought around A.D. 600 corresponding to a decline at Tikal and some other sites. Finally, around A.D. 760 there began the worst drought in the last 7,000 years, peaking around the year A.D. 800, and suspiciously associated with the Classic collapse.

Careful analysis of the frequency of droughts in the Maya area shows a tendency for them to recur at intervals of about 208 years. Those drought cycles may result from small variations in the sun's radiation, possibly made more severe in the Maya area as a result of the rainfall gradient in the Yucatán (drier in the north, wetter in the south) shifting southwards. One might expect those changes in the sun's radiation to affect not just the Maya region but, to varying degrees, the whole world. In fact, climatologists have noted that some other famous collapses of prehistoric civilizations far from the Maya realm appear to coincide with the peaks of those drought cycles, such as the collapse of the world's first empire (the Akkadian Empire of Mesopotamia) around 2170 B.C., the collapse of Moche IV civilization on the Peruvian coast around A.D. 600, and the collapse of Tiwanaku civilization in the Andes around A.D. 1100.

In the most naïve form of the hypothesis that drought contributed to causing the Classic collapse, one could imagine a single drought around A.D. 800 uniformly affecting the whole realm and triggering the fall of all Maya centers simultaneously. Actually, as we have seen, the Classic collapse hit different centers at slightly different times in the period A.D. 760–910, while sparing other centers. That fact makes many Maya specialists skeptical of a role of drought.

But a properly cautious climatologist would not state the drought hypothesis in that implausibly oversimplied form. Finer-resolution variation in rainfall from one year to the next can be calculated from annually banded sediments that rivers wash into ocean basins near the coast. These yield the conclusion that "The Drought" around A.D. 800 actually had four peaks, the first of them less severe: two dry years around A.D. 760, then an even drier decade around A.D. 810–820, three drier years around A.D. 860, and six drier years around A.D. 910. Interestingly, Richardson Gill concluded, from the latest dates on stone monuments at various large Maya centers, that collapse dates vary among sites and fall into three clusters: around A.D. 810, 860, and 910, in agreement with the dates for the three most severe droughts. It would not be at all surprising if a drought in any given year varied locally in its severity, hence if a series of droughts caused different Maya centers to collapse in different years, while sparing centers with reliable water supplies such as cenotes, wells, and lakes.

The area most affected by the Classic collapse was the southern lowlands, probably for the two reasons already mentioned: it was the area with the densest population, and it may also have had the most severe water problems because it lay too high above the water table for water to be obtained from cenotes or wells when the rains failed. The southern lowlands lost more than 99% of their population in the course of the Classic collapse. For example, the population of the Central Petén at the peak of the Classic Maya period is variously estimated at between 3,000,000 and 14,000,000 people, but there were only about 30,000 people there at the time that the Spanish arrived. When Cortés and his Spanish army passed through the Central Petén in 1524 and 1525, they nearly starved because they encountered so few villages from which to acquire corn. Cortés passed within a few miles of the ruins of the great Classic cities of Tikal and Palenque, but he heard or saw nothing of them because they were covered by jungle and almost nobody was living in the vicinity.

How did such a huge population of millions of people disappear? By analogy with the cases of the Anasazi and of subsequent Pueblo Indian societies during droughts in the U.S. Southwest, we infer that some people from the southern Maya lowlands survived by fleeing to areas of the northern Yucatán endowed with cenotes or wells, where a rapid population increase took place around the time of the Maya collapse. But there is no sign of all those millions of southern lowland inhabitants surviving to be accommodated as immigrants in the north, just as there is no sign of thousands of Anasazi refugees being received as immigrants into surviving pueblos. As in the U.S. Southwest during droughts, some of that Maya population decrease surely involved people dying of starvation or thirst, or killing each other in struggles over increasingly scarce resources. The other part of the decrease may reflect a slower decrease in the birthrate or child survival rate over the course of many decades. That is, depopulation probably involved both a higher death rate and a lower birth rate.

In the Maya area as elsewhere, the past is a lesson for the present. From the time of Spanish arrival, the Central Petén's population declined further to about 3,000 in A.D. 1714, as a result of deaths from diseases and other causes associated with Spanish occupation. By the 1960s, the Central Petén's population had risen back only to 25,000, still less than 1% of what it had been at the Classic Maya peak. Thereafter, however, immigrants flooded into the Central Petén, building up its population to about 300,000 in the 1980s, and ushering in a new era of deforestation and erosion. Today, half of the Petén is once again deforested and ecologically degraded. One-quarter of all the forests of Honduras were destroyed between 1964 and 1989.

To summarize the Classic Maya collapse, we can tentatively identify five strands. I acknowledge, however, that Maya archaeologists still disagree vigorously among themselves—in part, because the different strands evidently varied in importance among different parts of the Maya realm; because detailed archaeological studies are available for only some Maya sites; and because it remains puzzling why most of the Maya heartland remained nearly empty of population and failed to recover after the collapse and after regrowth of forests.

With those caveats, it appears to me that one strand consisted of population growth outstripping available resources. As the archaeologist David Webster succinctly puts it, "Too many farmers grew too many crops on too much of the landscape." Compounding that mismatch between population and resources was the second strand: the effects of deforestation and hillside erosion, which caused a decrease in the amount of useable farmland at a time when more rather than less farmland was needed, and possibly exacerbated by an anthropogenic drought resulting from deforestation, by soil nutrient depletion and other soil problems, and by the struggle to prevent bracken ferns from overrunning the fields.

The third strand consisted of increased fighting, as more and more people fought over fewer resources. Maya warfare, already endemic, peaked just before the collapse. That is not surprising when one reflects that at least 5,000,000 people, perhaps many more, were crammed into an area smaller than the state of Colorado (104,000 square miles). That warfare would have decreased further the amount of land available for agriculture, by creating no-man's lands between principalities where it was now unsafe to farm. Bringing matters to a head was the strand of climate change. The drought at the time of the Classic collapse was not the first drought that the Maya had lived through, but it was the most severe. At the time of previous droughts, there were still uninhabited parts of the Maya landscape, and people at a site affected by drought could save themselves by moving to another site. However, by the time of the Classic collapse the landscape was now full, there was no useful unoccupied land in the vicinity on which to begin anew, and the whole population could not be accommodated in the few areas that continued to have reliable water supplies.

As our fifth strand, we have to wonder why the kings and nobles failed to recognize and solve these seemingly obvious problems undermining their society. Their attention was evidently focused on their short-term concerns of enriching themselves, waging wars, erecting monuments, competing with each other, and extracting enough food from the peasants to support all those activities. Like most leaders throughout human history, the Maya kings and nobles did not heed long-term problems, insofar as they perceived them.

Finally, while we still have some other past societies to consider in this book before we switch our attention to the modern world, we must already be struck by some parallels between the Maya and the past societies discussed in Chapters 2–4. As on Easter Island, Mangareva, and among the Anasazi, Maya environmental and population problems led to increasing warfare and civil strife. As on Easter Island and at Chaco Canyon,

Maya peak population numbers were followed swiftly by political and social collapse. Paralleling the eventual extension of agriculture from Easter Island's coastal lowlands to its uplands, and from the Mimbres floodplain to the hills, Copán's inhabitants also expanded from the floodplain to the more fragile hill slopes, leaving them with a larger population to feed when the agricultural boom in the hills went bust. Like Easter Island chiefs erecting ever larger statues, eventually crowned by pukao, and like Anasazi elite treating themselves to necklaces of 2,000 turquoise beads, Maya kings sought to outdo each other with more and more impressive temples, covered with thicker and thicker plaster—reminiscent in turn of the extravagant conspicuous consumption by modern American CEOs. The passivity of Easter chiefs and Maya kings in the face of the real big threats to their societies completes our list of disquieting parallels.

UNIT 3
Techniques in Archaeology

Unit Selections

Key Points to Consider

- How can soil analysis identify past human activities?

- What advances have been made in techniques to date archaeological sites in the last 50 years? Discuss the use of laser technology, nuclear physics, and computers.

- How has DNA been used to help date archaeological materials? Please explain.

- How can a wasp's nest possibly be used to date archaeological sites? Explain the technique of "optical luminescence." How is it that this technique can go back in time about 17,000 years?

- What have archaeologists been able to borrow from physical anthropologists in terms of dating techniques? Give examples.

- How is forensics used in archaeology?

- How has computer modeling helped to unravel the archaeological mysteries of the American Southwest?

- How can techniques such as a gas chromatograph/mass spectrometer be used to identify and date archaeological materials? Give an example of this using a prehistoric unglazed piece of pottery.

Student Web Site
www.mhcls.com

Internet References

American Anthropologist
   http://www.aaanet.org
NOVA Online/Pyramids—The Inside Story
   http://www.pbs.org/wgbh/nova/pyramid/
Radiocarbon Dating for Archaeology
   http://www.rlaha.ox.ac.uk/orau/index.html

Archaeology has evolved significantly from being an exercise in separating the remains of past human behavior from the "dirt." And as such, archaeology in turn employs a diversified group of highly sophisticated techniques. Digging in itself has gone through its own evolution of techniques, ranging from the wild thrashings of Heinrich Schielmann to the obsessive, military-like precise technique of Sir Mortimer Wheeler. Archaeology continues to expand the use of a multidisciplinary approach, and is therefore incorporating more techniques that will prove to enlighten us about our human past.

The most well known technique to be developed in archaeology was radiocarbon dating. This provides archaeologists with one of their most valuable means of establishing the age of archaeological materials. This technique was a major revolution in archaeology, and was developed by W. F. Libby at UCLA in 1949. It has enabled archaeologists, for the first time (in all of history and prehistory) to have an empirical means of determining the age of archaeological sites in terms of absolute years. This dating technique is based on the principle of radioactive decay in which unstable radioactive isotopes transform into stable elements at a constant rate. In order to qualify their accuracy, dates are presented with a standard statistical margin of error. Great care is taken with respect to any factors that may skew the results of materials being dated. Radiocarbon dating is limited to the dating of organic materials, as it cannot date such things as stone tools. It can date materials as far back as 45,000 B.P. (before present). The word "present" was designated to be 1950 C.E. As the technique is perfected, it may be able to date organic matter of even earlier times.

The preservation of archaeological materials is dependent upon many variables. These include the original material of the artifact and the conditions of the site in which it is preserved. For example, a nineteenth-century adobe mission on the Mojave Desert in California may be so weathered as to be unrecognizable. This is due to the fact that extreme temperatures, varying from very hot to very cold, typical of a low-desert region, tend to rapidly destroy any kind of organic matter. On the other hand, consistently wet or consistently dry conditions tend to preserve organic matter in a relatively pristine state for a long period of time. Thus human remains tend to be well preserved in bogs—as in Denmark and in the arid coastal deserts of Peru. In Denmark, the conditions are constantly moist. In the coastal deserts of Peru, the conditions remain dry. Therefore archaeological material may be preserved for many thousands of years.

Since the discovery of radiocarbon dating, numerous other techniques have been invented that have their applications to archaeology to further clarify dates, preserve, and in general, add to the ability of archaeologists to do cultural historical reconstruction. Discussed in this section are some of the extraordinary applications of such varied hard sciences as nuclear physics, laser technology, and computers. We can now describe sites in terms of time–space systemics and virtual reality in a way that

© Nancy R. Cohen/Getty Images

exceeds recent science fiction. Remote sensing devices from outer space allow sites to be reconstructed without invasive excavation. New, cleverly devised radiometric techniques are being developed to suit specific conditions to date archaeological remains by association. The use of wasp's nests is one such example. Archaeologists sometimes rely on the use of forensic specialists to present images of the past that we could never before see. Used in conjunction with the exponential knowledge from DNA analysis, our images of the past became as detailed as that captured on a digital camera. Unglazed cooking pots have been tested to yield information on prehistoric diets through molecular analysis.

In spite of the ever-increasing sophistication of tools available to the archaeologist, the simple time-tested technique of archaeological surveying still helps reconstruct sites, again without invasive excavation. The future of archaeology will increasingly depend on techniques to maximize preservation of sites and minimize archaeological excavation.

Gritty Clues
How Soil Can Tell Stories of the Past

AIMEE CUNNINGHAM

At the base of Monticello Mountain, just below Thomas Jefferson's historic estate in Charlottesville, Va., sits a 90-meter-long greenstone wall. The Rivanna River runs on one side. On the other, earth has piled up to the wall's top. Built up from sediments washing down the mountain for centuries, this soil holds clues to history. But rather than bits of tools or pottery, the clues are chemical elements in the soil.

A complex ecosystem, soil is home to matter animal, vegetable, and mineral. Numerous chemical, biological, and geological processes take place continuously among these players. Yet within this dynamic world, an imprint of the past appears in the variety and abundances of soil's chemical elements.

People directly influence these imprints. "As people live on a landscape, they leave all kinds of chemical residues around" says geoarchaeologist Vance T. Holliday of the University of Arizona in Tucson. Some elements build up over time, while others diminish. Studying these changes "can provide us with a record of how a landscape evolves," he says.

While archaeologists have long scrutinized soils to find traces of the past, advances in analytical technologies in the past 10 to 15 years have made the detection of dozens of chemical elements rapid and cost-effective for the first time. With that additional information, archaeologists are tying chemical signatures to agricultural practices and other human activities. But while soil chemistry, offers new insights, it's most instructive in combination with artifacts and other historical evidence.

"Archaeology brings together many different lines of evidence to understand the narrative of the past," says Lisa Frink of the University of Nevada at Las Vegas. Soil chemistry is "another piece of evidence that adds to the understanding."

Dirt Diversity

Both dirt's parent material—the bedrock that slowly fragments into soil particles—and its living constituents affect soil's natural chemical composition. Magnesium, calcium, phosphorus, and numerous other elements can show up within chemical compounds among soil particles or as ions bound to those particles.

When people occupy an area, they influence the amounts of the elements in the soil. In agriculture, fertilizer adds some elements to the soil and crops deplete it. Furthermore, domestic activities, such as preparing food, maintaining fires, and disposing of waste, concentrate certain elements in the soil, says archaeologist T. Douglas Price of the University of Wisconsin-Madison.

Archaeologists have the most experience with phosphorus, an element long recognized to indicate human activity. Burial sites, waste from people and animals, and meat, fish, and other food remains all add phosphorus to the soil, where it combines with ions to form stable phosphate minerals, says Holliday. Phosphorus accumulates while people occupy an area, and concentrations can rise orders of magnitude higher than those in soil relatively free of human contact, he notes.

Although many scientists have suspected for decades that "there ought to be other things besides phosphorus lying around," says Price, finding additional tell tale elements has only recently become practical. For example, instruments that perform an analytical technique called inductively coupled plasma spectroscopy are now available at many universities, notes Price. These machines identify elements extracted from a soil sample by weighing ions or by detecting characteristic wavelengths.

Having identified the elements in a collection of samples, archaeologists can map a plot of ground according to the elements' concentrations. By combining that information with details of artifacts and other evidence of people's presence, scientists are deciphering chemical signatures of various human activities. For instance, potassium and magnesium tend to be higher where wood ash once entered the soil from a hearth.

The evidence so far "makes us think that we are seeing some real patterns in the [chemistry] data," says Price. However, he notes that there are differences in conditions among sites, so archaeologists still "have to learn each site in a different way."

Ephemeral Activities

Soil-chemistry data can be especially useful in detecting human activities at sites of occasional gatherings. In such places, people carried away their food vessels or tools once they ended a ceremony or broke camp, so few artifacts typically remain for archaeologists to find.

An archaeological site in the northwestern part of Honduras, for example, has two main areas: a ceremonial plaza surrounded by pyramids and a residential patio encircled by dwellings. E. Christian Wells of the University of South Florida at Tampa works with his research group at this site, called Palmarejo, which dates to between A.D. 400 and 1,000.

As they expected, the researchers found almost no artifacts within the boundaries of either the plaza or patio. But near the plaza, they found large serving platters, grinding stones, and incense burners. Areas just off the patio held smaller versions of these items as well as bowls and cups.

This evidence suggests that the community cooked, ate, and held religious ceremonies in both places, but in larger groups in the plaza than in the patio.

To get a sense of where in these open spaces the activities occurred, Wells' group turned to soil chemistry. The researchers took 324 samples—one every 2 m in the plaza and every 5 m in the patio. They sampled from about 15 centimeters below the areas' current surface, which is the level of the original patio and plaza. By identifying elements such as barium, magnesium, and phosphorus, Wells and his team discerned several patterns, which they reported at the 2006 American Chemical Society meeting in Atlanta in March.

Phosphorus concentrations in the plaza displayed greater variation than those in the patio did, which suggests that cooking and eating occurred throughout the patio but only in certain spots on the plaza, says Wells. The team also observed variations in barium and magnesium concentrations in the southern part of the plaza but doesn't know what activities those patterns might represent.

To learn more about the ancient site, Wells' team is observing the activities and studying the soils of indigenous people currently living in the area. Such information is critical for "making inferences between soil chemistry and ancient activities that took place," says Wells.

Similarly, Frink and Kelly J. Knudson of Arizona State University in Tempe are examining modern-day indigenous communities in Western Alaska. The people there collect enough food in the short summers to last through harsh winters. Frink, Knudson, and their colleagues work in the Yukon-Kuskokwim Delta, about halfway up the state's coast along the Bering Sea, where the Yup'ik catch and process salmon and other fish at camps that exist only during the summer season.

Before the researchers begin excavating archaeological sites, they're observing activities and collecting samples from present-day Yup'ik fish camps. Families at the camps live in tents and set up fish-processing areas that include a fish-cutting station and covered drying racks. "If the site is ephemeral—you don't have people building large houses—then soil chemistry can be very helpful" in revealing a signature that might also locate an ancient camp, says Knudson.

In 2004, the team reported on three fish camps, one a site revisited by the same family for 30 years and two others that had each been inhabited for just one summer. At the older camp, the group found that manganese, phosphorus, and strontium concentrations in soil were an order of magnitude higher under the drying racks than in soils outside the camp. Drippings from the fish probably caused the difference.

The newer camps displayed a similar, but weaker, chemical signature under the drying racks. The poorly draining Alaskan soils appear ideal for retaining elements for analysis, the researchers say.

The group plans to look for chemical signatures at archaeological sites in the area. Ultimately, says Knudson, the goal is to "use the data we have from the fish camps to look at the past."

Growing Season

The soil also holds clues to past farming practices. Fraser D. Neiman, director of archaeology at Monticello, and his colleagues have excavated the layers of soil behind the meter-high greenstone wall at Monticello Mountain to study how changes in agricultural strategies affected the landscape as well as the lives of the plantation's slave community.

Jefferson's father, Peter, began growing tobacco and corn on a small field at Monticello in the mid-18th century. His slaves used hand hoes and slashed and burned trees to clear fields, leaving behind the tree stumps. This type of agriculture typically leads to some erosion, but stumps keep much of the sediment in a field, says Neiman.

Thomas Jefferson took over the farm around 1764. He continued his father's practices while establishing additional fields. In the early 1790s, Jefferson switched to growing wheat, a crop that required a completely different strategy. Because wheat fields need to be plowed, the younger Jefferson had his slaves remove the tree stumps. He also rotated the wheat crop with clover and other plants and, to keep fields fertile, added manure and gypsum, which is calcium sulfate.

"The plowing totally stripped the fields and set up a process in the mountain environment for lots more erosion," says Neiman. After Jefferson's death, farming on the mountain slopes ceased.

At the 2006 Society for Historical Archaeology meeting in Sacramento, Calif., in January, Neiman's colleagues presented their analysis of a 1-by-2-meter chunk of soil roughly 2 meters deep that they had removed from the area behind the greenstone wall. Its color and texture indicated rich, dark topsoil in both the top, modern layer and the fourth layer down, which was probably from the time when Peter Jefferson began the farm. The researchers took 50 sediment samples at regular intervals from the top to the bottom of the excavated material.

The chemistry data ties the soil's layers to past events at the farm. For example, the researchers observed a spike in the sulfur concentrations between the fourth and third layers of soil, which indicated the point at which Thomas Jefferson switched to wheat.

"Thomas Jefferson was a huge fan of gypsum as a fertilizer," says Neiman. "The sulfur spike tells us when we are beginning to see the use of fertilizer on permanent fields."

The researchers plan to test additional sites around Monticello.

In all of its work, the team incorporates soil-chemistry data, pollen analysis, and studies of artifacts and historical documents to learn more about how changing patterns of land use affected slaves. The work "gives us physical traces of changes in slave-labor routines [such as] going from tobacco to wheat, hoeing to plowing," says Neiman. "We can begin to think about the social implications for the kind of work slaves had to do and how they did it."

Soil-chemistry data also reveal how farming practices affect the soil itself. Jonathan A. Sandor of Iowa State University in Ames and his colleagues study sites in New Mexico that the Zuni people have farmed for at least 1,000 years. These are some of the oldest agricultural fields identified in the United States. Zunis and other Native Americans still farm in these areas today.

The Zuni people have farmed in the dry Southwest without using irrigation or fertilizers, says Sandor. Instead, their success rested in the placement of their fields at the base of hills. During summer in the Southwest, intense, brief rains brought water and organic debris tumbling down the slopes onto the fields. The runoff not only waters the fields but also replenishes the soil's fertility, notes Sandor.

To study how this roughly 1,000-year-long farming practice affected the soil's fertility, the researchers compared soil samples from hillside sites that are still being farmed with samples from sites that have no evidence of ever having been farmed and from sites that were historically farmed but are now abandoned. The team measured the soil concentrations of phosphorus and nitrogen, two nutrients that plants need to grow.

The researchers report in an upcoming *Geoarchaeology* that they found no significant differences in the elements' concentrations at the various sites, which suggests that the Zunis' agricultural practices maintained soil fertility. "What they did was apparently fairly sustainable over long periods of time," says Sandor.

This is in contrast to some modern cultivation practices, which can degrade the soil, he notes.

Sandor is also analyzing the elements in crops now grown on these fields and in the water and sediments that run off the mountains.

"Soil is an important natural resource," he says, "and understanding the long-term effects of human beings on soil is important to coming up with management practices that help us conserve it."

"As people live on a landscape, they leave all kinds of chemical residues around."

—Vance T. Holliday, University of Arizona

In Context

While soil chemistry is gaining ground in archaeology, scientists remain cautious about how much the data can say. "When people do chemistry work in soils, they can't do it just in that isolated context," says Sandor. He notes that soil is also a product of biological and physical processes.

Neiman observes that "most of the work that's been done more recently has tended to be empirical rather than driven by a well grounded theoretical understanding of [soil] processes." To fully evaluate patterns of chemicals in the soil, scientists need a much better understanding of the mechanisms involved, he says.

Chemicals' movement within soil can confound interpretation of the data as well, says Holliday. While phosphorus tends to stay fixed, other elements, such as calcium, can be mobile. "If you are trying to make archaeological interpretations, you have to know that what you are measuring hasn't moved around," Holliday says.

Despite such difficulties, many researchers still consider soil chemistry an illuminating addition to other archaeological evidence. Says Neiman, "The payoff really comes in putting all this stuff together."

Digging Deep

Revolutionary technology takes archaeologists to new depths.

MARIANNE ALFSEN

A tiny crawfish popped out of a 300-year-old ceramic jar and stared in disbelief at the creature threatening to evict him from his home. At 560 feet down on the muddy bottom of the Norwegian Sea, visitors from the surface are rare—even more so when its a hulking, brightly lighted robot reaching a hydraulic arm toward you.

High above the jar, in the control room of a research ship, the technician running the remotely operated vehicle (ROV) watched a camera screen as he steered the robot's arm around the jar, nimbly avoiding the field of fragile wine bottles and Asian ceramics that lay half-buried in the mud around it. The thick tether connecting the ROV to the control room transmitted a response from the robot's hydraulic "fingers," essentially enabling the operator to "feel" the object as he watched himself pick it up through the "eyes" of the remote camera. As the jar was carefully deposited in a basket for delivery to the surface, the now homeless crawfish hurriedly swam away.

Originally developed more than half a century ago by the U.S. Navy to locate weapons and ships lost in depths beyond the reach of scuba divers, increasingly more sophisticated ROVs are now commonly used by world navies and natural-resource industries for deep-water exploration and construction. The first glimpse of robots' enormous potential in marine archaeology came in 1989, when a team led by Robert Ballard and Anna Marguerite McCann used an ROV to successfully investigate and sample a late Roman wreck more than 2,000 feet deep near Skerki Bank, off the coast of Sicily. Since then, engineers and archaeologists have endeavored to advance from mere visual survey and random removal of artifacts with ROVs, to full-blown robotic excavations.

There were two major problems to solve in excavating underwater sites with ROVs. First the robots, which generally operate independently underwater, attached only by a tether to the command vessel, are bulky and weigh hundreds or thousands of pounds; there is a risk that they may disturb or even destroy the very sites they are sent to investigate. Second, accurate and delicate maneuvering of an ROV (which relies on powerful thrusters to maintain a steady position) on an archaeological site has been a challenge. "This is why most deep-sea archaeological operations have been limited to documentation, sampling, and digging trial trenches," explains Marek E. Jasinski of the Norwegian University of Science and Technology in Trondheim, pointing to recent ROV surveys in the Black Sea and the eastern Mediterranean by Ballard's Institute for Exploration, and an ongoing survey in Greece by MIT and the Woods Hole Oceanographic Institute.

"All groups working on deep-sea excavation arrived at the same conclusion—that the best way forward was an ROV attached to a frame," says Brendan Foley of Woods Hole. While a frame set over an archaeological site would prevent the robot from accidentally coming into contact with fragile artifacts, and allow archaeologists to maneuver the ROV with more precision, the cost of developing and testing the new technology was prohibitive for academic researchers.

But then, in 2003, Jasinski and his colleague, Fredrik Søreide, had a magnificent stroke of luck.

S ince the early 1990s, Søreide and Jasinski have been collaborating on deep-sea survey and excavation technology. So when Norsk Hydro, operator for the development phase of the enormous Ormen Lange gas field off Norway's central coast, was required by national law to perform an archaeological survey of the subsea pipeline tracks in waters far too deep for human divers to explore— Søreide and Jasinski's research team at the university was a natural choice.

The survey, performed in 2003 using traditional ROVs with cameras, sonar, and geophysical survey equipment, revealed a historic shipwreck equal in size to the famous Swedish warship *Wasa.* (The 225-foot-long vessel sank on its maiden voyage in 1628 and was raised in 1961.) By archaeological standards, the ship was in good condition, splayed open on the muddy bottom with most of its deck and upperworks long gone. The timbers of the lower half of the vessel were well preserved in the sediment, with many of them sticking out from the surface. "Most Norwegian wrecks are found based on reports from divers and fishermen. It is rare that archaeologists locate a wreck themselves as in this case," says Søreide, who was the first to spot the remains of the ship. "It looked like someone had partied hard. Wine bottles were scattered everywhere. Soon we saw more objects: china, ceramics. I realized that it was an historic wreck buried in the mud, probably dating back to the second half of the eighteenth century. That was a good day," Søreide recalls.

In the Norsk Hydro boardroom, the response was less enthusiastic. Norwegian heritage laws require Hydro to preserve national heritage threatened by construction at their own cost, and the extreme underwater topography made it impossible for Hydro to choose an alternative track for its pipeline from the offshore gas field to a processing plant at Nyhamna. Jasinski, Søreide, and the rest of their nine-person scientific team were put in charge of excavating the site ahead of the pipeline construction, at a calculated cost of about 40 million Norwegian kroner—or $5.6 million. (This was not even the biggest archaeological project associated with the Ormen Lange gas field. Norsk Hydro had already paid about $9.8 million to excavate Stone Age settlements on the site of a natural gas-treatment facility on the island of Gossa—the most expensive excavation in Norwegian history.)

"One of the major obstacles for us and other scientists trying to solve these issues has been funding," says Jasinski. "Receiving the kind of money we did is almost unheard of in the world of marine archaeology." Where other ROV researchers have scratched the surface, Jasinski says the Norwegian team got "the resources, time, and stamina" to go deep, literally and figuratively, and achieve what has never been done before: the world's first deep-sea scientific excavation of a shipwreck.

On top of the bountiful resources available to the archaeologists, the condition of the shipwreck itself, lying only some 600 yards off the coast of what was once one of Norway's busiest fishing villages, provided a unique opportunity. "Most ships wrecked along the coast of Norway were smashed to pieces. This ship seems to have sunk intact," says Søreide.

In the eighteenth century, up to 500 boats fished the surrounding waters of the village of Bud. Myths or stories about shipwrecks normally survive for centuries in the local community. But nobody in the area knows anything about this particular wreck. "The lack of handed-down knowledge is very unusual," confirms Jasinski.

"We got more information about the Pontiac we found dumped close to the site than we got about the wreck itself," says Søreide with a laugh referring to a car dumped off the coast in 1963.

The ship's identity might be a mystery, but nobody questions how a ship and its crew could meet such a cruel end in these waters. The strait off Bud was a point of no return for ships venturing into the treacherous waters of Hustadvika—one of Norway's most notorious coastal waters. "You could hardly find a more classic site for shipwrecks in Norwegian waters," Jasinski and Søreide wrote in their project description. Even on a quiet summer day you can feel that nature rules in this area. The sun is shining, the wind is slight, but the current makes the sea boil between the islets.

Norsk Hydro was required to have the team excavate just the stern area of the ship—the only area that would be disturbed by pipeline construction. (To attempt to excavate the entire ship at that depth would take several years and tens or even hundreds of millions of dollars). The excavation area was mapped and surveyed by ROV and then the university team worked with ROV manufacturer Sperre AS to design a 1,000-square-foot steel frame to be suspended above the site. The ROV would be sent down from the research vessel to the site, where it would dock on a rolling bar inside the frame, allowing it to sit only inches above the excavation site. In May 2005, the scientists were ready to start. After some initial technical hiccups, the ROV and frame worked beautifully, allowing precise remote excavation that could extract a maximum amount of data from the sea floor. Advanced sensors transmitted data to the surface—the precise size and location of each artifact, and their relation to each other. Digital images provided the archaeologists with visual information on the in situ artifacts and their environment. Dredges carefully removed sediment and organic remains, while small suction devices and hydraulic arms excavated artifacts with the sensitivity of a fingertip and brush.

Preliminary investigations uncovered artifacts from seven different countries. None of them gave any clues to the identity of the ship, or why it met its destiny in these waters.

"We are fairly certain we are dealing with a trade ship from the mid to late eighteenth century," Jasinski said as he started his investigations of the recovered material last autumn.

The archaeologists found parts of the wooden hull relatively intact in the mud. The size and shape was consistent with a trade ship of Western European design. More than 100 wine bottles found on the wreck pointed to the same conclusion. Wine was an important trade item throughout Europe and was also extensively used when crews bartered with the locals.

"We also found luxurious Chinese porcelain, far too extravagant to have been used in the ship's mess. The same goes for the three compasses and two octants of uncertain nationality. It was highly unusual to carry more than one set of expensive navigation equipment, unless it was for trade," says Jasinski.

The archaeologists looked east as they continued their study of the more than 500 recovered objects, organic material, and piles of archive material. Russian coins, a Russian flour sack, and buckwheat, a Russian staple, pointed toward Russia, even if the ship's design was Western European.

"In his youth Tsar Peter the Great went incognito to Europe to study shipbuilding and work as a carpenter. When he became tsar he forbade traditional Russian shipbuilding. Only Western European constructions were allowed, where the wooden hull was nailed rather than stitched together. This ship might be a result of his policies," Jasinski speculated early in the investigation.

Despite thousands of objects scattered on the seabed off Bud, huge parts of the cargo were missing.

"These ships carried several tons of merchandise. The ship might have been empty on a return voyage, or the cargo was organic—such as salt or flour—and long ago dissolved in the seawater," he added. But now, seawater," he added. But now, the analysis of the pottery has recently been completed, and Jasinski may have to drop his theory that the vessel was a Russian ship on its return voyage from Europe. While the bulk of ceramics are German, English, and Chinese, there is also pottery with origins in Spain, the Netherlands, and Southeast Asia.

"The English stoneware does not have traces of use, and was probably part of the cargo. The ceramic pots from Southeast Asia, on the other hand, seem to have been in use on board," says Jasinski. Such evidence leads him to believe this may be a Dutch merchant ship, due to the presence of Dutch colonies in Southeast Asia at the time. "Bearing in mind that the Dutch at this time were deeply involved in trade with northern Russia, the find strengthens another hypothesis—that we are dealing with a Dutch

trade ship on its outbound journey to Russia, rather than a Russian ship on its way home from Europe," he adds.

Much of the material has yet to be analyzed, such as strange insects recovered from the wreck, which biologists have not been able to identify.

It may take months, even years, before the true identity of the ship is uncovered. In the meantime, the artifacts are being studied, conserved, and stored at the university's Museum of Natural History and Technology (Vitenskapsmuseet) in Trondheim.

Many countries are now looking to Norway for the technological key to unlock their own deep-sea mysteries. The Russian Academy of Science and research organizations collaborating with the largest Russian gas company, Gazprom, wish to use the Norwegian technology for similar purposes in Russia: preserving cultural heritage sites in conflict with pipeline tracks. The Trondheim team is also talking with Greek authorities about using their robotic excavation technology on ancient shipwrecks in the Aegean.

Woods Hole archaeologist Foley notes that it is not necessarily the technology that has changed the face of maritime archaeology, stressing that it was more the will and ability to bring these technologies to bear. He attributes the uniqueness of the Norwegian project to the way a wide range of resources and sciences came together—how engineers, archaeologists, and geologists from the universities worked together with the oil industry and the state to make it happen. "It is rare to see a government recognize the value of shipwrecks and other underwater cultural resources to such an extent," comments Foley. He also does not expect that the advanced deep-sea excavation technology will become a regular household appliance with most marine archaeologists. Because of the high costs involved, only the most precious of wrecks will get a visit from "robot-archaeologists" looking to do a full-blown excavation. "The financial barrier will actually help protect wrecks. As any first year archaeology student will learn, excavations are by nature intrusive," says Foley. "Only when the site is very compelling and important will we excavate."

This summer, Jasinski and Søreide will join up with a team from Texas A&M University to work on a nineteenth-century wreck located in a pipeline track in the Gulf of Mexico. "However, the task we have been given is different," explains Søreide. "The depth is 4,000 feet and we will not conduct a full excavation, but only collect visible artifacts and document the site." For this challenge, the team has decided to forego the frame, and instead will give the ROV legs that fold out like a spider and enable it to "sit" on top of the shipwreck and do the work.

"The project in Bud removed the last technological barrier for archaeological excavations at great depths," says Jasinski. But he points out that now that true excavation by remote control has been achieved, there is a bigger hurdle for the archaeological establishment to overcome.

"Marine archaeologists must get used to not having direct, physical contact with the cultural layers and artifacts. But there is no methodological difference between remote control and a more hands-on approach."

MARIANNE ALFSEN is a Norwegian-based freelance journalist.

A Wasp's-Nest Clock

With a highly unusual dating technique, two Australian researchers have identified what may be the world's oldest portrait of a human.

RACHEL F. PREISER

The rock outcroppings of the Kimberley region of northwestern Australia are painted, pecked, and engraved with vestiges of aboriginal art. Unfortunately, except for the odd charcoal sketch, most aboriginal rock art is nearly impossible to date—it is often colored with ocher, a mineral pigment that lacks the organic carbon compounds required by radioactive-dating techniques. Without an absolute scale, archeologists have had to rely on informed guesswork to date most aboriginal art. But that may soon change. Some Australian researchers have found a way to use fossilized wasps' nests to determine the age of ancient art.

Grahame Walsh, a rock-art specialist at the Takarakka Rock Art Research Center at Carnarvon Gorge, was studying the Kimberley paintings when he noticed that a nearby wasp's nest he had assumed to be of recent origin was in fact fossilized. Wasps' nests—made of a loosely packed fabric of sand, silt, and pollen grains—are not generally durable. But Walsh found that silica carried by water apparently seeped through the sandstone overlying the rock shelters and filled in the pores in the nest, reinforcing it to withstand the ravages of time.

Walsh realized that the sand grains worked into the nest would make it possible to date the nest. He contacted Richard Roberts, a geologist at La Trobe University in Melbourne who specializes in reading these grainy timepieces using a method known as optical luminescence dating. Radiation from radioactive trace elements in the sand bombards the grains. The radiation causes atoms in the grains to spit out electrons that become trapped in imperfections in the grains' crystalline structure. Here the displaced electrons remain until ultraviolet radiation in sunlight frees them from their crystal prisons. As the electrons return to more stable positions, each emits a photon of light. By exposing sand grains to light and measuring the intensity of the light emitted by the grains, geologists can estimate how long ago they were last exposed to sunlight.

Two years ago Roberts joined Walsh on an expedition to Kimberley in search of petrified wasps' nests built on top of rock art. While clambering around the rocky outcroppings, the researchers came across two fossilized nests overlying a mulberry-colored painting of a human figure whose elongated

(Photo © Richard Roberts)

A fossilized wasp's nest lies just to the left of the painted figures.

body, narrow head, and semicircular headdress suggested it belonged to a style believed by most archeologists to date back some 5,000 years. The researchers pried the fossilized nests free and extracted sand grains from their cores.

Using luminescence dating, Roberts discovered that the nests were more than 17,000 years old. That makes the underlying aboriginal rock painting the oldest depiction of a human figure in the world. Roberts believes the figure may actually be much older than the nest, since the Ice Age had reached its height at that time and the Kimberley region would thus have been arid and inhospitable to humans.

"Presumably the paintings were made during a previous, wetter period," says Roberts, "perhaps 25,000 to 30,000 years ago or even earlier, before the peak of the last glacial maximum." If he's right, the mulberry-colored figure may rival the oldest known paintings of animals—from the Chauvet cave in France—thought to be about 30,000 years old.

Although too sparse to date, the pollen found in the petrified nests can be used to identify the plants the wasps visited while building their homes many thousands of years ago.

The nests Walsh and Roberts found contain mostly eucalyptus pollen and smatterings of pollen from an array of flowering plants and grasses. For Roberts, that makes the nests a still more important record, enabling a detailed reconstruction of the environment in which the ancient artists lived. "My feeling is that the greatest global application of the approach will be to examine past vegetation histories and infer past climate from preserved nests," says Roberts. "That wasn't the main aim of our project—the presence of pollen was pure luck but the combination of being able to date the rock art and reconstruct past environments makes wasp nests extremely versatile time capsules."

Profile of an Anthropologist: No Bone Unturned

PATRICK HUYGHE

The research of some physical anthropologists and archaeologists involves the discovery and analysis of old bones (as well as artifacts and other remains). Most often these bones represent only part of a skeleton or maybe the mixture of parts of several skeletons. Often these remains are smashed, burned, or partially destroyed. Over the years, physical anthropologists have developed a remarkable repertoire of skills and techniques for teasing the greatest possible amount of information out of sparse material remains.

Although originally developed for basic research, the methods of physical anthropology can be directly applied to contemporary human problems. . . . In this profile, we look briefly at the career of Clyde C. Snow, a physical anthropologist who has put these skills to work in a number of different settings. . . .

As you read this selection, ask yourself the following questions:

- Given what you know of physical anthropology, what sort of work would a physical anthropologist do for the Federal Aviation Administration?
- What is anthropometry? *How might anthropometric surveys of pilots and passengers help in the design of aircraft equipment?*
- What is forensic anthropology? *How can a biological anthropologist be an expert witness in legal proceedings?*

Clyde Snow is never in a hurry. He knows he's late. He's always late. For Snow, being late is part of the job. In fact, he doesn't usually begin to work until death has stripped some poor individual to the bone, and no one—neither the local homicide detectives nor the pathologists—can figure out who once gave identity to the skeletonized remains. No one, that is, except a shrewd, laconic, 60-year-old forensic anthropologist.

Snow strolls into the Cook County Medical Examiner's Office in Chicago on this brisk October morning wearing a pair of Lucchese cowboy boots and a three-piece pin-striped suit. Waiting for him in autopsy room 160 are a bunch of naked skeletons found in Illinois, Wisconsin, and Minnesota since his last visit. Snow, a native Texan who now lives in rural Oklahoma, makes the trip up to Chicago some six times a year. The first case on his agenda is a pale brown skull found in the garbage of an abandoned building once occupied by a Chicago cosmetics company.

Snow turns the skull over slowly in his hands, a cigarette dangling from his fingers. One often does. Snow does not seem overly concerned about mortality, though its tragedy surrounds him daily.

"There's some trauma here," he says, examining a rough edge at the lower back of the skull. He points out the area to Jim Elliott, a homicide detective with the Chicago police. "This looks like a chopping blow by a heavy bladed instrument. Almost like a decapitation." In a place where the whining of bone saws drifts through hallways and the sweet-sour smell of death hangs in the air, the word surprises no one.

Snow begins thinking aloud. "I think what we're looking at here is a female, or maybe a small male, about thirty to forty years old. Probably Asian." He turns the skull upside down, pointing out the degree of wear on the teeth. "This was somebody who lived on a really rough diet. We don't normally find this kind of dental wear in a modern Western population."

"How long has it been around?" Elliott asks.

Snow raises the skull up to his nose. "It doesn't have any decompositional odors," he says. He pokes a finger in the skull's nooks and crannies. "There's no soft tissue left. It's good and dry. And it doesn't show signs of having been buried. I would say that this has been lying around in an attic or a box for years. It feels like a souvenir skull," says Snow.

Souvenir skulls, usually those of Japanese soldiers, were popular with U.S. troops serving in the Pacific during World War II; there was also a trade in skulls during the Vietnam War years. On closer inspection, though, Snow begins to wonder about the skull's Asian origins—the broad nasal aperture and the jutting forth of the upper-tooth-bearing part of the face suggest Melanesian features. Sifting through the objects found in the abandoned building with the skull, he finds several loose-leaf albums of 35-millimeter transparencies documenting life among the highland tribes of New Guinea. The slides, shot by an anthropologist, include graphic scenes of ritual warfare. The skull, Snow concludes, is more likely to be a trophy from one of these tribal battles than the result of a local Chicago homicide.

"So you'd treat it like found property?" Elliott asks finally. "Like somebody's garage-sale property?"

"Exactly," says Snow.

Clyde Snow is perhaps the world's most sought-after forensic anthropologist. People have been calling upon him to identify skeletons for more than a quarter of a century. Every year he's involved in some 75 cases of identification, most of them without fanfare. "He's an old scudder who doesn't have to blow his own whistle," says Walter Birkby, a forensic anthropologist at the University of Arizona. "He know's he's good."

Yet over the years Snow's work has turned him into something of an unlikely celebrity. He has been called upon to identify the remains of the Nazi war criminal Josef Mengele, reconstruct the face of the Egyptian boy-king Tutankhamen, confirm the authenticity of the body autopsied as that of President John F. Kennedy, and examine the skeletal remains of General Custer's men at the battlefield of the Little Bighorn. He has also been involved in the grim task of identifying the bodies in some of the United States' worst airline accidents.

Such is his legend that cases are sometimes attributed to him in which he played no part. He did not, as the *New York Times* reported, identify the remains of the crew of the *Challenger* disaster. But the man is often the equal of his myth. For the past four years, setting his personal safety aside, Snow has spent much of his time in Argentina, searching for the graves and identities of some of the thousands who "disappeared" between 1976 and 1983, during Argentina's military regime.

Snow did not set out to rescue the dead from oblivion. For almost two decades, until 1979, he was a physical anthropologist at the Civil Aeromedical Institute, part of the Federal Aviation Administration in Oklahoma City. Snow's job was to help engineers improve aircraft design and safety features by providing them with data on the human frame.

One study, he recalls, was initiated in response to complaints from a flight attendants' organization. An analysis of accident patterns had revealed that inadequate restraints on flight attendants' jump seats were leading to deaths and injuries and that aircraft doors weighing several hundred pounds were impeding evacuation efforts. Snow points out that ensuring the survival of passengers in emergencies is largely the flight attendants' responsibility. "If they are injured or killed in a crash, you're going to find a lot of dead passengers."

Reasoning that equipment might be improved if engineers had more data on the size and strength of those who use it, Snow undertook a study that required meticulous measurement. When his report was issued in 1975, Senator William Proxmire was outraged that $57,800 of the taxpayers' money had been spent to caliper 423 airline stewardesses from head to toe. Yet the study, which received one of the senator's dubious Golden Fleece Awards, was firmly supported by both the FAA and the Association of Flight Attendants. "I can't imagine," says Snow with obvious delight, "how much coffee Proxmire got spilled on him in the next few months."

It was during his tenure at the FAA that he developed an interest in forensic work. Over the years the Oklahoma police frequently consulted the physical anthropologist for help in identifying crime victims. "The FAA figured it was a kind of community service to let me work on these cases," he says.

The experience also helped to prepare him for the grim task of identifying the victims of air disasters. In December 1972, when a United Airlines plane crashed outside Chicago, killing 43 of the 61 people aboard (including the wife of Watergate conspirator Howard Hunt, who was found with $10,000 in her purse), Snow was brought in to help examine the bodies. That same year, with Snow's help, forensic anthropology was recognized as a specialty by the American Academy of Forensic Sciences. "It got a lot of anthropologists interested in forensics," he says, "and it made a lot of pathologists out there aware that there were anthropologists who could help them."

Each nameless skeleton poses a unique mystery for Snow. But some, like the second case awaiting him back in the autopsy room at the Cook County morgue, are more challenging than others. This one is a real chiller. In a large cardboard box lies a jumble of bones along with a tattered leg from a pair of blue jeans, a sock shrunk tightly around the bones of a foot, a pair of Nike running shoes without shoelaces, and, inside the hood of a blue windbreaker, a mass of stringy, blood-caked hair. The remains were discovered frozen in ice about 20 miles outside Milwaukee. A rusted bicycle was found lying close by. Paul Hibbard, chief deputy medical examiner for Waukesha County, who brought the skeleton to Chicago, says no one has been reported missing.

Snow lifts the bones out of the box and begins reconstructing the skeleton on an autopsy table. "There are two hundred six bones and thirty-two teeth in the human body," he says, "and each has a story to tell." Because bone is dynamic, living tissue, many of life's significant events—injuries, illness, childbearing—leave their mark on the body's internal framework. Put together the stories told by these bones, he says, and what you have is a person's "osteobiography."

Snow begins by determining the sex of the skeleton, which is not always obvious. He tells the story of a skeleton that was brought to his FAA office in the late 1970s. It had been found along with some women's clothes and a purse in a local back lot, and the police had assumed that it was female. But when Snow examined the bones, he realized that "at six foot three, she would have probably have been the tallest female in Oklahoma."

Then Snow recalled that six months earlier the custodian in his building had suddenly not shown up for work. The man's supervisor later mentioned to Snow, "You know, one of these days when they find Ronnie, he's going to be dressed as a woman." Ronnie, it turned out, was a weekend transvestite. A copy of his dental records later confirmed that the skeleton in women's clothing was indeed Snow's janitor.

The Wisconsin bike rider is also male. Snow picks out two large bones that look something like twisted oysters—the innominates, or hipbones, which along with the sacrum, or lower backbone, form the pelvis. This pelvis is narrow and steep-walled like a male's, not broad and shallow like a female's. And the sciatic notch (the V-shaped space where the sciatic nerve passes through the hipbone) is narrow, as is normal in a male. Snow can also determine a skeleton's sex by checking the size of the mastoid processes (the bony knobs at the base of the skull) and the prominence of the brow ridge, or by measuring the head of an available limb bone, which is typically broader in males.

From an examination of the skull he concludes that the bike rider is "predominantly Caucasoid." A score of bony traits help the forensic anthropologist assign a skeleton to one of the three major racial groups: Negroid, Caucasoid, or Mongoloid. Snow notes that the ridge of the boy's nose is high and salient, as it is in whites. In Negroids and Mongoloids (which include American Indians as well as most Asians) the nose tends to be broad in relation to its height. However, the boy's nasal margins are somewhat smoothed down, usually a Mongoloid feature. "Possibly a bit of American Indian admixture," says Snow. "Do you have Indians in your area?" Hibbard nods.

Age is next. Snow takes the skull and turns it upside down, pointing out the basilar joint, the junction between the two major bones that form the underside of the skull. In a child the joint would still be open to allow room for growth, but here the joint has fused—something that usually happens in the late teen years. On the other hand, he says, pointing to the zigzagging lines on the dome of the skull, the cranial sutures are open. The cranial sutures, which join the bones of the braincase, begin to fuse and disappear in the mid-twenties.

Next Snow picks up a femur and looks for signs of growth at the point where the shaft meets the knobbed end. The thin plates of cartilage—areas of incomplete calcification—that are visible at this point suggest that the boy hadn't yet attained his full height. Snow double-checks with an examination of the pubic symphysis, the joint where the two hipbones meet. The ridges in this area, which fill in and smooth over in adulthood, are still clearly marked. He concludes that the skeleton is that of a boy between 15 and 20 years old.

"One of the things you learn is to be pretty conservative," says Snow. "It's very impressive when you tell the police, 'This person is eighteen years old,' and he turns out to be eighteen. The problem is, if the person is fifteen you've blown it—you probably won't find him. Looking for a missing person is like trying to catch fish. Better get a big net and do your own sorting."

Snow then picks up a leg bone, measures it with a set of calipers, and enters the data into a portable computer. Using the known correlation between the height and length of the long limb bones, he quickly estimates the boy's height. "He's five foot six and a half to five foot eleven," says Snow. "Medium build, not excessively muscular, judging from the muscle attachments that we see." He points to the grainy ridges that appear where muscle attaches itself to the bone. The most prominent attachments show up on the teenager's right arm bone, indicating right-handedness.

Then Snow examines the ribs one by one for signs of injury. He finds no stab wounds, cuts, or bullet holes, here or elsewhere on the skeleton. He picks up the hyoid bone from the boy's throat and looks for the tell-tale fracture signs that would suggest the boy was strangled. But, to Snow's frustration, he can find no obvious cause of death. In hopes of identifying the missing teenager, he suggests sending the skull, hair, and boy's description to Betty Pat Gatliff, a medical illustrator and sculptor in Oklahoma who does facial reconstructions.

Six weeks later photographs of the boy's likeness appear in the *Milwaukee Sentinel.* "If you persist long enough," says Snow, "eighty-five to ninety percent of the cases eventually get positively identified, but it can take anywhere from a few weeks to a few years."

Snow and Gatliff have collaborated many times, but never with more glitz than in 1983, when Snow was commissioned by Patrick Barry, a Miami orthopedic surgeon and amateur Egyptologist, to reconstruct the face of the Egyptian boy-king Tutankhamen. Normally a facial reconstruction begins with a skull, but since Tutankhamen's 3,000-year-old remains were in Egypt, Snow had to make do with the skull measurements from a 1925 postmortem and X-rays taken in 1975. A plaster model of the skull was made, and on the basis on Snow's report—"his skull is Caucasoid with some Negroid admixtures"—Gatliff put a face on it. What did Tutankhamen look like? Very much like the gold mask on his sarcophagus, says Snow, confirming that it was, indeed, his portrait.

Many cite Snow's use of facial reconstructions as one of his most important contributions to the field. Snow, typically self-effacing, says that Gatliff "does all the work." The identification of skeletal remains, he stresses, is often a collaboration between pathologists, odontologists, radiologists, and medical artists using a variety of forensic techniques.

One of Snow's last tasks at the FAA was to help identify the dead from the worst airline accident in U.S. history. On May 25, 1979, a DC-10 crashed shortly after takeoff from Chicago's O'Hare Airport, killing 273 people. The task facing Snow and more than a dozen forensic specialists was horrific. "No one ever sat down and counted," says Snow, "but we estimated ten thousand to twelve thousand pieces or parts of bodies." Nearly 80 percent of the victims were identified on the basis of dental evidence and fingerprints. Snow and forensic radiologist John Fitzpatrick later managed to identify two dozen others by comparing postmortem X-rays with X-rays taken during the victim's lifetime.

Next to dental records, such X-ray comparisons are the most common way of obtaining positive identifications. In 1978, when a congressional committee reviewed the evidence on John F. Kennedy's assassination, Snow used X-rays to show that the body autopsied at Bethesda Naval Hospital was indeed that of the late president and had not—as some conspiracy theorists believed—been switched.

The issue was resolved on the evidence of Kennedy's "sinus print," the scalloplike pattern on the upper margins of the sinuses that is visible in X-rays of the forehead. So characteristic is a person's sinus print that courts throughout the world accept the matching of antemortem and postmortem X-rays of the sinuses as positive identification.

Yet another technique in the forensic specialist's repertoire is photo superposition. Snow used it in 1977 to help identify the mummy of a famous Oklahoma outlaw named Elmer J. McCurdy, who was killed by a posse after holding up a train in 1911. For years the mummy had been exhibited as a "dummy" in a California funhouse—until it was found to have a real human skeleton inside it. Ownership of the mummy was eventually traced back to a funeral parlor in Oklahoma, where McCurdy had been embalmed and exhibited as "the bandit who wouldn't give up."

Using two video cameras and an image processor, Snow superposed the mummy's profile on a photograph of McCurdy that was taken shortly after his death. When displayed on a single monitor, the two coincided to a remarkable degree. Convinced by the evidence, Thomas Noguchi, then Los Angeles County corner, signed McCurdy's death certificate ("Last known occupation: Train robber") and allowed the outlaw's bones to be returned to Oklahoma for a decent burial.

It was this technique that also allowed forensic scientists to identify the remains of the Nazi "Angel of Death," Josef Mengele, in the summer of 1985. A team of investigators, including Snow and West German forensic anthropologist Richard Helmer, flew to Brazil after an Austrian couple claimed that Mengele lay buried in a grave on a São Paulo hillside. Tests revealed that the stature, age, and hair color of the unearthed skeleton were consistent with information in Mengele's SS files; yet without X-rays or dental records, the scientists still lacked conclusive evidence. When an image of the reconstructed skull was superposed on 1930s photographs of Mengele, however, the match was eerily compelling. All doubts were removed a few months later when Mengele's dental X-rays were tracked down.

In 1979 Snow retired from the FAA to the rolling hills of Norman, Oklahoma, where he and his wife, Jerry, live in a sprawling, early-1960s ranch house. Unlike his 50 or so fellow forensic anthropologists, most of whom are tied to academic positions, Snow is free to pursue his consultancy work full-time. Judging from the number of miles that he logs in the average month, Snow is clearly not ready to retire for good.

His recent projects include a reexamination of the skeletal remains found at the site of the Battle of the Little Bighorn, where more than a century ago Custer and his 210 men were killed by Sioux and Cheyenne warriors. Although most of the enlisted men's remains were moved to a mass grave in 1881, an excavation of the battlefield in the past few years uncovered an additional 375 bones and 36 teeth. Snow, teaming up again with Fitzpatrick, determined that these remains belonged to 34 individuals.

The historical accounts of Custer's desperate last stand are vividly confirmed by their findings. Snow identified one skeleton as that of a soldier between the ages of 19 and 23 who weighed around 150 pounds and stood about five foot eight. He'd sustained gunshot wounds to his chest and left forearm. Heavy blows to his head had fractured his skull and sheared off his teeth. Gashed thigh bones indicated that his body was later dismembered with an ax or hatchet.

Given the condition and number of the bodies, Snow seriously questions the accuracy of the identifications made by the original nineteenth-century burial crews. He doubts, for example, that the skeleton buried at West Point is General Custer's.

For the last four years Snow has devoted much of his time to helping two countries come to terms with the horrors of a much more recent past. As part of a group sponsored by the American Association for the Advancement of Science, he has been helping the Argentinian National Commission on Disappeared Persons to determine the fate of some of those who vanished during their country's harsh military rule: between 1976 and 1983 at least 10,000 people were systematically swept off the streets by roving death squads to be tortured, killed, and buried in unmarked graves. In December 1986, at the invitation of the Aquino government's Human Rights Commission, Snow also spent several weeks training Philippine scientists to investigate the disappearances that occurred under the Marcos regime.

But it is in Argentina where Snow has done the bulk of his human-rights work. He has spent more than 27 months in and around Buenos Aires, first training a small group of local medical and anthropology students in the techniques of forensic investigation, and later helping them carefully exhume and examine scores of the *desaparecidos,* or disappeared ones.

Only 25 victims have so far been positively identified. But the evidence has helped convict seven junta members and other high-ranking military and police officers. The idea is not necessarily to identify all 10,000 of the missing, says Snow. "If you have a colonel who ran a detention center where maybe five hundred people were killed, you don't have to nail them with five hundred deaths. Just one or two should be sufficient to get him convicted." Forensic evidence from Snow's team may be used to prosecute several other military officers, including General Suarez Mason. Mason is the former commander of the I Army Corps in Buenos Aires and is believed to be responsible for thousands of disappearances. He was recently extradited from San Francisco back to Argentina, where he is expected to stand trial this winter [1988].

The investigations have been hampered by a frustrating lack of antemortem information. In 1984, when commission lawyers took depositions from relatives and friends of the disappeared, they often failed to obtain such basic information as the victim's height, weight, or hair color. Nor did they ask for the missing person's X-rays (which in Argentina are given to the patient) or the address of the victim's dentist. The problem was compounded by the inexperience of those who carried out the first mass exhumations prior to Snow's arrival. Many of the skeletons were inadvertently destroyed by bulldozers as they were brought up.

Every unearthed skeleton that shows signs of gunfire, however, helps to erode the claim once made by many in the Argentinian military that most of the *desaparecidos* are alive and well and living in Mexico City, Madrid, or Paris. Snow recalls the case of a 17-year-old boy named Gabriel Dunayavich, who disappeared in the summer of 1976. He was walking home from a movie with his girlfriend when a Ford Falcon with no license plates snatched him off the street. The police later found his body and that of another boy and girl dumped by the roadside on the outskirts of Buenos Aires. The police went through the motions of an investigation, taking photographs and doing an autopsy, then buried the three teenagers in an unmarked grave.

A decade later Snow, with the help of the boy's family, traced the autopsy reports, the police photographs, and the grave of the three youngsters. Each of them had four or five closely spaced bullet wounds in the upper chest—the signature, says Snow, of an automatic weapon. Two also had wounds on their arms from bullets that had entered behind the elbow and exited from the forearm.

"That means they were conscious when they were shot," says Snow. "When a gun was pointed at them, they naturally raised their arm." It's details like these that help to authenticate the last moments of the victims and bring a dimension of reality to the judges and jury.

Each time Snow returns from Argentina he says that this will be the last time. A few months later he is back in Buenos Aires. "There's always more work to do," he says. It is, he admits quietly, "terrible work."

"These were such brutal, cold-blooded crimes," he says. "The people who committed them not only murdered; they had a system to eliminate all trace that their victims even existed."

Snow will not let them obliterate their crimes so conveniently. "There are human-rights violations going on all around the world," he says. "But to me murder is murder, regardless of the motive. I hope that we are sending a message to governments who murder in the name of politics that they can be held to account."

What Did They Eat?

Eleanora Reber

Most archaeologists know that visible food residues can appear on potsherds, offering a possibility of dietary reconstruction. Visible residues are not, however, the only means of identifying the contents of pots. When an unglazed pottery vessel is used for cooking, lipids and water-soluble compounds from the contents absorb into the vessel walls. These absorbed residues, which are protected by the unyielding clay matrix from chemical degradation, can be extracted and identified.

Makings of Prehistoric Stew

As a meal is cooked in an unglazed vessel, the prehistoric cook may have added a variety of foods into a stew. From the cook's point of view, she was boiling food until properly cooked, serving, then rinsing the vessel for its next use. On the molecular level, as the foods were added to the stew, heat and the circulation of water caused fats, vitamins, starches, proteins and other substances to circulate through the water, and to be absorbed by the walls of the pot. Bacteria may have begun to work on the foods even before they were added to the pot; if the vessel was not washed for several hours following cooking, even more spoilage could occur. Water-soluble chemicals—such as most vitamins—absorbed into the pot are easily washed out by groundwater following archaeological deposition of the pot. Less water-soluble chemicals, however, once safely absorbed into the walls of the pot become a fixture until polluted by modern solvents or chemicals, or removed for study.

Extraction to Reconstruction

The procedure for residue identification involves extraction of preserved residue from the walls of a vessel. Because these residues are held in the walls of the vessel by weak chemical bonds, their recovery involves powdering 1–3 grams of the sherd, and then extracting the powder with solvent. This destructive procedure is painful for both the archaeologist and analyst, and is not undertaken lightly.

The precious residue-impregnated solvent is then evaporated to produce a tiny amount of unimpressive grease, which is injected into a chemical instrument called a gas chromatograph/ mass spectrometer. This instrument separates the residue into its component compounds, and identifies each compound through its molecular fragments.

With the habits of our prehistoric cook in mind, however, it is clear that identifying diet from a residue is not a simple task. Many pottery vessels were used for more than one type of food. If a vessel was used for cooking, we need to consider the effect of heat on the foods. Furthermore, even when absorbed into a pot, some degradation of the chemicals can slowly occur. Polyunsaturated fats tend to degrade first, then monounsaturated fats, leaving the saturated fats behind. Bacterial action complicates matters further. So, the analyst looks for marker compounds—compounds that are unique to a particular food or group of foods, such as cholesterol in meat, theobromine in cocoa, or leaf waxes in turnips or cabbage. Ratios of lipids can also tell the analyst something about the basic classes of foods. If a high ratio of unsaturates to saturates survives, it suggests the presence of vegetables or grain.

Identifying Maize

Although analysis of absorbed residues is not infallible, and cannot identify everything cooked in a pot, the technique is already useful. Stable isotopic data give a snapshot of the residue. The presence of meat or vegetable can be determined with a fairly high degree of certainty. In an ambiguous pot it is also possible to tell whether or not food in a pot has been cooked, thereby answering questions about vessel function. If marker compounds are present, the corresponding food can be identified. Many, or perhaps even most foods may have marker compounds, but to discover this, each food must be carefully investigated. This is a worthy goal, and one that attracts students to the field, but progress is, of necessity, slow.

One archaeological application of residue is my own research, in which I am developing a technique using stable isotope and lipid analysis to identify maize residues. When established I will apply the technique to Mississippian pottery from a variety of temporal and geographical locations. The appearance of maize in residues should correspond to the change in cooking vessel thickness and temper, which has generally been attributed to the appearance of maize in the region. Thus, residue analysis can answer a variety of archaeological and anthropological questions by any researcher with questions about diet and pottery.

Save Your Residues!

Once an absorbed residue is safely preserved inside the matrix of the clay, few things can remove or damage it. One of these culprits, unfortunately, is post-excavation washing or treatment of a sherd. Acid-washing and varnishing both damage absorbed residues irretrievably. Labeling a sherd with a nail polish and white-out will also contaminate residues, though they may be salvageable. Touching a sherd during excavation or storing it in a plastic bag can result in modern residues which may make the

analysis of older remains difficult. A sherd submitted for residue study should not be washed, it should be touched as little as possible and stored and sent to the lab in tin foil or acid-free paper.

ELEANORA REBER is presently in the doctoral program at Harvard U, Department of Anthropology. Following an undergraduate career at Beloit College as a chemistry/anthropology major, she spent time digging for contract firms. She is presently working on a preliminary study involving the identification of maize residues in pottery from around the world. One hundred sherds are needed, and analysis will be free of charge. If you have a sherd which you believe has been used to cook maize, please send samples and inquires, by March 1, to: Eleanora Reber, Dept of Anthropology, Harvard, 11 Divinity Ave, Cambridge, MA 02138; 617/495-4388, reber@fas.harvard.edu.

UNIT 4

Historical Archaeology

Unit Selections

Key Points to Consider

- What is historical archaeology? Give some examples.

- What is the evidence for the early development of medicine?

- What are the implications of the archaeological evidence of Jesus' place of birth for modern Christianity?

- How did the archaeological investigation at Jamestown provide new insight about the success of the United States of America?

- What has the excavation of the Medici tombs revealed about the lives and deaths of Florence's first family?

- How is the Donner Pass story an example of cultural/historical reconstruction, even though it is not strictly archaeology?

Student Web Site

www.mhcls.com

Internet References

GIS and Remote Sensing for Archaeology: Burgundy, France
http://www.informatics.org/france/france.html
Society for Historical Archaeology
www.sha.org
Zeno's Forensic Page
http://forensic.to/forensic.html

How many times have you misplaced your car keys? Locked yourself out of the house? Lost your wallet? Your address book? Eyeglasses? Sometimes these artifacts are recovered and brought back into the historical present. Sometimes they are lost forever, becoming part of the garbage of an extinct culture. Have you ever noticed that lost things, when found, are always in the last place you look? Is this a law of science? Be skeptical. Here is an opportunity to practice historical archaeology. You may wish to try this puzzler in order to practice thinking like an archaeologist. (Do not forget to apply the basics discussed in unit 1.) The incident recounted here is true. Only the names, dates, and places are changed to protect the privacy of the famous personages involved in this highly-charged mystery.

Problem: Dr. Wheeler, a British archaeologist at a large university left his office on Friday December 17, 2003, around 10 P.M. on a cold Friday evening. This was his last night to be at the university because he would not be back again until after the holidays.

Right before he left his office, he placed a thin, reddish, three-ring notebook in an unlocked cupboard.

Dr. Wheeler then proceeded to go directly to his designated campus parking space, got into his Mini Cooper S, and drove directly to his flat in Marshalltown Goldens. When he arrived home, he went straightaway to his study. He remained at his flat with his family and never left his flat during the entire holiday.

Dr. Wheeler and his family had a jolly good holiday, and Dr. Wheeler thought nothing more of his notebook until the university resumed its session on Wednesday, January 5, 2004, at the beginning of the New Year.

Upon returning to his office, Dr. Wheeler could not find his notebook in the cupboard, and he became very agitated. He chased his assistant, Miss Mortimer, around the office, wielding a wicked looking Acheulean hand ax. Poor Miss Mortimer claimed that she had no knowledge of the whereabouts of the notebook.

But Dr. Wheeler had always suspected that Miss Mortimer pinched pens and pencils from his desk, so, naturally. . . . But Miss Mortimer protested so earnestly that Dr. Wheeler eventually settled in, had a cup of tea, and decided that perhaps he had absentmindedly taken the notebook home after all.

However, a thorough search of his flat indicated that the notebook was clearly not there. It was lost! Dr. Wheeler had almost lost himself when his wife, Sophia, caught him excavating her rose garden in the vain hope that Tut, the family dog, had buried the lost article there. It was a professor's nightmare, since the notebook contained the only copy of all his class records for the entire term. What could he do? He knew he was in danger of being fired for incompetence.

So, Dr. Wheeler approached the problem in the manner of a proper, eccentric archaeologist. He had another cup of tea and generated several hypotheses about where his notebook might have gone. He tested several hypotheses, but to no avail!

© Hisham F. Ibrahim/Getty Images

His notebook still remained missing. However, being the good archaeologist he was, he kept on generating hypotheses. But his notebook was still not found. Then he began to wonder if maybe the post-processualists weren't right after all!

Dr. Wheeler was at his wits' end when, pure luck intervened, as it often does in archaeology. You just get lucky sometimes. Everyone does. His faithful assistant Miss Mortimer received a phone call on January 9, 2004, from a woman who had found the missing notebook on the evening of December 31, 2003. The helpful lady found his notebook in a gutter! To be precise, she found it in a family neighborhood located on the corner of Olduvai Drive and East Turkana Avenue in Hadar Heights, about a mile away from the university. Please note that this area is in the opposite direction from Dr. Wheeler's flat in Marshalltown Goldens. The notebook was wet and muddy, and furthermore, it was wedged down into a gutter grill in the street.

Greatly relieved, the next day, January 10, 2004, Dr. Wheeler had Miss Mortimer run over to the kind woman's flat. It was in this mysterious way that he recouped his class records. Dr. Wheeler was so delighted that when Miss Mortimer returned with the notebook, he invited her to sit and join him for a pot of tea (which was not his habit, being a misogynist). Yet, Dr. Wheeler was not satisfied with merely recovering his notebook. He was curious to know what had happened to it and why! He continued to generate more sophisticated hypotheses to solve the mystery.

Challenge to the Student

Try to place yourself in Dr. Wheeler's position. Attempt to generate your own hypotheses as to the whereabouts of the lost notebook from the night of Friday, December 17, 2003, to the time of its return on January 10, 2004.

How do you go about doing this? First, review everything you "believe" to be true. Be very careful and skeptical about what is true and what is not. Then convert this into your original database. From that point, again set up more hypotheses and/or make alternative hypotheses until you arrive at the simplest possible explanation. The simplest possible explanation is most likely to be the correct answer. Support your answer with your database.

Pretend that you are doing historical archaeology. Ask your living informant(s) for information first. What could you ask Dr. Wheeler? You could ask, "Did you go back to the lavatory before you left the building on December 17, 2003? Are you sure of where your motorcar was parked or could you be mistaken? What was the weather like? Was it raining? Is it possible that you in fact stopped and talked to someone on your way to your motorcar? Are you sure you were home on December 31, 2003 and not out to celebrate the New Year?" Be very precise with your questioning. Also, let your imagination run wild with possibilities. Brainstorm. Sometimes this is when you are most likely to get the answer. Creativity is the essence of all science.

Hints

Dr. Wheeler's university office was never broken into. Poor Miss Mortimer and the kind lady who found the notebook had nothing to do with the disappearance of the notebook. Dr. Wheeler's dog Tut did not bury his notebook. So what did happen? There is in fact a correct answer that will explain the mystery. Try to find that answer! To do this, you will have to think like an archaeologist. It is a lot of fun, and it will reward you well!

Artful Surgery

Greek archaeologists discover evidence of a skilled surgeon who practiced centuries before Hippocrates.

ANAGNOSTIS P. AGELARAKIS

Sometime before 600 B.C., a surgeon in the settlement of Abdera on the north coast of the Aegean faced a difficult case. Standing back from his patient, a young woman in her late twenties lying on the table before him, he examined the wound cautiously. Normal practice required that the healer ask how an injury occurred, but here it was clear from the broken flesh and hair matted with blood. A stone or lead missile, hurled from a sling by one of the native Thracians intent on the colony's destruction, had bit her on the back of the head. Stepping closer, a grave expression on his face, the surgeon gently explored the wound by hand and with a bronze probe. As he feared, the impact was at a point where the bones came together, joining in a suture—the weakest point of the skull.

Today, most medical students take a solemn vow, repeating the Hippocratic Oath, named for Hippocrates, the ancient Greek physician we call the "Father of Medicine." Although we know little about him—he has been described as the "most famous but least known Greek physician"—in his own day, Hippocrates (ca. 460–370 B.C.) was spoken of with respect by Plato and Aristotle. He was born at the island of Kos, near Ionia (the eastern coast of the Aegean Sea), and after practicing medicine throughout Greece, he devoted considerable time to teaching students.

None of the surviving late fifth- and early fourth-century B.C. Greek medical treatises—numbering about 70 and collectively known as the Hippocratic corpus—can be securely ascribed to the great physician himself. They could have been compiled by his students, who conceivably added to their master's notes, handbooks, and lecture materials. Perhaps in part from a library on Kos, the texts—gathered together in Alexandria at a later date—reflect the rich legacy of the Ionian school of medicine.

Some of the works are instructional, such as *About the Physician* and *In the Surgery*. Others, such as *Fractures* and *On Head Wounds,* appear to have been written as practical handbooks. Of these, the *Oxford Classical Dictionary* notes that, "The directions for bandaging and for diagnosis and treatment

of dislocations and fractures, especially of depressed fractures of the skull, are very impressive." And it describes *On Head Wounds* "as a practical work by a highly skilled craftsman, and every sentence suggests experience." Indeed, it was still in use as a medical text in Europe more than two millennia after it was written.

But new evidence, on which the story of the wounded young woman at the head of this article is based, will rewrite our history of the development of ancient medical practice. The patient was among those sent north by Clazomenae, a Greek city in Ionia, to establish a colony at Abdera around 654 B.C. She was successfully treated—a difficult operation performed by a master surgeon saved her—and lived for another 20 years. Her remains, which were excavated at Abdera by Eudokia Skarlatidou of the Greek Archaeological Service and which I have had the privilege to study, provide incontrovertible evidence that two centuries before Hippocrates drew breath, surgical practices described in the treatise *On Head Wounds* were already in use.

According to the historian Herodotus, the Clazomeneans at Abdera were "driven out by the Thracians" who perhaps conducted a war of attrition, contesting the colonists' access to land for agriculture and timber or plundering and destroying their crops. Yet the archaeological record indicates that the Clazomenean settlers persisted for at least eight decades, and excavations have revealed many traces of their colony, including its 13-foot-thick fortification walls and cemeteries. In one burial ground was the grave with the well-preserved skeleton of the woman who had survived the wound and subsequent surgery.

From her bones, I could determine that apart from some dental pathologies and arthritis of the spine and limbs, she had been relatively healthy and quite physically active before she died of an unknown cause. The healed wound itself is dramatic: a hole about the size of a quarter (14.8 by 9.2 mm) on the back right side of her skull is surrounded by a larger oval area (66.4 by 19.9 mm) where the surgeon scraped the bone with a rasp, leaving faintly discernible marks that radiate outward from the opening.

When the young woman was hit, the stone or lead missile crushed the soft tissues of her scalp and caused a serious depressed fracture, possibly with the projectile embedded in the bone. Sharp edges on fissure fractures extending from the wound endangered the dura mater (the fibrous membrane enveloping the brain). Surgery was needed to remove bone splinters and possibly the lodged missile, eliminate fissures, evaluate the condition of the dura mater if exposed, and apply "healing drugs."

To judge by procedures set out in *On Head Wounds,* the surgeon first evaluated the injury without touching the patient, then by touching and subsequently by using a probe to better diagnose the type, extent, and severity of the trauma. He asked about the injury and the patient's physiological responses to it. Then he cut and opened up the soft tissues surrounding the wound for better visual inspection and preparation for surgical intervention before dressing the wound with a paste of fine barley wheat boiled with vinegar. The next day, he further cleaned and dried the soft tissues around the wound and made a final diagnosis of the bone injury And he might have spread black ink on the cleaned bone; it would seep into and reveal any hairline fissures that might not be visible otherwise.

On Head Wounds sets forth diagnostic procedures for identifying and treating a range of cranial injuries caused by different weapons. In most cases, a wound on the back of the head—"where the bone is thicker and oozing puss will take longer to reach the brain"—was less likely to be fatal than one in the front. But, as in the case of the woman from Abdera, "When a suture shows at the exposed bone area of the wound—of a wound anywhere on the head—the resistance of the bone to the traumatic impact is very weak should the weapon get wedged in the suture." So, according to the Hippocratic text, the case was a serious one. It was made more so because of the nature of the weapon, a missile from a sling, because, "Of those weapons that strike the head and wound close to the cranial bone and the cranium itself, that one that will fall from a highest level rather than from a trajectory parallel to the ground, and being at the same time the hardest, bluntest, and heaviest . . . will crack and compress the cranial bone."

For compressed head fractures, *On Head Wounds* recommends trepanation, removal of a disk of bone from the skull using a drill with a serrated circular bit. This would eliminate the danger of bone splinters and radiating fracture fissures. It would also permit the removal of bone fragments that had been crushed inward, allowing the brain to swell from the contusion without pressing against loose bone fragments with sharp edges that might puncture the dura mater. But there was one cranial area where a scraping approach was strongly recommended instead of trepanation: "It is necessary, if the wound is at the sutures and the weapon penetrated and lodged into the bone, to pay attention for recognizing the kind of injury sustained by the bone. Because . . . he who received the weapon at the sutures will suffer far greater impact at the cranial bone than the one who did not receive it at the sutures. And most of those require trepanation, but you must not trepan the sutures themselves . . . you are required to scrape the surface of the cranial bone with a rasp in depth and length, according to the position of the wound, and then cross-wise to be able to see the hidden breakages and

crushes . . . because scraping exposes the harm well, even if those injuries . . . were not otherwise revealed."

Should you determine that the bone is denuded of flesh and that it is not healthy as a consequence of the trauma, it is necessary to carry out a diagnosis of its condition: the extent of the impact and the nature of the surgical intervention required . . . if the wound is at a suture and the weapon penetrated and lodged in the bone, it is necessary to pay attention to recognize the kind of injury sustained by the bone. . . .

— Attributed to Hippocrates

Faced with a compressed fracture with radiating fissure fractures and fearing damage to the dura mater, the surgeon scraped the bone in length, width, and depth, removing fragments and eliminating the fissures through scraping and not trepanation. He then would have tended to any adjacent injured tissues.

While the reconstruction of the patient's treatment is in part conjecture, based on the Hippocratic text itself, the size and shape of the surgical intervention and use of the rasp rather than trepanation is certain from traces on the bone itself. So the surgical procedure matches perfectly what was recommended two centuries later in *On Head Wounds* for this type of injury in this location.

Ancient Greek sources offer little aid in tracing the development of medicine before Hippocrates. It is not surprising that medical historian Guido Majno wrote in *The Healing Hand* that "the beginnings of Greek medicine, which should fill a library, are mostly blank pages." Medical writings from before the Hippocratic corpus have not survived. Moreover, we only know of one real Greek physician before Hippocrates. The historian Herodotus notes that some time after 522 B.C., a Democedes successfully treated the Persian king Darius I for a sprained ankle *after* Egyptian doctors had failed. But that is still a century after the unknown physician of Abdera performed his masterful surgery.

If we look to earlier times, Homer, before 700 B.C., describes more than 140 combat injuries in the *Iliad* and, in a few cases, tells how they were treated—the arrow or spear extracted, ointment applied to reduce the pain and stop the bleeding, and the wounds bound. But in all the Greek army there are only two trained healers, Machaon and Podalirios, both sons of the legendary hero-physician Aesclepius, son of the god Apollo. The healers were highly valued, and when Machaon is wounded, he is rushed off the battlefield in a chariot because, says Homer, "the physician who knows how to extract arrowheads and with herbal ointments to cure the wounds" is worth the lives of many men.

But medicine has an element of the supernatural in Homer. When Machaon and Podalirios are unavailable, it falls to Achilles' comrade Patroclus to treat a wounded warrior. He does so using a method he learned from Achilles. Who taught both Aesclepius and Achilles? According to Homer it was Chiron, the wisest of all the centaurs. And in the *Odyssey,* when the young prince Odysseus is injured by a boar, a charm is recited over the wound to staunch the blood.

Medicine in the Iliad, composed just a century before the Clazomenean physician at Abdera, is rather simplistic. Clearly, significant advances in medical thought took place during the eighth and early seventh centuries B.C. Perhaps the sociopolitical changes that occurred with the emergence of city-states favored the rapid evolution of medical practice. While one cannot argue that the Ionian Greeks developed sophisticated medical practices entirely in isolation, there is no strong evidence that they drew on an outside source in making the jump from simple battlefield first aid or reciting a charm over a wound to performing the sophisticated skull surgery exhibited on the young woman from Abdera.

We do not know exactly how the Clazomeneans chose the colonists who sailed to Abdera. Were they an elite group, the less wealthy who were willing to risk the venture, or the politically and socially disfavored? We do know, however, that among them there was a masterful surgeon, Hippocrates' predecessor, who was among the earliest of the Ionian school of medical practitioners.

ANAGNOSTIS P. AGELARAKIS is a professor of physical anthropology at Adelphi University; the translations of Hippocratic and Homeric excerpts are his. He would like to thank Evi Skarlatidou, excavator of Abdera cemetery K, and Ntina Kallintzi, head archaeologist of the Museum at Abdera.

From *Archaeology,* March/April 2006, pp. 26–29. Copyright © 2006 by Archaeological Institute of America. Reprinted by permission.

Where Was Jesus Born?

**Theologians question biblical accounts of the Nativity.
Now archaeologists are doing the same.**

AVIRAM OSHRI

The town of Bethlehem in the West Bank, some six miles south of Jerusalem, is revered by millions as the birthplace of Jesus. According to the New Testament account of the apostle Matthew, Joseph and Mary were living in Bethlehem in the southern region of Judea at the time of Jesus' birth and later moved to Nazareth in the northern Galilee region. In the more popular account of the apostle Luke, Joseph and a very pregnant Mary traveled more than 90 miles from their residence in Nazareth to Joseph's Judean hometown of Bethlehem to be counted in a Roman census. Regardless of the variation, both apostles agree that Jesus was born in Bethlehem in Judea, the city where King David had been born a thousand years earlier. The Christian Messiah could thereby be considered a descendant of the House of David—a requirement for followers of the Judeo-Christian tradition.

But while Luke and Matthew describe Bethlehem in Judea as the birthplace of Jesus, "Menorah," the vast database of the Israel Antiquities Authority (IAA), describes Bethlehem as an "ancient site" with Iron Age material and the fourth-century Church of the Nativity and associated Byzantine and medieval buildings. But there is a complete absence of information for antiquities from the Herodian period—that is, from the time around the birth of Jesus.

During the earliest excavations of the church, carried out by the Antiquities Department of the British Mandate in Palestine in the mid-1930s, archaeologists found a mosaic floor dating to the sixth century A.D., and below that, the remains of a church from the reign of Constantine in the first half of the fourth century A.D. Artifacts from the Middle Ages were recovered from trenches six feet deep in the church courtyard. Excavations in the 1920s revealed a Late Roman lead coffin and Byzantine Christian graves. Following the Six-Day War in 1967, surveys in Bethlehem showed plenty of Iron Age pottery, but excavations by several Israeli archaeologists revealed no artifacts at all from the Early Roman or Herodian periods. In fact, with the single exception of a 50-year-old Jordanian publication that mentions Herodian pottery sherds found in a corner of the church, there is surprisingly no archaeological evidence that ties Bethlehem in Judea to the period in which

Jesus would have been born. Furthermore, in this time the aqueduct from Solomon's Pools to Jerusalem ran through the area of Bethlehem. This fact strengthens the likelihood of an absence of settlement at the site, as, according to the Roman architect Vitruvius, no aqueduct passes through the heart of a city. Only about a half-mile outside Bethlehem in Judea have some Herodian-period remains been found, and it may be possible that people had resettled elsewhere nearby during this time.

I had never before questioned the assumption that Jesus was born in Bethlehem in Judea. But in the early 1990s, as an archaeologist working for the IAA, I was contracted to perform some salvage excavations around building and infrastructure projects in a small rural community in the Galilee. When I started work, some of the people who lived around the site told me how Jesus was really born there, not in the south. Intrigued, I researched the archaeological evidence for Bethlehem in Judea at the time of Jesus and found nothing. This was very surprising, as Herodian remains should be the first thing one should find. What was even more surprising is what archaeologists had already uncovered and what I was to discover over the next 11 years of excavation at the small rural site—Bethlehem of Galilee.

Bethlehem of Galilee is mentioned for the first time in Joshua 19:14, as one of the towns allotted to the tribe of Zebulun. Its name is recorded again in a list of priest guardians who moved to the Galilee after the destruction of the Second Temple, and again by Eusebius, who notes there are two Bethlehems: one in "the Zebulun region" and one in Judea. Today, the 200-household community, some four miles west of Nazareth, is a quiet agricultural center that also attracts tourists with its bed-and-breakfasts and holistic spas.

Religious scholars had long questioned whether the Bible's only Nativity narratives set in Bethlehem in Judea were a deliberate attempt by Matthew and Luke to associate Jesus with the House of David and reinforce his status as Messiah among the early Jewish convert communities. Indeed, there is a passage in John (7:41–43) in which Jesus' legitimacy is questioned because he is from the Galilee and not Judea. But the generally accepted alternative to Bethlehem of Judea was the town in which Jesus grew up—Nazareth. Scholars only began to unite about the possibility of Bethlehem of Galilee being the birthplace of Jesus in the late nineteenth century.

Between 1992 and 2003, I carried out five salvage excavations in Bethlehem of Galilee. The ancient ruins cover 37 acres immediately west of the modern settlement, and a small portion still contains standing remains. A nineteenth-century survey of the Galilee describes two ruins at this site, a synagogue and church. The synagogue has not been identified, but it has been tentatively located in an unexcavated area. The church was first exposed in 1965, when a road from Nazareth to Bethlehem was built, destroying the main hall and revealing sixth-century mosaic floors decorated with medallions of vines with figures of animals and plant motifs.

We know that Bethlehem of Galilee was a bustling center of Jewish life around the time of Jesus' birth. Among the archaeological evidence we have for this is a workshop that made stone vessels used for Jewish purification rituals, which are otherwise a very rare find in the Galilee in this period. There are also the remains of a Herodian-period residential area with ceramic and stone vessels that would have been used by a Jewish population.

When I first arrived at Bethlehem of Galilee in 1992 and saw the ruins, I didn't think that there was much left to find. But soon I discovered the church's baptismal font as well as more mosaic floor remains from the church, indicating a structure 145 feet long and between 80 and 100 feet wide. This makes it among the largest Byzantine churches in Israel and raises the question of why such a huge house of Christian worship was built in the heart of a Jewish area.

During that same year, my team found another building from the same period just northeast of the church containing an oil press, an underground vault with candles bearing cross decorations, and an abundance of pig bones. On the basis of these and many other findings, we identified the building as a monastery. Five years later, excavations near the monastery revealed the remains of a large public building, possibly a hotel or inn, with horse troughs on the ground floor and well-appointed facilities on the second floor, which included a lavish mosaic floor, All three buildings—the church, monastery, and inn—appear to have been violently destroyed during the Persian invasion of the Holy Land in the early seventh century A.D.

Over the years, segments of a three-foot-thick fortification wall with ramparts and towers have been discovered by myself and others around Bethlehem of Galilee. Ceramic evidence dates the wall to the sixth–eventh century A.D., before the Persian invasion. If this is a Byzantine-era fortification, its meaning is significant. At this time, Bethlehem of Galilee was not a large or significant city, and the fact that it was fortified shows that its existence was in danger. Jews had been expelled from Jerusalem from the second century A.D. to the end of the Byzantine period, but we know from contemporary accounts that the population in the Galilee during this time was overwhelmingly Jewish. Is it possible that, because of the hostility the Jews had toward Christians in this period, the residents of Bethlehem of Galilee fortified the site which they held to be the birthplace of the Christian Messiah?

Texts from the Middle Ages describe an Eastern Christian community living in Bethlehem of Galilee, and we have archaeological evidence that agrees with this. It is unclear what, if any, Christian population resided in Bethlehem of Galilee during the Ottoman period, but at the beginning of the twentieth century, a group of missionaries from a German organization known as the Temple Society settled in Bethlehem of Galilee. Although there is no recorded reason for their settlement, it is widely believed that the religious order chose this Bethlehem because they identified it with the site of the birth of Jesus. They were eventually exiled to Australia because they supported the Nazis in World War II.

Today, the residents of Bethlehem of Galilee make a comfortable living through agriculture and tourism and are quite happy to leave the crowds of religious pilgrims to Bethlehem in Judea. One man in town grows Christmas trees for Christians living in nearby Nazareth. My government-funded salvage excavations are over, but I am trying to find support to continue the project, as there is still so much left at the site to discover and understand.

If the historical Jesus were truly born in Bethlehem, it was most likely the Bethlehem of Galilee, not that in Judea. The archaeological evidence certainly seems to favor the former, a busy center a few miles from the home of Joseph and Mary, as opposed to an unpopulated spot almost a hundred miles from home. At the very least, it is an improbable trip for a pregnant women to have made on a donkey.

AVIRAM OSHRI is a senior archaeologist with the Israeli Antiquities Authority.

From *Archaeology*, Nov/Dec 2005, pp. 42–45. Copyright © 2005 by Archaeological Institute of America. Reprinted by permission.

Legacy *of the* Crusades

The ruins of castles on hillsides throughout the Middle East are mute reminders of a bloody chapter in medieval history.

SANDRA SCHAM

A story is told in Kerak, a small city in Jordan dominated by a well-preserved crusader castle, about the fortress' most notorious denizen, Reynauld of Chatillon. According to this tale, the Hajj route to Mecca during Reynauld's time, the late twelfth century A.D., passed beneath his castle walls. Attracted by the richness of one caravan, Reynauld swooped down on the unfortunate pilgrims, capturing all and relieving them of their worldly goods. At the end of his foray, he found, to his immense glee, that one of his hostages was the sister of the legendary Islamic leader Saladin. Reynauld's fellow crusaders were appalled by his brazen violation of a rather tenuous truce. Baldwin IV, king of Jerusalem, sent a message forthwith, demanding that Reynauld release his distinguished prisoner. Reynauld's answer reflects his customary bravado: "You are king of Jerusalem," he wrote, "but I am king in Kerak."

Kerak, though, never had a king, a fact well known to both Reynauld and the local guides who repeat this story. Nevertheless, although it was within the boundaries of the crusader kingdom of Jerusalem, Kerak was also far enough away from the center of power to enable its ruler to do pretty much as he pleased—that is, summarily executing prisoners, whether they were men, women, or children, in the most brutal manner imaginable. Reynauld eventually got his just desserts, and has the dubious distinction of being the only important crusader to have been personally executed by Saladin.

The castle of Kerak is built on a spur to take advantage of the natural defense accorded by this topography. The town of Kerak has grown all around the spur and it is usually a lively tourist destination. I visited the site, familiar to me from previous sojourns in Jordan, on a beautiful day this past summer, when one would normally expect to see tour buses and guides hustling large groups through the castle gates. The streets were empty. Abdul Hamied, one of Kerak's more knowledgeable local guides, explained, "Tourism in Jordan is down by 70 percent-I worked only seven days this year." Jordan is feeling the effects of the prolonged Israeli-Palestinian struggle, despite the fact that it has been relatively free from conflict itself.

The castle of Kerak in Jordan was once home to notorious crusader knight Reynauld of Chatillon, who preyed on pilgrims traveling to Mecca. A popular tourist destination in modern times, the castle has recently seen a drop in visitors because of the ongoing Israeli-Palestinian conflict.

Reflecting on battles both past and present, and the physical legacy of these conflicts ever-present in the landscape, I asked Hamied what he learned about crusader history growing up in Kerak in the shadow of this looming medieval structure. "We were taught that they came from Pharaoh's Island [off the coast of the Sinai Peninsula] and built this line of castles here [from Aqaba to Turkey] to control the trading business," he replied. "When these crusaders came, they came as invaders—killing thousands. And they were not coming for religion or 'holy war.' It was an economic war that used religion."

Aziz Azayzeh, another guide at Kerak, agrees with this assessment. "As a Jordanian, I learned in school that the crusaders came and took our lands just because of greed and gave us nothing in return." Both men, however, true to their professions, say similar things about the crusader sites. Azayzeh continues, "Later, when I studied more about them, I think they did give us something—they were good architects. You know Saladin was smart. He asked the best architects and artists from the crusaders to stay and work." Hamied is more philosophical: "The crusaders—they came as invaders, the Romans came as invaders, in Hellenistic times also. The big powers everywhere—they look to their own interests, but they left something behind for us at these places."

Listening to these remarks, as I stood at the summit of Kerak, I recalled a conversation I had with a colleague before leaving the United States. Salman Elbedour, an American psychology professor who is also an Israeli Bedouin, told me that there is a "Crusader Complex" in the Middle East. Consequently, it was no surprise to him that President Bush's rather bizarre juxtaposition of ideas, promising to rid the world of the perpetrators of violence in the name of religion, while at the same time labeling the American incursion in Afghanistan a "crusade," was perceived as a major affront by the Arab world. Elbedour and other Muslims, whose ancestors lived in the very heart of crusader territory, see the crusaders as the ultimate vicious usurpers. Archaeologist Adel Yahyeh, who lives in Ramallah on the West Bank, adds, "When we were children in Palestine, our nightmares were about monsters coming after us, wearing crosses on their chests. We even started to see Israeli soldiers that way—strange as it seems."

You go to Lebanon, Syria, Jordan today . . . you can see that many of the crusaders stayed and married, and that today we are a mixture of people.

Crusader sites, like the crusader tradition, inspire a variety of emotions and thoughts. The castles are what most people think of when they envision the crusader period (1097–1291), and many Arabs, says Yahyeh, take a measure of pride in them, since it was the Arabs who liberated the castles from their Christian enemy. But there are other effects of the period to be considered, as well. "You go to Lebanon, Syria, Jordan today . . . you can see that many of the crusaders stayed and married, and that today we are a mixture of people," says Azayzeh. This casual statement actually reflects the focus of a great deal of new archaeological activity relating to crusader sites in the region. Although it was long believed that European culture did not penetrate rural areas in the Levant, excavations of villages and farmsteads with crusader architecture, sugar refining equipment (a fairly new industry in the medieval period), and a general increase in pig bones at rural sites now indicate otherwise.

Of course, Muslims are not the only ones to have suffered at the hands of the crusaders. Eastern Orthodox Christians and Jews have their own perspectives on this period. As Jörg Bremer, a German historian and journalist who is now living in Jerusalem, says, "Today, we talk of special [collective] memories of the Crusades." Jews see the Crusades, he continues, "as having started in Germany with killing of Jews." Then, there is "the tradition of the Eastern Church relating to the sack of Byzantium" (by crusaders in 1204—when it was an entirely Christian city). Finally, he speaks of the revival of crusader consciousness among Muslims who see "the state of Israel today as neo-crusader."

Bremer is a latter-day member of the Order of the Knights of St. John (the Hospitallers), as were his ancestors, and explains, "The Hospitallers were in the Holy Land long before the Crusades and were not called 'knights' until the real crusaders came." Hospitaller tradition, he says, avers that "we were the only European group that was allowed to stay [after the crusaders]

were defeated]." Bremer laments the fact that the Hospitallers, originally a peaceful group, were forced by the coming of the Templars to bear arms. The Templars were founded in 1119 for the purpose of defending Christian pilgrims in the Holy Land, while the Hospitallers, so-called because their principal mission was to care for the sick, did not become a military order until 1130, some 60 years after having been founded in Jerusalem.

The historical and cultural legacy of the Crusades is accompanied by a concrete, or rather stone, legacy, dotting hillsides throughout the Middle East. Less obvious than the isolated castles like Kerak are the crusader remains in the cities, many of which were built upon in subsequent eras. Jerusalem and Akko (Acre), the two most important cities of medieval times, are replete with varied examples of crusader architecture. In Jerusalem, the centerpiece of the crusader kingdom, many sites were modified by the crusaders, but they built from the ground up as well. Not surprisingly, most of these activities centered on churches; the complete rebuilding of the Church of the Holy Sepulchre was a major project. The church was consecrated in 1149, a half-century after the crusaders first seized Jerusalem, and stands today largely in its crusader form.

Akko's harbor served as the primary port of entry for pilgrims to the Holy Land. Today, local residents take a plunge into the Mediterranean from the city's crusader fortifications.

Despite this fact, many members of Eastern Orthodox denominations think of the Church of the Holy Sepulchre as Byzantine. "It was first built in the fourth century, and there are still Byzantine structures," explains Ardin Sisserian, an Eastern Orthodox gatekeeper and guide at the Church. The reason for his de-emphasis on crusader architecture here may have something to do with tensions between the Catholics, "whose ancestors came with the sword and the Cross," says Sisserian, and the other four faiths that have access to the Church—all Eastern Christian.

Bremer encountered similar tensions when he and other modern Hospitallers asked to pray at Jerusalem's twelfth-century Church of St. John the Baptist, patron saint of their order. Although the Greek Orthodox Church now owns the structure, it was once so important to the Hospitallers that they maintained guards there after the expulsion of other crusaders and the retaking of Jerusalem by Saladin in 1244. The Hospitallers were denied permission to pray there until 2001, when, Bremer says, they went to Greek Orthodox officials to open what he calls a "diplomatic channel," with the formal admission that "this part of our history is horrible" and that they wanted to go "on the record as recognizing special ties with the Eastern Church." As a result, Bremer says, they "could pray in the church for the first time in 800 years."

These days, most visitors to the Church of the Holy Sepulchre appear to be Israelis rather than Christian pilgrims—who, like many others, are leery of coming to what they perceive to be a war zone. Among the groups speaking Hebrew and touring the church on one Shabbat (Jewish Sabbath) afternoon were several people wearing yarmulkes, as well as seemingly secular Jews. A nonreligious member of a group of mixed religious and secular students, Hagai Dror, explained, "Christians today seem closer to Jews than Muslims do. We see these sites as European, and many of us who have a European background are interested in them." His friend, Gal Ariely, added, "The main reason we are here is because we live here. This is my city, and it's my duty to know about it." This last statement reflects the sense of ownership that many young Israelis feel about Jerusalem. Yossi is an ultra-orthodox Jewish resident of the Mt. Zion's Diaspora Yeshiva, which is housed in a building that was at one time a fourteenth-century crusader monastery. Yossi, who had a strictly religious education in Jerusalem, says that he knows nothing about crusaders except that "I live in a crusader house."

The city of Akko was the last major crusader foothold in Palestine—finally falling to the Muslim forces in 1291, after 100 years of renewed crusader rule. Akko's crusader remains can now be seen below the city's current street level in the northern part of today's walled Old Town. It's a fascinating labyrinth of underground structures unearthed by excavations that began in the late 1950s and continue today. There are barracks for the knights, a hall of the crusader palace, an underground sewage system with a number of public toilets, and portions of crusader streets and walls—all visible beneath the bustling Ottoman city above.

Akko's Ottoman structures, largely built on top of the crusader ruins, represent the Arab character of the city, past and present. The people who live in most of the houses in the Old City, however, were moved there from the Galilee after 1948 (the year of the establishment of the state of Israel), when Akko's older indigenous Arab population fled the city. Ron Be'eri, an archaeologist from the University of Haifa who works at Akko, says that the people who live there today "feel little connection with the city's history" and generally view the historical character of their own houses as an annoyance. Considered abandoned property owned by the State of Israel, these places are occupied mostly by Arab renters who are not permitted, even if they have the funds, to buy them. They are also not permitted, because these are historic structures, to alter them in any way. Consequently, most of the Old City's residences are in great disrepair.

Nevertheless, Erica Gal of the Akko Development Corporation insists that Akko's locals take an interest in the heritage of their city. "Schools visit the subterranean [crusader] site all the time and, from the fifth grade, local students take a course called 'Akko, My Town' in which they learn all of the local history." She does suggest that visits by local people to Akko underground may be limited by the fact that they must buy tickets to gain access to it. Be'eri believes that "very few" of the Old City's residents have ever visited the crusader site, but this may reflect their hostility toward "heritage sites" in general, given their experience with them, rather than any residual resentment of crusaders.

Although the schools of Akko may take an interest in crusader sites as part of the local history, education in most of Israel, as distinct from Jordan, glosses over the crusader occupation. "We learn nothing about this period in school," says Salman Elbedour, who received an Israeli education. According to Israeli archaeologist Adrian Boas, the crusader period, which is his area of specialization, is not a favored subject for Israeli historians and archaeologists, although he points out that a recent crusader exhibit at the Israel Museum in Jerusalem drew large crowds. As to the historical antagonism, "If you asked the average Jew here about this," he says, "they wouldn't have a clue what you were talking about." Attitudes toward crusader sites in Israel are a reflection of cultural ties to, or antipathies toward, the Crusades as well as individually held beliefs. Boas, originally from Australia, says that his interest in the Crusades and crusader sites comes "from basically having grown up in an Anglo-Saxon country. As a child, I was always interested in the medieval period." Elbedour says that he has no interest in visiting crusader sites. Bremer, who has visited the sites, says that many of the castles look "so militant—like tank posts on top of a hill."

While Boas admires the "tactical advantages" of Kerak and other spur castles, he says that he is most impressed with Belvoir, a Hospitaller castle overlooking the Jordan River and the Damascus to Jerusalem Road. In this case, the strategical importance of Belvoir's location in the past is repeated in the present as today, it overlooks the boundaries between Israel and the West Bank, and Israel and Jordan. One of the earliest examples of the "concentric castle" or castrum, a building with one fortification wall entirely enclosing another, Belvoir remains one of the most remarkable buildings of this type.

On the coast south of Akko is probably one of the few crusader sites in the Middle East that is regularly visited by people who live there. Elbedour admits to having been to only one crusader site, Caesarea, but only "because it's on the [Mediterranean] Sea." Although the town witnessed few historical events in the past, some crusader buildings at Caesarea have an interesting modern history. One of them, the citadel, became a mosque after the defeat of the crusaders. With the founding of the state of Israel and subsequent displacement of the local population of Muslims, the mosque became a restaurant and bar, a state of affairs that was bound to offend those Muslims remaining in the region. The restaurant, called "The Castle," is now closed.

Caesarea's crusader—and Roman-era ruins were restored to attract foreign tourists. Its location on a stretch of sandy Mediterranean beach makes it popular with Israeli visitors.

Caesarea, according to Pennsylvania State University archaeologist Ann Killebrew, was among those sites that the Israel Antiquities Authority decided early on to develop. Crusader remains and Roman ruins, although they do not precisely reflect the ethnic or religious character of the country today, were restored specifically to attract foreign tourists, she says. In the 1990s, Caesarea was further embellished as a result of the government's efforts to provide employment to workers from the nearby town of Or Akiva. As a result, says Killebrew, the site has been "completely uncovered, and has become unattractive to tourists."

Some writers who have recently looked at the legacy of the Crusades, such as Karen Armstrong (*Holy War*) and, to a lesser extent, Bernard Lewis (*What Went Wrong?*) believe they are the source of the troubles afflicting the Middle East today. Whether or not the Crusades were responsible for bringing West and East together or, conversely, the origin of the struggles now taking place in the region, it seems certain that a crusader legacy, lasting almost 1,000 years, is not a media fantasy. In few places in the world is ancient history given such immediacy as in the Middle East. The founding of the state of Israel in 1948 was partially predicated on the biblical history of the region during the Iron Age—a period some 3,000 years in the past. A trauma that is only 900 years old is relatively recent in a place where history is marked by millennia rather than centuries.

SANDRA SCHAM, a contributing editor for *Archaeology,* is an archaeologist who has been living and working in Israel since 1996. A former curator of the Pontifical Biblical Institute Museum in Jerusalem, she is currently affiliated with the department of anthropology at the University of Maryland at College Park.

From *Archaeology,* September/October 2002 , pp. 24–30. Copyright © 2002 by Sandra Scham. Reprinted by permission of the author.

Secrets of the Medici

Excavation of Florence's first family reveals clues to the lifestyles of the Renaissance rich, solves a murder mystery, and turns up a lost treasure.

GINO FORNACIARI, BOB BRIER, AND ANTONIO FORNACIARI

The Medici were among the most powerful families in the world. Beginning in the fourteenth century, they built a fortune bankrolling popes and kings. Through their wealth and their political abilities, they went from being one of many patrician clans in Florence to the city's hereditary rulers. They married into the royal houses of Austria and France, and two of their number were made pope. Scholars and lovers of art, the Medici were patrons of Leonardo, Raphael, Botticelli, Galileo, Michelangelo, and Cellini. And under their rule, Florence became the intellectual hub of the Western world.

The Medici were also legendary for their adeptness at intrigue and murder. In 1537, for example, Cosimo I came to power when the reigning duke, Alessandro Medici, was assassinated by a cousin. The 18-year-old Cosimo—son of Giovanni Medici, the family's greatest military captain, but from a junior branch—was not accepted by many of the leading families of Florence. They took up arms against him, but Cosimo was victorious on the battlefield. And those of his opponents who survived, including Alessandro's murderer, met with "unfortunate accidents" shortly thereafter.

Many of the leading Medici were buried in the Chapel of San Lorenzo in Florence, which long enjoyed the family's patronage. In 2004, we obtained Superintendent Antonio Paolucci's permission to examine 47 of the Medici interred there, including Cosimo. The multiyear project is a unique opportunity to study the health of the Medici (a rare look at a single family over a long period) and might settle allegations of murder to be found in legends about the dynasty.

We had no idea what we would find. In 1857, after it was discovered that the Medici tombs, then above ground in the chapel, had been plundered, their remains were buried below its floor for protection. Brass plaques set into the floor indicate where they were buried, but there were no precise records of how they were buried. Moreover, in 1947 researchers intent primarily on examining the skulls exhumed several Medici but left virtually no record of what they found or how they reburied them. A final uncertainty was what effect the disastrous 1966 flood of the Arno River, which inundated the chapel, might have had on the remains.

Our first subjects were Cosimo I; his wife, Eleonora of Toledo; and two of their sons, Giovanni and Garzia. Cosimo married Eleonora, daughter of the Spanish viceroy of Naples, in 1540 when she was 16 years old. She was young, charming, well educated, and very rich. She shared her husband's love of the arts and she financed the family's purchase of the Pitti Palace so their children would have more room to play. It was a politically smart marriage for Cosimo, but all indications are that it was also a happy marriage.

We started with Cosimo and his family because they were buried together in an area of the chapel that could easily be screened from the thousands of tourists that visit San Lorenzo daily. We would examine the remains in a field lab set up in the chapel's New Sacristy, with its beautiful Michelangelo sculptures commissioned by the Medici.

We lifted the marble flooring where a plaque indicated Eleonora was buried, and found a layer of rubble—plaster, brick fragments, and small stones—with some human bones, mostly small bones of the hands and feet. Apparently this was the work of the 1940s excavators, who had exhumed several bodies at once, then examined and reburied them. (Their research, relating skull shapes to intelligence and personality, is now discredited.) Then they apparently discovered a few small bones left over and threw them in the rubble before replacing the floor. Beneath this we found three stone slabs sealing a rectangular chamber lined with bricks and then plastered. We were surprised to see two metal boxes within, but Eleonora and her husband, Cosimo, had been reburied together, each in a zinc ossuary, in 1947. So we had two Medici for the price of one.

The bottom of the chamber was covered with dried-out mud left by the Amo flood, and we were concerned that water might have penetrated the ossuaries and led to the decay of the remains. But when we opened Eleonora's box, we found that although no soft tissue was preserved, the bones were in good condition.

We know quite a bit about Eleonora, and it was interesting to compare her skeleton with the historical record. In their 24 years of marriage, Eleonora gave birth 11 times in 14 years, when she was 18, 19, 20, 21, 23, 24, 25, 26, 27, 31, and 32. She was pregnant for most of her adult life, and her skeleton showed it.

Every birth is a trauma to the mother's pelvis and leaves its mark. In Eleonora's case, the bones that come together at the front of the pelvis were extremely rough and irregular. She was a small woman, and every time she had a child there was damage to the bones, followed by regrowth and remodeling of them. And the back of her pelvis, which is normally somewhat angular, was flattened by the many children coming down the birth canal.

All those pregnancies, during which calcium is leached from the mother for the bone development of the fetus, had had a serious effect on Eleonora's teeth. She had lost several, and others were abscessed. Even today in Italy there is the expression "For each baby a tooth." Eleonora was one of the richest women in the world, but her wealth didn't protect her from dental distress or an early death from malaria at the age of 40.

Cosimo's life, too, is mirrored in his bones. He was a sportsman who lifted weights, rode, and hunted regularly. Strenuous physical activity causes muscle size to increase, and this, in turn, causes bone to thicken and strengthen. Not surprisingly, his skeleton is what anthropologists call "robust." His upper leg bones have marked protuberances where the thigh muscles used to grip a horse during riding attached to them. His shoulder blades were asymmetrical, the right considerably larger than the left. Cosimo was a righty. But he did not sail into old age smoothly. Three of his vertebrae were fused, the result of a metabolic disorder, which would have caused him difficulty bending in old age. His teeth also gave him problems. Many were fractured from a lifetime of eating hard foods such as nuts and raw vegetables. The dentist on our team said it looked as if Cosimo had had a diet of wood.

What was unexpected was that someone had rather crudely sawed off the top of Cosimo's skull, probably to remove the brain. They knew that to preserve the body you must remove the brain or else it will putrefy. Perhaps a family physician who had never done anything like that before was given the job of preserving the great Cosimo for posterity.

With Cosimo and Eleonora's sons Giovanni and Garzia, we moved into the darker side of the Medicis. Archival evidence suggests that the boys succumbed to malaria a few days apart in 1562. But there is also a legend, preserved in histories of the family, that Giovanni, then aged 19, and Garzia, then 16, quarreled during a hunting trip and that Garzia stabbed and killed his brother. When their father, Cosimo, learned of the murder of his favorite son, in a fit of rage he ran Garzia through with his sword. Their mother, Eleonora, died six days later, supposedly of a broken heart. Which was the real story? Would the brothers' remains show evidence of violence or preserve clues that point to malaria? Giovanni's tomb proved to be covered by a single large limestone slab. On the lid of the zinc box in the chamber was a lead plaque from his original burial that read: *Ossa Iohanuis Cardinalls Cosimo I Filli*—the bones of Cardinal Giovanni, son of Cosimo I. (That he had been made a cardinal at the age of 17 attests the power of the Medici.)

Skeletal age markers—his molars, long bones, and pelvis—indicated that Giovanni had indeed died at around 19. While his lower teeth were perfect, one of the uppers had a terrible abscess. And the evidence for murder? Often the truth is less sensational than the legend, and that seems to be the case with Giovanni. His skeleton showed no signs of violence, no cut marks to the breastbone, ribs, or vertebrae. But we still had his brother Garzia's remains to examine. Supposedly he died by his father's sword. Perhaps we would find evidence of fatal trauma there.

Garzia's tomb proved similar to his brother's and parents'. He was about three years younger than his brother, and his skeleton confirmed his age. At Corregi Hospital, the team's radiologist did a full study of Garzia's bones. Medici biographers mention that the child was chronically ill, and the x-ray images of his leg bones revealed horizontal "growth-arrest" lines indicating serious illness at around two years old and at least four more times before he was 10. But as with Giovanni, the skeleton showed no signs of violence. Both brothers died within weeks of each other. So what killed them?

Our team's historian, Donatella Lippi of the University of Florence, knows as much about the Medici as anyone and is familiar with Italy's National Archives. Several letters in the archives revealed a probable cause of death. One from the family physician warns Cosimo not to take the boys on a hunting trip to the Marema, an area infested with malaria southwest of Florence. Cosimo didn't listen to the doctor, and on November 20, 1562, wrote to another son, "on the 15th Giovanni suffered from a high fever but became worse and died." Soon after his brother's death, Garzia also died. It is possible that Cosimo's letter was a cover-up for his violent rage, but our examination of the bones showed no evidence of violence. Malaria probably was the cause of their deaths, and also of their mother, Eleonora, who nursed them through their illnesses. Our team's pathologists are now trying to find clinical evidence of malaria in small bone samples from Giovanni, Garzia, and Eleonora. They are looking for the DNA of the parasite that causes malaria, but it is pioneering work and will be difficult, as the Arno flood waters might have washed away the evidence.

We had examined the bodies of four Medici, revealing aspects of their health unknown in the archival record and confirming other conditions that were. And we showed that, at least with Giovanni and Garzia, the Medici were not murderers. Our first season was coming to a close, and we had time for just one more Medici: Gian Gastone, the last Medici to rule Florence, who died in 1737. Renowned as an eccentric, Gian Gastone had an interest in botany and led a dissipated life. He spent the last five years of his life in bed—he wasn't sick, he just liked it there—and reportedly never bathed.

The 1857 commission that reburied the Medici recorded the funerary equipment that accompanied each corpse, and this gave us an idea of what we might find with Gian Gastone:

In a cypress coffin, which was very well preserved, covered with black velvet and a small golden braid, there was another lead coffin, that had on its lid a cross on three mountains. After having opened it, a corpse was found, enveloped in a black silky sheet. Unrolled, it was clear that this corpse belonged to a Grand Duke because he wore the Grand-Ducal crown of golden metal on his head and he was dressed with a silky Great Cape, the sign of the Grand Master of Saint Steven. There were two gold medals, the first near the head, the other on the breast . . .

The researchers who exhumed the Medici in 1947 did not examine Gian Gastone, so there was some hope that we might find him just as he was described.

We thought that exhuming him would be simple, but when we raised the brass plaque and removed the floor tiles, we found a solid brick-and-stone masonry floor. We removed more floor tiles but still encountered the same masonry. Almost all the flooring stones were rectangular, but one was a perfect circle set inside a square. I asked several chapel employees what was beneath it, but they had no idea. One suggested a sewer. We decided to lift the stone and see if it led to Gian Gastone.

Inserting a thin file between the circle and the rectangle it was set into, one of our workmen removed the cement between the two. Then with the aid of suction cups, we lifted the marble circle, revealing a layer of sand. Beneath this was another circular stone, with an iron ring in its center, and below it we found stairs going down to a crypt. Peering in, I could see that a layer of undisturbed mud covered all the stairs: no one had been down since the 1966 flood. I could see several coffins, perhaps a dozen, many for children. They had clearly been disturbed. Some had the lids off and some lay smashed on the floor, which was littered with human bones. In addition to Gian Gastone's coffin, the crypt held the remains of a man and seven children, and a skull lacking the rest of its skeleton. (We do not yet know who these individuals are.) What caused this chaos? Gian Gastone's gold crown and medallions would have been a tempting treasure for tomb robbers.

Once we photographed and recorded the state of the tomb, various team members came down to have a look. Donatella Lippi peered into the lead coffin of Gian Gastone and surveyed the mass of wood fragments inside it but found no sign of his bones or crown or gold medals. She asked, "What happened to the gold?" We concluded that it had probably been melted down by thieves long ago.

Photographing and recording the crypt took weeks, and only after that was completed did we focus on Gastone. When we cleared the wood debris from inside his lead coffin, we found that the lid had in fact fallen into it. And beneath the lid, there was Gian Gastone, with his crown and medals! Our guess that robbers had rifled the tomb was wrong; the flood was the culprit. As a result of these finds, our next year will be spent conserving the artifacts from Gian Gastone's tomb and preparing publications on the findings. When that is done, we have several dozen more Medici buried in the chapel, waiting to be studied, including Cosimo's father, the great general Giovanni Medici. Historical accounts say that Giovanni had captured Milan on behalf of Pope Leo X (another Medici), but at the siege of Pavia in 1525, was hit in the leg by a bullet. In 1526 he was shot again in the same leg, which had to be amputated. He is said to have survived the operation, but died a week later. Certainly Giovanni's bones, and likely those of his relatives, have tales to tell.

GINO FORNACIARI is professor of the history of medicine and pathology at the University of Pisa. **BOB BRIER** is senior research fellow at the C.W. Post Campus of Long Island University and a contributing editor of *Archaeology.* **ANTONIO FORNACIARI** is an archaeologist with the Medici project.

Digging for Truth

Forget what you've learned about Pilgrims and Plymouth Rock. Stunning new archaeological evidence reveals that the real roots of American independence and the entrepreneurial spirit which drove it were thriving in Virginia's Tidewater.

NICK D'ALIO

You probably know about John Smith and Pocahontas, but not much more. Jamestown in 1607 was English America's first permanent settlement and, since then, perhaps its most unjustly maligned. According to many histories, Jamestown was a false start in the New World: a colony founded on greed that ultimately failed due to poor location, infighting and highborn colonists resistant to hard work. The colony's very physical legacy, its original fort, was believed to have long ago washed away into the James River.

Enter Dr. William Kelso, chief archaeologist for the Jamestown Rediscovery Project sponsored by the Association for the Preservation of Virginia Antiquities. Using computer technology, centuries-old accounts written by the colonists themselves and the eye of a historical detective, Kelso has rediscovered James Fort and with it a trove of priceless artifacts that illuminate the lives, struggles and surprising accomplishments of those first English Americans.

The pioneering settlement Kelso describes in his book *Jamestown: The Buried Truth* is an astonishing place. Still, you may find it strangely familiar. This is the real story of the birth of a nation—America before the Pilgrims.

Dr. Kelso, most people probably think that an archaeologist would be more likely to dig for King Tut than John Smith.
So did I! Until I discovered that there was an American history that archaeologists could make a contribution to.

What led you to believe James Fort was still there, when previous experts agreed that the fort was gone?
When I first came to James Island, I realized that story didn't have any particular backing to it—no real evidence—it was just agreed upon. When I looked at one of the earlier trenches, I could see that there was a dark layer underneath everything. I questioned it, but I didn't get an answer. I came to realize how little was known about the area.

Your project is called Jamestown Rediscovery. Why would we need to rediscover where English America began? Why don't we know it?
Because it keeps getting swept under the rug. I think this all goes back to the American Civil War. You know, the victors write the history. That's the North. That's the Pilgrims in 1620. It's not a Southern colony in 1607. In the standard history books, Jamestown comes off as a bunch of greedy men, coming here to make money.

I've read they were lazy, too.
That's been the story. But that's not at all what we're finding. The artifacts we've unearthed indicate people very hard at work, performing long, strenuous labor. Sure, they were trying to make a profit for the corporation. Now, how un-American is that?

It's very American. But not like the Jamestown I learned about in social studies class. For example, in your book you talk about knights in shining armor.
There were at least three sirs—knighted men—at Jamestown. We've found armor all over the place. They brought more helmets than heads to put them on. American history does go back to knights in armor. Shakespeare himself drew on the Jamestown experiences [for his play *The Tempest*]. To me, this means that to really understand the beginnings of America, we need to look back to a much older European tradition.

You say that almost immediately on arriving, the colonists began felling trees and splitting them into planks, not just to build homes but to ship the lumber back to England.
That first summer, they loaded three ships for exporting. That was the idea: Find items of value and send them back. We've also found evidence that the colonists were attempting to manufacture glass, bronze and other valuables for export, using the resources here.

Even searching for gold?
We've recovered state-of-the-art crucibles, the kind used to assay gold deposits. It's also documented that the colonists even

sent back an entire shipload of dirt. They thought it was gilded. Which is ironic.

Why?

Because the dirt was the gold, the actual land—what the settlers couldn't have back home.

So this was starting a nation and starting a business?

Oh, absolutely. After all, it was called the Virginia Company. We're not digging up columns and tombs here. We're finding a legacy that isn't made of bricks—it's the remains of a system of commerce.

For example, right now, I'm looking our on the James River, and there's a barge that's loaded with gravel and it's headed, I think, for Japan. So the whole thing is still in operation. And from this same place.

That's a really different take on how America began. Every schoolchild learns that the Pilgrims came here for religious freedom. These entrepreneurial Jamestown pioneers sound much different.

Yes, but also more like modern Americans.

How difficult would it have been for the original colonists to construct James Fort?

Building this palisade in just 19 days is probably the main reason that half the original colonists died. The colonists erected, say, 600 logs, weighing up to 800 pounds each, in the hot Virginia summer, after being raised in England. And working under fire, literally, from the natives. It must have been a panicking thing.

Was this the wrong place to land?

No. The perceived threat to the colony was Spain. Against a Spanish sea attack, the colonists chose the right strategic position: an island. There's no other place along the James River as defensible as this one.

So this one triangular fort, about 100 yards on a side, was how big America was in 1607?

English America, yes, you could say that. The dwellings, warehouses and other buildings that made up the colony were inside the fort. The building remains we're excavating now are the buildings that John Smith and the other colonists lived and worked in.

Since the precise location of the fort had been lost, you used the colonists' own writings to find it. Were the Jamestowners accurate record keepers? Can we believe what they wrote?

Yes. There's no doubt. Especially William Strachey, one of the colony scribes. His location for the fort was very exact.

Poring through these archaically written documents, Jamestown takes on an almost mythological quality. You know about John Smith and Pocahontas. But it becomes real historical science when we retrace the steps. The stories become true. I have a friend who teaches colonial history, and after seeing the digs he said, "Now I believe what I've always taught."

You mentioned William Strachey. I understand you may have actually unearthed something of his.

Very likely his signet ring. It was recovered in the corner of the fort.

The Jamestown You Know

1607 • 105 colonists establish the first permanent English settlement in North America. Named for King James I, Jamestown is expected to turn a profit for investors in the Virginia Company of London. Only 38 colonists survive the harsh conditions and warfare with Indian tribes.

1608 • Some 200 new settlers arrive in Jamestown, including Dutch and Polish glassmakers, artisans skilled in producing naval stores and the first European women in the colony. John Smith is elected president of the governing council. Smith is sent back to England the following year and never returns to Virginia.

1609–10 • The "Starving Time" claims 155 of 215 colonists. The survivors prepare to abandon Virginia but are met at the mouth of the James River by supply ships and additional settlers from England.

1611 • English settlement pushes west with the establishment of Henricus (now Henrico) on the James River near present-day Richmond. Hostilities with the Indians continue.

1613 • Pocahontas, daughter of the powerful chief Powhatan, is captured and held at Jamestown. Peace negotiations begin between the colonists and Powhatan.

1614 • Pocahontas marries John Rolfe, who successfully cultivated tobacco for export to England. In the absence of the gold and jewels the colonists had hoped to find, the crop guarantees Jamestown's economic survival.

1617 • Pocahontas dies in England.

1619 • The first representative governing body in English America meets at Jamestown. The first African slaves are brought into the colony aboard Dutch ships.

1620 • Plymouth colony is established by the Pilgrims in Massachusetts.

1622 • Indian attacks on Jamestown's outlying settlements kill more than 300 colonists. Henricus is destroyed.

1624 • James I revokes the Virginia Company's charter, making Virginia a royal colony.

1646 • A peace treaty unravels the powerful confederation of local Indian tribes and cedes large amount of land to English settlers.

1699 • The capital of Virginia moves from Jamestown to Williamsburg.

Is that the closest anyone has ever come to connecting an artifact with a specific colonist?

It's one of three. We've also found a pewter flagon—drinking mug—in a well outside the fort, which bears the initials of settlers Richard and Elizabeth Pierce.

And the captain's staff?

Unearthed in one of the burials. We believe the remains are those of Captain Bartholomew Gosnold. You think people don't know much about Jamestown, but boy, they have never heard of this

Virginia Company of London

Eager to gain a foothold in North America but unable to fund an expedition out of royal coffers, James I chartered the Virginia Company of London in 1606 to establish a colony between the 34th and 41st northern parallels (roughly Cape Fear to the Long Island Sound). This joint-stock company raised capital by selling shares to private investors who, in turn, stood to profit from whatever riches the colonists might find.

Jamestown, however, offered no jewels or precious metals, and the sale of raw materials like lumber brought only minimal returns. When news of the terrible "Starving Time" and infighting among the colonists reached England, the Virginia Company faced financial ruin. To boost public interest in the venture and bring in much-needed cash, the company instituted a lottery to raise funds. Its treasurer, Sir Edwin Sandys, also promoted "headrights," a system that allowed investors to obtain land in Virginia by paying a settler's passage to the colony. In turn, the settler paid off that debt by working on the investor's land for a specified period of time. This marked a significant shift in the Virginia Company's mission, moving from colonization for profit to securing new territory for the Crown.

The company's debt continued to grow, however, and James revoked its charter in 1624, making Virginia a royal colony led by a governor appointed by the king. Although the Virginia Company failed to enrich its shareholders, it provided an opportunity for England to compete with Spain and France for a stake in the New World.

The Jamestown You Don't Know

Putting a Face to a Name

In 1996 archaeologists unearthed the skeleton of a white male, age 18 to 20. A lead musket ball and shot were still lodged in bone just below the right knee, and it is likely the man bled to death. Labeled JR102C (for Jamestown Rediscovery, 102nd excavation), his identity is unknown. Researchers used modern crime lab techniques to create a face for JR. Forensic anthropologists partially reconstructed the skull with surviving bone fragments; computer imagery filled in the rest. An artist then cast a plaster mold of the skull, created skin tissue with clay and modeled facial features. It's not known who shot JR, but the position of the lead indicates that the shooter was 8 to 15 feet away and suggests that JR was the victim of friendly fire.

Buried Treasures

Although corn was a staple of the settlers' diets, only one cob has been found at Jamestown. It survived as a "pseudomorph," or false form. Corrosive material from metal objects buried with the corn coated the cob and retained its shape as the food decayed.

A silver ear picker would have been owned by a gentleman, but less costly models were common throughout 17th-century English society. Earwax was removed with the spoon-shaped end, while the pick was used to scrape plaque from teeth.

---

guy! According to John Smith, Gosnold was the main reason the colony survived that first year. That would make this a very important find—an unsung hero in American history.

Your work has even put a face on the Jamestowners.
Yes, using modern forensics. That's another reason I think we're revealing a forgotten century in American history. It's what archaeology does. In a document, you can have someone's point of view. But what you find in the ground, no one's putting a spin on that.

We're getting a fairer picture of the settlement. There were mistakes made. A lot of people died needlessly. It was paradise, and it wasn't. People want to know: Did Jamestown succeed or fail? Well, it did both. These remains, their number, location and condition, point up how terribly hard life was in early Jamestown.

Especially during the "Starving Time" in 1609–10. After 400 years, how can you dig down and say definitively that these colonists very nearly starved to death?
It's clear from what they butchered. We've found the remains of rats, dogs, horses—I mean, you're chopping up your transportation. They were eating poisonous snakes, stuff that's really taboo unless you're absolutely desperate. Then there's a question: Why didn't they leave the fort for food? They couldn't.

Documentary evidence says if they ventured out of the fort, they were picked off.

By the natives?
Yes, but we've also found evidence of natives working inside the compound. We have evidence that someone was actually making stone tools in the fort. They were flaking points and making beads. What we've found represents the greatest evidence of contact between the Powhatan Indians and the English: Powhatan artifacts like pottery, beads and native pipes.

Again, this brings another sense of reality that you wouldn't think of before. There were Indians in the fort, as well as outside. Not like a Western—the settlers on one side of the fort, and the Indians on the other.

You've recovered more than a million artifacts. Some look remarkably modern, like they were lost last year. Is there one artifact that stands out in your mind?
So many are astonishing. But I'd have to say, the fort itself. Individual artifacts can also present several interpretations. The one absolute that we've found is James Fort. It exists on dry land; it didn't wash away. That's undeniable. And in archaeology, it's very seldom that you can come up with something undeniable.

The Jamestown you're discovering is nothing like what most of us have seen in pictures. You know, the little stick huts.
That was one of the biggest surprises to me. I thought of little "Hansel & Gretel" cottages. In fact, Jamestown never had those.

Spain Cedes Control

The English founded the first permanent colony in Virginia, but they were not the first European settlers there. In 1570 the Spanish established a Jesuit mission, Ajacan, on the York River, just a few miles from where Jamestown would be founded 37 years later. The mission's priests were all killed by Indians, and the site was soon abandoned.

Spain and England had long competed for influence in both the Old World and the New. A 1604 peace treaty ended 20 years of war between the two nations, but the Jamestown settlers were on constant guard against possible attacks from Spanish ships. Spain, on the other hand, viewed Jamestown as a potential base for English pirates. After all, when the celebrated privateer Sir Walter Raleigh tried to colonize the Outer Banks of present-day North Carolina in the 1580s, one motivation was the area's proximity to Spanish treasure ships plying the Caribbean.

Political intrigue added to the danger. Don Pedro de Zúñiga, the Spanish ambassador to London, kept King Philip III of Spain informed about Jamestown, and he pressed his monarch to send troops to destroy it. In 1608 Philip approved a plan to do "whatever was necessary to drive out the people who are in Virginia," but it was never implemented.

Zúñiga advanced a second scheme involving Baron Thomas Arundel, an English Catholic who had taken part in a failed attempt to establish a Catholic colony in North America in 1605. Arundel offered to plant a spy in Jamestown who would determine "by what means those people can be driven out without violence in arms." It's unclear what Arundel had in mind, but Philip advised Zúñiga not to deal with him.

In 1611 Don Diego de Molina, a Spanish spy, was taken prisoner in Jamestown. Molina managed to send reports about the colony to agents in London; when he eventually returned to Spain, Molina urged Philip to eliminate the English presence in Virginia. Again, Philip demurred.

In the end, England's success in North America was helped along by Spain's failure to curb those first efforts at Jamestown.

'A World of Miseries'

Now all of us at James Town beginning to feel that sharp prick of hunger which no man truely describe but he which has Tasted the bitterness thereof.

A world of miseries ensued as the Sequel will express unto you in so much that some to satisfy their hunger have robbed the store for the which I caused them to be executed. Then having fed upon horses and other beasts as long as they Lasted we were glad to make shift with vermine as dogs, Cats, Rats, and mice All was fish that came to Net to satisfy cruel hunger as to eat Boots shoes or any other leather some could Come by And those being Spent and devoured some were enforced to search the woods and to feed upon Serpents and snakes and to dig the earth for wild and unknown Roots where many of our men were Cut off of and slain by the Savages.

And now famine beginning to Look ghastely and pale in every face that nothing was spared to maintain Life and to do those things which seem incredible As to dig up dead corpses out of graves and to eat them and some have Licked up the Blood which has fallen from their weak fellows And amongst the rest this was most Lamentable That one of our Colony murdered his wife Ripped the child out of her womb and threw it into the River and after chopped the Mother in pieces and salted her for his food The same not being discovered before he had eaten Part thereof for the which cruel and inhumane fact I ajudged him to be executed the acknowledgement of the deed being enforced from him by torture having hung by the Thumbs with weights at his feet a quarter of an hour before he would confess the same.

—George Percy led the Jamestown colony through the winter of 1609–10, the infamous "Starving Time."

Considered one of the most important documents from the early settlement period, Percy's account describes the colonists' desperation in chilling detail.

Source: "'A True Relation,' by George Percy, 1609–1612," Virtual Jamestown, Virginia Center for Digital History, University of Virginia (www.virtualjamestown.org).

there's a section on how, by the mid-17th century, the Jamestowners insisted on the same rights as Englishmen. So when Jefferson writes about justifications for the Revolution, he says we want to maintain our rights that we established here 160 years ago.

Jefferson's sentiment was "Keep your promise that started in Jamestown."
Yes, exactly.

Did Jamestown eventually decline because the colonial capital moved to Williamsburg?
Yes, the area reverted to farmland. Jamestown is not really a good deep-water port; there are better ports at Yorktown.

So Jamestown didn't disappear because it failed, but because the American experiment it started grew so successful.
That's my point. The Virginia Company, the colony's sponsors, failed, so everyone concludes that Jamestown failed. But

The little huts didn't last long. We can see in the ground when they were torn down.

Jamestown started as poles in the ground, with tents over the tops. Then it went to something that would look at home in Ireland, one-story structures. Later, Jamestown becomes more of a city facade; they put up buildings which would have looked perfectly logical in London. Half-timber buildings. Finally it goes to brick, by statute, to make things permanent.

And while building that city, you say that Jamestown also built American independence, long before it happened at Independence Hall.
Absolutely. The basis of the American Revolution started at Jamestown. Jefferson knew that. In his book *A History of Virginia*,

it didn't. By the time the Pilgrims step on Plymouth Rock in 1620, there were over a thousand people living up and down the James River on various prosperous plantations. And the ideas of Jamestown, that legacy, moved to Williamsburg, and then to Richmond.

And the site of James Fort even has a second history after that.
As a Confederate fort. Again, this was the most defensible position in the area. In fact, the Confederates used Jamestown's surviving church steeple as an observation tower. Their fort was earthen walls. Today, those walls are full of Jamestown artifacts.

Did the Confederates know that?
Oh, yes. Their journals record finding logs from the fort, and burials. The Confederates found a piece of armor that is still in our collection.

Another new nation, trying to start on this same spot?
In a way. And Union forces saw Jamestown as important to take. It was the beginnings of their country.

So this really is about "becoming American." In your book, you've said that the Jamestown colonists arrived here as quintessential Englishmen.
Yes they did. We've found their teacups and porcelain. We've found hundreds of sewing pins for fine garments. They were bringing their lives here. As far as I can determine, Jamestown was the first permanent English colony anywhere on earth.

When did these Englishmen become American?
We can see it happening in the archaeological record. The Englishmen become Americans when they figure out how to use this new environment. They came to this place where the forests were endless, where you could have land. The Virginia Company sent them for gold, but they found valuables that you couldn't get back home.

That's what drove them to endure the risks of this place. Then they adapted to it. They learned to make native pottery. We've found Powhatan-type bowls with feet on them, made to sit on English tables. They adapted their European armor for guerrilla fighting, by chopping it up and making smaller pieces—like flak jackets. We've found the pieces. They even recast some of their armor into kettles and other implements when the fighting was over.

Like swords into ploughshares. In many ways, its sounds like the America we know today started in this one tiny settlement. What can Jamestown teach us now, 400 years later?
The most important lesson for Americans today? Probably how precariously this whole thing started.

Living through the Donner Party

The nineteenth-century survivors of the infamous Donner Party told cautionary tales of starvation and cannibalism, greed and self-sacrifice. But not until now are we learning why the survivors survived.

JARED DIAMOND

"Mrs. Fosdick and Mrs. Foster, after eating, returned to the body of [Mr.] Fosdick. There, in spite of the widow's entreaties, Mrs. Foster took out the liver and heart from the body and removed the arms and legs. . . . [Mrs. Fosdick] was forced to see her husband's heart broiled over the fire." "He eat her body and found her flesh the best he had ever tasted! He further stated that he obtained from her body at least four pounds of fat." "Eat baby raw, stewed some of Jake and roasted his head, not good meat, taste like sheep with the rot."

—George Stewart,
Ordeal by *Hunger: The Story of the Donner Party*

Nearly a century and a half after it happened, the story of the Donner Party remains one of the most riveting tragedies in U.S. history. Partly that's because of its lurid elements: almost half the party died, and many of their bodies were defiled in an orgy of cannibalism. Partly, too, it's because of the human drama of noble self-sacrifice and base murder juxtaposed. The Donner Party began as just another nameless pioneer trek to California, but it came to symbolize the Great American Dream gone awry.

By now the tale of that disastrous journey has been told so often that seemingly nothing else remains to be said—or so I thought, until my friend Donald Grayson at the University of Washington sent me an analysis that he had published in the *Journal of Anthropological Research*. By comparing the fates of all Donner Party members, Grayson identified striking differences between those who came through the ordeal alive and those who were not so lucky. In doing so he has made the lessons of the Donner Party universal. Under more mundane life-threatening situations, who among us too will be "lucky"?

Grayson's insights did not depend on new discoveries about the ill-fated pioneers nor on new analytical techniques, but on that most elusive ingredient of great science: a new idea about an old problem. Given the same information, any of you could

extract the same conclusions. In fact, on page 163 you'll find the roster of the Donner Party members along with a few personal details about each of them and their fate. If you like, you can try to figure out for yourself some general rules about who is most likely to die when the going gets tough.

The Lewis and Clark Expedition of 1804 to 1806 was the first to cross the continent, but they didn't take along ox-drawn wagons, which were a requirement for pioneer settlement. Clearing a wagon route through the West's unmapped deserts and mountains proved far more difficult than finding a footpath. Not until 1841 was the first attempt made to haul wagons and settlers overland to California, and only in 1844 did the effort succeed. Until the Gold Rush of 1848 unleashed a flood of emigrants, wagon traffic to California remained a trickle.

As of 1846, when the Donner Party set out, the usual wagon route headed west from St. Louis to Fort Bridger in Wyoming, then northwest into Idaho before turning southwest through Nevada and on to California. However, at that time a popular guidebook author named Lansford Hastings was touting a shortcut that purported to cut many miles from the long trek. Hastings's route continued west from Fort Bridger through the Wasatch mountain range, then south of Utah's Great Salt Lake across the Salt Lake Desert, and finally rejoined the usual California Trail in Nevada.

In the summer of 1846 a number of wagon parties set out for California from Fort Bridger. One, which left shortly before the Donner Party, was guided by Hastings himself. Using his shortcut, the party would eventually make it to California, albeit with great difficulty.

The pioneers who would become the members of the Donner Party were in fact all headed for Fort Bridger to join the Hastings expedition, but they arrived too late. With Hastings thus unavailable to serve as a guide, some of these California-bound emigrants opted for the usual route instead. Others, however, decided to try the Hastings Cutoff anyway. In all, 87 people in 23 wagons chose the cutoff. They consisted of 10 unrelated families and 16 lone individuals, most of them well-to-do midwestern farmers and townspeople who had met by chance and joined forces for protection. None had had any real experience of the western mountains or Indians. They became known as the Donner Party because they elected an elderly Illinois farmer named George Donner as their captain. They left Fort Bridger on July 31, one of the last parties of that summer to begin the long haul to California.

Within a fortnight the Donner Party suffered their first crushing setback, when they reached Utah's steep, brush-covered Wasatch Mountains. The terrain was so wild that, in order to cross, the men had first to build a wagon road. It took 16 backbreaking days to cover just 36 miles, and afterward the people and draft animals were worn out. A second blow followed almost immediately thereafter, west of the Great Salt Lake, when the party ran into an 80-mile stretch of desert. To save themselves from death by thirst, some of the pioneers were forced to unhitch their wagons, rush ahead with their precious animals to the next spring, and return to retrieve the wagons. The rush became a disorganized panic, and many of the animals died, wandered off, or were killed by Indians. Four wagons and large quantities of supplies had to be abandoned. Not until September 30—two full months after leaving Fort Bridger—did the Donner Party emerge from their fatal shortcut to rejoin the California Trail.

By November 1 they had struggled up to Truckee Lake—later renamed Donner Lake—at an elevation of 6,000 feet on the eastern flank of the Sierra Nevada, west of the present-day California-Nevada border. Snow had already begun to fall during the last days of October, and now a fierce snowstorm defeated the exhausted party as they attempted to cross a 7,200-foot pass just west of the lake. With that storm, a trap snapped shut around them: they had set out just a little too late and proceeded just a little too slowly. They now faced a long winter at the lake, with very little food.

Death had come to the Donner Party even before it reached the lake. There were five casualties: on August 29 Luke Halloran died of "consumption" (presumably tuberculosis); on October 5 James Reed knifed John Snyder in self-defense, during a fight that broke out when two teams of oxen became entangled; three days later Lewis Keseberg abandoned an old man named Hardkoop who had been riding in Keseberg's wagon, and most of the party refused to stop and search for him; sometime after October 13 two German emigrants, Joseph Reinhardt and Augustus Spitzer, murdered a rich German named Wolfinger while ostensibly helping him to cache his property; and on October 20 William Pike was shot as he and his brother-in-law were cleaning a pistol.

They cut off and roasted flesh from the corpses, restrained only by the rule that no one partook of his or her relative's body.

In addition, four party members had decided earlier to walk out ahead to Sutter's Fort (now Sacramento) to bring back supplies and help. One of those four, Charles Stanton, rejoined the party on October 19, bringing food and two Indians sent by Sutter. Thus, of the 87 original members of the Donner Party, 79—plus the two Indians—were pinned down in the winter camp at Donner Lake.

The trapped pioneers lay freezing inside crude tents and cabins. They quickly exhausted their little remaining food, then killed and ate their pack animals. Then they ate their dogs. Finally they boiled hides and blankets to make a glue-like soup. Gross selfishness became rampant, as families with food refused to share it with destitute families or demanded exorbitant payment. On December 16 the first death came to the winter camp when 24-year-old Baylis Williams succumbed to starvation. On that same day 15 of the strongest people—5 women and 10 men, including Charles Stanton and the two Indians—set out across the pass on homemade snowshoes, virtually without food and in appallingly cold and stormy weather, in the hope of reaching outside help. Four of the men left behind their families; three of the women left behind their children.

O n the sixth morning an exhausted Stanton let the others go on ahead of him; he remained behind to die. On the ninth day the remaining 14 for the first time openly broached the subject of cannibalism which had already been on their minds. They debated drawing lots as to who should be eaten, or letting two people shoot it out until one was killed and could be eaten. Both proposals were rejected in favor of waiting for someone to die naturally.

Such opportunities soon arose. On Christmas Eve, as a 23-year-old man named Antoine, a bachelor, slept in a heavy stupor, he stretched out his arm such that his hand fell into the fire. A companion pulled it out at once. When it fell in a second time, however, no one intervened—they simply let it burn. Antoine died, then Franklin Graves, then Patrick Dolan, then Lemuel Murphy. The others cut off and roasted flesh from the corpses, restrained only by the rule that no one would partake of his or her own relative's body. When the corpses were consumed, the survivors began eating old shoes.

On January 5, 23-year-old Jay Fosdick died, only to be cut up and boiled by Mrs. Foster over the protests of Mrs. Fosdick. Soon after, the frenzied Mr. Foster chased down, shot, and killed the two Indians to eat them. That left 7 of the original 15 snowshoers to stagger into the first white settlement in California, after a midwinter trek of 33 days through the snow.

On January 31 the first rescue team set out from the settlement for Donner Lake. It would take three more teams and two and a half months before the ordeal was all over. During that time many more people died, either in the winter camp or while fighting their way out with the rescue teams. There was never enough food, and by the end of February, cannibalism had established itself at the lake.

When William Eddy and William Foster, who had gotten out with the snowshoers, reached the lake with the third rescue team on March 13, they found that Keseberg had eaten their sons. The Foster child's grandmother accused the starving Keseberg of having taken the child to bed with him one night, strangling him, and hanging the corpse on the wall before eating it. Keseberg, in his defense, claimed the children had died naturally. When the rescuers left the lake the next day to return to California, they left Keseberg behind with just four others: the elderly Lavina Murphy, the badly injured George Donner, his 4-year-old nephew Samuel and his healthy wife Tamsen, who could have traveled but insisted on staying with her dying husband.

The fourth and last rescue team reached the lake on April 17 to find Keseberg alone, surrounded by indescribable filth and mutilated corpses. George Donner's body lay with his skull split open to permit the extraction of his brains. Three frozen ox legs lay in plain view almost uneaten beside a kettle of cut-up human flesh. Near Keseberg sat two kettles of blood and a large pan full of fresh human liver and lungs. He alleged that his four companions had died natural deaths, but he was frank about having eaten them. As to why he had not eaten ox leg instead, he explained that it was too dry: human liver and lungs tasted better, and human brains made a good soup. As for Tamsen Donner, Keseberg noted that she tasted the best, being well endowed with fat. In a bundle held by Keseberg the rescuers found silk, jewelry, pistols, and money that had belonged to George Donner.

After returning to Sutter's Fort, one of the rescuers accused Keseberg of having murdered his companions, prompting Keseberg to sue for defamation of character. In the absence of legal proof of murder the court verdict was equivocal, and the issue of Keseberg's guilt remains disputed to this day. However, Tamsen Donner's death is especially suspicious since she had been in strong physical condition when last seen by the third rescue team.

Experience has taught us that the youngest and oldest people are the most vulnerable even under normal conditions, and their vulnerability increases under stress.

Thus, out of 87 Donner Party members, 40 died: 5 before reaching Donner Lake, 22 in their winter camp at the lake, and 13 (plus the two Indians) during or just after efforts to leave the lake. Why those particular 40? From the facts given in the roster, can you draw conclusions, as Grayson did, as to who was in fact the most likely to die?

As a simple first test, compare the fates of Donner Party males and females irrespective of age. Most of the males (30 out of 53) died; most of the females (24 out of 34) survived. The 57 percent death rate among males was nearly double the 29 percent death rate among females.

Next, consider the effect of age irrespective of sex. The worst toll was among the young and the old. Without exception, everyone over the age of 50 died, as did most of the children below the age of 5. Surprisingly, children and teenagers between the ages of 5 and 19 fared better than did adults in their prime (age 20 to 39): half the latter, but less than one-fifth of the former, died.

By looking at the effects of age and sex simultaneously, the advantage the women had over the men becomes even more striking. Most of the female deaths were among the youngest and oldest, who were already doomed by their age. Among those party members aged 5 to 39—the ones whose ages left them some reasonable chance of survival—half the men but only 5 percent of the women died.

The dates of death provide deeper insight. Of the 35 unfortunates who died after reaching the lake, 14 men but not a single woman had died by the end of January. Only in February did women begin to buckle under. From February onward the death toll was essentially equal by sex—11 men, 10 women. The differences in dates of death simply underscore the lesson of the death rates themselves: the Donner Party women were far hardier than the men.

Thus, sex and age considered together account for much of the luck of the survivors. Most of those who died (39 of the 40 victims) had the misfortune to be of the wrong sex, or the wrong age, or both.

Experience has taught us that the youngest and oldest people are the most vulnerable even under normal conditions, and their vulnerability increases under stress. In many natural disasters, those under 10 or over 50 suffered the highest mortality. For instance, children under 10 accounted for over half the 240,000 deaths in the 1970 Bangladesh cyclone, though they constituted only one-third of the exposed population.

Much of the vulnerability of the old and young under stress is simply a matter of insufficient physical strength: these people are less able to walk out through deep snow (in the case of the Donner Party) or to cling to trees above the height of flood waters (in the case of the Bangladesh cyclone). Babies have special problems. Per pound of body weight a baby has twice an adult's surface area, which means double the area across which body heat can escape. To maintain body temperature, babies have to increase their metabolic rate when air temperature drops only a few degrees below body temperature, whereas adults don't have to do so until a drop of 20 to 35 degrees. At cold temperatures the factor by which babies must increase their metabolism to stay warm is several times that for adults. These considerations place even well-fed babies at risk under cold conditions. And the Donner Party babies were at a crippling further disadvantage because they had so little food to fuel their metabolism. They literally froze to death.

But what gave the women such an edge over the men? Were the pioneers practicing the noble motto "women and children first" when it came to dividing food? Unfortunately, "women and children last" is a more accurate description of how most men behave under stress. As the *Titanic* sank, male crew

Manifest of a Tragic Journey

Donner Family

Name	Sex	Age	Notes
Jacob Donner	M	65	died in Nov. in winter camp
George Donner	M	62	died in Apr. in winter camp
Elizabeth Donner	F	45	died in Mar. in winter camp
Tamsen Donner	F	45	died in Apr. in winter camp
Elitha Donner	F	14	
Solomon Hook	M	14	
William Hook	M	12	died Feb. 28 with first rescue team
Leanna Donner	F	12	
George Donner	M	9	
Mary Donner	F	7	
Frances Donner	F	6	
Isaac Donner	M	5	died Mar. 7 with second rescue team
Georgia Donner	F	4	
Samuel Donner	M	4	died in Apr. in winter camp
Lewis Donner	M	3	died Mar. 7 or 8 in winter camp
Eliza Donner	F	3	

Murphy-Foster-Pike Family

Name	Sex	Age	Notes
Lavina Murphy	F	50	died around Mar. 19 in winter camp
William Foster	M	28	
William Pike	M	25	died Oct. 20 by gunshot
Sara Foster	F	23	
Harriet Pike	F	21	
John Landrum Murphy	M	15	died Jan. 31 in winter camp
Mary Murphy	F	13	
Lemuel Murphy	M	12	died Dec. 27 with snowshoers
William Murphy	M	11	
Simon Murphy	M	10	
George Foster	M	4	died in early Mar. in winter camp
Naomi Pike	F	3	
Catherine Pike	F	1	died Feb. 20 in winter camp

Graves-Fosdick Family

Name	Sex	Age	Notes
Franklin Graves	M	57	died Dec 24. with snowshoers
Elizabeth Graves	F	47	died Mar. 8 with second rescue team
Jay Fosdick	M	23	died Jan. 5 with snowshoers
Sarah Fosdick	F	22	
William Graves	M	18	
Eleanor Graves	F	15	
Lavina Graves	F	13	
Nancy Graves	F	9	
Jonathan Graves	M	7	
Franklin Graves Jr.	M	5	died Mar. 8 with second rescue team
Elizabeth Graves	F	1	died soon after rescue by second team

Breen Family

Name	Sex	Age	Notes
Patrick Breen	M	40	
Mary Breen	F	40	
John Breen	M	14	
Edward Breen	M	13	
Patrick Breen Jr.	M	11	
Simon Breen	M	9	
Peter Breen	M	7	
James Bren	M	4	
Isabella	F	1	

Reed Family

Name	Sex	Age	Notes
James Reed	M	46	
Margaret Reed	F	32	
Virginia Reed	F	12	
Patty Reed	F	8	
James Reed Jr.	M	5	
Thomas Reed	M	3	

Eddy Family

Name	Sex	Age	Notes
William Eddy	M	28	
Eleanor Eddy	F	25	died Feb. 7 in winter camp
James Eddy	M	3	died in early Mar. in winter camp
Margaret Eddy	F	1	died Feb. 4 in winter camp

Keseberg Family

Name	Sex	Age	Notes
Lewis Keseberg	M	32	
Phillipine Keseberg	F	32	
Ada Keseberg	F	3	died Feb. 24 with first rescue team
Lewis Keseberg Jr.	M	1	died Jan. 24 in winter camp

Mccutchen Family

Name	Sex	Age	Notes
William McCutchen	M	30	
Amanda McCutchen	F	24	
Harriet McCutchen	F	1	died Feb. 2 in winter camp

Williams Family

Name	Sex	Age	Notes
Eliza Williams	F	25	
Baylis Williams	M	24	died Dec. 16 in winter camp

Wolfinger Family

Name	Sex	Age	Notes
Mr. Wolfingter	M	?	killed around Oct. 13 by Reinhardt and Spitzer
Mrs. Wolfinger	F	?	

Unrelated Individuals

Name	Sex	Age	Notes
Mr. Hardkoop	M	60	died around Oct. 8, abandoned by Lewis Keseberg
Patrick Dolan	M	40	died Dec. 25 with snowshoers
Charles Stanton	M	35	died around Dec. 21 with snowshoers
Charles Burger	M	30	died Dec. 29 in winter camp
Joseph Reinhardt	M	30	died in Nov. or early Dec. in winter camp
Augustus Spitzer	M	30	died Feb.7 in winter camp
John Denton	M	28	died Feb. 24 with first rescue team
Milton Elliot	M	28	died Feb. 9 in winter camp
Luke Halloran	M	25	died Aug. 29 of consumption
William Herron	M	25	
Samuel Shoemaker	M	25	died in Nov. or early Dec. in winter camp
James Smith	M	25	died in Nov. or early Dec. in winter camp
James Smith	M	25	died in Nov. or early Dec. in winter camp
John Snyder	M	25	killed Oct. 5 by James Reed
Jean Baptiste Trubode	M	23	
Antoine	M	23	died Dec. 24 with snowshoers
Noah James	M	20	

members took many places in lifeboats while leaving women and children of steerage class below decks to drown. Much grosser male behavior emerged when the steamship *Atlantic* sank in 1879: the death toll included 294 of the 295 women and children on board, but only 187 of the 636 men. In the Biafran famine of the late 1960s, when relief agencies tried to distribute food to youngsters under 10 and to pregnant and nursing women, Biafran men gave a brutally frank response: "Stop all this rubbish, it is we men who shall have the food, let the children die, we will make new children after the war." Similarly, accounts by Donner Party members yield no evidence of hungry men deferring to women, and babies fared especially poorly.

Instead, we must seek some cause other than male self-sacrifice to account for the survival of Donner Party women. One contributing factor is that the men were busy killing each other. Four of the five deaths before the pioneers reached the lake, plus the deaths of the two Indians, involved male victims of male violence, a pattern that fits widespread human experience.

However, invoking male violence still leaves 26 of 30 Donner Party male deaths unexplained. It also fails to explain why men began starving and freezing to death nearly two months before women did. Evidently the women had a big physiological advantage. This could be an extreme expression of the fact that, at every age and for all leading causes of death—from cancer and car accidents to heart disease and suicide—the death rate is far higher for men than for women. While the reasons for this ubiquitous male vulnerability remain debated, there are several compelling reasons why men are more likely than women to die under the extreme conditions the Donner Party faced.

The Donner Party records make it vividly clear that family members stuck together and helped one another at the expense of the others.

First, men are bigger than women. Typical body weights for the world as a whole are about 140 pounds for men and only 120 pounds for women. Hence, even while lying down and doing nothing, men need more food to support their basal metabolism. They also need more energy than women do for equivalent physical activity. Even for sedentary people, the typical metabolic rate for an average-size woman is 25 percent lower than an average-size man's. Under conditions of cold temperatures and heavy physical activity, such as were faced by the Donner Party men when doing the backbreaking work of cutting the wagon road or hunting for food, men's metabolic rates can be double those of women.

To top it all off, women have more fat reserves than men: fat makes up 22 percent of the body weight of an average nonobese, well-nourished woman, but only 16 percent of a similar man. More of the man's weight is instead made up of muscle, which gets burned up much more quickly than does fat. Thus, when there simply was no more food left, the Donner Party men burned up their body reserves much faster than did the women. Furthermore, much of women's fat is distributed under the skin and acts as heat insulation, so that they can withstand cold temperatures better than men can. Women don't have to raise their metabolic rate to stay warm as soon as men do.

These physiological factors easily surpass male murderousness in accounting for all those extra male deaths in the Donner Party. Indeed, a microcosm of the whole disaster was the escape attempt by 15 people on snowshoes, lasting 33 days in midwinter. Of the ten men who set out, two were murdered by another man, six starved or froze to death, and only two survived. Not a single one of the five women with them died.

Even with all these explanations, there is still one puzzling finding to consider: the unexpectedly high death toll of people in their prime, age 20 to 39. That toll proves to be almost entirely of the men: 67 percent of the men in that age range (14 out of 21) died, a much higher proportion than among the teenage boys (only 20 percent). Closer scrutiny shows why most of those men were so unlucky.

Most of the Donner Party consisted of large families, but there were also 16 individuals traveling without any relatives. All those 16 happened to be men, and all but two were between 20 and 39. Those 16 unfortunates bore the brunt of the prime-age mortality. Thirteen of them died, and most of them died long before any of the women. Of the survivors, one—William Herron—reached California in October, so in reality only 2 survived the winter at the lake.

Of the 7 men in their prime who survived, 4 were family men. Only 3 of the 14 dead were. The prime-age women fared similarly: the 8 survivors belonged to families with an average size of 12 people, while Eleanor Eddy, the only woman to die in this age group, had no adult support. Her husband had escaped with the snowshoers, leaving her alone with their two small children.

The Donner Party records make it vividly clear that family members stuck together and helped one another at the expense of the others. A notorious example was the Breen family of nine, every one of whom (even two small children) survived through the luck of retaining their wagons and some pack animals much longer than the others, and through their considerable selfishness toward others. Compare this with the old bachelor Hardkoop, who was ordered out of the Keseberg family wagon and abandoned to die, or the fate of the young bachelor Antoine, whom none of the hungry snowshoers bothered to awaken when his hand fell into the fire.

Family ties can be a matter of life and death even under normal conditions. Married people, it turns out, have lower death rates than single, widowed, or divorced people. And marriage's life-promoting benefits have been found to be shared by all sorts of social ties, such as friendships and membership in social groups. Regardless of age or sex or initial health status, socially isolated individuals have well over twice the death rate of socially connected people.

For reasons about which we can only speculate, the lethal effects of social isolation are more marked for men than for women. It's clear, though, why social contacts are important for both sexes. They provide concrete help in case of need. They're our source of advice and shared information. They provide a sense of belonging and self-worth, and the courage to face tomorrow. They make stress more bearable.

All those benefits of social contact applied as well to the Donner Party members, who differed only in that their risk of death was much greater and their likely circumstances of death more grotesque than yours and mine. In that sense too, the harrowing story of the Donner Party grips us because it was ordinary life writ large.

JARED DIAMOND is a contributing editor of *Discover,* a professor of physiology at UCLA School of Medicine, a recipient of a MacArthur genius award, and the author of *The Third Chimpanzee.*

UNIT 5

Contemporary Archaeology

Unit Selections

Key Points to Consider

• What are the differences between "creationism," "alternative archaeology," and "the science" of archaeology? What needs do each satisfy and why can they not be reconciled?

• In the absence of government funding, should archaeological fieldwork be financed by the private sector if it means getting there before the looters?

• Should a badly needed highway be allowed to cover a World War I battlefield or should the area be preserved as a memorial?

• What happens if archaeologists themselves lie about their findings to suit their own purposes? Give an example of this based on the findings at the Nazi death camps.

• Did Brazil's rain forest once support an ancient civilization? Support your position.

• What is the evidence that suggests that modern humans replaced the Neandertals? Why were the Neandertals unable to resist encroachment?

• How have the new methods of "virtual paleoanthropology" revised our views on the Neandertal?

Student Web Site
www.mhcls.com

Internet References

Archaeology and Anthropology: The Australian National University
   http://online.anu.edu.au/AandA/
WWW: Classical Archaeology
   http://www.archaeology.org/wwwarky/classical.html
Al Mashriq-Archaeology in Beirut
   http://almashriq.hiof.no/base/archaeology.html
American Indian Ritual Object Repatriation Foundation
   http://www.repatriationfoundation.org/
ArchNet—WWW Virtual Library
   http://archnet.asu.edu/archnet/
Current Archaeology
   http://www.archaeology.co.uk
National Archaeological DataBase
   http://www.cast.uark.edu/other/nps/nagpra/nagpra.html
Society for Archaeological Sciences
   http://www.socarchsci.org/

The origins of contemporary archaeology may be traced back to the nineteenth century. Several currents of thought and beliefs coalesced in that unique century. Some say it started with a Frenchman named Boucher de Perthes who found odd-shaped stones on his property, stones that could comfortably be held by a human hand. Undoubtedly, thousands of other people made such finds throughout history. But to Monsieur de Perthes, these stones suggested a novel meaning. He wondered if these odd rocks might be tools made by humans long lost in the mists before history.

Other exciting changes were occurring in the epistemology of the nineteenth century that would soon lend credibility to this hypothesis. In 1859, there was the publication of "On the Origin of Species" by Charles Darwin. In this book (which, by the way, never mentioned humans or any implied relationship they might have to apes), Darwin suggested a general process that became known as natural selection. The theory suggested that species could change gradually in response to the environment. This was an idea counterintuitive to scientific thought. Even biologists believed that species were immutable. But this theory changed forever the way human beings regarded their place in nature. If species could change, then the implication was—so could humans. And that idea knocked humankind down from the loft and into the archaeological record.

There was the concurrent emergence of uniformitarianism, which implied that the Earth was old, very old. (It is, in fact, about 5 billion years old.) But with this idea, the revolutionary possibility that human beings could have existed before history became more plausible. Such a serious challenge to the established wisdom that the Earth was only about 6,000 years old additionally contributed to the new age speculation about the meaning of being human.

The newly emerging science of paleontology, and the discovery and recognition of extinct fossil species seriously challenged the traditional, elevated status of human beings. Nineteenth-century philosophers were forced to reexamine the nature of humanity. Among the intellectuals of the Western world, the essential anthropocentrism of the Christian view gradually shifted to a more secular view of humankind as a part and parcel of nature. Therefore humans became subject to the rules of nature and natural events, without reference to theology.

So, it was within this new nineteenth-century enlightenment, that Boucher de Perthes suggested his hypothesis regarding the antiquity of his stone tools. The time had come, and others came forward saying that they too had found these same, odd-shaped stones, and had thought similar thoughts. The study of archaeology had begun.

As a science evolves, it naturally diversifies. In fact, because mainstream archaeology is being pulled in different directions, some have had concerns that archaeologists will specialize

© IT Stock Free

themselves right out of the mainstream of anthropology. The other side of the coin, however, is that our shared cultural concept and holistic approach should help us to maintain our traditional relationships with each other, and with the field of anthropology.

Current economic climate presents challenges in yet another realm, that of financing future archaeological endeavors and finding additional sources of labor. And then, there are the ethical questions that archaeologists must consider. Because an archaeological site is a nonrenewable resource, excavation results in the systematic destruction of the site and its ecological context. Anything overlooked, mislaid, not measured, or in some way not observed is a lost piece of the past, and if the information that is retrieved is never shared with an audience, it is a complete loss. Yet, as the world population continues to expand, we are destined to impact this scarce and valuable resource. The applied field of archaeology, commonly referred to as Cultural Resource Management (CRM), deals with the complex needs of developers and state and federal agencies. Its practitioners derive their livelihood from this work, even if it means physically destroying archaeological sites. They do so while striving to mitigate adverse impact, and collect data in a way that will enable the archaeological community of the future to answer questions that have yet to be asked.

One saving grace in the field may be found in the current trend toward a more "public archaeology." There is awareness that archaeologists should present their findings in a more palatable, story format. Now is the time for the archaeological community to start a give-and-take dialogue with the public; by portraying their projects within the larger picture that expresses more than a set of tedious details in archaeological lingo. It is for these reasons that the articles presented in this section deal with the archaeological community's current interest in the preservation, conservation, and reconstruction of archaeological sites, and their educational and aesthetic value.

Thracian Gold Fever

Archaeologist and showman Georgi Kitov's spectacular discoveries raise questions about managing Bulgaria's past.

MATTHEW BRUNWASSER

On a soft, gray fall afternoon, a crowd of several hundred waited patiently outside the Iskra History Museum in Kazanluk, the unprepossessing main town in central Bulgaria's rose-growing region. The blank concrete facade of the museum, like that of most Communist-era cultural institutions, created a notably joyless impression.

But inside, the 15 visitors allowed at a time into the small exhibition hall were awed by fantastic Thracian gold, silver, bronze, and ceramic objects, 28 in all, recently discovered only eight miles away and on public display for the first time. An ancient amphora housed on a wobbly metal stand rocked ominously as a woman brushed by. The excitement of the visitors washed over the tiny provincial museum as they carefully studied the objects that have been heralded across the world.

"We are filled with history from the land to the sky," remarked Albena Mileva, who is 24 and unemployed. She hitchhiked 20 miles from the neighboring city of Stara Zagora with two friends to see the exhibit. "So long ago the Thracians were so developed in so many ways. You can touch their spirit and their way of life."

"I have no words," sighed Nadka Nenkova, a 66-year-old retired economist who had just seen the exhibit. "All this time it's been underground, and we didn't even know it was there."

While the sensational finds from a 2,500-year-old necropolis dubbed the "Valley of the Thracian Kings" have fired the imagination of the Bulgarian public and the world beyond, the story behind the discoveries, centered around the controversial methods of the archaeologist who made them—unorthodox excavation practices, shady business deals, allegations of collaborations with looters—raises questions about how this poor former Eastern Bloc nation will manage the future of its past.

It all started on August 19 of last year, when Georgi Kitov of the Bulgarian Academy of Sciences discovered a gold mask in a late fifth-century B.C. burial mound outside the town of Shipka, eight miles from Kazanluk.

The discovery made headlines worldwide ("Putting a New Face on Thrace," November/December 2004), and the 61-year-old Kitov, an archaeologist specializing in Thracian tomb studies who has been in the field for more than 30 years, became

a household name in Bulgaria. Photographs of the robust man with the bushy Abraham Lincoln beard cradling the exquisite mask were splashed across national and international newspapers. In different press statements he attributed the mask to two different Thracian kings who lived more than a century apart, although it was later determined to be the death mask of a warrior, and proudly pointed out to journalists that, at 1.5 pounds, the mask was much more impressive than the Mycenaean Mask of Agamemnon, which, he said, was made of only a paltry 2.5 oz. of gold leaf (in fact, it weighs in at 6 oz. of gold).

Although it may seem amusing to outsiders, Kitov's game of artifact one-upmanship played right to the hearts of his countrymen. Today's Bulgarians are not considered direct descendants of the Thracians, powerful but illiterate Indo-European tribes who were commonly described by their Greek neighbors as "barbarians." Rather, Bulgarians are descended from Central Asian proto-Bulgars who came to the area in the seventh century A.D. and mixed with the remains of local Thracian tribes and Slavs. Nonetheless, the Thracians offer an unusually strong common identity of which all Bulgarians can feel proud—not just because they share the same real estate, but because they offer a comforting association in Bulgaria's current period of post-Communist social dislocation. "Bulgarians need to go back before the divisive historical memories of the Turks and the Russians to find an identity they can agree on," says anthropologist Margarita Karamihova of the Bulgarian Ethnological Institute. "We can't even agree on who to hate anymore. We love to have bigger and better things which increase our self-confidence in comparison with our neighbor countries. And we are so proud that our gold mask is bigger than their gold mask!"

Adding to the wellspring of national pride that the discovery engendered, Kitov allowed himself to speculate generously on an elegant gold ring with a depiction of a seated, spear-wielding athlete that was also found in the tomb along with Greek pottery and bronze and iron weapons. Six days into the 2004 Olympic Games in Athens, and the day after he opened the tomb, the archaeologist was quoted telling Reuters that he believed the ring featured an Olympic rower. "We are dedicating this find to our rowers in Athens," said Kitov. "It's a sign that they should win a gold medal." What he failed to mention was that the ancient games had never hosted the sport of rowing.

A month later, on September 21, together with his team of 12 specialists, a crew of workers, and the ever-present crowd of onlookers, Kitov found what many say is the most exquisite object of his career, a 26-pound bronze head that appears to have been crudely severed at the neck from a life-size statue. As if acting as a sentry, it was found buried deep in a stone-lined pit some 15 feet in front of the entrance to Golyamata Kosmatka, "The Big Shaggy One," a burial mound more than 60 feet high and 10 times as long, located less than a mile from the tomb of the gold mask. Due to the size of the mound and its location some seven miles from Seuthopolis, a city built by the late-fourth-century B.C. king Seuthes III, the tomb is believed to be the burial site of the ruler.

Using three large earthmoving machines, Kitov located the entrance to the Golyamata Kosmatka tomb three days after the discovery of the bronze head. Miners on his team spent approximately a week removing dirt from the 40-foot corridor that lay beyond the entrance; scorch marks on stones indicated that a fire had caused the wooden infrastructure of the corridor to collapse, protecting it from looters for millennia. Ninety-nine percent of Thracian tombs were looted during antiquity, and Kitov and other experts say the fire was likely to have been set deliberately to protect the tomb.

While the crowds of locals and reporters buzzed around, limited air and cramped space kept outsiders from entering the tomb. Finally, in the early afternoon of October 4, Kitov stood at the head of his assembled team at the end of the corridor, facing an enormous marble door beyond which, most likely, was something every archaeologist dreams organ unlooted tomb. Could this enormous burial mound be in fact the very resting place of Seuthes III?

The narrow first room, about five feet wide and twice as long, contained the intact skeleton of a sacrificed horse. A blocked-up doorway lay on the opposite side of the chamber. The doorway was cleared to reveal a second room, empty but much larger, with stone walls and a graceful domed ceiling 15 feet high. The "perfect acoustics" led Kitov to believe it had a ritual purpose. And there across the room was yet another doorway, again packed with rocks and dirt.

That night, Kitov and his team entered the third and final chamber, the centerpiece of which was a sarcophagus tall enough to stand in, carved from a single piece of granite and weighing more than 60 tons. Amid thick dust, exactly as they were laid out 2,300 years ago on the bed and the floor, were more than 70 gold, silver, bronze, and ceramic objects fit for a king, including armor, a gold kylix (drinking cup) and wreath, bronze coins depicting Seuthes III, and three human teeth.

But then, as often happens in Bulgarian life, the story of this amazing archaeological discovery took a sharp turn for the absurd. According to Kitov's account in later press reports—as no journalists were present in the tomb—the archaeologist called the Kazanluk police chief and requested a few policemen to help escort the treasure back to expedition headquarters at a Shipka hotel. Kitov reportedly did not consider the private security firm he used to guard the entrance of the tomb up for

the job. Witnesses say more than 50 Bulgarian law enforcement officers, ordered by the Interior Ministry, showed up outside the tomb: regular uniformed police, masked special forces armed with Kalashnikov assault rifles, and even a local prosecutor.

Adding to the circus was the presence of Ivan Juchnovski, president of the Bulgarian Academy of Sciences, and Vassil Nikolov, director of the National Archaeological institute and Museum. The police frisked them, as well as everybody else present, for artifacts each time they exited the tomb. Tempers flared all around.

The cops insisted that they would have to take the priceless objects to a Kazanluk police station. Kitov refused, insisting that they be taken to his hotel headquarters. At a standoff, the archaeologist, his team, and his guests instead decided to sit it out in the tomb, where they stayed up all night drinking wine in celebration of their discovery and in defiance of the masked and armed authorities outside. Kitov refused to let any outsiders enter, so the police spent a chilly night camped out in their cars parked outside the tomb. The next morning, team members packed the artifacts into expedition cars and authorities escorted them to the hotel.

When Kitov's latest bonanza made news across the country that day, the government's storm-trooper reaction to the discovery elicited boundless amusement among the press and public. The police justified their response by saying it was suspicious that the team needed to remove precious artifacts in the middle of the night, and that one of Kitov's private security guards had a criminal record. The archaeologist fired back by demanding, in the country's biggest national daily, Trud Daily, the resignation of the Interior Minister.

After the team went home and got some sleep, the anger evaporated. There had never been a better time to be an archaeologist in Bulgaria. A photograph of Kitov smiled from the front page of Trud Daily, sipping from the gold kylix while 39-year-old Diana Dimitrova, his deputy expedition leader and mother of his child, held the gold wreath over his head like a halo. The huge headline announced KITOV wanes IN GOLD. Other papers showed masked policemen guarding the tomb with automatic rifles. Political cartoons ridiculed the Interior Ministry.

A few days later, Kitov, dressed casually in a white T-shirt, welcomed the Foreign Minister at Golyamata Kosmatka and was awarded the Gold Honorary Badge of the Foreign Ministry. The minister said the finds were exceptional significance for the future of cultural tourism and tourism in Bulgaria in general" and announced that the government would give Kitov's expedition 50,000 levs (about $35,000) to continue its work. The Construction Minister even promised to fix the roads in the depressed region around the tombs. "I will be the Bulgarian Schliemann," Kitov had once boasted to colleagues years ago. His lifetime of talk had become reality.

Among his colleagues, however, Kitov does not receive nearly the same respect as he does from the local media, public, and politicians. The archaeological community in Bulgaria is very small, perhaps only 250 professionals in all, so most agreed to talk only anonymously. Kitov clearly prefers to dig, focusing his energy on discovering objects, and appears to have little interest in documenting or scientifically analyzing his finds. Several specialists noted that he rarely published his discoveries until several years ago, when he was publicly criticized by colleagues. A former colleague, who recalled that Kitov once bragged that he hadn't been to the library of the Bulgarian Archaeological Institute "since 1977," characterizes him as "a typical villager, the worst example of those who succeeded in the late Communist system, not academic at all." Nonetheless, he has recently excavated some of the country's most significant Thracian sites, including the Alexandrovo tomb, which contains elaborate painted depictions of Thracians, and Starosel, perhaps the largest Thracian sanctuary yet discovered.

A maestro of heavy earthmoving equipment—even orchestrating four machines at the same time—Kitov has pioneered what his detractors say is its overuse on archaeological sites in Bulgaria. Many archaeologists are bewildered by his hastiness. While established Bulgarian archaeologists have spent 20 years investigating one site, he excavated six sites this summer alone, and had permission for at least 10. "Ninety percent of us reject his methods," says a colleague.

If we didn't hurry, [looters] would've entered the grave, and taken out everything. That's why we hurry, and that's why we use machines.

Kitov is unapologetic. "The looters were one step away from the town where the ring and mask were found," said Kitov in a recent telephone conversation (granted only grudgingly on the condition that it be quick). "If we didn't hurry, if we were a week late, for example, they would've entered the grave, and taken out everything that was inside and no one would have ever known what was there in Shipka. That's why we hurry and that's why we work very hard, and that's why we use machines without damaging the archaeological site. We once found 27 beads from a gold necklace in a huge mound, which means that the machines don't stop us from finding objects. Nothing is destroyed, nothing is damaged."

Kitov was censured in February 2001 by the Council for Scientific Field Studies at the National Archaeological Institute and Museum (AIM), to which he belonged. The other 13 members voted unanimously to take away his permission to lead expeditions for a year, based on violations that included excavating three sites without permission; "nonprofessional digging" and "covering a site without consideration of conservation"; working 10 sites in one season, including two at the same time; the uncontrolled use of earthmoving equipment and metal detectors despite complex geological deposits; working with a team lacking any sufficiently qualified or experienced members; and not leaving any unstudied sites for future generations. Kitov defended himself by saying he was morally

obligated to work the sites without permission because he had seen looters nearby and needed to save them.

Then in September the same year, the institute's Scientific Council voted unanimously to expel Kitov from his leadership post of the Thracian Section of AIM, which he had held for 11 years, as well as to form a commission to investigate all his expedition documentation for the previous five years. Among an even longer series of professional issues such as those featured at the February meeting, Kitov was accused of acting like a "spoiled child," and the council chair protested at his accusing her in the media of "filling orders for the looter's Mafia" and calling her a "moron."

But Kitov still has one very well-placed ally. Vassil Nikolov, who was present for the opening of the Golyamata Kosmatka tomb and as director of AIM is responsible for approving excavation licenses in the country, says he has no concerns about control over archaeological activity in Bulgaria, or about Kitov, although he could not say how many dig permissions Kitov holds. The archaeologist himself believes he had "12 or 15 [permissions in 2004], somewhere around there." Nikolov said the high number is the result of a new and improved system whereby a separate permit is given for each mound, instead of one permission for a whole complex of mounds. And because Nikolov was working in the area and visited Kitov every day, he says, he personally saw that the archaeologist never worked more than one site at a time.

Bulgarian scholars are deeply concerned not only about Kitov and his methods, or the respectability he commands, but also about the broader repercussions for archaeology in their country. The attention he receives risks shifting public and financial focus onto "treasure" and Thracians at the expense of all other archaeological investigations. There is a wealth of heritage in Bulgaria from other cultures as well, including Greek, Roman, Ottoman, Byzantine, and ancient Bulgarian. "Colleagues say it is offensive that the government awards Kitov because he finds gold," says one archaeologist, "but others who don't live with their families for six years because of their work get nothing."

Such attitudes are most likely a result of jealousy, Kitov says. "It's not a matter of finding gold, it's a matter of gathering a lot of facts about the Thracians. We only work four, five months a year like other colleagues and we get results. We work 10, 12 hours a day. While some of the other colleagues might work four, five, six hours and want to have our results, they won't have them."

It was two days after the Golyamata Kosmatka finds were put on display for the first time in Kazanluk that I met Kitov. Bulgaria was still buzzing about the Thracians. When I arrived, he was sitting alone at a folding table near the tomb entrance, doing a newspaper crossword puzzle—the stereotypical pursuit of the bored Communist-era worker. He was wearing a mobile phone promo T-shirt, cheap plastic sunglasses, and a black Speedo. "Should I grab a chair?" I asked. "No," he said, "we'll stand." He clearly did not welcome scrutiny of his work, but perhaps he was fatigued by the insatiable press interest.

The conversation was very strained, but Kitov became animated when the topic steered into what is clearly favorite territory: state neglect and incompetence in archaeological affairs, in particular with regard to the Valley of the Thracian Kings. He complained that the area was awash with looters and that the authorities did nothing to stop them or preserve the sites. "We want to turn this into a tourist site," he said. "Little by little, we hope to have a person stay here, sell tickets, another to take people inside. You need very little money; fortunately, most of these mounds are near the road." Kitov described how, because of tourism at Starosel, more than 20 people "have bread and work thanks to our work." If tourism were to come to Shipka, he argued, he could put more than 50 people to work. "We simply want the local government to not stop us, to look favorably on our work, and turn the tombs into tourist sites."

When tourists come and there is no road, no electricity, no lights and water, and nowhere to eat or sleep, they are not going to come back.

Bulgaria's infatuation with its self-styled Schliemann got its first dose of reality a few weeks later on October 30, when the cover of the weekly Politika featured a picture of Kitov wearing a T-shirt with the bronze head, shrugging his shoulders with his arms upraised. The two-inch headline exclaimed: GEORGI KITOV—THE CASHIER OF THE THRACIAN GOLD. The accompanying story accused Kitov of illegally trying to develop the concessions for the tomb area, and showed images of an admitted looter in the tomb at the moment he entered the third chamber of Golyamata Kosmatka.

A contract had been signed by Kitov, the director of the Kazanluk Museum, which financed the expedition, and a third party known as the Bulgarian Investment Fund to develop the Golyamata Kosmatka site for tourism. It was not yet a legal contract because the mayor of Kazanluk had not signed (the Kazanluk municipality owns the land beneath the site). But even if he had, the contract would not have been valid because the Culture Ministry is required by law to develop any archaeological site anywhere in the country.

Still, an initiative in developing sites where the state does nothing is somewhat difficult to fault. All Bulgarian archaeologists work for local, regional, or national museums or institutes and all artifacts are property of the state, but the state has little money available for fieldwork, let alone for protection or maintenance of monuments after they are opened. "State administration has no relationship to science," laments one archaeologist. The Culture Ministry also recommended that prosecutors investigate Kitov's nonprofit association TEMP (the Bulgarian acronym for "Thracian Expedition for Tomb Studies") because of clauses in its association's registration that allow for activities which under law only licensed archaeologists or the state can perform.

Of particular concern to the archaeological community was Kitov's association with the Bulgarian Investment Fund, which provided private security guards for Golyamata Kosmatka and also claims to have supplied a $90,000 "scanner" used to locate sites during Kitov's expeditions. The fund employee who operated the equipment, Mario Shopov, also freely admitted a grave-robbing background. Asked by *Politika* whether he dealt with looting or archaeological expeditions, Shopov replied, "Both. I'm interested in history, and separately I work with the equipment of Mr. Dinov," [co-owner of the Bulgarian Investment Fund]. Shopov is a signatory for the finds in Golyamata Kosmatka, and a Kitov-produced DVD about the excavations confirms his presence in the third chamber just after it was opened—shaking hands with Kitov. Shopov also says he was a responsible party for the finds in the gold-mask burial and another Kitov tomb. Shopov declined to tell ARCHAEOLOGY anything about the scanner used in Kitov's discoveries, citing "commercial secrets." A police source is quoted in the Politika story saying Shopov is "operationally interesting."

Kitov described the admitted looter to ARCHAEOLOGY as someone who was in the tomb "coincidentally" at 2:30 A.M. when the third chamber was opened, although he previously told the magazine that not even the police were allowed to enter the tomb. Nikolov and others confirm the latter version of events.

A police investigator later revealed that the official list of artifacts found at Golyamata Kosmatka was incomplete enough for some objects to have gone unaccounted for—an administrative but not a criminal offense. Konstantin Dimitrov, chief expert of the investigative branch of Crimes Against Cultural Artifacts in the National Police, says the police have never "investigated" Kitov—a formal term for the beginning of a law-enforcement operation on specific charges. He does say that the police were "checking signals" from the Culture Ministry about various possible violations, but would not be more specific.

The press attention given to Kitov has raised fresh debate on how to protect Bulgaria's cultural heritage. There is currently no law against buying antiquities in Bulgaria, only for digging for them or selling them—and even those laws are rarely enforced, making the country, according to Bozhidar Dimitrov, director of the National History Museum, the largest exporter of illicit antiquities in Europe. The parliament passed a law that went into effect January 1 giving all private collectors one year to register their collections with local museums, without having to establish origins or ownership.

The gold mask and ring, as well as the bronze head, are on display in the National Archaeological Museum in Sofia, while the Golyamata Kosmatka artifacts are in Kazanluk. Some are being restored but others are on display. There are no plans for any of the artifacts to travel abroad before the summer.

Kitov is currently in Sofia, where he says he is writing up his finds for the Bulgarian journal *Archaeologia*. At the end of 2004, readers of the country's second-largest daily named him one of the year's 55 "Most Honorable Bulgarians." Next spring he plans to return to the Valley of the Thracian Kings to continue work on other tombs in the same area, some of which he has worked on before, and some of which he hasn't.

Back in Shipka, people are readying themselves for the tourists they think will come. An unusual example of private initiative is being undertaken by Ali Kachan, a 58-year-old former tractor driver who owns a restaurant 300 yards from the burial mound where the gold mask was found. Within three weeks of the discovery, he had received all the required permissions and already begun building a defensive "house" around the tomb with his own money. "Private people need help," he says. "They are not used to having initiative. The moment the state gives serious money for the infrastructure of the burial mounds, things will happen as they should."

Kachan is not the only one thinking about what the finds might mean in concrete terms for Bulgarians. There is serious talk about basing the national tourism strategy on the Valley of the Thracian Kings. "Gold masks, bronze heads, tombs—all this makes me very happy," says Ivan Kalchev, who rents rooms to tourists in his enormous house in Shipka. He began construction work on a separate hotel just weeks before the first discovery. Most agree the Valley of the Kings is right now more a business strategy than scientific fact, but few fault the idea. "If someone wants to advertise it, that's great," says Vassil Nikolov, who is helping Bulgaria's president develop a strategy for managing the country's cultural heritage. "But first real money needs to be invested to develop the sites. When the foreign tourists come and there is no road, no electricity, no lights and no water, and nowhere to eat or sleep, they are not going to come back." As a start, the government recently allotted 1.2 million levs (about $800,000) to build roads and bring water and electricity to a few of the valley's tombs, including Golyamata Kosmatka.

Driving back toward Kachan's restaurant, a car cuts across the muddy field passing us in the opposite direction, toward the tomb of the golden mask. Kachan shakes his head and clicks his tongue against his teeth with disappointment. "No one will be there to show them anything," he tells me. Sometimes the restaurant owner gives tours himself. He feels each visitor who comes to the valley is a precious opportunity to share his pride and help the impoverished local economy. His vision for the future includes hotels, restaurants, and shops rising in the desolate fields where socialist agricultural cooperatives once raised roses. Kachan expects plenty of problems for at least a few years until the area develops enough infrastructure for feeding and housing foreign tourists. "In Bulgaria, people still aren't adapted to doing things 100 percent privately. When they learn to accept this, things will be different."

MATTHEW BRUNWASSER is an investigative journalist based in Sofia, Bulgaria.

In Flanders Fields
Uncovering the Carnage of World War I

Neil Asher Silberman

The Belgian City of Ieper—better known by its French name, Ypres—is really two cities. One is a growing center of high-tech entrepreneurship and commerce with light manufacturing, biotechnology laboratories, and software-development firms clustered around the city in office complexes and industrial parks. The other is a place of cemeteries and war monuments: Flanders fields is where "the poppies blow/between the crosses, row on row," according to the poem by World War I Canadian combat surgeon John McCrae. For four hellish years during World War I, huge armies were bogged down here in a bloody stalemate. By the time of the Armistice in November 1918, this once-proud city, with its massive gothic Cloth Hall, step-gabled shop facades, cathedral, and medieval town square, had been pulverized by incessant bombardment. Its surrounding farmlands were transformed into a cratered, treeless wasteland. It was here that brutal trench warfare claimed the lives of nearly half a million British, Irish, Canadian, Australian, Indian, South African, New Zealand, German, French, and Belgian soldiers. Today, battlefield tours of the "Ypres Salient," as the Allied position deep in German-held territory was known during the war, the 144 official war cemeteries, and memorial ceremonies annually attract hundreds of thousands of visitors to Ieper. A new, state-of-the-art museum, In Flanders Fields, offers a sobering multimedia vision of trench warfare for tourists, descendants of World War I veterans, and a steady stream of school groups.

Now archaeologists have been thrust into a new battle for the soul of Ieper that pits the city's physical expansion against the commemoration of its tragic past. A plan for a new major highway, intended to bring economic development to the region, threatens its vast archaeological remains. Just beneath the surface of the fields, farmyards, and roads all around Ieper for at least three miles in every direction are the remains of trenches, fortifications, ammunition dumps, bunkers, and dugouts; unexploded munitions; discarded equipment; and the unrecovered bodies of at least one hundred thousand soldiers who are listed as missing in action on the various memorials erected throughout the battlefield.

The struggle over Ieper's future has highlighted many of the challenges facing battlefield archaeology the world over. What right does a community have to expand and develop land that is the site of a historic battlefield? What are the obligations of the present generation to preserve the integrity of battlefield landscapes as a memorial to the fallen and a reminder of the horrors of the past? And what role can archaeology play in examining the nature of modern warfare and preserving its physical remains?

High-tech Ieper and war-memorial Ieper have always lived in polite coexistence, but in 2002, a new regional transportation plan suddenly brought their conflicting interests into sharp relief. The A19, a major eight-lane highway that currently ends at the edge of the battlefield, was slated to continue its northward extension from France, eventually connecting Ieper to the Belgian coast of the English Channel, with its heavily visited tourist spots and ferry ports. Supporters argued that A19 would be a boon to Ieper's economy and draw off summertime traffic congestion from its narrow secondary roads. The plan for an initial four-and-a-half-mile extension was approved by Ieper's city council and sent for final approval and funding to the regional Flemish government.

Naturally, the farmers whose lands would be expropriated for road building immediately objected. But wider and more pervasive protests soon began to be heard: Historians, veterans' groups, preservation activists, and commemorative organizations were outraged that the new highway would rip through a four-and-a-half-mile swath of Flanders fields, almost certainly obliterating all traces of the bodies, trenchworks, and fortifications.

In response to these complaints, the Flemish ministry of culture ordered the Institute for Archaeological Patrimony (IAP), the public research body responsible for excavation and archaeological preservation in Flanders, to undertake a detailed assessment of the proposed route of the A19 extension. The project would provide an opportunity to learn more about Ieper's World War I artifacts. Archaeology in the region has long been focused on the prehistoric, Roman, and medieval periods. Twentieth-century archaeology, and particularly twentieth-century battlefield archaeology, was something new. "At first, I wasn't particularly enthusiastic about his assignment," says Marc DeWilde, head of the IAP West Flanders regional office and a specialist in the area's medieval period. "But we all now recognize how interesting and important this work is."

Over the years, battlefield archaeology at Ieper has been a sporadic, ad hoc affair. Year after year, a grim harvest of bones, twisted metal, and unexploded ordnance has complicated and sometimes endangered the inhabitants' lives. Even today, more than eighty-five years after the end of fighting, a Belgian army bomb-disposal truck makes weekly rounds of the rural roads around the city collecting bombs, artillery shells, and rusted clumps of ammunition and hand grenades that have turned up in the plowing and tending of fields. On rare occasions local farmers have been injured or killed. At building sites and roadworks on the expanding fringes of Ieper, workers regularly uncover trenches, bunkers, military equipment, and human remains. It is impossible to tell how many finds have been dug up and kept or sold as relics by the area's World War I buffs, working with metal detectors and digging in secrecy. Buried artifacts from World War I are protected by the antiquities laws of Flanders, but in practice they are vulnerable: Because the region is so archaeologically rich, it has been impossible for local IAP archaeologists to effectively patrol the entire area.

In other places along the Western Front, World War I archaeology has been limited to small-scale research projects on select French and Belgian battlefields. But here at Ieper the potential size of the dig was unprecedented. To get a better sense of the nature of the fighting and the places most likely to contain extensive battlefield remains, an enormous cache of contemporaneous documents was studied: military maps, reports, requisition orders, personal snapshots, diaries and letters, and World War I aerial photos.

Assisted by British colleagues from the University of Greenwich, the Imperial War Museum, the National Army Museum, and University College London, De Wilde and his team began work in the spring of 2002. Using the archival maps and documents, first they plotted the recorded locations of trench lines and other fortifications on modern topographical maps of the survey area. They then field walked the entire four-and-a-half-mile strip to spot concentrations of artifacts on the surface and tie them into documented battle sites. This turned up several intense concentrations of material: wire, supplies, tracks, bunkers, dugouts, pipelines, glass bottles with markings, shovels, helmets, concretized sandbags, bullets, cartridges, shells, and indications of trenches. The location of the finds closely matched the documentary record.

Nine areas were selected for excavation on the basis of the surface finds, and digging on two started right away. The IAP archaeologists began with a site identified from the WWI maps and accounts as "The High Command Redoubt," the German front established after the second Battle of Ieper, In April 1915, when the Germans' devastating chemical attack using canisters of acrid, blinding chlorine gas cleared the way to this strategic point. The English war chronicler Edmund Blunden, an Ieper veteran himself, noted that this redoubt was the highest strategic significance to the German forces, as it directly overlooked the Allied frontlines. The excavation revealed a system of trenches and machine-gun positions linked to substantial wooden structures. One of the walls still bore the initials "K.W.," carved by one of the builders or soldiers stationed there. It was eerily empty except for a rusted bayonet blade and a cache of unexploded

hand grenades. Luckily, the IAP team had been trained to handle such potentially dangerous finds by the bomb-disposal unit of the Belgian army. "Once we learned how to deal with the grenades, shell cases, and unexploded bombs, we had no problem with these types of finds," says archaeologist Pedro Pype.

Within the shell craters were the shattered remains of five soldiers, two of them still wearing leather webbing, entrenching tools, pistol, bayonet, and ammunition packs.

At the second site, known in war accounts as Turco Farm, the discoveries were much more numerous and grisly. According to historical sources, this was the place where first the French and later the British established their frontlines after 1915. Excavations revealed a network of narrow trenches with "duckboards"—wood planks laid to keep soldiers above the mud—that had been lined with now-rusted sheets of corrugated iron. Within these trenches, the team recovered digging tools, a copper teaspoon, shoes, a water-logged woolen sock, and a shattered skeleton, identified as British from the distinctive uniform buttons found with it. Nearby they discovered the bones of a lower leg, with the foot still intact, inside a well-preserved military boot. The French factory marks stamped into the sole indicated the likely nationality of the fallen soldier.

The discovery of human remains changed everything. Over the years, whenever bones were found in the Ieper area, local police had been called in to determine whether they were those of battle casualties or evidence of a more recent crime. If war related, the bones were taken to a government morgue and eventually given over to the appropriate combatant nation. Often the remains could be linked to a particular army, unit, or even individual by the equipment, uniform buttons, or personal possessions found with them. England's Commonwealth War Graves Commission (CWGC) had been particularly active in identifying the remains of British and Commonwealth soldiers and burying them with full military honors in national cemeteries. Since one of the bodies from Turco Farm was British, it was transferred to the CWGC for proper burial. Though no German archaeologists or scholars have been involved in the excavations, had the bodies of the country's soldiers been recovered, German authorities would have been contacted to repatriate the remains.

The excavation at the next site, Crossroads Farm, was not merely a battlefield recovery operation. The archaeologists were also able to verify the hellish dynamics of trench warfare. The level farmland between the outer ring of the city and the low ridges that surrounded it—through which A19 would run—had been the deadly no man's land between the Allied trenches and those of the besieging German forces on the ridges above. Here, the IAP team traced the complex trench system that the Allies had expanded in preparation for an assault on the German positions during the Third Battle of Ieper in the summer of 1917. A variety of structural details and artifacts were uncovered, including duckboards, a deep concrete bunker, a wooden dugout, and cap badges representing the Royal King's Rifle Corps, the Dorsetshire Regiment, and the East Kent Regiment known as the "Buffs." The archaeologists also examined the clearly defined shell craters that pockmarked the entire area. Within the shell craters were the shattered remains of five soldiers, two of them still wearing leather webbing, entrenching tools, pistol, bayonet, and ammunition packs. British visitors to the excavation created a temporary memorial there, marking the places where the bodies were found with the familiar poppy-decorated wooden crosses used in Ieper's military cemeteries; formal military burials are planned for the coming months. From these remains and the location of the trenches, the archaeologists were able to trace in precise detail how the British had expanded and shifted the orientation of their trenches as they edged closer to the German frontlines.

At the very start of the project, the IAP had convened a panel of military historians and preservation experts from the United Kingdom, France, and Belgium to compile a background report on the historical significance of the threatened section of the Ieper battlefield. Though the panel was cautious in expressing its political opinions about the wisdom of the proposed highway plan, they were unambiguous in their opinion about the site's enormous historical and archaeological value as one of the most important battlefields of World War I. The excavations dramatically confirmed this conclusion.

Yet for the problem of the proposed highway, there are no easy answers. The panel recommended that the area be declared a protected heritage zone, but the supporters of the road project countered that the extent of the battlefield is so vast that any attempt to shift the road's path to skirt the entire area would be too expensive and inefficient to achieve the region's development aims. Alternatively, raising the highway on pillars to protect the human remains and archaeological deposits beneath it would also be costly and, as the preservationists pointed out, would forever destroy the visual context of the open ground and low ridges where the battles of Ieper were fought. Excavating the entire four-and-a-half-mile stretch would be far beyond the capacity of the IAP—or of any similar archaeological organization—considering the hundreds of bodies, dense network of trenches and fortifications, and tons of equipment that would almost certainly be found.

Something will have to be done to prevent the total destruction of the World War I remains, says Marc DeWilde. "I am concerned about any destruction of archaeological deposits. If the highway plan is approved and the archaeological remains are in danger, it's our responsibility to excavate what we must and preserve what we can."

At the time of this writing, no decision on the A19 extension has been made, and the archaeological project goes on. More finds—and more funerals—can be expected. And with elections for the Flemish Parliament in June, no decision is anticipated soon. As the preservation and development debates continue, only one thing is certain: The pioneering project at Ieper has demonstrated archaeology's essential role in preserving and understanding the great historical trauma of modern warfare, whose gruesome traces lie beneath the surface of this now-peaceful ground.

Neil Asher Silberman is an author, a historian, and the coordinator of international programs for the Ename Center for Public Archaeology in Belgium. He thanks Marc Dewilde, Pedro Pype, Mathieu de Meyer, Frederik Demeyere, Wouter Lammens, Janiek Degryse, and Franky Wyffels of the IAP West Flanders regional office for their assistance with this article.

Germany's Nazi Past

The Past as Propaganda

How Hitler's archaeologists distorted European prehistory to justify racist and territorial goals.

BETTINA ARNOLD

The manipulation of the past for political purposes has been a common theme in history Consider Darius I (521—486 B.C.), one of the most powerful rulers of the Achaemenid, or Persian, empire. The details of his accession to power, which resulted in the elimination of the senior branch of his family, are obscured by the fact that we have only his side of the story, carved on the cliff face of Behistun in Iran. The list of his victories, and by association his right to rule, are the only remaining version of the truth. Lesson number one: If you are going to twist the past for political ends, eliminate rival interpretations.

The use of the past for propaganda is also well documented in more recent contexts. The first-century Roman historian Tacitus produced an essay titled "On the Origin and Geography of Germany." It is less a history or ethnography of the German tribes than a moral tract or political treatise. The essay was intended to contrast the debauched and degenerate Roman Empire with the virtuous German people, who embodied the uncorrupted morals of old Rome. Objective reporting was not the goal of Tacitus's *Germania;* the manipulation of the facts was considered justified if it had the desired effect of contrasting past Roman glory with present Roman decline. Ironically, this particular piece of historical propaganda was eventually appropriated by a regime notorious for its use and abuse of the past for political, imperialist, and racist purposes: the Third Reich.

The National Socialist regime in Germany fully appreciated the propaganda value of the past, particularly of prehistoric archaeology, and exploited it with characteristic efficiency. The fact that German prehistoric archaeology had been largely ignored before Hitler's rise to power in 1933 made the appropriation of the past for propaganda that much easier. The concept of the *Kulturkreis,* pioneered by the linguist turned-prehistorian Gustav Kossinna in the 1920s and defined as the identification of ethnic regions on the basis of excavated material culture, lent theoretical support to Nazi expansionist aims in central and eastern Europe. Wherever an artifact of a type designated as "Germanic" was found, the land was declared to be ancient Germanic territory. Applied to prehistoric archaeology, this perspective resulted in the neglect or distortion of data that did not directly apply to Germanic peoples. During the 1930s scholars whose specialty was provincial Roman archaeology were labeled *Römlinge* by the extremists and considered anti-German. The Römisch Germanische Kommission in Mainz, founded in 1907, was the object of numerous defamatory attacks, first by Kossinna and later by Alfred Rosenberg and his organization. Rosenberg, a Nazi ideologue, directed the Amt Rosenberg, which conducted ethnic, cultural, and racial research.

Altered prehistory also played an important role in rehabilitating German self-respect after the humiliating defeat of 1918. The dedication of the 1921 edition of Kossinna's seminal work *German Prehistory: A Preeminently National Discipline* reads: "To the German people, as a building block in the reconstruction of the externally as well as internally disintegrated fatherland."

According to Nazi doctrine, the Germanic culture of northern Europe was responsible for virtually all major intellectual and technological achievements of Western civilization. Maps that appeared in archaeological publications between 1933 and 1945 invariably showed the Germanic homeland as the center of diffusionary waves, bringing civilization to less developed cultures to the south, west, and east. Hitler presented his own views on this subject in a dinner-table monologue in which he referred to the Greeks as Germans who had survived a northern natural catastrophe and evolved a highly developed culture in southern contexts. Such wishful thinking was supported by otherwise reputable archaeologists. The *Research Report of the Reichsbund for German Prehistory,* July to December 1941, for example, reported the nine-week expedition of the archaeologist Hans Reinerth and a few colleagues to Greece, where they claimed to have discovered major new evidence of Indogermanic migration to Greece during Neolithic times.

This perspective was ethnocentric, racist, and genocidal. Slavic peoples occupying what had once been, on the basis of the distribution of archaeological remains, Germanic territory, were to be relocated or exterminated to supply true Germans with *Lebensraum* (living space). When the new Polish state was created in 1919, Kossinna published an article, "The German Ostmark, Home Territory of the Germans," which used archaeological evidence to support Germany's claim to the area. Viewed as only temporarily occupied by racially inferior "squatters," Poland and Czechoslovakia could be reclaimed for "racially pure" Germans.

Prehistoric archaeologists in Germany who felt they had been ignored, poorly funded, and treated as second-class citizens by colleagues specializing in the more honored disciplines of classical and Near Eastern archaeology now seemed to have everything to gain by an association with the rising Nazi party. Between 1933, the year of Hitler's accession to power, and 1935, eight new chairs were created in German prehistory and funding became available for prehistoric excavations across Germany and eastern Europe on an unprecedented scale. Numerous institutes came into being during this time, such as the Institute for Prehistory in Bonn in 1938. Museums for protohistory were established, and prehistoric collections were brought out of storage and exhibited, in many cases for the first time. Institutes for rune research were created to study the *futhark,* or runic alphabet in use in northern Europe from about the third to the thirteenth centuries A.D. Meanwhile, the Römisch Germanisches Zentral Museum in Mainz became the Zentral Museum für Deutsche Vor- und Frühgeschichte in 1939. (Today it has its pre-war title once again.)

Open-air museums like the reconstructed Neolithic and Bronze Age lake settlements at Unteruhldingen on Lake Constanz were intended to popularize prehistory. An archaeological film series, produced and directed by the prehistorian Lothar Zotz, included titles like *Threatened by the Steam Plow, Germany's Bronze Age, The Flames of Prehistory and On the Trail of the Eastern Germans.* The popular journals such as *Die Kunde (The Message), and Germanen-Erbe (Germanic Heritage)* proliferated. The latter publication was produced by the Ahnenerbe ("Ancestor History") organization, run as a personal project of Reichsführer-SS and chief of police Heinrich Himmler and funded by interested Germans to research, excavate, and restore real and imagined Germanic cultural relics. Himmler's interests in mysticism and the occult extended to archaeology; SS archaeologists were sent out in the wake of invading German forces to track down important archaeological finds and antiquities to be transported back to the Reich. It was this activity that inspired Steven Spielberg's *Raiders of the Lost Ark.*

The popular journals contained abundant visual material. One advertisement shows the reconstruction of a Neolithic drum from a pile of meaningless sherds. The text exhorts readers to "keep your eyes open, for every *Volksgenosse* [fellow German] can contribute to this important national project! Do not assume that a ceramic vessel is useless because it falls apart during excavation. Carefully preserve even the smallest fragment!" An underlined sentence emphasizes the principal message: "Every single find is important because it represents a document of our ancestors!"

Amateur organizations were actively recruited by appeals to patriotism. The membership flyer for the official National Confederation for German Prehistory (*Reichsbund für Deutsche Vorgeschichte*), under the direction of Hans Reinerth of the Amt Rosenberg, proclaimed: "Responsibility with respect to our indigenous prehistory must again fill every German with pride!" The organization stated its goals as "the interpretation and dissemination of unfalsified knowledge regarding the history and cultural achievements of our northern Germanic ancestors on German and foreign soil."

For Himmler objective science was not the aim of German prehistoric archaeology. Hermann Rauschning, an early party member who became disillusioned with the Nazis and left Germany before the war, quotes Himmler as saying: "The one and only thing that matters to us, and the thing these people are paid for by the State, is to have ideas of history that strengthen our people in their necessary national pride. In all this troublesome business we are only interested in one thing—to project into the dim and distant past the picture of our nation as we envisage it for the future. Every bit of Tacitus in his *Germania* is tendentious stuff. Our teaching of German origins has depended for centuries on a falsification. We are entitled to impose one of our own at any time."

Meanwhile archaeological evidence that did not conform to Nazi dogma was ignored or suppressed. A good example is the controversy surrounding the Externsteine, a natural sandstone formation near Horn in northern Germany In the twelfth century Benedictine monks from the monastery in nearby Paderborn carved a system of chambers into the rock faces of the Externsteine. In the mid-1930s a contingent of SS Ahnenerbe researchers excavated at the site in an attempt to prove its significance as the center of the Germanic universe, a kind of Teutonic mecca. The excavators, led by Julius Andree, an archaeologist with questionable credentials and supported by Hermann Wirth, one of the founders of the SS Ahnenerbe, were looking for the remains of an early Germanic temple at the Externsteine, where they claimed a cult of solar worshipers had once flourished. The site was described in numerous publications as a monument to German unity and the glorious Germanic past, despite the fact that no convincing evidence of a temple or Germanic occupation of the site was ever found.

So preposterous were the claims made by Andree, Wirth, and their associates that numerous mainstream archaeologists openly questioned the findings of the investigators who became popularly known as *German omanen* or "Germanomaniacs." Eventually Himmler and the Ahnenerbe organization disowned the project, but not before several hundred books and pamphlets on the alleged cult site had been published.

By 1933 the Nazis had gone a step further, initiating a movement whose goal was to replace all existing religious denominations with a new pseudopagan state religion based loosely on Germanic mythology, solar worship, nature cults, and a Scandinavian people's assembly or *thing,* from which the new movement derived its name. Central to the movement were open-air theaters or *Thingstätten,* where festivals, military ceremonies, and morality plays, known as *Thingspiele,* were to be staged. To qualify as a Thingstätte, evidence of significant Germanic occupation of the site had to be documented. There was considerable competition among municipalities throughout Germany for this honor. Twelve Thingstätten had been dedicated by September 1935, including one on the summit of the Heiligenberg in Heidelberg.

The Heiligenberg was visited sporadically during the Neolithic, possibly for ritual purposes; there is no evidence of permanent occupation. It was densely settled during the Late Bronze Age (1200–750 B.C.), and a double wall-and-ditch system was built there in the Late Iron Age (200 B.C. to the Roman occupation), when it was a hillfort settlement. Two provincial Roman watchtowers, as well as several Roman dedicatory inscriptions, statue bases, and votive stones, have been found at the site.

When excavations in the 1930s failed to produce evidence of Germanic occupation the Heiligenberg was granted Thingstätte status on the basis of fabricated evidence in the published excavation reports. Ironically, most of the summit's prehistoric deposits were destroyed in the course of building the open-air arena. The Heiligenberg Thingstätte actually held only one Thingspiel before the Thing movement was terminated. Sensing the potential for resistance from German Christians, the Ministry of Propaganda abandoned the whole concept in 1935. Today the amphitheater is used for rock concerts.

Beyond its convenience for propaganda and as justification for expansion into countries like Czechoslovakia and Poland, the archaeological activities of the Amt Rosenberg and Himmler's Ahnenerbe were just so much window dressing for the upper echelons of the party. There was no real respect for the past or its remains. While party prehistorians like Reinerth and Andree distorted the facts, the SS destroyed archaeological sites like Biskupin in Poland. Until Germany's fortunes on the eastern front suffered a reversal in 1944, the SS Abhenerbe conducted excavations at Biskupin, one of the best-preserved Early Iron Age (600–400 B.C.) sites in all of central Europe. As the troops retreated, they were ordered to demolish as much of the site's preserved wooden fortifications and structures as possible.

Not even Hitler was totally enthusiastic about Himmler's activities. He is quoted by Albert Speer, his chief architect, as complaining: "Why do we call the whole world's attention to the fact that we have no past? It's bad enough that the Romans were erecting great buildings when our forefathers were still living in mud huts; now Himmler is starting to dig up these villages of mud huts and enthusing over every potsherd and stone axe he finds. All we prove by that is that we were still throwing stone hatchets and crouching around open fires when Greece and Rome had already reached the highest stage of culture. We should really do our best to keep quiet about this past. Instead Himmler makes a great fuss about it all. The present-day Romans must be having a laugh at these revelations."

"Official" involvement in archaeology consisted of visits by Himmler and various SS officers to SS-funded and staffed excavations, like the one on the Erdenburg in the Rhineland, or press shots of Hitler and Goebbels viewing a reconstructed "Germanic" Late Bronze Age burial in its tree-trunk coffin, part of the 1934 "Deutsches Volk—Deutsche Arbeit" exhibition in Berlin. Party appropriation of prehistoric data was evident in the use of Indo-European and Germanic design symbols in Nazi uniforms and regalia. The double lightning bolt, symbol of Himmler's SS organization, was adapted from a Germanic rune. The swastika is an Indo-European sun symbol which appears in ceramic designs as early as the Neolithic in western Europe and continues well into early medieval times.

German archaeologists during this period fall into three general categories: those who were either true believers or self-serving opportunists; those (the vast majority) who accepted without criticism the appropriation and distortion of prehistoric archaeology; and those who openly opposed these practices.

Victims of the regime were persecuted on the basis of race or political views, and occasionally both. Gerhard Bersu, who had trained a generation of post–World War I archaeologists in the field techniques of settlement archaeology, was prematurely retired from the directorship of the Römisch Germanische Kommission in 1935. His refusal to condone or conduct research tailored to Nazi ideological requirements, in addition to his rejection of the racist Kossinna school, ended his career as a prehistonian until after World War II. The official reason given for the witchhunt, led by Hans Reinerth under the auspices of the Amt Rosenberg, was Bersu's Jewish heritage. By 1950 Bersu was back in Germany, again directing the Römisch Germanische Kommission.

It should be noted that some sound work was accomplished during this period despite political interference. The vocabulary of field reports carefully conformed to the dictates of funding sources, but the methodology was usually unaffected. Given time this would have changed as politically motivated terms and concepts altered the intellectual vocabulary of the discipline. In 1935, for example, the entire prehistoric and early historic chronologies were officially renamed: the Bronze and pre-Roman Iron Ages became the "Early Germanic period," the Roman Iron Age the "Climax Germanic period," the Migration period the "Late Germanic period," and everything from the Carolingians to the thirteenth century the "German Middle Ages."

It is easy to condemn the men and women who were part of the events that transformed the German archaeological community between 1933 and 1945. It is much more difficult to understand the choices they made or avoided in the social and political contexts of the time. Many researchers who began as advocates of Reinerth's policies in the Amt Rosenberg and Himmler's Ahnenerbe organization later became disenchanted. Others, who saw the system as a way to develop and support prehistory as a discipline, were willing to accept the costs of the Faustian bargain it offered. The benefits were real, and continue to be felt to this day in the institutions and programs founded between 1933 and 1945.

The paralysis felt by many scholars from 1933 to 1945 continued to affect research in the decades after the war. Most scholars who were graduate students during the 12-year period had to grapple with a double burden: a humiliating defeat and the disorienting experience of being methodologically "deprogrammed." Initially there was neither time nor desire to examine the reasons for the Nazi prostitution of archaeology. Unfortunately prehistoric archaeology is the only German social-science discipline that has still to publish a self-critical study of its role in the events of the 1930s and 1940s.

The reluctance of German archaeologists to come to terms with the past is a complex issue. German prehistoric archaeology is still a young discipline, and first came into its own as a result of Nazi patronage. There is therefore a certain feeling that any critical analysis of the motives and actions of the generation and the regime that engendered the discipline would be ungrateful at best and at worst a betrayal of trust. The vast majority of senior German archaeologists, graduate students immediately after the war, went straight from the front lines to the universities, and their dissertation advisers were men whose careers had been determined by their connections within the Nazi party.

The reluctance of German archaeologists to come to terms with the past is a complex issue.

The German system of higher education is built upon close bonds of dependence and an almost medieval fealty between a graduate student and his or her dissertation advisor. These bonds are maintained even after the graduate student has embarked on an academic career. Whistle-blowers are rare, since such action would amount to professional suicide. But in the past decade or so, most of the generation actively involved in archaeological research and teaching between 1933 and 1945 have died.

Their knowledge of the personal intrigues and alliances that allowed the Nazi party machine to function has died with them. Nonetheless, there are indications that the current generation of graduate students is beginning to penetrate the wall of silence that has surrounded this subject since 1945. The remaining official documents and publications may allow at least a partial reconstruction of the role of archaeology in the rise and fall of the Nazi regime.

The future of prehistoric archaeology in the recently unified Germany will depend on an open confrontation with the past. Archaeologists in the former East Germany must struggle with the legacy of both Nazi and Communist manipulation of their discipline. Meanwhile, the legacy of the Faustian bargain struck by German archaeologists with the Nazi regime should serve as a cautionary tale beyond the borders of a unified Germany: Archaeological research funded wholly or in part by the state is vulnerable to state manipulation. The potential for political exploitation of the past seems to be greatest in countries experiencing internal instability. Germany in the years following World War I was a country searching for its own twentieth-century identity. Prehistoric archaeology was one means to that end.

Earth Movers

Archaeologists say Brazil's rain forest, once thought to be inhospitable to humans, fostered huge ancient civilizations. The proof is in the dirt.

MARION LLOYD

High along bluffs overlooking the confluence of the mighty Negro and Solimões Rivers here, supersize eggplants, papayas, and cassava spring from the ground.

Their exuberance defies a long-held belief about the Amazon. For much of the last half century, archaeologists viewed the South American rain forest as a "counterfeit paradise," a region whose inhospitable environment precluded the development of complex societies. But new research suggests that prehistoric man found ways to overcome the jungle's natural limitations—and to thrive in this environment in large numbers.

The secret, says James B. Petersen, an archaeologist at the University of Vermont who has spent the past decade working in the Brazilian Amazon, is found in the ground beneath his feet. It is a highly fertile soil called *terra preta do indio,* which is Portuguese for "Indian black earth." By some estimates, this specially modified soil covers as much as 10 percent of Amazonia, the immense jungle region that straddles the Amazon River. And much of that area is packed with potsherds and other signs of human habitation.

"This was one of the last archaeological frontiers on the planet. It's as if we know nothing about it," says Mr. Petersen, as he analyzes the discovery of the day, a series of circular carbon deposits that might indicate the outline of a prehistoric house.

Scientists are now working to determine whether *terra preta,* which contains high levels of organic matter and carbon, was deliberately created by pre-Columbian civilizations to improve upon the notoriously poor rain-forest soil, or whether the modified earth was an accidental byproduct of sustained habitation by large groups of people.

Either way, Mr. Petersen believes it likely that pre-Columbian societies in the Amazon were not the primitive tribal societies they were once thought to be, but highly complex chiefdoms.

"We're providing the proof," he says during a several-week-long dig in August near the Brazilian jungle city of Manaus. His team of American and Brazilian archaeologists, who call themselves the Central Amazon Project, have excavated more than 60 sites rich in *terra preta* near where the Negro and Solimões Rivers merge to form the Amazon River proper.

One of the group's founders, Michael J. Heckenberger of the University of Florida, is bolstering the new findings with research on large prehistoric earthworks farther east along the upper Xingu River. Studying this area, which now is inhabited by the Kuikuru Indians, has allowed him to compare data of prehistoric land management with modern ethnographic studies.

On some pre-Columbian sites explored by Mr. Petersen and his team, several miles of earth are packed with millions of potsherds. The archaeologists have also found evidence that they say points to the existence of giant plazas, bridges, and roads, complete with curbs, and defensive ditches that would have taken armies of workers to construct.

Intriguingly, the earliest evidence of large, sedentary populations appears to coincide with the beginnings of *terra preta.*

"Something happened 2,500 years ago, and we don't know what," says Eduardo Góes Neves, a Brazilian archaeologist at the Federal University of São Paulo, who is co-director of the Central Amazon Project. He dusts off the flanged edge of a bowl from around 400 BC that one of his Brazilian graduate students pulled from a layer of *terra preta* eight feet down. The team got lucky when the landowner at Açutuba, the largest of their excavation sites, bulldozed a huge pit in one of his fields. The "swimming pool," as the team jokingly calls the 15-yard-wide hole, is giving them a rare chance to compare levels of *terra preta* over a large area.

The research has implications not only for history, but also for the future of the Amazon rain forest. If scientists could discover how the Amerindians transformed the soil, farmers could use the technology to maximize smaller plots of land, rather than cutting down ever larger swaths of jungle. The benefits of what Mr. Petersen calls this "gift from the past" are already well known to farmers in the area, who plant their crops wherever they find *terra preta.*

Rich in Controversy

The claims made for *terra preta* extend far beyond a legacy passed down from farmer to farmer. The archaeologists now reject the idea that pre-contact Amerindians were—as one team member says, ironically—"Stone Age primitives frozen at the dawn of time."

"It's made by pre-Columbian Indians and it's still fertile," says Bruno Glaser, a soil chemist from the University of Bayreuth, in Germany, who was taking samples of *terra preta* from another site discovered by Mr. Petersen's team. "If we knew how to do this, it would be a model for agriculture in the whole region."

It's made by pre-Columbian Indians and it's still fertile. If we knew how to do this, it would be a model for agriculture in the whole region.

Ideally what researchers dub "slash and char" agriculture, the indigenous technique that returns nutrients to the soil by mixing in organic waste and carbon, could replace slash-and-burn, a contemporary technique that consumes tens of thousands of acres of rain forest every year. Mr. Glaser is part of an international team of scientists studying the chemical composition of *terra preta* in an effort to recreate it.

The research into *terra preta* fuels a revisionist school of scientists who argue that pre-Columbian Amazonia was not a pristine wilderness, but rather a heavily managed forest teeming with human beings. They believe that advanced societies existed in the Amazon from before the time of Christ until a century after the European conquest in the 1500s decimated Amerindian populations through exploitation and disease. The theory is also supported by the accounts of the first Europeans to travel the length of the Amazon in 1542. They reported human settlements with tens of thousands of people stretching for many miles along the river banks.

But not everyone working in the field of Amazonian research buys the new theory.

"The idea that the indigenous population has secrets that we don't know about is not supported by anything except wishful thinking and the myth of El Dorado," says the archaeologist Betty J. Meggers, who is the main defender of the idea that only small, tribal societies ever inhabited the Amazon. "This myth just keeps going on and on and on. It's amazing."

Ms. Meggers, director of the Latin American Archaeology Program at the Smithsonian Institution's Museum of Natural History, in Washington, has spent her life trying to prove that Amazonia is a uniquely untrammeled and hostile wilderness. Now 82, Ms. Meggers has been working in the field since the late 1940s, when she and her husband, Clifford Evans, now deceased, began pioneering fieldwork on Marajó Island, at the mouth of the Amazon. She summarized their findings in a seminal 1954 article, "Environmental Limitation on the Development of Culture," which was published in *American Anthropologist*.

Ms. Meggers's 1971 book, *Amazonia: Man and Culture in a Counterfeit Paradise* (Aldine-Atherton), converted her views into gospel for a generation of Amazonian archaeologists. In it, she argued that modern Amerindian groups, generally composed of a few hundred people, follow ancient practices of infanticide and other population-control measures to exist in a hostile environment.

"It had a huge impact," says Susanna B. Hecht, a geographer at the University of California at Los Angeles who has spent three decades studying traditional farming practices in Amazonia. "Virtually every Anthropology I class read that book." Ms. Hecht's most recent research is with the Kayapó Indians in the upper Xingu River, the same region where Mr. Heckenberger is working. To her surprise, she discovered the Indians were creating a version of *terra preta* by burning excess vegetation and weeds and mixing the charcoal into the soil.

"One of the things we found rather unusual was how much burning was going on all the time," she says. "It wasn't catastrophic burning. It was that the whole landscape was smoldering all the time."

Ms. Hecht says the technique was probably more widespread before Indian societies were devastated by the arrival of the Europeans, who introduced measles, typhoid, and other diseases to which the Indians had no resistance. By some estimates, 95 percent of the Amerindians died within the first 130 years of contact. While their numbers were once estimated in the millions, there are now roughly 250,000 Amerindians living in Brazil.

"I think you could have had very dense populations, and what you had was a real holocaust in various forms," she says. However, Ms. Hecht notes, little was known about the impact of those epidemics when Ms. Meggers was first writing, and her persuasive arguments against large civilizations discouraged archaeologists from probing deeper into the Amazon. "Everyone said, 'Nobody was there anyway. Why bother?'" says Ms. Hecht.

The difficulty and dangers of conducting research in the Amazon also played a part. The region was largely impassible until the 1960s, when the Brazilian government began encouraging settlement in the jungle's interior.

A few researchers did challenge Ms. Meggers's theories early on. The most outspoken figure was Donald Lathrap, a University of Illinois archaeologist who worked in the Peruvian Amazon in the 1950s. He argued that Amazonia could and did support complex societies with advanced technology, and that the cradle of those civilizations was very likely in the central Amazon, where Mr. Petersen is working.

Another pioneer was William M. Denevan, a geographer emeritus at the University of Wisconsin, whose discovery of huge earthworks in lowland Bolivia in the early 1960s suggested that pre-Columbian peoples modified their environment for large-scale agriculture. In a 1992 article, "The Pristine Myth: The Landscape of the Americas in 1492," he argued that the modern Amazon rain forest was the result of human management over millennia, not a virgin wilderness.

"The key issue here can be summed up in two words: environmental determinism," he says, referring to the once-popular school of thought, favored by Ms. Meggers, that says environment dictates man's ability to progress. "We are saying people always have options," he says. "We can farm in outer space. And we can farm in the Antarctic. Or we can crop in the driest part of the Sahara Desert. It may be very expensive, but that's a different issue."

Building a Mystery

Other researchers working in Amazonia go even further. They suggest that prehistoric man may have created cities that rivaled those of the Aztecs and Maya. Again, they say, the proof is in the dirt.

William I. Woods, a geographer at Southern Illinois University at Edwardsville, has been studying *terra preta* deposits extending over 100,000 acres around the Brazilian jungle city of Santarém, where the Tapajós River meets the Amazon. He believes as many as 500,000 people might once have inhabited the area, implying a civilization larger than the Aztec capital of Tenochtitlán, once the largest city in the Americas.

"There is some fussing about the magnitude, from" he says. "But I don't think there are too many scholars who have any problems with chiefdoms existing and lots of people being supported for long times in various places in the Amazon."

Ms. Meggers has not taken challenges to her life's work lying down. In a 2001 article in *Latin American Antiquity,* she accuses the revisionist camp of endangering the rain forest by suggesting that large-scale farming was feasible in the region. Her view is shared by some biologists and environmentalists.

"Adherence to 'the lingering myth of Amazonian empires' not only prevents archaeologists from reconstructing the prehistory of Amazonia, but makes us accomplices in the accelerating pace of environmental degradation," she writes.

Mr. Neves, the Brazilian archaeologist, disagrees. "It's not like loggers are revving up the chainsaws after reading our articles," he says as he walks along a winding dirt road littered with pre-Columbian potsherds on his way to the dig site at Açutuba, a jungle-shrouded stretch of farmland overlooking the Negro River. "Deforestation through ranching isn't how the Amerindian interacted with the landscape," he says. "The Amerindians weren't destroying the environment. They were enriching it."

The rain forest is not inherently hostile to man, says Mr. Neves. He argues that pre-Columbian peoples knew how to use the huge diversity of species to their advantage, through a combination of farming, fishing, and managed tree harvesting. Cassava, a starchy root that grows well in the acidic rain-forest soil, was probably the Amerindians' main food source, which the Indians could have supplemented with corn and other vegetables grown on *terra preta.* But they also relied heavily on fish and turtles for protein, he says.

Blowing Dust from the Pages

Terra preta proponents also argue that historical accounts support their theories. The Rev. Gaspar de Carvajal, a Spanish priest who accompanied the first exploratory expedition down the Amazon in 1542, reported seeing hundreds of tortoises kept in corrals and "an abundance of meat and fish . . . that would have fed 1,000 men for a year." The friar also recounts an ambush by more than 10,000 Indians at a point in the river just west of modern-day Manaus, suggesting that the area was heavily populated as recently as the 16th century. He also describes armies of Indians who repelled attempts by the Spaniards to come ashore near modern-day Santarém.

Ms. Meggers is skeptical. "How could these people, when they're fleeing, count 10,000 warriors?" she says. "It's silly."

She notes that other portions of Father Carvajal's account, in particular his description of female Amazon warriors, which gave the river its name, have since been dismissed by historians as inventions to impress the Spanish crown.

> **They have not done enough work to establish whether it was a single large settlement or a result of intermittent occupation over longer periods of time.**

She also challenges estimates by the Central Amazon Project that between 5,000 and 10,000 people may have once inhabited Açutuba, possibly the largest site under excavation in the Brazilian Amazon. "They have not done enough work to establish whether it was a single large settlement or a result of intermittent occupation over longer periods of time," she says. She also accuses the group of ignoring the results of surveys in the region backed by the Smithsonian Institution over several decades.

Mr. Petersen shrugs off the criticism. "We're not here to fight Betty Meggers," he says, while taking a break from digging under the broiling jungle sun. "We're here to build on her work and refine it." He says that Ms. Meggers made a major contribution to the field by highlighting the enormous challenges involved in inhabiting the Amazon rain forest, even if he argues that later research shows that pre-Columbian peoples found ways of overcoming those natural limitations.

His team has several dozen radiocarbon dates from potsherds and carbon deposits collected throughout Açutuba, which they say show that the entire site was continuously inhabited during two waves from about 360 BC to as late as 1440 AD. The evidence also supports the existence of stratified societies, says Mr. Petersen. He picks up an ornate, white- and black-painted potsherd from the *terra preta* under a field of glistening eggplants. "This is probably from about AD 800, and look how sophisticated it is. It's like fine dinnerware," he says, comparing the sherd with that from a coarser vessel from about the same period, which he calls "everyday china." His team has unearthed more than 100,000 potsherds dating from 500 BC to about AD 1500 at the three-square-mile site, including roughly a dozen burial urns.

Digging through earth packed with tons of pottery is slow going. Particularly when you only have about eight pairs of hands.

"We've been working here nine years, and we've barely scratched the surface," says Mr. Neves, who has raised the bulk of the money from his university and the São Paulo state government. He estimates that there are at least 100 unexcavated sites within their research area, which extends over 40 square miles around the town of Iranduba. Some of the sites might be even larger than Açutuba.

Ecological Edge

Unlike the Maya in northern Central America, the inhabitants of the Amazon lacked stone for building. So they had to resort to organic and man-made materials. As a result there are few permanent markers of earlier civilizations, forcing archaeologists to extrapolate from small scraps of evidence.

"The only reason that everyone accepts large, socially complex societies in Maya land is that they have surviving pyramids and stelae," says Mr. Petersen. "If the Maya and others had used mostly organic perishables in their architecture, like the Amazon people, then I would bet there would be much more mystery and debate about the nature of pre-Columbian Amerindians in Central America, too."

At a nearby site, called Hatahara, the team recently excavated 11 human skeletons dating to about AD 800 from one nine-yard trench dug into a large burial mound. Believing it unlikely that they would have stumbled upon the only evidence in the mound, they estimate there may be hundreds more bodies buried there, suggesting a population of at least a few thousand people.

The skeletons provided the team with other insights into the previous inhabitants. "These were not famine-stricken people," Mr. Neves says, noting that the skeletons measured about 5-foot-7. In contrast, modern indigenous inhabitants often do not grow taller than five feet, a fact used by earlier archaeologists to argue that the jungle was unsuited for human habitation.

"I don't think there were ever severe limitations here," says Mr. Neves.

He points at the acres of glistening vegetables that seem to grow effortlessly throughout the Açutuba site. Settlers throughout the Iranduba area take advantage of the abundant *terra preta* deposits to grow vegetables and fruit for the nearby city of Manaus, supplying much of the produce consumed by its 1.4 million people.

"I know *terra preta* is very good and that it was made by the Indians," says Edson Azevedo Santos, a 48-year-old farmer drenched in sweat from weeding his zucchini patch. Unlike the acidic soil found in most of the rain forest, which can only sustain crops for a three-year period, *terra preta* plots can withstand constant farming for decades, if properly managed.

Even more striking, *terra preta* may have the capacity to regenerate itself, says Mr. Woods, the Southern Illinois geographer. He recently tested that possibility by removing a large section of *terra preta* on a plot near Santarem. To his amazement, the soil grew back within three years. "I suggested that the soil should be treated as living organism and that microorganisms are the secret," he says, adding that more research is needed to allow scientists to repeat the process. "This is very sophisticated stuff."

The New Neandertal

**Virtual fossils and real molecules are changing
how we view our enigmatic cousin.**

JEAN-JACQUES HUBLIN

Next year will mark the 150th anniversary of the discovery at Neandertal, a little valley near Düsseldorf in western Germany, of the first recognized fossil humans. The occasion will be commemorated with conferences and exhibitions at major German museums. As a warm-up for this "Neandertal Year," two dozen scholars gathered at New York University this past January, in a Manhattan suffering near-glacial conditions, to exchange views on the latest advances in the field.

Our fascination with Neandertals is well founded. They were the first known example of an extinct species of human, they evolved mostly in Europe, and we now have an unrivaled fossil record accumulated by a century and a half of research. Because there are more specimens of Neandertals than any other premodern human, any new techniques or approaches in paleoanthropology are usually applied to them first. And in recent years we have learned a great deal about these humans that once seemed unattainable, including aspects of their biology such as genetics. Studies have also revealed unexpected features of their growth, development, and life history. Even more traditional approaches, such as the comparison of Neandertal and modern human bone shapes, continue to yield new data.

Visions of the Neandertals as brutish cave dwellers prevailed for many years following their discovery. The first reconstruction, in 1908, was based on the partial skeleton of an old male found at La Chappelle aux Saints in France, but the individual had been stooped from arthritis. That fact, and its projecting face, heavy brow, and generally robust bones gave rise to our earliest, though inaccurate, view of Neandertals. But in the last decades of the twentieth century, the pendulum began to swing in the opposite direction. For some, Neandertals appeared only as a slightly different population of our own species, adapted to the cooler climates of the Paleolithic world. The most politically correct version saw them as almost indistinguishable from modern humans in abilities and behaviors, and hardly differing in many anatomical aspects. The New York conference provided a more balanced picture of a "New Neandertal" that is both very similar to and very different from us.

Emblematic of this New Neandertal is a composite skeleton created at the American Museum of Natural History in New York and discussed at the conference by Ian Tattersall, one of its curators. Most scholars have focused on analyzing particular parts of the skeleton, such as the skull or pelvis, so the reconstruction is our first look at an entire one. It is a large male, built from casts of bones from several individuals (most are from two finds, one at La Ferrassie, France, and the other at Kebara, Israel). Tattersall emphasized how different it is from our own skeletons, not only in the anatomy of the skull, which is well known, but in entire body shape. If any living Neandertals had come to the conference dressed in a suit and tie, they still would have stood out. But this composite skeleton was only one of many innovative approaches to finding the new Neandertal that were presented in New York.

Virtual Fossils

Human fossils are precious and fragile, and to study them scientists have embraced or developed new methods in recent years. CT scanning, for example, is used with increasing frequency to assess fine internal details of specimens, such as the inner ear of Neandertals. Imaging techniques, combined with sophisticated software for manipulating digitized fossils, allow us to work with virtual objects rather than the originals. One can now reconstruct fragmentary specimens, piecing them together on the computer and supplying missing parts. If a skull's right side is damaged, the left can be copied and a mirror image of it substituted instead. Even specimens warped and distorted in the fossilization process can be straightened out.

The new methods of "virtual paleoanthropology" have been used to investigate how modern humans and Neandertals differ even in childhood. At the New York meeting, Marcia Ponce de Leon and Christoph Zollikofer of the University of Zurich presented a computer model and simulation comparing skull growth, showing the divergence of shape began early in development and reflected different growth patterns in the bones. Another comparison of Neandertal and modern human childhood development was recently undertaken by Fernando

Ramirez–Rozzi of the French Centre National de la Recherche Scientifique in Paris and José Maria Bermudez de Castro of Madrid's Natural History Museum. They looked at tooth enamel, which has microscopic striations that can be counted like the growth rings in a tree trunk, and concluded that Neandertals reached adulthood at about 15 rather than 18 years of age, as in present-day human populations. Further analysis will confirm whether or not this was the case.

Modern human specimens are also being digitized, allowing us to assess bone shape and size variations and understand their significance in anatomical evolution. In a remarkable contribution at the conference, Katerina Harvati and Tim Weaver of the Max Planck Institute for Evolutionary Anthropology in Leipzig, Germany, looked at skull variation in modern humans from different climates and cultures. They found that the shape of the face is linked to local environmental conditions, which fits well with the current belief that the Neandertal's projecting face is a cold-climate adaptation. By contrast, the shape of the brain case, particularly the temporal bone (on the side of the skull), proved to be a good indicator of genetic closeness among populations.

Real Molecules

Meanwhile, the genuine specimens have been the object of increased attention through the study of DNA, proteins, and chemical elements that can be found in bones and teeth—giving us a completely new source of valuable information about our remote relatives' biology and their daily lives.

In 1997, a fragment of DNA was reconstructed from the same bones that the quarry workers found in Neandertal in 1856. The DNA of the Neandertal fell outside modern human variation, and suggested a divergence between the ancestors of Neandertals and modern humans nearly half a million years ago. Since the original DNA study, nine other Neandertal individuals have yielded some genetic information, all similar to one another yet distinct from that of modern humans. Although this number is small, the evidence gives us insight into the demography of the Neandertals. The limited variability of their DNA suggests that there were times perhaps during glacial advances, when their population was greatly reduced, resulting in genetic bottlenecking. The population recovered in size afterward but with fewer surviving different genetic lines. In this respect, humans—modern, Neandertal, and others—strongly contrast with African apes which evolved in a much less stressful environment during the last several hundred thousand years, and therefore have much greater genetic variability. Interestingly, while we can now study Neandertal DNA, it is very difficult to analyze DNA from the early modern humans who replaced them between 40,000 and 30,000 years ago. Because Neandertal DNA is different from our own, modern contamination (from excavators, museum curators, or laboratory personnel) can be identified and discounted. With fossils of our own forebears, however, differentiating ancient DNA from recent contamination is virtually impossible. Such research can only be undertaken with new fossil finds that are kept in sterile conditions from the field to the lab.

There is no evidence that the last Neandertals were evolving toward a physical appearance like our own, but the issue of the possible contribution of Neandertals to the modern European genetic makeup is still fervently debated. Even if Neandertals represented a distinct, although very close, species separate from modern humans, we know that in nature, hybridization is a common process under such circumstances. At the conference, Trenton Holliday of Tulane University surveyed the zoological evidence, pointing out many hybrids among large mammals including members of the camel, horse, dog, and cat families. Did Neandertals and modern humans interbreed? It is quite possible in some instances, but it had no major biological results.

Proteins can now be recovered from bones and examined with methods similar to those used with DNA. This year, for the first time, Christina Nielsen-Marsh of the Max Planck Institute was able to extract and analyze a protein from Neandertal teeth from Shanidar, Iraq. In Neandertals, this particular protein (osteocalcin) displays a sequence similar to that of modern humans, indicating it has changed little over a long period of time. In the near future, extraction and sequencing of fossil proteins may open new ways to study evolutionary relationships between extinct species, and may allow us to go farther back in time than is possible with ancient DNA, which is more complex and degrades more quickly.

Scientists are investigating other molecules and chemical elements found in Neandertal bones. Collagen, routinely extracted from bone today for radiocarbon dating, yields carbon and nitrogen, while strontium and calcium can be sampled from the mineral parts of bone. These four elements can give us indications of an individual's diet, since they come from foods. Studies by Herve Bocherens of the Centre National de la Recherche Scientifique in Montpellier and Michael Richards of the Max Planck Institute suggest the European Neandertals were highly carnivorous, a pattern not unlike that observed in modern hunter-gatherers in cold regions. In the future, such analyses may also reveal indicators of population movements, since bone chemistry also reflects, for example, specific elements in ground water that vary from region to region.

The Last Neandertals

The possible interactions between Neandertals and modern invaders between 40,000 and 30,000 years ago in Europe remains one of paleoanthropology's most debated issues, so it was no surprise that it surfaced in New York. There is little doubt that the presence of another group of humans in Europe played a major role in the extinction of the Neandertals, through competition for resources if nothing else. But other factors in the Neandertals' demise have been discussed recently. For example, Chris Stringer of the Natural History Museum, London, has shown that this period was characterized by repeated and extreme climatic changes occurring in rapid succession. Although Neandertals had faced and survived severe climatic crises along the course of their evolution, the coincidence of this climatic instability with the invasion of the European territory by modern humans presented a double challenge for the last Neandertals. Both groups must have tried adapting during this confrontation in a very difficult environment. At the conference, Shara Bailey of the Max Planck Institute and I showed that Neandertals at the French cave site of Arcy-sur-Cure are indisputably associated with stone tools and bone ornaments formerly thought to have been made only by modern humans. The acquisition during this period of new techniques and habits, such as the use of body ornaments, by the last Neandertals is much debated by specialists. Many scholars believe it may have resulted from their encounters with modern humans, who had developed this behavior more than 100,000 years ago, even before leaving Africa. These contacts, they argue, may have been seldom, but resulted in imitation by the Neandertals or even trade between the two populations. But modern humans might have been affected as well. It has been proposed that the burst of artistic expression—cave art, figurines, and the like—observed in our forebears at this time relates to group identification and may have resulted from the interaction with these indeed human, but very different, beings.

Because Neandertals are the best-known group of fossil humans, they are the group that always raises the most questions. As the last branching of the human evolutionary tree and our closest relatives in the recent past, they will remain an object of popular fascination as well as scientific interest. In fact, how we envision Neandertals may tell us as much about the way we see ourselves as about them. With the "New Neandertal" we have definitively shed two such images, one in which our ancient cousin was brutish and far different from us, the other in which we were nearly identical. But perhaps our newfound knowledge, from virtual fossils and molecular studies, is taking us to a deeper understanding of Neandertals.

JEAN-JACQUES HUBLIN, director of the Department of Human Evolution at the Max Planck Institute in Leipzig, has led fieldwork in France, Spain, and Morocco, and is now participating in an international project at Dikika, Ethiopia.

Whither the Neanderthals?

Richard G. Klein

The Neanderthals are the longest known and best understood of all fossil humans. In 1856, quarry workers cleaning out a limestone cave in the Neander Valley, Germany, found a partial skeleton for which the group is named. Today, several thousand Neanderthal bones are known from more than 70 individual sites. Yet, paleoanthropologists still debate just how much the Neanderthals differed from living humans and whether the differences help explain why the Neanderthals disappeared.

Most Neanderthal specimens are isolated skeletal elements, especially teeth and jaws, but nearly every part of the skeleton is represented in multiple copies. There are also more than 20 partial skeletons from individuals of both sexes and different ages.[1] More than 300 archaeological sites have yielded artifacts and broken-up animal bones that illuminate Neanderthal behavior and ecology.[2]

The Neanderthals evolved in Europe. Some of their distinctive anatomical features already mark European fossils that are more than 350,000 years old.[3] Through a process of natural selection and random genetic drift, they emerged in full-blown form by 130,000 years ago. From then on, they were distributed more or less continuously from Spain to southern Russia; by 80,000 years ago, they had extended their range to western Asia (see the figure). They persisted in Europe and western Asia until at least 50,000 years ago and perhaps in some places until 30,000 years ago.

Everywhere they lived, the Neanderthals were the immediate predecessors of modern humans, and it has often been suggested that they were ancestral to living populations. However, at the same time that the Neanderthals occupied Europe and western Asia, other kinds of people lived in the Far East and Africa.[4] The Africans were anatomically much more modern than the Neanderthals, and are therefore more plausible ancestors of living humans. Furthermore, surveys show that variants of mitochondrial DNA[5] and the Y chromosome[6] in living Eurasian humans derive exclusively from African variants that probably existed no more than 100,000 years ago.

Further support for this argument comes from mitochondrial DNA extracted from Neanderthal bones. The data indicate that the last shared ancestor of Neanderthals and living humans lived 500,000 to 600,000 years ago.[7] Non-sex chromosomes of living humans may conceivably retain some Neanderthal genes,[8] but the combined fossil and genetic evidence suggests that any Neanderthal contribution to living populations was small. The Neanderthals may thus be regarded as a fascinating but extinct side branch of humanity.

Modern humans invaded the west Asian part of the Neanderthal range about 45,000 years ago. They subsequently swept northward and westward through Europe, swamping or replacing the Neanderthals within 10,000 to 15,000 years. The modern human triumph depended on technological, economic, and demographic advantages that were apparently grounded in an enhanced ability to innovate. This ability probably appeared first in Africa, but debate continues on how rapidly it evolved and whether it was rooted in biological change or in population growth and social reorganization. Fossils and artifacts are unlikely to resolve this issue, but genes underlying cognition might.

Neanderthal Physical Form

The Neanderthals were distinguished by large heads, massive trunks, and relatively short, powerful limbs.[1] Their average brain size equaled or exceeded that of modern humans, but their skulls also exhibit specializations that are unknown in any other people, fossil or living.[9] These unique features underscore the likelihood that the Neanderthals represent a divergent evolutionary lineage.

The specializations include the extraordinary forward projection of the face along the midline, the tendency for the braincase to bulge outwards at the sides, a depressed elliptical area of roughened bone on the back of the skull, and an array of bumps and crannies in the vicinity of the mastoid process. In addition, high-resolution computed tomography has revealed a singular configuration of the bony labyrinth of the inner ear.[10]

These features apparently had a genetic basis, because they are already visible in young children. The labyrinth configuration was fixed even before birth. There is no indication that the specialized features attenuated through time: The latest Neanderthals, 60,000 to 30,000 years ago, express them just as strongly as their more remote ancestors. Modern humans completely lack them. The skull alone then is sufficient to preclude a major Neanderthal contribution to living human populations.

High activity levels and a strenuous life-style explain the power of Neanderthal limbs. The short limbs and massive trunk, which would conserve body heat, were probably an adaptive response to the mostly glacial climatic conditions under which the Neanderthals evolved. Among living humans, such features particularly characterize Arctic peoples. The Neanderthals had even more massive trunks and shorter limbs, yet never faced true Arctic cold. The degree to which they adapted physically may reflect their limited ability to adapt culturally.

Neanderthal Behavior and Ecology

The modern successors to the Neanderthals are often known colloquially as the Cro-Magnons, after a French site where their bones were uncovered in 1868. In general, Neanderthal bones occur with artifact assemblages that archaeologists assign to the Middle Paleolithic cultural (or artifactual) complex, whereas Cro-Magnon bones occur with artifacts of the succeeding Upper Paleolithic complex. The use of separate names for the physical types and the artifact complexes allows for deviations from the usual rule of association.

Middle and Upper Paleolithic people shared many advanced behaviors, including a refined ability to flake stone, burial of the dead (at least on occasion), an interest in naturally occurring mineral pigments, full control over fire, and a heavy dependence on meat (probably obtained mainly through hunting). Both Neanderthal and Cro-Magnon skeletal remains sometimes reveal debilitating disabilities, indicating that both kinds of peoples cared for the old and the sick. There could be no more compelling indication of shared humanity.

Yet, archaeology also suggests many important behavioral differences. Unlike Upper Paleolithic Cro-Magnons, Middle Paleolithic Neanderthals left little compelling evidence for art or jewelry. Their graves contain nothing to suggest burial ritual or ceremony. They produced a much smaller range of readily distinguishable stone tool types; much more rarely crafted artifacts from plastic substances like bone, ivory, shell, or antler; and left no evidence for projectile (as opposed to thrusting) weapons. Their cave sites are generally poorer in cultural debris and richer in bones of bears and other cave dwellers (suggesting less dense human populations). They failed to build structures durable enough to leave an archaeological trace, and were confined to relatively mild, temperate latitudes. Finally, the Middle Paleolithic artifact assemblages that Neanderthals produced varied little through time and space. The Upper Paleolithic assemblages that Cro-Magnons made varied far more and are the oldest from which we can infer identity-conscious ethnic groups.

Hence, only the Upper Paleolithic anticipates the material record of historic hunter-gatherers, and only Upper Paleolithic people were fully modern in the sense that all historic people were.

Neanderthal/Cro-Magnon Contact

Consistent with an African origin for the Cro-Magnons, radiocarbon dating suggests that they displaced the Neanderthals about 45,000 years ago in western Asia and only 5000 to 15,000 years later in Europe. In Europe, the Neanderthals may have succumbed much earlier in the far east (Russia) than the far west (Iberia), but the supporting dates are sparse. There is also the ever-present possibility of minute, undetectable contamination with recent carbon, which can make a sample that is 50,000 to 40,000 radiocarbon years old appear 20,000 to 10,000 years younger.

Such contamination may explain radiocarbon dates that suggest the survival of Neanderthals in southern Russia,[11] Croatia[12], and Spain[13] for 7000 years or more after Cro-Magnons had appeared nearby. Only the alternation of Neanderthal and Cro-Magnon layers within a single site could provide unequivocal evidence for substantial chronological overlap. No known site provides such alternation. Wherever Middle Paleolithic and early Upper Paleolithic layers occur in the same site, the Upper Paleolithic layers directly overlie the Middle Paleolithic ones, with no indication for a significant gap in time. The implication is that in most places the Neanderthals disappeared abruptly.

Neanderthal/Cro-Magnon interbreeding has been suggested from occasional fossils, including a recently discovered Upper Paleolithic child's skeleton from Portugal.[14] However, in each case, the anatomical indications are at best ambiguous, and few experts recognize any hybrids. Evidence for cultural contact is also sparse, except for one well-documented case from central France. Here, a site occupied by Neanderthals shortly before their disappearance has provided an undeniable mix of Middle and Upper Paleolithic artifact types, including well-made bone tools and jewelry.[10] It also contains the only indisputable house ruin from a Neanderthal site.

The mix may mean that Neanderthals could imitate Upper Paleolithic/Cro-Magnon neighbors. But if Upper Paleolithic technology allowed more effective use of natural resources and larger human populations, it is puzzling that Neanderthals failed to adopt it more widely. If they had done so, then their unique skeletal traits and genes would be more obvious in succeeding populations.

Cognition and Neanderthal Extinction

Except for the French site just cited, there is little to suggest that Neanderthals could behave in a modern, Upper Paleolithic way. This inability may explain why they disappeared so quickly and completely. However, Neanderthal brains were no smaller than those of modern humans. If there was a difference in brain function, it resided in soft tissue that cannot be inferred from empty skulls. Hence, neither archaeology nor fossils can reveal Neanderthal cognitive capacity.

This issue is important not only for illuminating Neanderthal disappearance. Fossils show that between 130,000 and 50,000 years ago, the African contemporaries of the Neanderthals were more modern in anatomy, but archaeology suggests that they closely resembled the Neanderthals in behavior.[4] A change in brain function about 50,000 years ago could explain why modern Africans subsequently expanded to Eurasia.

The discovery that FOXP2, a gene involved in speech and language, achieved its modern sequence less than 200,000 ago years ago[15] provides tentative support for such a change in brain function. A truly persuasive case may depend on the isolation of genes that are expressed differently in the brains of apes and people.[16] Many human gene variants will turn out be very ancient, but if there was a brain change around 50,000 years ago, one or more variants should coalesce to about this time. Fossil bones could provide a further test, now that some have been shown to retain organic compounds that bear on brain function.[17]

The longest continuous debate in paleoanthropology is nearing resolution. Modern humans replaced the Neanderthals with little or no gene exchange. Almost certainly, the Neanderthals succumbed because they wielded culture less effectively. The main question that remains open is whether Neanderthal genes explain their failure to compete culturally.

References

1. E. Trinkaus, P. Shipman, *The Neandertals: Changing the Image of Mankind* (Knopf, New York, 1993).

2. P. A. Mellars, *The Neanderthal Legacy: An Archaeological Perspective from Western Europe* (Princeton Univ. Press, Princeton, NJ, 1996).

3. J. L. Bischoff et al., *J. Archaeol. Sci.* **30,** 275 (2003).

4. R. G. Klein, *The Human Career: Human Biological and Cultural Origins* (Univ. of Chicago Press, Chicago, ed. 2, 1999).

5. M. Ingman, H. Kaessmann, S. Pääbo, U. Gyllensten, *Nature* **408,** 708 (2000).

6. P. A. Underhill et al., *Nature Genet.* **26,** 358 (2000).

7. M. Hofreiter, D. Serre, H. N. Poinar, M. Kuch, S. Pääbo, *Nature Rev. Genet.* **2,** 353 (2001).

8. A. R. Templeton, *Nature 416,* **45** (2002).

9. A. P. Santa Luca, *J. Hum. Evol.* **7,** 619 (1978).

10. J.-J. Hublin, F. Spoor, M. Braun, F. Zonneveld, *Nature* **381,** 224 (1996).

11. I. V. Ovchinnikov et al., *Nature* **404,** 490 (2000).

12. F. H. Smith, E. Trinkaus, P. B. Pettitt, I. Karanovic, M. Paunovic, *Proc. Natl. Acad. Sci. U.S.A.* **96,** 12281 (1999).

13. J.-J. Hublin et al., *C. R. Acad. Sci. Paris Ser. IIA* **321,** 931 (1995).

14. C. Duarte et al., *Proc. Natl. Acad. Sci. U.S.A.* **96,** 7604 (1999).

15. W. Enard et al., *Nature* **418,** 869 (2002).

16. W. Enard et al., *Science* **296,** 340 (2002).

17. H.-H. Chou et al., *Proc. Natl. Acad. Sci. U.S.A.* **99,** 11736 (2002).

RICHARD G. KLEIN is with the Program in Human Biology, Stanford University, Stanford, CA 94305, USA. E-mail: rklein@stanford.edu

Children of Prehistory

Stone Age kids left their marks on cave art and stone tools.

BRUCE BOWER

Walk about 300 meters into Rouffignac Cave in southern France, turn left into a dark chamber, raise a lantern, and gaze up at a prehistoric marvel. A welter of undulating, curving, crisscrossing lines blankets the ceiling in abstract abandon. Single, double, and triple sets of lines zigzag and run together in swirls. In other parts of the cave, similarly configured lines appear beside, inside, underneath, and on top of drawings of now-extinct mammoths. Archaeologists refer to such marks as finger flutings, the lines that human fingers leave when drawn over a soft surface. In Rouffignac Cave, finger flutings cut through pliable red clay to expose hard white limestone underneath.

Soon after the discovery of Rouffignac's finger flutings about 50 years ago, researchers started speculating about the mysterious marks. One influential account referred to the decorated ceiling as the "Serpents' Dome." Others interpreted the finger flutings as depictions of mythical creatures or streams of water, symbols from initiation rites into manhood, or shamans' ritual signs.

New evidence, gathered by Kevin Sharpe of the University of Oxford in England and Leslie Van Gelder of Walden University in Minneapolis, challenges those assertions. They argue that 2-to-5-year-old kids generated the bulk of Rouffignac's ancient ceiling designs. Teenagers or adults must have hoisted children so that the youngsters could reach the ceiling and run their fingers across its soft-clay coat.

Sharpe and Van Gelder's study joins a growing number of efforts aimed at illuminating the activities of Stone Age children. Researchers who conduct such studies regard much, but certainly not all, of prehistoric cave art as the product of playful youngsters and graffiti-minded teenagers.

Stone Age adults undoubtedly drew the famous portrayals of bison, mammoths, and other creatures at sites such as France's Lascaux Cave and Spain's Altamira Cave. However, less attention has focused on numerous instances of finger fluting, pigment-stained handprints and hand outlines, and crude drawings of animals and people, all of which may have had youthful originators.

"Kids undoubtedly had access to the deep painted caves [during the Stone Age], and they participated in some of the activities there," says Jean Clottes, a French archaeologist and the current president of the International Federation of Rock Art Organizations. "That's a hard fact."

Moreover, archaeologists suspect that many of the relics found at prehistoric stone-tool sites around the world are the largely unexamined handiwork of children and teenagers who were taking early cracks at learning to chisel rock.

"I suspect that children's products dominate stone-tool remains at some of those sites," remarks archaeologist John J. Shea of Stony Brook (N.Y.) University.

Cave Tots

Sharpe and Van Gelder have long speculated that prehistoric kids created many of the patterned lines that adorn caves such as Rouffignac. Their suspicion was kindled in 1986, when Australian archaeologist Robert G. Bednarik published the first of several papers contending that the walls and ceilings of caves in western Europe and southern Australia contained numerous examples of child-produced grooves as well as some made by adults. He coined the term finger fluting for this practice.

Bednarik, who heads the Australian Rock Art Research Association in Caulfield South, noted that, because of the spacing and width of the marks, a large proportion of the grooves must have been the work of small fingers. "Approximately half the markings were clearly made by children, even infants," he says.

To date, Bednarik has investigated finger fluting in about 70 Australian and European caves. Analyses of wall and ceiling sediment in a portion of these caves indicate that the line designs originated at least 13,000 years ago, and in some cases 30,000 years or more ago.

At Rouffignac, Sharpe and Van Gelder took Bednarik's ideas an empirical step further. First, the researchers asked children and adults to run the fingers of one hand across soft clay. The scientists then measured the width of the impressions of each individual's central three fingers. Participants included 124 pupils and 11 teachers from four schools—three in the United States and one in England. Their ages ranged from 2 to 55. The volunteers held their fingers close together during the exercise, mimicking the fingerfluting style at Rouffignac. Even with adult assistance, 2-to 3-year-olds usually just smacked the clay with an open hand.

Comparisons of modern finger widths with those arrayed on the French cave's ceiling indicate that 2-to-5-year-olds made the vast majority of Rouffignac markings, Sharpe and Van Gelder reported in the December 2006 *Antiquity*. Either teenagers or adults crafted a few finger flutings at the site, since members of these age groups possess similar, larger finger widths than children do. In the modern sample, a 12-year-old girl and a 14-year-old boy displayed wider fingers than any adult did. Hand sizes of late Stone Age people are comparable to those of people today, Sharpe says.

A 5 foot, 10 inch-tall person standing on tiptoes could just reach the ceiling of the Rouffignac chamber, Sharpe notes. Adults must have hoisted children on their shoulders while weaving their way through the inner sanctum, so that their passengers could trace curved, elongated lines. This activity occurred sometime between 27,000 and 13,000 years ago, according to estimates of the extinction dates of animals depicted in drawings in the cave.

Perhaps finger fluting was simply a playful exercise, a form of ancient finger painting, Sharpe suggests.

While Bednarik welcomes the new evidence on youthful finger fluting, he suspects that such marks mimicked visual sensations produced by reactions of the brain in response to prolonged darkness and sensory deprivation deep inside caves. In such situations, people—and especially children, in Bednarik's view—temporarily see wavy lines, points of light, and other geometric shapes.

Stone Age kids at Rouffignac may have translated these visions into finger fluting without adult assistance, Bednarik holds. Since soil movements can alter the height of cave floors, prehistoric children might once have been able to reach the chambers' ceilings on their own, he suggests.

In contrast, Clottes accepts the notion that prehistoric adults lifted young finger fluters at Rouffignac. However, he hypothesizes that ancient people regarded caves as portals to spirit worlds and as places for important rituals. "Children were brought inside the caves to benefit from the supernatural power the caves held by touching the walls, putting or printing their hands on the walls, drawing lines, and perhaps occasionally sketching animals or geometric signs," Clottes says.

Paul Bahn, an independent archaeologist in England, sees no way to confirm Clottes' contention. "Finger fluting may have been deeply significant or may have been almost mindless doodling," Bahn remarks. "The fact that some kids were lifted up by bigger people in no way helps us to decide."

Handy Boys

In September 1940, three teenage boys in rural France set out to find a rumored underground passage to an old manor. Their search led them to a small opening in the ground that had been blocked off to keep away livestock. After returning the next day with a lamp, the boys crawled into the hole and entered the Lascaux cave with its gallery of magnificent Stone Age drawings.

Caves exerted a hypnotic pull on boys long before Lascaux's discovery, says zoologist R. Dale Guthrie of the University of Alaska in Fairbanks. In fact, he contends, teenage boys played a big part in producing the prehistoric cave art, not just in finding it thousands of years later.

Guthrie, who studies the remains of Stone Age animals and is himself an artist, made his case in a 2005 book titled *The Nature of Paleolithic Art* (University of Chicago Press).

Adolescent boys, at times joined by female peers and children, decorated cave walls and ceilings for fun, not to commune with spirits, Guthrie holds. Exploring caves and decorating underground chambers with personal marks provided an outlet for creative play that readied boys for the rigors and challenges of big-game hunting as adults, he suggests.

Youngsters made up a hefty proportion of ancient populations. In a Stone Age band of roughly 35 people, about two dozen individuals were in their twenties or younger, Guthrie estimates. Few elders lived past age 40.

Several European Stone Age caves contain sets of footprints of teens and children, suggesting that prehistoric kids of different ages went exploring together, Guthrie says.

The most extensive evidence of a youth movement in ancient cave art comes from Guthrie's comparison of the size of hand impressions at some sites with corresponding measurements of people's hands today. In at least 30 European caves, ancient visitors rendered hand images by pressing a pigment-covered palm and fingers against a wall or by blowing pigment against an outspread hand held up to a wall to create a stenciled outline.

Guthrie assessed nine different dimensions characterizing each of 201 ancient hand impressions. He obtained the corresponding hand measurements for nearly 700 people, ages 5 to 19, in Fairbanks.

Teenagers ranging in age from 13 to 16 left most of the prehistoric handprints, Guthrie concludes. He classifies 162 prints as those of adult or teenage males, based on traits such as relatively wide palms and thick fingers. The remaining 39 prints belong either to females or to young boys.

Guthrie contends that much Stone Age cave art was concocted hastily, yielding simple, graffitilike images with no deep meaning. For instance, a few caves contain hand outlines with missing fingers or other deformities that teenage boys with normal hands made for fun, in Guthrie's view. He has replicated the "maimed-hand look" by spattering paint around his own bent fingers onto flat surfaces.

Stone Age caves also contain many unfinished or corrected sketches of animals as well as drawings of male and especially female sexual parts. Small groups of boys, flush with puberty but not yet old enough for adult duties, probably invested considerable energy in exploring caves and expressing their hopes and fears on chamber walls, Guthrie proposes.

"Paleolithic art books are really biased in showing only beautiful, finished cave images," he asserts. "The possibility that adolescent giggles and snickers may have echoed in dark cave passages as often as did the rhythm of a shaman's chant demeans neither artists nor art."

Sharpe, a supporter of Guthrie's conclusions, notes that teenage boys apparently jumped up and slapped the walls of chambers in Rouffignac and in a nearby French cave, making hand marks about 2.5 m above the floor.

Clottes, however, doubts that youthful thrill seekers took the lead in generating prehistoric European cave art. "In most caves, images were made by adults" he says. "A majority of those images display both artistic mastery and technical expertise."

Knap Time

Guthrie's labeling of prehistoric teenagers as big-time cave artists stimulated a related insight by John Shea. The Stony Brook researcher realized, after reading Guthrie's book, that nearly every set of stone tools and tool-making debris found at Stone Age sites includes the likely handiwork of children.

"Almost every stone-tool assemblage includes unusually small, simple artifacts, overproduced in an obsessive way, that children could have made," Shea says.

These tiny, rudimentary implements—many dating to hundreds of thousands of years ago—were made from poor-quality rock, an additional sign that they were fashioned by kids taking early whacks at tool production, Shea asserts. Seasoned stone-tool makers used high-quality rock.

Shea teaches a college class in stone-tool making, also known as flint knapping. Observations of novice flint knappers, combined with the likelihood that prehistoric people learned to make stone tools at young ages, bolster his argument—published in the November-December 2006 *Evolutionary Anthropology*—that children produced many previously discovered small stone artifacts. Researchers have already established that modern children can learn to make basic stone tools starting at age 7.

Shea plans to develop criteria to distinguish beginners' stone artifacts from those of experienced flint knappers. For instance, he has noted that beginners create lots of debris as they experiment with tool-making techniques. Also, the shape and quality of their finished products vary greatly from one piece to the next, unlike experts' uniform implements.

As early as 1998, Harvard University archaeologist Ofer BarYosef suggested that Stone Age kids may have watched adults making tools, picked up toolmakers' discarded stones, and tried to imitate what their elders had done. At the time, his suggestion went largely unnoticed.

"Children's activities have been ignored at [Stone Age] sites and at most later archaeological sites as well," remarks archaeologist Steven L. Kuhn of the University of Arizona in Tucson.

Questions remain about whether children and other novices invariably generated smaller stone artifacts than experienced tool makers did, Kuhn says. Research into children's activities in modern hunter-gatherer societies might offer clues to youngsters' behavior long ago, in his view.

Stone Age kids may eventually rewrite what scientists know about ancient stone tools and cave art. It's enough to make a pre-historic parent proud.

Watery Tombs

Testimony coerced from shamans by Spanish priests may, ironically, be a key to understanding more about Maya spiritual life.

KRISTIN M. ROMEY

On the eighth day of August, 1562, a Maya man named Diego Te sat nervously on a wooden bench inside a church in the Yucatec town of Sotuta, under the careful gaze of senior apostolic judge Juan de Villagómez. With a priest serving as translator, Te made the sign of the cross before the judge, swore to tell the truth, and finished with "Amen."

His account is preserved today in the Archivo General de Indias in Seville. About a year earlier, said Te, he had gone to the church at midnight to light a candle for his ill father when he encountered Lorenzo Cocom, the main *cacique,* or leader, of Tixcamahel, along with a man named Mateo and Francisco Uicab, a Maya shaman. The men had brought two "idols," representations of Maya gods, into the church. Standing next to the idols were two young boys the witness identified as Juan Chel and Juan Chan, kidnapped by the men from their home villages of Kantunil and Usil. As Te watched from the back of the church, Cocom and Mateo cut the hearts from the boys and handed them to the shaman, who, in turn, rubbed them on the mouths of the idols.

> **Cocom and Mateo cut the hearts from the boys and handed them to the shaman, who, in turn, rubbed them on the mouths of the idols.**

The following day, town bailiff Melchor Canche appeared before the apostolic judge and described a similar event. He had gone to the church late at night five years earlier to say his prayers, and saw the chief caciques of Tixcamahel and a number of shamans making sacrifices to their idols inside the church. Two children were killed and tied to wooden crosses; as the crosses were raised inside the church, the assembled men announced: "Behold the figure of Jesus Christ." As Canche looked on, two men he identified as Juan Cime and Luis Ku "opened them up and removed their hearts, and gave them to the *ah-kines* [shamans], who offered the hearts to the idols." The bodies of the children were later thrown into a *cenote,* or sinkhole.

The gods of the Maya pantheon were sustained with human blood. In turn, they provided mankind with the necessities for life. This fundamental relationship between man and god reached its peak during the Classic Period (A.D. 250–900) and took on various forms, from the self-bloodletting of kings to the mass execution of war prisoners after ritual ballgames. Although the practice varied in intensity throughout the Maya world, the purposes of blood sacrifice stayed the same: to appease an angry god; to balance the forces of nature; to beseech a higher power; or to divine the future.

Most native ritual practice in Yucatán went underground with the arrival of Spanish rule and Christian missionaries the 1540s, and a few decades later Franciscan leader Diego de Landa launched a zealous campaign to root out idolatry that culminated in 1562 with the destruction of thousands of ritual objects and most of the Maya books in existence. Landa and his men held trials in and around the town of Maní, forcing the Maya, under torture or threat of torture, to renounce their beliefs and confess their rituals, particularly the reviled practice of human sacrifice.

Landa was eventually recalled to Spain for his excessive behavior, was tried and acquitted, and before returning to the New World in 1573 as Bishop of Yucatán, recorded oral traditions of the Maya in *An Account of the Things of the Yucatán.* He included variations on the ritual of human sacrifice, including tossing idols and live victims into Chichén Itzá's duly named Cenote of Sacrifice. The Maya saw cenotes as gateways to Xibalba, the Underworld, and home of Chac, god of rain. Bishop de Landa wrote that the sacrifice was performed during times of drought, noting that the Maya believed that the victims would not die, "although they never saw them anymore." Dredging operations at Chichen Itzá by archaeologists in 1910 and the 1960s recovered the remains of at least 120 individuals and a variety of ritual objects, seemingly confirming Bishop de Landa's account. With the advent of the cave-diving exploration era in the 1980s, scientists began to realize that countless other cenotes, formed when acidic rain-water eats away at the porous limestone bedrock of the Yucatán Peninsula, also housed a wealth of ancient cultural material and human remains ("Diving the Maya Underworld," May/June 2004). Few archaeologists are trained for the dangerous diving required to search these deep, dark, underwater caverns, and thousands of sites across the peninsula still await discovery and exploration. Now, researchers at the Universidad Autónoma de Yucatán in Merída are trying to narrow their search for cenotes of enormous ritual importance to the Maya by using the detailed colonial accounts of human sacrifice.

Archaeologist Guillermo de Anda first began to look into Seville's Archivo General de Indias and Madrid's Archivo Histórico Nacional for information on cenotes in 2001, and was particularly struck by the testimony recorded in 1562, the year of Diego de Landa's auto de fé. "The confessions from that year are so numerous and complete," explains Anda. "They mention the names of the shamans and their *nacomes* [assistants], the kinds of sacrifices and where they took place, the names of the victims and where they were from, how they were procured, and where they were deposited at the end of the ritual." In the 1562 archives in Seville, 99 instances of human sacrifice were described involving 196 victims, of which the deposition sites of 143 are noted. Four-fifths of those were thrown into cenotes by Maya priests at the end of the ritual. "It's like a guide for finding sacrifice victims in cenotes," says the archaeologist.

Despite his enthusiasm, Anda is careful to point out the context in which the confessions were generated. Many of the "witnesses," for instance, who claimed to be at the village church in the middle of the night and stumbled upon the sacrifices were actually participants in the rituals. "We have accounts where the witnesses happen to know the names of the victims, the fact that they were kidnapped, and the names of the villages that they were kidnapped from," observes Anda. "These men knew that they would be tortured if they didn't talk, so they gave the Church what it wanted—they just left themselves out of it."

Other scholars are less enthusiastic regarding the veracity of the confessions generated by Landa and his men. "You can certainly get a window into many Maya practices and beliefs through the accounts preserved in the colonial archives," says John Chuchiak, a professor of Colonial Latin American History at Southwest Missouri State, "but I've never come across human sacrifice in confessions after the Landa trials. And within those trials, there's this syncretic blending of Christian and Maya ritual, like sacrifice *and* crucifixion. I think it's probably an attempt by Landa and his men to beef up their accounts. Then again," he concedes, "we know there was human sacrifice taking place in Central Mexico 50 years after the Spanish Conquest."

But there are accounts of human sacrifice among the Yucatec Maya outside the church archives that continue up to the eighteenth century, argues Anda. "After the Landa debacle, the Church took a softer line in public," he says, "but many scholars believe that the trials continued in secret. These are the confessions we're trying to find now." Anda also believes that, to the Maya, it may have made sense to appropriate elements of Christianity. The Spanish destroyed Maya temples and built churches from their remains on the same site, and the Maya may have viewed these Christian houses of worship as their own sacred spaces. He also cites elements in Maya religious belief and practice that had similarities to Christianity, such as the story of the young maize god, who dies and is reborn, and the practice of tying a victim to a wooden scaffold before performing a sacrifice. "Of course

there will be made-up material," says Anda, "but we can trace a pattern—with the shaman and the nacomes, the objects they use, the heart extraction—from representations of sacrifice in the Classic Period up through the time of these documents. And within these confessions, you have the same shaman named over and over again by different people, performing different kinds of sacrifices in events a year apart. It's not just a coincidence, and these are not just stories—there's a continuity here. Maya sacrifice is a long-standing tradition."

At least 15 cenotes were specifically named in the confessions extracted during the Landa trials, and others gave the names of nearby towns such as Sotuta and Homun where Maya priests were allegedly active in sacrifices and where Bishop Landa's men later held their interrogations. Anda began to dive in cenotes in areas mentioned in the archives and realized that there was an unusually high number of human remains in many of them compared to other sites in Yucatán State. Right now he is only performing nonrecovery surveys, which means that no artifacts are touched. All discoveries are reported to the Instituto Nacional de Antropología e Historia, Mexico's federal anthropology and history institute.

This spring, I met up with Anda and his six-person survey team for a week of exploring cenotes on the outskirts of Homun, a small town some 25 miles southeast of Merída, the capital of Yucatán State. The weathered church of St. Buenavista, built on the remains of an enormous Precolumbian temple platform, commands the center of town. Inside this church, Maya shamans were hanged by their thumbs until they confessed their "idolatrous" religious practices to Spanish authorities.

The beam of light draws through the transparent water towards our slowly treading fins, glancing off three human skulls resting on the cenote floor some 50 feet below.

Homun's jumble of concrete-block shacks and traditional thatch-roof huts on the outskirts of town quickly gives way to the jungle, and many of the cenotes we visited lay at the end of meager dirt paths that snake through miles of spiky scrub and palms still shredded by last year's pounding of successive hurricanes. Anda relies on his local Maya guides to help him find specific cenotes cited in the archives, whose names may have changed over the centuries, as well as other sites that may be worth investigating. Today's Maya still regard certain cenotes as particularly sacred or even cursed, and Anda actively seeks them out.

The biggest puzzle facing the university's research team, which also includes historian Pilar Zabala, physical anthropologist Vera Tiesler, and Anda's graduate students, is that according to the archives, Maya shamans traveled an average of 12 miles—and up to 40 miles—from the site of the sacrifice to deposit a victim in a specific cenote. A victim might be sacrificed in Sotuta, for example, and his body would be dumped 25 miles away in the Sacred Cenote at Chichén Itzá. Other victims would be sacrificed in Homun and deposited 15 miles away in the village of Yaxcaba. As Anda continues his survey of the sacrificial cenotes, he has yet to find if there is a physical or geographical "key," some sort of common characteristic that knits these sites together and gives them their particular ritual value—that special something that made it worth transporting a dead body many miles through the jungle, often in the middle of the night, all the time evading colonial authorities, when there were perfectly serviceable cenotes in the immediate sacrifice site.

I'm thinking about this "key" as we unload our equipment from Anda's van at the first dive site (to deter looting, names and distinguishing characteristics of unprotected cenotes are not included in this article). The site is deep inside an abandoned plantation, and the cenote was modified during colonial times into a well, with a two-person-wide opening to the water below. On closer inspection, we realize the opening itself sits atop a small square Precolumbian platform, each corner oriented in a cardinal direction, aligned with the four corners of the Maya vision of the earth.

Anda's assistants lower us to the water on the "elevator," a rope with a wooden T-bar tied to the end, which is scarily efficient at getting divers down dark 40-foot-deep well shafts. We bob in the cool water and wait for our dive gear to follow on a rope down the tiny hole, gauging the size of the black cavern by the echoes of our voices. The air is thick and tastes like an old coat. Anda is first to gear up, and he flips on his high-intensity dive light. The beam crosses a two-story-high wall of stalactites, which loom like a collection of enormous, battered ivory tusks. It fades out into the emptiness of the cavern beyond, then draws back through the transparent water towards our slowly treading fins, glancing off of three human skulls resting on the cenote floor some 50 feet below.

The pop-culture view of cenote sacrifice has been the Maya maiden standing on the edge of an enormous void, ready to be tossed to the gods.

For archaeologists used to poking around and dusting things off for a better look, non-recovery surveys can be frustrating; the law forbids you from even fanning sediment off of an object. But there are certain things Anda looks for in the cenotes that may suggest a connection to the activity mentioned in the confessions. A fully articulated skeleton on the cenote floor means, of course, that a body was thrown in whole. (It's impossible to put people back together from various bones spotted on site, as individual body parts were also thrown into cenotes.) Ribs and breastbones are examined for fractures or cut-marks resulting from heart removal, and he also looks for foot and wrist injuries that may be a byproduct of crucifixion, as well as wood, cord, or nails accompanying remains.

We begin our dive, and everywhere I cast my light I see bones. Leg bones, ribs, fully articulated skeletons. I glide down through a narrow crevasse at 100 feet and spot a skull wedged in at the bottom. We come back around a tower of stalagmites to a small plateau of rock, on which a pair of skeletal legs are stretched out. There are blocks of wood where the feet should be. I pose a question to Anda, forming the symbol of the cross with my hands. He shrugs.

At the end of the dive, we ascend slowly along a wall pocked with fossil sea urchins, a reminder that the peninsula was covered by ocean some 15 million years ago. I notice a polished ivory knob poking out of the powdery crystalline wall, then slowly recognize a series of thin, ragged human ribs emerging from the rock. Looking up, I realize the wall of the cavern is set with human bones—femurs, vertebrae, a random pelvis—and mortared with centuries of ceaseless drip from the magnificent stalactites that just break the surface of the water. At the top of the wall, in 10 feet of water, is a small ledge where two skulls rest. Both are flattened on the sides and slightly peaked, a custom of deliberate skull modification that the Maya stopped practicing for the most part well before the Spanish arrived.

Anda counts more than 40 complete sets of remains and 12 children's skulls at the site. It turns out to be our most spectacular dive in terms of the number of human remains, but we're even more intrigued by the wooden objects we consistently come across in several of the cenotes: trays or lidless boxes, about six feet long and five inches deep, carved from a single piece of wood. One is covered in stucco, and most are found in proximity to bones. Nothing similar seems to exist at other Maya sites; in fact, very few wooden objects are preserved from the ancient Maya world. They're also unlike anything known from colonial sites. It's impossible to say whether these "trays" are Maya or Spanish until one is raised and dated.

Overall, with the exception of a cenote in Sotuta that turned up nothing but a single Classic pot, our focus on "archival" cenotes resulted in some rich dives with an unusually high amount of human remains and wooden artifacts compared to cenotes outside of the area mentioned in the archives. These sites also contain a lot of Postclassic (A.D. 900–1500) ceramics, which may be a result of their proximity to the Postclassic center of Mayapán ("Last Great Capital of the Maya," March/April 2005). Interestingly, many of these sites also contained skulls with apparent cranial deformations, suggesting that these cenotes held a ritual significance over several centuries.

The pop culture view of cenote sacrifice has been the Maya maidèn standing on the edge of an enormous void, ready to be tossed to the gods. Most of the victims in the archives from 1562, however, were male (85 percent), and predominantly young, with nearly all of them purchased for the sacrifice or stolen from their homes while their parents worked in the fields. And while no bones from the recently surveyed cenotes have yet been recovered and scientifically examined, the Instituto Nacional de Antropología e Historia has given Anda the opportunity to analyze the human remains excavated from Chichén Itzá's Cenote of Sacrifice. So far, he's discovered

60 percent of the identifiable remains from the cenote are male and 69 percent range from seven to 15 years old. Many remains also show unusually severe signs of malnourishment, reflected in bone porosity and tooth enamel, which seems to correspond with children poor enough to be commodities that were bought and sold. There are also burn marks on skulls and hack marks on ribs recovered from the site, which confirms that, contrary to Bishop Landa's oft-cited account, not everyone was thrown into the Cenote of Sacrifice alive.

The archives also give us a good idea of why the Maya were performing these sacrifices. Twelve of the 99 rituals performed in 1562 made reference to a "great hurricane" that ravaged Yucatán a year earlier. Two sacrifices were performed to request good harvests, one for long life, and three for the well-being of a cacique. Two sacrifice victims were used for divinatory purposes.

Anda's research team is now focusing its attention on later periods in Yucatec history to trace how long into the Colonial Period sacrifice in Maya communities continued. Although there are accounts of human sacrifice occurring among the Maya into the eighteenth century, research into the official archives has so far only turned up records of animal sacrifice in cenotes. There are suspicions the practice may have even continued into the Caste War, the last great uprising of the Maya that swept the peninsula in the second half of the nineteenth century.

Within the relatively young subdiscipline of underwater archaeology, cenote research is a brave new world. The handful of professionals equipped to explore these difficult sites are still trying to understand how to efficiently survey and properly excavate them. And Anda recognizes the historical accounts from the period of contact between the Maya and the Spanish are merely a tool to further his work, and not an answer. "I don't want to fall into the trap of saying, well, the archives say that a lot of sacrifice victims are in Cenote A, and then we go and find many bodies in Cenote A, so we immediately conclude that they're sacrifice victims, because we're just at the beginning of our research," he says.

Instead, the hope is that one day, archaeologists will be able to use the Spanish archives to understand why some cenotes held such enormous ritual significance to the Yucatec Maya, and why others contain nothing more than a single pot. Perhaps this information was once contained in the countless manuscripts destroyed by Landa and the inquisition he launched—and it would be an ironic justice if the confessions wrought from the Maya, often under extreme duress, ended up being the key to unlocking some of their lost spiritual history.

KRISTIN M. ROMEY is deputy editor and senior writer at *Archaeology*.

Test-Your-Knowledge Form

We encourage you to photocopy and use this page as a tool to assess how the articles in *Annual Editions* expand on the information in your textbook. By reflecting on the articles you will gain enhanced text information. You can also access this useful form on a product's book support Web site at *http://www.mhcls.com.*

NAME: DATE:

_____

TITLE AND NUMBER OF ARTICLE:

_____

BRIEFLY STATE THE MAIN IDEA OF THIS ARTICLE:

_____

LIST THREE IMPORTANT FACTS THAT THE AUTHOR USES TO SUPPORT THE MAIN IDEA:

_____

WHAT INFORMATION OR IDEAS DISCUSSED IN THIS ARTICLE ARE ALSO DISCUSSED IN YOUR TEXTBOOK OR OTHER READINGS THAT YOU HAVE DONE? LIST THE TEXTBOOK CHAPTERS AND PAGE NUMBERS:

_____

LIST ANY EXAMPLES OF BIAS OR FAULTY REASONING THAT YOU FOUND IN THE ARTICLE:

_____

LIST ANY NEW TERMS/CONCEPTS THAT WERE DISCUSSED IN THE ARTICLE, AND WRITE A SHORT DEFINITION:

We Want Your Advice

ANNUAL EDITIONS revisions depend on two major opinion sources: one is our Advisory Board, listed in the front of this volume, which works with us in scanning the thousands of articles published in the public press each year; the other is you—the person actually using the book. Please help us and the users of the next edition by completing the prepaid article rating form on this page and returning it to us. Thank you for your help!

ANNUAL EDITIONS: Archaeology, 9/e

ARTICLE RATING FORM

Here is an opportunity for you to have direct input into the next revision of this volume.
We would like you to rate each of the articles listed below, using the following scale:

1. **Excellent: should definitely be retained**
2. **Above average: should probably be retained**
3. **Below average: should probably be deleted**
4. **Poor: should definitely be deleted**

Your ratings will play a vital part in the next revision.
Please mail this prepaid form to us as soon as possible.
Thanks for your help!

RATING	ARTICLE	RATING	ARTICLE
	1. The Awful Truth about Archaeology		18. The Maya Collapses
	2. Archaeology: The Next 50 Years		19. Gritty Clues
	3. All the King's Sons		20. Digging Deep
	4. Maya Archaeologists Turn to the Living to Help Save the Dead		21. A Wasp's-Nest Clock
	5. The Fantome Controversy		22. Profile of an Anthropologist: No Bone Unturned
	6. Distinguished Lecture in Archaeology: Communication and the Future of American Archaeology		23. What Did They Eat?
	7. Prehistory *of* Warfare		24. Artful Surgery
	8. The Mystery of Unknown Man E		25. Where Was Jesus Born?
	9. Who Were the First Americans?		26. Legacy *of the* Crusades
	10. Poop Fossil Pushes Back Date for Earliest Americans		27. Secrets of the Medici
	11. Archaeologists Rediscover Cannibals		28. Digging for Truth
	12. A Coprological View of Ancestral Pueblo Cannibalism		29. Living through the Donner Party
	13. Modern Humans Made Their Point		30. Thracian Gold Fever
	14. New Women of the Ice Age		31. In Flanders Fields
	15. Woman the Toolmaker		32. The Past as Propaganda
	16. Yes, Wonderful Things		33. Earth Movers
	17. Bushmen		34. The New Neandertal
			35. Whither the Neanderthals?
			36. Children of Prehistory
			37. Watery Tombs

NO POSTAGE
NECESSARY
IF MAILED
IN THE
UNITED STATES

ABOUT YOU

Name

Date

_____

Are you a teacher? ☐ A student? ☐
Your school's name

_____

Department

_____

Address   City   State   Zip

_____

School telephone #

_____

YOUR COMMENTS ARE IMPORTANT TO US!

Please fill in the following information:
For which course did you use this book?

_____

Did you use a text with this ANNUAL EDITION? ☐ yes ☐ no
What was the title of the text?

_____

What are your general reactions to the Annual Editions concept?

_____

Have you read any pertinent articles recently that you think should be included in the next edition? Explain.

_____

Are there any articles that you feel should be replaced in the next edition? Why?

_____

Are there any World Wide Web sites that you feel should be included in the next edition? Please annotate.

_____

May we contact you for editorial input? ☐ yes ☐ no
May we quote your comments? ☐ yes ☐ no